Competitive Success

Competitive Success

How Branding Adds Value

JOHN A. DAVIS

A John Wiley and Sons, Ltd, Publication

Library of Congress Cataloging-in-Publication Data

Davis, John A.
 Competitive success : how branding adds value / John A. Davis.
   p. cm.
 Includes bibliographical references and index.
  ISBN 978-0-470-99822-9 (pbk.)
 1. Brand name products. 2. Branding (Marketing) I. Title.
 HD69.B7D37 2010
 658.8'27—dc22
                                                        2009033764
A catalogue record for this book is available from the British Library.

Set in 10/12 Goudy by Macmillan Publishing Solutions
Printed in Great Britain by Bell and Bain, Glasgow

Dedication

As always, to my family Barb, Kate, Chris and Bridget you are the best!

Also, a special dedication in memory of my dad Robert T. Davis. An amazing father and beloved marketing Professor from Stanford.

Contents

Preface

A Different Brand Book

The title of this book, *Competitive Success: How Branding Adds Value*, was chosen because books on branding do not always explain the answers to *how* questions ("How do I derive value from branding?", "How is a brand built?", "How does a 'brand mentality' affect the organization?") whereas they are better at answering *what* questions ("What is a brand?" "What is brand management", "What is marketing communications?", "What are the marketing activities?", "What do various marketing terms mean?") Answering *how* branding adds value distinguishes this book from those that define *what* brand management is.

The mechanics of classic brand management have been thoroughly explained and examined over the years, with innumerable explanations of the myriad marketing activities and associated complexities. The point of this book is not to repeat what is already well covered. References to salient aspects of this are made where it is relevant to *how* they help companies build their brands. This highlights an issue that was raised repeatedly by business people over the past several years: "how does one make sense of all the brand-building theories and frameworks in a way that more clearly connects concepts to practices?" The research showed that many brand-management practices of top brands are adapted and even significantly altered, rendering familiar frameworks virtually unrecognizable. The challenge was how to explain this in a way that would capture the common patterns and practices of how top brands become successful, yet still convey the variation, at times extreme, that exists. The summary finding is that top brands act more often in a holistic manner, in contrast to a systematic one. This is an important distinction for students and practitioners of branding and is the primary emphasis of this book. Let's discuss the latter first.

Systematic branding implies operating in a particular way, adhering to a fixed plan. Indeed, most of the written material in brand management describes the importance of brand management as a systematic way of managing a business, defining terms, and parsing brand development decisions into a series of discreet, perfectly manageable, and logical choices. But the intrusion of reality often throws doubt on the applicability of the resulting plans. This is not meant to suggest that top brands abandon important business processes like planning. Instead, top brands elevate the holistic approach above purely systematic, often overtly working hard to blur the boundaries within organizations and thereby opening up the silos that otherwise create artificial barriers to interaction.

When the initial research for this book began, a frequent question from company leaders was "*How* do I actually build an organization that lives and breathes *brand*?" Early on, one senior manager even framed the issue this way: "I meet people from top brands everyday and it seems they *exude* branding in everything they do. Everybody seems 'together', like they naturally 'get it'. How can I get my organization to be like this?" The question revealed an interesting challenge: is it possible to transform an organization from one merely going through the motions into one that lives and breathes branding every day as if it were a natural part of every decision? The operative word in her question was *exude*, which seemed a very unlikely business term. One exudes sexuality, or energy, but one does not exude branding, or so the thinking goes. Such descriptive terminology is not typically heard in the staid world of business, where detached analytical calm is the preferred style. Yet exuding seemed to aptly describe the behavior of people within top brands and even the organizations themselves. Holistic branding means that the various parts of the organization are intimately connected through a myriad of formal and informal relationships, each creating associations that are observed, felt, and even directly shaped by the market. This makes the management of brands or, more accurately, the control over brands, much more challenging than many business people realize.

It implies a question of leadership or, more specifically, "how can company leadership bring about this transformation?" This issue took the research in a different direction, as each company studied was viewed from the standpoint of its ability to embody its reputation, not just advertise it.

Which brings us back to the senior manager's earlier question of getting her organization to *exude* branding, a notion that belies a systematic solution. The science of business, which suggests that data can be plugged into a formula and out spews the answer, is not always so logical or neat and tidy after all. Branding is downright blurry and often messy, with unclear boundaries and regular violations of 2 x 2 frameworks and decision trees. People make decisions involving emotion as well as logic and it turns out that successful brands work in a similar way.

This is a very different issue from the management of brands. Both are important. But the *how* question kept coming up and it became obvious that many managers were not as clear in their understanding of *how* a brand creates value. As stated, there are many very good textbooks about the specific management of brands from a pure marketing standpoint, but none that dealt with brands as an organization-spanning imperative involving the active coordination among marketing and nonmarketing departments alike.

The issue of terminology was a recurring theme. Specifically, what is meant by the term *brand*? Digging through reports and talking to company leaders brought forth a simple answer—*brand* is everything (no longer necessarily bound by product-specific attributes). This immediately posed another challenge. If brand is everything, then how does an organization manage one? After all, business schools teach that businesses should be *managed* by clearly defined processes overseen by functional experts and, furthermore, if something can't be measured, it isn't worth doing. Yet if brand is everything, then either a voluminous amount of additional management and measurement is required or organizations have to rethink fundamentally the practice of building brands. Many of the brands studied for this book had mostly figured this out, albeit with very different approaches. Which again stood in contrast to decades of business teaching that prescribed a relatively confined set of branding practices.

Other terms were questioned as well. What is marketing? How does it relate to branding? What is brand value? Brand equity? Inevitably, questions then arose about the differences in practices across organizations. Why does Procter & Gamble, well known for building a stable of strong consumer brands, manage its brands differently from Nestlé, another well-known consumer products company? Isn't there a set of universal brand management rules that always work? And there is the classic question: "what is the formula for brand success?" Of course, there are no single best answers to these questions because each top brand builds success in its own way, over years and even decades of trial, error, success, failure, reorganizing, and more.

Research

Since 2000, more than 200 companies around the world have been studied. Each company was researched by teams of students for major projects in multiple brand and marketing strategy courses taught first at University of Washington's Foster School of Business, then subsequently at Singapore Management University. The overarching premise of their projects was to identify the marketing and branding practices of their chosen firms compared against a primary competitor. Students often chose brands from Interbrand's and BrandFinance's published lists of the world's most valuable brands, or selected a well known alternative, as long as they could demonstrate that it was a reputable brand in its market. An important requirement was that the companies had to be publicly listed on a known stock exchange somewhere in the world so that access to annual reports and financial data was easily gathered. There was no restriction on B2C or B2B firms, or industry, so there is a wider variety of firms and corresponding practices. This yielded a more interesting set of findings, which confirmed that the term *brand* is much more than just a product.

The research was complemented by the input of over a thousand senior managers from companies around the world in dozens of executive education programs in which many of the findings were introduced, probed, and analyzed by these leaders in comparison to their own experiences.

From the research, it became clear that this book should have a different purpose: to show *how* organizations can create, develop, and cultivate an understanding of branding as an embedded, even natural, consideration of every decision. In effect, everyone must *live* the brand.

Who Benefits from this Book?

The short answer is anyone interested in marketing and branding issues will find this book useful, from senior management to entry level to students, with each gaining different insights depending on their own experiences and understanding. For students, this book serves as a natural complement to their studies in advertising, product development, and marketing management.

This book is also intended to offer insight for those not classically trained in marketing because, as discussed within, building a strong brand requires the active involvement of colleagues and departments across the company and not just marketing. This book emphasizes the benefits of strategic coordination and integration so that the holistic nature of successful branding can be seen and acted upon from the proper perspective. Nonmarketers will come away with a better appreciation of the complexities associated with branding as well as its strategic importance to the firm, recognizing that it requires more than managing advertising campaigns or writing marketing plans.

How this Book is Organized

We will show how to think about and pursue brand building so that value is created. Companies in the research repeatedly stated they needed people better prepared in *how* to build brands, not just able to describe what it means. Thus, the content combines proven academic theory *and* current practices. Throughout the book, each chapter will conclude with explanations of measures that are related to the content within. A word of caution here: no set of measures is complete or specific enough to address each chapter's topics thoroughly. The measures included are designed to inspire readers to consider them and the many ways their brand building can be assessed. The book also includes numerous examples and company briefs and discussion questions to stimulate the reader's understanding and use of the material.

Certain subtopics appear in multiple chapters, particularly various departments and management groups, referenced in the context of their role and influence within the topic being discussed. The reason is to illustrate that in top brands people do not interpret their title as a boundary or limit on what they can or can't do. It merely labels them for the benefit of outsiders. Instead, many employees in the top brands studied saw themselves as both caretakers of a respected societal institution and current owners (however temporary that might be) of its future, with all the responsibility that entails. This means that their contribution to the brand-building effort is not confined to one area of the new brand framework, but every area, either directly or indirectly.

There are three sections to this book.

Part 1

The first part encompasses Chapters 1–3 and focuses on understanding what is meant by "brand". It discusses why this topic is important for competitive success and explains how different brand architectures function. The background information in this part gives the necessary context for the new brand framework discussed in Part 2. The importance of history in helping us understand where we are today is well established, as it explains many of the contextual forces that influence current events. Chapter 1 has a brief historical background followed by a strategic overview of branding, including common definitions of the meaning of brand and the nature of the competitive arenas in which brands compete. The new definition of brand is introduced and implications assessed, inviting comparisons to its historical antecedents. Chapter 2 is devoted to brand value, describing methodological approaches to its measurement, and then discussing consumer-based brand equity frameworks. Chapter 3 describes established brand architectures, their strengths and weaknesses and how they help provide a structure for brand building. Some readers may be familiar with the topics in Chapter 3 but reviewing them provides an important backdrop for the new brand framework, since the old and new approaches will often be combined.

Part 2

Part 2 is the heart of the book, introducing and discussing the new brand framework. There are four components in the framework, discussed over seven chapters. Readers will quickly notice the importance of the interactions and interconnections among these four components in driving brand success. They work together to create a holistic brand that is vibrant and memorable, particularly in contrast with less successful rivals. Chapter 4 gives an overview of the new brand framework, showing the complete picture first so that readers can begin to see and understand the interdependencies between topics. There are four components within the framework that take the remaining chapters of this section. Chapter 5 addresses brand destiny, which captures the essence, or soul, of the brand, including the importance of understanding and working toward the brand's long-term ambitions. Chapter 6 focuses on brand distinction and the factors that influence the practices of top brands that help differentiate them. Chapter 7 examines brand culture from the individual employee and organizational points of view and considers why developing a strong brand culture is vital to long-term competitive success. Chapters 8–10 are dedicated to brand experiences, starting with the big picture and narrowing to specific subcomponents that influence what customers see and, quite literally, *experience.*

Part 3

Part 3 is a single chapter, focused on brand leadership. This is a purposeful departure from the term "brand management". At this point, readers will have learned about the complexity of building a successful brand, whether that brand is an entire company, or a single product. The brand's success in the future will be more likely to be due to thoughtful, strategic leadership that sets the brand on the right path than tactical execution that succeeds on one day but fails on another. Tactics alone simply won't enable a brand to adapt to competitor changes and market trends. This is where the concept of brand leadership comes in because leaders have the responsibility to look beyond the day to day and toward a better future. To facilitate this strategic understanding, Chapter 11 discusses a brand-planning approach that incorporates the new brand framework, which shows how to organize and use the new brand framework to create a holistic brand that adds measurable value to the business, and immeasurable psychic gain for stakeholders. It includes two important exercises that are designed to map out a given brand and its many variables.

For Faculty

Several educational tools are available that support the use of this book in the classroom.

Instructor's Resources

Competitive Success: How Branding Adds Value is designed for use in the classroom, with Instructor Resources designed to complement and inspire student learning. The Instructor's Resources include:

Instructor's Guide

- Chapter Objectives - a synopsis of key objectives discussed in each chapter.
- Chapter Overview - an outline and key terms summary providing instructors with summary bullet points, page references, and PowerPoint slide recommendations.
- Answers to Discussion Questions - suggested answers and explanations for discussion questions within each chapter. Instructors should feel free to expand on the answers and update company-specific information with current data.
- Latest Examples - each chapter uses concise company examples and/or concise cases to illustrate best practices.

Instructor's PowerPoint Slides

- Clear and concise slides from each chapter, including relevant graphics, guiding students and instructors through the main points of each chapter. Instructors should remind students that the slides are not a verbatim recitation of each chapter's content and that students are responsible for knowing all content in each chapter to maximize their learning.

Instructor's Online Resources

Useful descriptions, definitions, and examples from the text book and instructor's resources are available from **www.wileyeurope.com/college/davis.**

Acknowledgments

I am indebted to many wonderful people for making this book possible.

The John Wiley & Sons UK team of Nicole Burnett, Anneli Mockett, Steve Hardman, Georgia King, and Sarah Booth has been professional throughout and I sincerely appreciate their efforts. Indirectly, the Wiley Asia team of Nick Wallwork and C. J. Hwu that has been responsible for my previous four books on marketing metrics and sports marketing topics were instrumental in supporting this project in its infancy.

I cannot say enough about the literally hundreds of students I have worked with over the years whose brand research projects have been insightful and worthwhile. Many are cited within but there are many more. They have been an absolute pleasure to teach.

I have had the good fortune to work alongside a remarkable group of marketing colleagues at Singapore Management University (SMU) whose dedication and love of marketing and path-breaking research is inspiring. The entire group is committed to being among the very best in the world and their publication record in recent years has been admirable. I hold all of them in the highest esteem. In particular, Jin Han and Andre Bonfrer have been terrific supporters of my work in and out of the classroom. President Howard (Woody) Hunter, Provost Rajendra Srivastava, Deputy President Tan Chin Tiong, and Dean of Executive Education Annie Koh have been great supporters as well. During the final phases of writing I left SMU to join Emerson College in Boston as Department Chair and Professor of Marketing and am looking forward to working with the many great colleagues there. I will miss SMU but I am thrilled to be part of Emerson.

A wonderful network of global academic colleagues came from my relationship with Columbia University Business School's Center on Global Brand Leadership, led by Faculty Director Bernd Schmitt and Executive Director David Rogers. They have been actively involved in SMU conferences, even cosponsoring several, while also speaking and providing great new research content. Through them, and Jin Han at SMU, I have come to know Dae Ryun Chang, Professor of Marketing at Yonsei University. His enthusiastic speeches, seminars, and insightful research are motivating. Plus, his love of movie nostalgia makes for fun conversations.

A special note of appreciation for David Montgomery, the former Dean of the Lee Kong Chian School of Business at SMU and the Sebastian S. Kresge Professor of Marketing Strategy, Emeritus at Stanford University's Graduate School of Business. Dave has been a mentor for years whose advice and guidance I trust implicitly. Everyone should be so fortunate.

There are innumerable business leaders whose insights over the years opened many doors and inspired further digging into the findings. Several have been speakers at global conferences that I helped organize at SMU, as well as the Marketing Excellence Speakers Series that I ran. Others have been guests on the podcast series "LeadershipMatters" that I co-host with Michael Netzley, a corporate communications professor at SMU—in particular, Tom McCabe (Standard Chartered), Kevin Goulding (AIG), Mike McBrien (Genesys), David Haigh (BrandFinance) Frank Mars (Mars), Steve Leonard (EMC), Frederick Moraillon (BusinessObjects), Ravi Agarwal (NSX), Argus Ang (RV), Becky DiSorbo (EMC), Gavin Coombs (FutureBrand), Andrew Saks (Dell), David Shaw (Lenovo), Paul Iacovino (Four Seasons), Michael Issenberg (ACCOR), Chip Conley, (Joie de Vivre Hotels), and Rod Beckstrom (ICANN).

Of course, my family is the biggest source of support of all. My wife, Barb, is truly special and I am beyond fortunate. One cannot have a better pal to travel with through life. My globetrotting daughter, Kate, whose international relations expertise and her current work in the most troubled areas in Africa is definitely making the world a better place, never ceases to amaze me and gives me great confidence that the future is in superb hands. My son Chris, whose academic ambitions, musical interests, and general enthusiasm for life, is a constant source of inspiration. My youngest daughter, Bridget, whose love of relaxing to read a good book and snuggling with family and animals after slaughtering her opponents in tennis shows time and again the importance of balance in life.

Part I

Understanding the Importance of Brand

Competitive Success

1

Topics

Preview

As we will learn, brands come in many sizes, shapes and industries. The concept of brand is older than the commercial practices of the past century might suggest. The historical roots suggest a desire to highlight the unique characteristics of an organization and/or a business. The advent of the modern age introduced a more formal and professional approach to branding, an approach that has evolved over the years into a sophisticated and complex set of activities. Brands, like any business, start small and grow if fortune favors them. Growth is influenced by the brand's ability to adapt to changing customer tastes. At the same time, numerous variables act on and interact with brands to continually reshape them. Not all brands are the same, nor are all markets. There is a great deal of latitude surrounding what a brand becomes, where it is marketed and how it performs. An important point to remember is that a brand cannot exist without some level of public awareness. This chapter will explore the foundation of brands, what they are and how they have evolved, setting the stage for deeper exploration and analysis in subsequent chapters about how to effectively build strong brands that create competitive advantage.

Historical Snapshot

The idea of brands has been around for centuries, but it was not called or known as a brand in the modern sense. Images, insignia and names have been used throughout much of recorded history to designate property, famous people, official buildings, places of worship, and merchant activities.

Over 1700 years ago, workers began to organize themselves based on common skills. Eventually to become known as guilds, these early organizations were loose associations whose members specialized and refined their crafts. Guilds and their equivalents were found in different societies around the world, from Asia to the Middle East to Europe. Over the centuries, guilds became an important part of economic life, training skilled workers, organizing talent and producing goods. Guild members undertook long apprenticeships, working for master craftsmen (considered the recognized experts of their trade) in their hometown guilds for many years before venturing out on their own to work with master craftsmen in other towns. This learning experience earned them the label "journeyman," a term signifying the travels and varied work experiences undertaken. Eventually, journeymen would settle into a town and apply to the local guild to work as a master craftsman. In Europe, particularly during the period from the twelfth to the sixteenth centuries, guilds covered a wide range of crafts and skills, from tailors to smiths to carpenters to artisans (and much more), highlighting a simple form of differentiation. Merchant guilds also existed, which were associations of leading merchants that regulated commerce in their town. Merchants were considered of a higher social standing than craftsmen or, below them, servants and employees. They controlled many of the factors of production and economic success since they could determine which goods could be sold, how many, and by whom.

Trade fairs brought different guilds and their goods together for trade exchanges. While not frequent, when trade fairs were held a greater variety of goods was available to local townspeople, helping build societal expectations for greater choice and even introducing harder-to-acquire items, including luxury goods, setting up a more sophisticated structure of exclusive and commodity goods. The most successful guilds wielded power and influence, garnering additional attention that further enhanced their prestige and distinguishing them from lesser guilds. Royal and/or government recognition gave some higher status and privilege, essentially protecting their work from competition and raising their visibility. Guilds continued to evolve, acting in many capacities from training to production to quality control to the equivalent of certification, bestowing merchants and craftsmen with control over the production of goods in society.[1] In many ways, guilds were the forerunners to modern organizations because they controlled labor, production, determination of premium and commodity goods, and sought recognition in order to increase awareness and thereby increase demand and sales.

Josiah Wedgwood, founder of Wedgwood, a company specializing in ceramics and pottery started in 1759, remarked about the importance of recognition and visibility resulting from the Royal Commission his company received

> It is really amazing how rapidly ... (our china) has spread almost over the whole Globe, & how universally it is liked. How much of this general use, & estimation, is owing to the mode of its introduction & how much to its real utility & beauty? are questions in which we may be a good deal interested for the government of our future Conduct ... For instance, if a Royal, or Noble Introduction be as necessary to the sale of an Article of Luxury, as real Elegance & beauty, then the Manufacturer, if he consults his own interest will bestow as much pains, & expence too if necessary, in gaining the former of these advantages, as he would in bestowing the latter.[2]

To put this in a modern context, Wedgwood had discovered the importance of testimonials in conferring value, credibility and reputation, all cornerstones of a strong brand.

While modern corporations are far more varied in their work and structure, and more sophisticated in their branding practices, guilds gave society insight into how expertise and reputation were attained, two key building blocks in modern brand building.

The early years of the twenty-first century witnessed a rapidly changing business environment. The rapid technological advances of the 1990s saw the expansion and commercialization of the Internet, providing companies with new digital tools to sell products and reach customers. Customers were now accessible anywhere where there was a computer with an on-line connection, adding a new, direct channel for company managers. Companies in the West, eager to reduce costs, increasingly outsourced low-skill manufacturing to developing countries where labor was cheaper. New trade agreements fostered international expansion of companies around the world. The West's biggest multinational corporations expanded rapidly as access to the developing markets of Asia (particularly China, India, Thailand, Malaysia, Indonesia, Vietnam and Cambodia) opened up. At the same time, companies from these emerging markets began their own international expansion. The process of *globalization* was underway. But what is globalization? According to the *Stanford Encyclopedia of Philosophy*,

> ... globalization refers to fundamental changes in the spatial and temporal contours of social existence, according to which the significance of space or territory undergoes shifts in the face of a no less dramatic acceleration in the temporal structure of crucial forms of human activity.[3]

More simply, for the purposes of this book, globalization refers to the massive changes taking place in the global business environment that enable companies to compete across borders more easily and with increasing regularity. Innumerable political, economic, sociocultural and additional technological factors have been significant catalysts in this change, although new media, including the Internet and digital technology, have also served as catalysts. Globalization has reduced barriers to competitive entry, increasing the number of competitors in markets around the world. Customers have more choice as a result. To win over customers, company managers must develop a business strategy that differentiates their offerings from those of the competition.

Strategic Overview

Logically, management must have a *brand strategy* that clearly articulates the aims and objectives of the organization and how it will be perceived when each of these activities is aligned. Brand strategy guides management, and all employees, down a common path toward genuine differentiation. In this crowded global business environment, building a brand as a necessary means to create competitive advantage has become both important and urgent.

B2C and B2B Companies

The distinction between B2C and B2B firms is evident: B2C firms (*Business to Consumer*) are companies that produce and/or market products to consumers, whereas B2B firms (*Business to Business*) are companies that produce and/or market products to other companies. Having a clear brand strategy is both sensible and necessary for B2C and B2B companies. All companies are competing in complex markets, each with unique business characteristics that compel managers to tailor their offerings to conditions specific to each market. Developing a unique expertise and identity is vital to building a strong, sustainable business and reputation, and this will be explored in-depth in Chapter 6. But in this effort, what is a *brand*, and how does developing it help companies succeed?

Product versus Brand

Before discussing brand in greater detail, we need to answer an important question: "what is the difference between a product and a brand?" The definition of "product" is easier, so we will begin with that. The definition of brand underlies its many applications and benefits and, as the animating focal point of this book, requires a more in-depth explanation.

Product

A product is a generic term encompassing a good (tangible product) or service (intangible product) produced for transaction for the benefit of customers. Customers can be consumers or businesses, and transactions normally involved financial compensation, although trade and barter is another vehicle for compensating parties in a transaction. When individuals purchase a good, such as an MP3 player or a watch, they are likely also getting warranties, service and support information, image, and needs satisfaction all at once. A service is a more intangible product, such as a consulting recommendation, an insurance policy, or even an interaction between a restaurant food server and a customer. Like a good, a service is performed in exchange for compensation.

Brand Definitions

Brands have often been narrowly defined brands as *slogans, logos, and/or advertising campaigns*. Let's look at each briefly. They will be discussed in greater depth, along with additional marketing communications tools, in Chapter 10.

Slogans

Slogans are simplified messages designed to help position the company and/or its products for the market. Examples abound, including:

Slogan	Company
Just Do It[4]	Nike
Impossible is Nothing[5]	Adidas
We Try Harder®[6]	Avis
Open Happiness™[7]	Coca Cola
The World's Local Bank[8]	HSBC
Probably the Best Beer in the World[9]	Carlsberg
Sheer Driving Pleasure[10]	BMW
Don't Leave Home Without It[11]	American Express
A Great Way to Fly[12]	Singapore Airlines
The World's Best Low Cost Airline[13]	Air Asia
Good Food, Good Life[14]	Nestlé
New World. New Thinking™[15]	Lenovo
Think Different[16]	Apple
Affordable Solutions for Better Living[17]	IKEA

Slogans, developed and marketed correctly, provide a succinct means of making the thing being marketed more memorable. Slogans can also become the object of parody or negative counterpositioning. In the 1964 U.S. Presidential election, the Republican candidate was Barry Goldwater and the Democratic candidate was Lyndon Johnson, who was also the incumbent President. Goldwater's campaign slogan was

In your heart, you know he's right'[18]

The slogan benefited from a double meaning: *right* meant both "correct" and "right of center" on the political spectrum. However, Lyndon Johnson's campaign developed even more powerful and memorable counter-slogans:

In your guts you know he's nuts

and

In your heart he's too far right[19]

Goldwater lost the election to Johnson, although do not assume that the slogans were a significant cause because there were other, far more important contributing factors. Slogans, in this case, were nothing more than convenient taglines used by both political parties in an effort to shape public perception.

Logos

Logos are a graphical element such as a symbol, photo, emblem, or even a name. They are a visual aid and/or trademark that, like a slogan, are used for communication purposes (print and TV advertising, brochures, web sites, signage, and more) in an effort to make an organization and/or its products more memorable. Successful logos are rarely the result of a regimented formula. Designs cover a broad range of styles, from creative to conservative, from whimsical and colorful to serious and simple, from graphic to verbal. Today design firms specialize in creating unique logos, charging substantial fees for their services, yet not all logos require such extravagant investment. In 1971 Phil Knight, founder of Nike, hired Carolyn Davidson, who was a graphic design student at Portland State University. She developed several concepts from which the Swoosh was selected. The total cost was only $35. Many years later, Phil Knight thanked her more generously by give her a gold Swoosh ring with a diamond, along with Nike stock. The global familiarity that Swoosh now has was not at all obvious when first designed. As Phil Knight, Nike founder, told Davidson at the time, "I don't love it, but it will grow on me."[20]

Whether discussing the Nike Swoosh, the Mercedes star, the Coca-Cola Wave, or the Wedgwood "W," familiar brand logos trigger a reaction from customers. This trigger is a by-product of the company's brand-building efforts over time. While logos by themselves are simply a visual aid, they also serve as a shorthand way to remind us of the brand's *relevance*, *associations*, and its resulting *reputation* in the market. As companies mature and their recognition increases, logos and slogans are usually formalized in documents called corporate identity standards, developed to provide specific guidance in the appropriate and acceptable uses of logos and slogans in all company-related communications, whether internal or external. Furthermore, these corporate identity standards, when trademarked, provide a form of legal protection against copying and similar forms of infringement.

Advertising

Advertising is communication designed to persuade another party, usually businesses or consumers, to purchase a company's products, adopt a point of view, or behave in a certain way. It is usually a combination of verbal (or written) copy and visual imagery. Advertising is an important element of a larger brand-building strategy. Done well, advertising reveals to the market interesting insights about a company and its offerings and extends the company's public narrative, helping add to the company's reputation.

Many companies have successfully crafted advertising campaigns that last for years, embedding themselves deeply into society. Countless examples of advertising success and failure exist in most markets.

EXAMPLE 1-1:

Advertising Success Story: Intel Inside

In 1991, Intel was a large but relatively unknown high-tech company that sold sophisticated microprocessors to computer manufacturers for use in their consumer PCs. Each generation of Intel microprocessors was known as "X86" — for example 286, 386 and 486. But these numerical identities were not legally protectable as trademarks, so competitors frequently rode Intel's innovation coattails by designating their own rival products with the same numerical nomenclature. A team of Intel managers, led by marketing manager Dennis Carter, launched a new campaign, now famously known as "Intel Inside®," which was intended to tell the market that Intel's microprocessors were the market leaders and were vital to the smooth operation of a high quality and reliable PC. Intel offered a cooperative marketing program to PC manufacturers in which a portion of the advertising cost would be shared if the PC maker agreed to use the Intel logo on all print ads. The program succeeded, with more than 300 PC makers signing on and Intel's name recognition increasing dramatically in the market, causing a classic advertising "pull" effect whereby consumers asked for PC's that had "Intel Inside®." PCs without Intel microprocessors were less desirable. In 1993, Intel strengthened this campaign with the launch of its first named microprocessor, the "Pentium," a legally protectable trademark. The Intel Inside® campaign has been enormously successful and is recognized as a sign of high quality and innovation.[21]

Advertising Challenges: The Dot.com Era

Advertising money can be easily misused. The 2000 Super Bowl game in the U.S. (the most widely-watched sporting event in the U.S. with between 90 and 130 million fans tuning in each year)[22] offers instructive lessons for marketers as they weigh expensive advertising decisions. The dot.com era from the mid-1990s to around 2005 was a unique period in business history, with technology companies garnering high market valuations, often in the absence of sound business models or profitability. Over $40 million was collectively spent by more than a dozen dot.com firms for 30-second television commercials during the Super Bowl game, with the average commercial costing $2.2 million that year. The ads were as eye catching as they were odd, including a talking sock puppet ad for Pets.com and an E*TRADE Financial commercial highlighting a dancing chimpanzee. The connections between the ads and the companies were often tenuous at best, serving mostly to catch viewer attention but failing to earn ongoing consumer loyalty. The majority of the dot.com companies that advertised in 2000 went out of business. E*TRADE remains active, although its business has changed dramatically over time, particularly since the financial crisis of mid-2008.[23] One of the 2000 Super Bowl advertisers, OurBeginning.com—was a wedding invitation designer with little actual business. The company Super Bowl ads cost more than $4 million,[24] substantially more than revenues at the time. So why did the dot.coms spend so much on a one-time television advertisement on the Super Bowl? The temptation of

> the Super Bowl's large and diverse audience, many of whom tune in simply to watch the creative advertising and not the actual game, was simply too great. Yet as the dot.com failures demonstrate, advertising success requires far more than just a one-time investment in a creative ad, even if the audience is enormous. Advertising must be evaluated with the same rigor as other investments, with a keen eye on the long-term strategic objectives of the company firmly in mind and a series of shorter term tactics designed to reinforce the advertising message through daily activities and programs designed around the needs of consumers.

Expanded Brand Definitions

Certainly, slogans, logos, and advertising remain important components of a successful brand development effort, and we will discuss these in-depth in Chapter 10. But the rapid advancement of the Internet, two-way instantaneous communications via digital tools, and more sophisticated business models render these traditional interpretations as limited at best.

The concept of brand has been refined over the past 25 years, offering more sophisticated descriptions. A few examples are illustrated here. While differences do exist, note their commonality:

American Marketing Association Definition

The American Marketing Association (AMA) offers two definitions of brand,[25] reflecting both a traditional and an updated interpretation:

Traditional

A name, term, design, symbol, or any other feature that identifies one seller's good or service as distinct from those of other sellers. The legal term for brand is trademark. A brand may identify one item, a family of items, or all items of that seller. If used for the firm as a whole, the preferred term is trade name.

Updated

A brand is a customer experience represented by a collection of images and ideas; often, it refers to a symbol such as a name, logo, slogan, and design scheme. Brand recognition and other reactions are created by the accumulation of experiences with the specific product or service, both directly relating to its use, and through the influence of advertising, design, and media commentary.

An additional definition is:

A brand often includes an explicit logo, fonts, color schemes, symbols, sound, which may be developed to represent implicit values, ideas, and even personality.

The AMA's traditional definition is closer to previous managers' understanding of a brand. Technically correct, it is a useful starting point for understanding the importance of having a strong brand name. Practicing managers today define brands more expansively. The updated definition encompasses the concept of "experiences," an important aspect of management's brand development efforts that will be discussed in greater depth in this textbook.

Legal Definition

In the U.S., the legal definition states: "A brand is a name and/or symbol that uniquely identifies a seller's goods or services in the market."[26] Internationally, there is a common legal definition of a brand as "a sign or set of signs certifying the origin of a product or service and differentiating it from the competition."[27] The distinction between the two is slight. The unifying piece is the notion of a brand as a symbol or sign.

Academic Definitions

David Aaker, the E. T. Grether Professor of Marketing and Public Policy Haas Marketing Group at the Haas School of Business at University of California, Berkeley and one of the pre-eminent academic authorities on branding, views a brand through the concept of brand equity, described as "A set of assets (or liabilities) linked to a brand's name and symbol that adds to (or subtracts from) the value provided by a product or service ..."[28]

Aaker's definition introduces an important aspect of branding: the linkage, or associations that customers attach to a brand. Developing valuable associations is a powerful way to reinforce a brand's reputation and identity, which will be explored fully in Chapters 8, 9, 10 and 11.

Similarly, Kevin Lane Keller, the E. B. Osborn Professor of Marketing at the Tuck School of Business at Dartmouth, refers to industry practices he has observed in describing a brand as "... something that has actually created a certain amount of awareness, reputation, prominence ... in the marketplace"[29] and he contrasts this view with the American Marketing Association's definition, which while being technically correct, does not account for the broader range of associations and corresponding value attached to brands.

Bernd Schmitt, the Robert D. Calkins Professor of International Business at Columbia Business School suggests that branding has become so pervasive that everything will soon be a brand. He distinguishes between brands and products, "In the world in which the brands rule, products are no longer bundles of functional characteristics but means to provide and enhance customer experiences."[30]

Schmitt adds "... the very essence of a brand as a rich source of sensory, affective, and cognitive associations that result in memorable and rewarding brand experiences."[31]

Schmitt's inclusion of customer and brand experiences are an important part of his research. Indeed, the findings from much of the research conducted for this textbook found strong and compelling linkages between external customer experiences and internal company activities, described by the *Destiny, Distinction, Culture, Experiences* framework on which this book is based.

While there are minor differences, each of these definitions shares a common theme of brand as a strategy for differentiating companies and attracting customers, providing managers with clearer guidance in their brand development efforts. Marketers today must recognize that brands play a pivotal role in society by helping customers, both consumer and business, decide which products and services to purchase. How do brands influence this decision? By acting as *de facto* decision-making *filters* for customers when they are choosing among two or more comparable offerings. Globalization has created new opportunities for companies while also making markets more crowded. Products are copied more easily, making product-differentiation an increasing challenge for companies that once relied on quality and innovation as key to their identity. Managers today are required to think more boldly and must plan more thoughtfully about how to accentuate and reinforce their unique offerings to hinder the efforts of a clever competitor that can easily copy.

The pursuit of differentiation is hard work, because it encompasses operations, marketing, R&D, product development, culture building, and customer experience development. The combination of these activities is reflected in what the market understands your "brand" to be; the sum total is your company's reputation, and reputation is the same as brand, as will be demonstrated throughout this text.

Competitive Arenas

Brands can compete in any or all of several competitive categories:

- global;
- regional;
- national;
- local;
- niche.

Global

A company is a global brand when its reputation is consistent across geographies. Consistency is different from uniformity. The former describes *generally* consistent product approaches around the world owing for some local tailoring that does not depart dramatically from core ingredients, whereas the latter describes identical precision in every market, which is hard to execute on a practical level, nor is it necessarily desirable due to differing tastes across cultures.

Furthermore, product consistency is different than marketing communications consistency. Global brands do and usually must adjust their messages because of language and cultural differences. Marketing folklore is rife with tales of poor slogan translations embarrassing companies and cultures. In the 1960s, Pepsi-Cola's slogan "Come Alive! You're in the Pepsi Generation" was allegedly translated into Chinese as "Pepsi Brings Your Ancestors Back from the Grave." As impressive, or distressing, as that sounds, delivering on this expectation is a tall order.[32]

Nike, Procter & Gamble, IBM, LVMH, Lenovo, and Singapore Airlines are examples of global brands that meet the consistency criteria. Each creates a wide range of products every year that are marketed relatively similarly around the world while adapting messages to the tastes and sensibilities of local cultures. There are many more companies than this that are considered global brands. A helpful resource about the world's best brands is produced annually by Interbrand, a global brand consultancy, and printed in *BusinessWeek* magazine.[33] While it is not a comprehensive list of all global brands (it only features the top 100 global brands as measured by brand value), a quick review of companies listed provides an excellent introduction into the kinds of companies and products that are succeeding in multiple markets around the world, and have been for years.

Regional

Regional brands are consistent across a proximate geographic area. As with global brands, marketing communications do focus on common themes, although regional variation may still occur, particularly when the brand is marketed where language differences exist. Regions include: Europe, North America, Southeast Asia, South Africa, and the Middle East.

Granini, a popular German fruit juice, is marketed consistently across many countries in Europe. Apex-Pal is a Singapore-based food company specializing primarily in Asian-themed restaurants, including Sakae Sushi. Their locations are throughout Southeast Asia and China. Alaska Airlines is a U.S. airline that flies to cities in the U.S., Canada and Mexico.

Interbrand produces a variety of regional and country-specific reports about top brands as well. In addition, many regional business publications and online services produce annual surveys of the leading brands in their countries and regions, including:

- Asia: Branding Asia (www.brandingasia.com)
- Europe/UK: B2B (www.b2binternational.com)
- South America: (www.brandsoftheworld.com)

National

Companies with national brands are those that compete consistently *within* and *across* their national boundaries. The brand's reputation is well known across the entire national market, even though specific product offerings may differ by local markets within.

First American is a U.S. company offering mortgage, property title, valuation, and real estate data services to U.S. businesses and consumers purchasing real estate-related products and services. Nordstrom is an upscale department store chain in the U.S. with a long-established reputation for superior service in addition to its reputation for equally strong retail settings and merchandise selections. Similarly, Selfridges is an upscale U.K. department store with a flagship store in London and three other stores in England.

Local

Local brands range from established single-location mom-and-pop businesses with loyal clientele, such as a favorite restaurant or a specialty retail store, to limited-size chains concentrated in a tight geographic region. Local brands build reputations often by developing more personal relationships and familiarity with their customers, rather than investing in marketing campaigns to build awareness and/or position their business. Because their business is well known and understood by their customers, local brands can develop a uniquely deep relationship with customers and, since they are not concerned with attracting a large national or global audience, they can turn their attention on nurturing loyalty. Most cities boast haunts that are favorites for locals. Interestingly, local brands can be viewed as more authentic to visitors because of the cachet attached to what locals prefer, thereby helping the local brand extend its reputation beyond the geographic boundaries.

Joie de Vivre Hotels is a San Francisco-based boutique hotelier with more than 30 distinctive hotels located in California. The company emphasizes the eclectic and diverse cultures of California by making each hotel unique. Resisting the temptation to expand its successful business model, company founder and CEO Chip Conley has kept the company focused on growth in California.

Niche

Niche brands offer products or services that satisfy the needs of a particular audience, whether business or consumer. When properly executed, niche brands develop a specialty reputation in the market for expertise in a specific area, creating a competitive advantage over larger and better funded rival brands at the national and global level.

Leviathan is a Perth, Australia-based company that markets technologically advanced outerwear for use in outdoor activities, waters sports, and oceanographic research. Its expertise is in a focused niche (also known as a vertical market) with a clearly defined customer audience.

RV! Centre is a Southeast Asian firm specializing in marketing education programs and services to students in secondary schools seeking admission to universities outside of the region. The company also offers executive education programs and educational publications, providing an education-specific set of offerings designed to meet the needs of consumers in Myanmar, Vietnam, Cambodia, and Sri Lanka, seeking guidance in education opportunities outside their home countries.

M.A.S. Holdings is a Sri Lankan company specializing in apparel manufacturing. Its customers include Nike, Victoria's Secret, Speedo, and The Gap. M.A.S. Holdings has grown from a small local manufacturer when it began in the mid-1980s to a $700 million+ company with 45 000 employees.[34] Its expertise is primarily in the skilled manufacturing of performance textiles, although they have extended this into a wide range of apparel development over the years.

These brand distinctions are not absolute and it is quite possible for a company to be competing in more than one area, necessitating a different brand strategy in each of the markets and/or brand categories in which the company conducts business. Given these different competitive areas, past interpretations of the meaning of *brand* must be broadened beyond narrow functional or departmental definitions to capture the full complement of factors that now comprise a *brand*. Business leaders now view "brand" as synonymous with reputation, and reputation is affected by innumerable variables, many of which are far beyond the traditional purview of marketing as the caretaker of company communications to the market. Logically, brand development is like reputation development, and therefore must be viewed from an integrative perspective. Doing so introduces a new definition of brand.

New Brand Definition

Brands are the entire organization as seen through the eyes of stakeholders, as shown in Figure 1-1.[35] Stakeholders include people inside and outside the firm. When defined this way, the challenge of planning and implementing management's brand development efforts becomes apparent. Branding becomes the responsibility of the entire organization since every person and every department within directly or indirectly affects the perception of the brand.

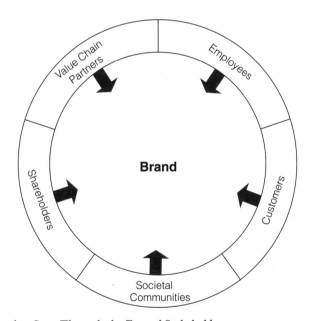

Figure 1-1   Brand as Seen Through the Eyes of Stakeholders

One-dimensional definitions of brand are clearly incomplete in this regard. To assume a brand is fully explained by its logo, slogan or legal trademark is akin to assuming a person's hair color describes everything about them. Such limitations are simplistic. While visual devices can trigger a range of responses from customers, they are but a microcosm of the many factors that influence customer perceptions and inform their judgment.

Creating a positive perception is vital to the success of any organization and the role of company leaders is to minimize the obstacles to smooth-running working environments for all employees so that they can concentrate on delivering on their portion of the brand perception. Perception is simply the process by which we become aware of something, triggered by a variety of stimuli as shown in Figure 1-2.

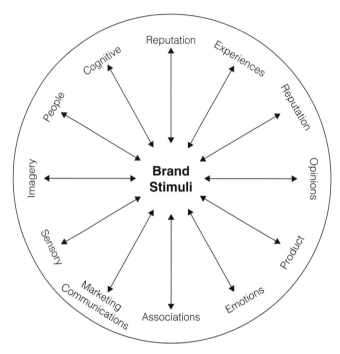

Figure 1-2　Brand Stimuli

The various stimuli create associations with the brand, provoking different responses from customers. Associations will be discussed throughout this book because nurturing them hopefully reinforces positive qualities about the brand that inspire customers to purchase.

Brand Value and Brand Equity Introduction

With brands, perceptions are created from a mix of tangible and intangible elements that send signals to the market about the quality of the company and its offerings. Positive perceptions lead to consumers favoring one brand over another, ultimately encouraging the purchase of the favored brand's products. This produces positive economic gain for the branded enterprise's management and shareholders, more commonly known as brand value. Brand value is simply a measure of the difference of the net present cash-flows from a branded offering over those of a lesser known or even unbranded competitor. Correspondingly, brand value captures the premium the market attaches to a stronger brand over a weaker one.

As we will learn in Chapter 2, brand value is often a substantial percentage of total firm value, so management is paying more attention to this measure than ever before. Brand equity is a related term that often creates confusion with brand value. Brand equity reflects the customer's perception either for or against the brand and, correspondingly, it can be positive or negative. To create brand equity firms must use tactics, including synchronized marketing and operations activities, to align their own organization toward a common set of objectives that ultimately attract and retain the interest of valuable customers. The accumulation of brand equity activities builds brand value. This can create organization tension, from determining clear brand objectives to internal accountability issues to delivering on brand promises, which will be discussed in Chapter 7. Interestingly, this holistic definition of brand applies to B2C and B2B organizations, although you will learn important differences in tactical execution in Chapters 8–10 that are relevant to each organization-type. Consider brand value analogous to the market value of your home and brand equity similar to the individual investments and contributions you make in your home over time. Each individual investment improves your home, increases your financial stake and, if the market agrees, enhances the overall value of your home. Of course, as we will see, external factors beyond our control can affect brand value. Management's task is organizing and monitoring firm actions (both people and program) to ensure the most effective use of resources so that brand value is enhanced.

Tactical Overview

Brand strategy is described and supported by the brand development plan. Brand development planning is the collections of activities marketers use to conceive, plan, develop, implement and, ultimately, measure the value contributed by the brand. These activities are more commonly called *tactics*. Marketers must ensure their plans and tactics are developed in conjunction with the firm's strategic and operational planners for proper alignment to occur. The absence of such coordination risks failure to deliver on promises made to the market. Promises are most often in the form of communication, both formal (initiated by the company, such as through advertising) and informal (initiated by consumers, such as through word of mouth), that conveys to consumers what they can expect from the company. The brand development effort will be fully discussed in Chapter 4.

Why Branding is Important

Marketers are responsible for identifying and attracting valuable customers. A variety of tools are used, from marketing communication to field sales, to accomplish this. But the companies and products that marketers represent compete in a crowded world, filled with a growing number of competitors each seeking customers as well. The challenge marketers face is convincing customers that their company's products are best suited for the customer's needs, especially as compared to the competitors'. This is no easy task especially because most markets have multiple competitors offering similar high-quality products. Competing on price to gain customers at the expense of the competition compels a company to pursue a low-cost business strategy over a long period of time. Such a strategy might increase the discounter's market share over the short term. Yet this is hard to sustain since the investment in operational excellence that is required to reduce costs and keep prices low often detracts from investment in product quality, people development, and customer service, each of which is also an important ingredient in long-term success.

Branding, or more accurately, treating a brand as a strategic asset that requires ongoing investment, is important for companies that want to differentiate their offerings and build a valuable reputation in the marketplace.

The logic of branding is clear: whether a company is small or large, local or global, B2C or B2B, having a positive reputation for making relevant products that customers value helps ensure competitive success over the long term. This is as true of the local restaurant as it is for Apple and Boeing.

Five Levels of Branding

The research for this book revealed five clear levels in brand sophistication, illustrated by Figure 1-3. The number of companies declines at each higher level, which stands to reason: Only the largest and best funded companies can invest significant resources across a broad range of marketing programs. However, a caveat is in order: new media is making it easier and less expensive (per customer) to reach customers and build a brand without investing as much, or at all, in traditional broadcast and large print campaigns. This means that companies in the lower levels can build brands in less traditional ways.

- *Level 1.* The majority of companies studied, particularly small and some mid-size, are level 1, "poorly branded." There is a handful of large companies at level 1. In some instances, they were simple operations, such as large warehouses or professional service organizations such as accountancies. Level 1 means that their basic identity is erratically executed, if at all. Identifying marks are typically worn, or missing, or small, or colors are faded, and there is general inconsistency in identity and message on collateral materials, particularly printed materials. Web sites are rudimentary, often used as an electronic brochure. Little or no use of new media is evident. Outside design experts were not used or, if they were, it was not obvious. These companies are mostly local, known to a close group of customers and some competitors, but are not highly visible nor do they have any discernable market-wide reputation.
- *Level 2.* Level 2 companies have a basic identity (logo, slogan, some ads) that is consistently deployed in signage, collateral materials, and simple advertising (usually vertical industry/trade publications versus horizontal print or broadcast). The range of businesses is more varied, although the number is lower than in level 5. More customers are aware of these firms, as are some of the surrounding business community members. These are local, niche, and some regional businesses.
- *Level 3.* Companies at this level have more diverse marketing communication and brand awareness practices. Many have more than one brand. Level 2 capabilities,

Figure 1-3   Brand Levels

plus addition of local or regional sponsorships, radio advertising, and a somewhat more sophisticated web site (perhaps with dynamic content and/or a simple shopping cart for online purchasing capability) characterize these companies. These firms are known locally, regionally, and possibly nationally in their home country. Niche brands are also represented here. To the extent that international customers are aware, some online sales are from overseas. This is also dependent on shipping practices. However, these companies focus their attention on their home markets and not international ones.

- *Level 4.* Level 4 companies have a competent, professional image using multiple marketing communication tools and sophisticated product management. Their communications are consistent and web sites are sophisticated. These companies are typically well known and considered high quality. The very best local and regional firms are sometimes in this category but level 4 is dominated by national and international firms with highly respected reputations. Niche brands, with global vertical market expertise also show up here. Their identities are well known to the public, their customer practices are well-developed, and they are considered at or near the top of their industries.

- *Level 5.* Level 5 companies demonstrate aspirational practices that inject the brand into the lifestyle of stakeholders (customers, employees, shareholders, value-chain participants) using numerous touchpoints, associations, and in-depth customer experiences. Aspirational branders create an indelible impression with their various audiences. Aspirational branders see their brand as part of a cause (not necessarily corporate social responsibility) in that the founders/brand owners believe deeply in what the brand stands for and the benefits/good it creates for people. They use a wide variety of traditional and nontraditional marketing, plus they exhibit many parts of the DDCE brand framework. While the most visible and largest global brands (by brand value) fit here, there are niche, regional, and national brands as well.

Most of this textbook is focused on Level 5 brands, although the other levels are referenced where appropriate.

Another important point is relevance. More specifically, updating the relevance of conventional branding practices. Indeed, this book may well surprise those familiar with the branding frameworks and practices of the past 30 years, many of which are still important today. But as much as there is known about brand management and associated benchmarked practices, more needs to be understood about the practices of those firms that rose above all others. Indeed, the story of today's top brands is less about the conventional wisdom they followed and more about their *defying* of it that led them to pre-eminent status. We will see many of the tried and true frameworks and models typical of brand management as it has been known for much of the second half of the twentieth century. But the companies studied for this book saw benchmarking more as a form of copying, not innovation, and consequently went their own route to brand building success. It is this route that is discussed in the *Destiny, Distinction, Culture, Experiences* framework.

Implications

Interestingly, brands have multiple owners. Of course, companies own the legal rights (including trademark) and receive the lion's share of the financial gains. Shareholders are legal owners as well, with little control at the individual level (unless they own a substantial percentage of the organization), and more control collectively, particularly in the selection of boards and, of course, the purchase and sale of shares. Customers, however, are the most interesting kind of owner. They may not own the brand in the legal sense, unless they are also shareholders, but they own the direction of the brand. This has never been more true than since the advent of Web 2.0 and associated digital media that enable instantaneous, two-way communication, increasingly customer led, that affirms (or rejects) the direction of the brand. This is a powerful sea change and one that companies everywhere must not only understand but build into their ongoing brand development. This will be discussed throughout this book, particularly in the chapters pertaining to brand experiences.

Brand Sustainability

This book is not a description of the newest brands *unless* there happens to be something sustainable and compelling, beyond being the flavor of the month. Instead, this book focuses on unique practices that make top brands successful. As a result, it is logical that few new brands are examined simply because they have yet to establish themselves over the years as formidable competitors in good times and bad. It is reasonable to suppose that a new brand, however exciting it might be, has yet to stand the test of time. Therefore, many familiar brands are discussed in this book. However, because of the global reach of the research, there are many more brands that may not be as familiar to all branding experts, let alone students of branding. This is because despite today's globalized world, there are many instances of successful brands in regional markets that have yet to grow into other global markets, even though being a global brand may one day be their destination.

Measurement

At the strategic level, measures will be broader in nature, assessing directional progress as opposed to specific program or campaign metrics. To determine useful measures, management must agree on common objectives, such as an increase in brand awareness and/or an improvement in reputation. Pragmatism should guide expectations since measurement precision, especially with strategic expectations, is unlikely because of the longer term time frame required to determine progress. The following metrics are discussed in this section:

- Awareness
- Brand Scorecards

Awareness

Metric
Awareness.[36]

Brand Benefits
Gives insight into whether consumers are aware of the brand, either directly or indirectly.

How
- *Recall.* Recall refers to a situation in which a consumer is surveyed and asked to name (or *recall*) a brand, product, or advertising campaign without prompting. This is also known as *unaided* recall. In aided recall research respondents are given a general hint to test whether a brand then comes to mind. The hints can be increasingly specific to determine how memorable a brand is. To illustrate, a consumer might be asked: "which brands do you recall when you think of MP3 players?"
- *Recognition.* Recognition asks consumers whether they recognize the company or product *after* being shown any of several prompts (advertising, product, or similar associations). For example, a consumer might be shown a selection of MP3 players and asked: "do you recognize these brands?" Note that recall and recognition can also be effective measures for short-term advertising campaigns.

Formula
Awareness measures are not specific formulas. The information is derived from questions specifically designed to test awareness. Different research techniques include surveys, focus groups, and interviews. The research can be conducted by an independent third-party market research firm, or through the brand's own, in-house research project. In either case, survey design is important, as the way that questions are asked can affect how

consumers answer. Focus groups must also be planned thoughtfully and led by an expert facilitator who can keep the discussion going and on track.

Impact on Brand

Recall is a basic measure of advertising effectiveness but it is not a measure of preference. Recall results do not indicate if a consumer has decided to purchase products advertised, or whether they even have a slight preference for the brand. Qualitative research, indeed even some quantitative research, is subject to bias and interpretation. This may discourage those seeking absolute answers about the strength of the brand. If so, then expectations must be adjusted. Recall is a reasonable, but not perfect, test of how successful company brand building has been. Important considerations include determining the specific time period being evaluated and, if possible, a comparison timeframe for benchmarking progress. Sales may show a significant increase in recent months, which might lead one to conclude that recent brand-building efforts paid off. This could also be misleading. The competition might have made a strategic blunder, causing customers to switch brands. Or, brand building from previous years might finally be working, in which case those efforts deserve at least some of the credit. But the exact cause will be unknown, so management must rely on judgment and experience.

Recall can also result from a negative association, which means the brand is at risk for being perceived poorly. Such associations can arise from many things, including:

- poor customer service when returning a product;
- product performance not meeting expectations.

Controversy can also boost awareness. Benetton, the Italian fashion apparel brand, has run brand campaigns that tackle sensitive social issues in a direct, almost confrontational way, virtually daring consumers to use their products despite their bold messages.[37] Nike has courted controversy over the years with its athlete endorsements and outsourcing practices. In Brazil, pedestrian safety advertisements featuring crushed people on the front of public buses, have brought attention to the hazards pedestrians face while they also create a buzz around their shocking images.[38] The Red Cross of Australia has run promotions featuring a donation box filled with blood (as opposed to money), giving a more visceral appeal than normally seen.[39]

Recall can even affect entire industries. Prior to April 2000, it was considered glamorous to be working for a dot.com, irrespective of what it did or whether it actually made money. In the post-April 2000 world, dot.coms are often derided and labeled as the poster child of immature, poor businesses with bad planning.

Improving reputation is an underlying premise of this book. As such, no single formula exists. Instead, a myriad of contributions from across the organization are required to improve reputation. Certainly, improving awareness is an important step in gaining acceptance in the marketplace. But to translate awareness into action whereby the public actively supports and buys the brand is beyond the scope of a single brand campaign or simple formula.

Brand value and brand equity will be discussed in Chapter 2. However, the concept of brand equity is useful as a device for assessing areas of a brand's strength and weakness.

In learning about the definition and meaning of brand, introducing the concept of brand equity begins the process of getting comfortable and acquainted with branding. The following brand scorecards shed light on this important topic.

Brand Scorecards

Metric
Brand Scorecards[40]

Brand Benefits
Identifies and scores the intangible factors that are the sources of brand equity.

How
Brand assets and liabilities are scored compared to the average brand in that market.

Formula/How Determined
Roger J. Best, Emeritus Professor of Marketing from the University of Oregon, views brand equity as the analog to the owner's equity in the balance sheet, except that brand equity is determined by subtracting brand liabilities from brand assets. He suggests two useful scorecards: one measures brand assets and the other measures brand liabilities.

Brand Assets

Best sees brands as comprised of five primary assets:

- *Brand awareness*: how aware are consumers of your company and/or its products?
- *Market leadership*: what is your market share?
- *Reputation for quality*: are you perceived as offering superior quality?
- *Brand relevance*: are your products relevant to the consumers you target?
- *Brand loyalty*: do customers stay with your products over time?

Brands are compared to the average brand in their market. There are five categories of brand assets, scored on a 1–20 point scale (20 being most valuable), with a maximum score of 100 for all five assets combined as represented by Figure 1-4.

Brand Liabilities

There are five brand liabilities:

- *Customer dissatisfaction*: how high are customer complaint levels?
- *Environmental problems*: are your environmental practices poor?
- *Product or service failures*: is product quality low?
- *Lawsuits and boycotts*: is your company facing legal problems?
- *Questionable business practices*: are there ethical lapses?

Corporate social responsibility (CSR) is increasingly important as a determinant of reputation. Does a company ignore the communities in which it operates? If so, then a low CSR score would follow.

Brand assets	Below average (0)	Somewhat below (5)	About average (10)	Somewhat above (15)	Top performer (20)	Brand asset score
Brand awareness						
Market leadership						
Reputation for quality						
Brand relevance						
Brand loyalty						
Total brand assets						

Figure 1-4   Brand Assets Scorecard

As with brand assets, marketers would want to score their companies and/or products on the chart in Figure 1-5.

The final step is to subtract brand liabilities from brand assets. The difference is a subjective interpretation of brand equity. Best[40] provides a useful diagram to illustrate the methodology—see Figure 1-6.

Impact on Brand

Marketers can assess their brand relative to the average competitor and derive a score that indicates the relative strength of the brand.

Brand assets	Below average (0)	Somewhat below (5)	About average (10)	Somewhat above (15)	Top performer (20)	Brand liability score
Customer dissatisfaction						
Environment						
Product failure						
Lawsuits						
Questionable practices						
Total brand liabilities						

Figure 1-5   Brand Liabilities Scorecard

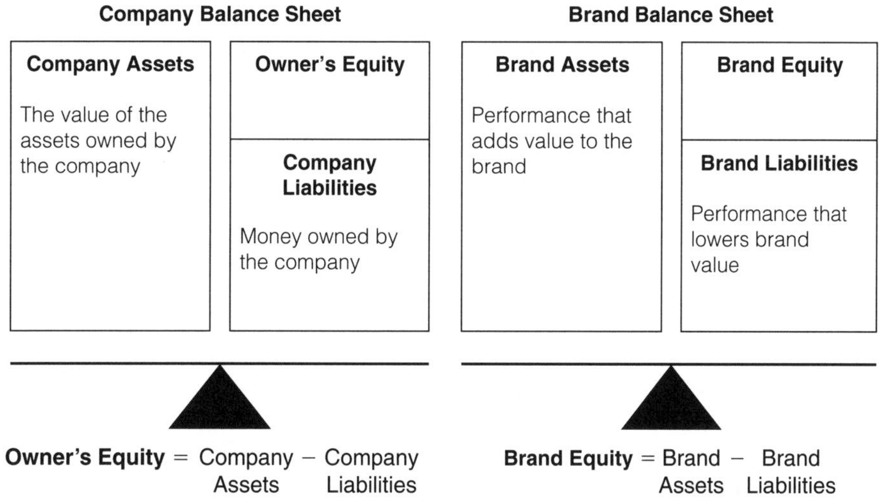

Company Balance Sheet

Company Assets	Owner's Equity
The value of the assets owned by the company	**Company Liabilities**
	Money owned by the company

Brand Balance Sheet

Brand Assets	Brand Equity
Performance that adds value to the brand	**Brand Liabilities**
	Performance that lowers brand value

Owner's Equity = Company − Company
Assets   Liabilities

Brand Equity = Brand − Brand
Assets   Liabilities

Figure 1-6   Brand Equity Calculation
Source: Best, 2005.

Summary

Over the centuries, businesses that succeed have done so by being distinctive, identifying ways to improve and finding a growing base of customers that believe the brand is relevant to their needs. This chapter introduced the concept of brand as an important strategic asset in helping companies grow in an increasingly globalized world, enabling them to develop a differentiated reputation that is relevant to customers. Understanding the definition of a brand today is the first step in knowing what questions to ask to build a successful brand. We learned that a brand is no longer defined as a logo, slogan, or ad. While these are useful representations of the brand, they represent only a small part of the total brand. A brand today is "the entire organization as seen through the eyes of stakeholders." Stakeholders include not just customers but employees, shareholders, and value-chain participants. Each of them views a brand through their own lens, which ultimately influences public perceptions as well. This establishes an important point that will be discussed throughout this book: brands are not completely controlled by companies. Indeed, particularly because of social media, the public increasingly controls brands today. As controversial as this might sound, it also represents an opportunity for brands to integrate themselves more deeply into the fabric of society. Concurrently, brands are further shaped by stimuli generated by the company and by events in the market, each interacting with the other, adding layers of meaning and attributes that give brands added depth and dimension.

Popular press can sometimes steer us into believing that brands are large, global companies with extensive resources against which smaller companies cannot effectively compete. But there are many different types of brands, competing at the local, regional, and national levels. Furthermore, there are niche brands that compete in vertical or narrow markets that are well known to their customers, even if they are not global in scope and influence.

As we learned, there are 5 levels of brand in the world today. This book will emphasize the factors that make Level 4 and Level 5 brands successful including their combination of a wide array of internal practices and external tools that create a truly holistic brand.

Discussion Questions

1. What is the difference between a product and a brand? Can they be the same thing? Are they always the same thing?
2. Why is it important to understand the definition of a brand? What is the benefit to the company?
3. How has branding evolved? What are the factors that have influenced this evolution?
4. Describe what you believe the effect each stakeholder has on the brand? Which is most important? Why do you believe that?
5. Select a popular consumer products brand and list stimuli that affect its reputation.
6. Give an example each of a Level 1 and a Level 5 brand. Can the Level 1 brand become Level 5? What will it need to do?

Case Briefs

While the concept of brand is basic at this stage, its fundamental meaning can be explored further. The following case briefs describe two companies: one is B2C and the other is a B2B firm. These two companies will be revisited later in this book adding more depth to their stories and providing contrasting yet provocative illustrations of brand building.

Case Brief: Joie de Vivre Hotels[41]
Joie de Vivre Hotels (JDV), based in San Francisco, California, is the second largest boutique hotelier in the United States, with over 30 hotels. The company's name means "Joy of Life" and this directly influences the operating philosophy. Chip Conley is JDV's CEO and founder. He has developed JDV around creating great guest experiences, defined by the philosophy of "inspiring all five senses in the first five minutes," which means that each of guests' five senses (taste, touch, sight, hearing, smell) must be ignited upon entering any of their properties. Akin to three-dimensional branding, Conley's philosophy has enabled JDV to grow to over $200 million in revenues during its 20-year history, winning awards and media

recognition from around the world. Each hotel is tightly themed, targeting very narrow customer niches.

For example, the Hotel Rex® is designed around literature and art themes, attracting a clientele with similar tastes. The Phoenix Hotel is JDV's "rock and roll" hotel, with irreverent color schemes, musical influences, art, and unusual music piped throughout the property. The Hotel Carlton emphasizes a cross-cultural theme, with photographs from exotic locations around the world. The hotel is also one of JDV's green hotels, complete with solar panels, and has been certified as a Green Business by the city of San Francisco. This eclectic hotel attempts to capture the cacophony of influences from the increasingly globalized word.

JDV's unique themes run counter to most modern hotel companies. JDV does not use a business model focused on repeating the same experiences from one hotel to the next, irrespective of the location. Instead, each JDV hotel is individualistic, creating highly original experiences for guests. The company's philosophy of inspiring all five senses in the first five minutes translates into experience-based marketing activities that make the hotels come to life for guests, from unique fabrics and textures to music, to interesting visuals and scents, all consistent with each hotel's theme. This unusual approach to marketing and product themes has produced strong results for JDV. Occupancy rates are among the highest in the U.S., revenues and profits are superior and the company has won a wide range of awards and industry recognition.

1. What is Joie de Vivre's brand strategy? What differentiates them from competitors?
2. How can brand consistency be achieved when each hotel is tailored to a different market?
3. What are the challenges management faces in running Joie de Vivre?
4. What are the advantages and disadvantages of vertical niche themes and their impact on employee transferability?
5. What are the key takeaways of Joie de Vivre's branding efforts?
6. Are their lessons useful for other organizations? If so, what types and why? If not, why not?
7. What measures would you use to determine the success of Joie de Vivre's strategy?

Case Brief: MAS Holdings[42]

MAS Holdings is a Sri Lanka-based company specializing in apparel design and manufacturing. In its 20+-year history, the company has grown to over $700 million in revenue with 45 000 employees. Customers include many of the world's leading brands: The Gap, Nike, Adidas, Speedo, and Victoria's Secret. The company is regularly acknowledged for its people development program called "Women Go Beyond," a unique recognition program that selects top performers based on their contributions at work and in their communities. The highlighted employees have posters of them on display at all MAS facilities, stories of their success in the company's newsletter, and annual movies made of them and their other selected colleagues. Since 92% of their employees are women, this program has proven to be an important catalyst for top performance over the years.

1. What is MAS Holdings' point of differentiation? What makes them unique? Is it textiles? Apparel manufacturing? People development?
2. Which one affects their brand reputation the most? How would you determine this?
3. As a competitor, how would you beat MAS?

Notes

1. 1) "Medieval Society," retrieved May 7, 2008 from www.the-orb.net/textbooks/westciv/medievalsoc.html. 2) "Urban Government and Society," retrieved May 21, 2008 from www.the-orb.net/wales/h3h03/h3h03r11.htm. 3) Braudel, F., "The Wheels of Commerce," 1982, vol. II of *Civilization and Capitalism,* Harper & Row.
2. Koehn, N., *Brand New,* © 2001 Harvard Business School Publishing Corporation, p. 12.
3. "Globalization," *The Stanford Encyclopedia of Philosophy,* retrieved July 1, 2008 from http://plato.stanford.edu/entries/globalization/.
4. "History and Heritage," retrieved October 23, 2008 from www.nikebiz.com/company_overview/history/1980s.html.
5. Adidas corporate web site, retrieved October 7, 2008 from www.adidas.com/campaigns/usiin/content/.
6. "Historical Chronology," Avis corporate web site, retrieved October 23, 2008 from www.avis.com/car-rental/content/display.ac?navId=T6M21S03.
7. "Open Happiness Press Release," Coca-Cola company web site, retrieved October 23, 2008 from www.thecoca-colacompany.com/presscenter/presskit_open_happiness_press_release.html.
8. Source: HSBC corporate web site, retrieved February 2, 2009 from www.hsbc.com/1/2/.
9. Carlsberg corporate web site, retrieved January 29, 2009 from www.carlsberg.com/.
10. BMW corporate web site, retrieved February 2, 2009 from www.bmw.com/.
11. "About Us. American Express Timeline of the Card," retrieved February 2, 2009 from http://home3.americanexpress.com/corp/50/timeline.asp.
12. "The Experience," Singapore Airlines corporate web site, retrieved February 28, 2009 from www.singaporeair.com/saa/en_UK/content/exp/index.jsp.
13. Air Asia corporate web site, retrieved March 11, 2009 from www.airasia.com/.
14. Nestlé corporate web site, retrieved May 1, 2009 from www.nestle.com/.
15. Lenovo corporate web site, retrieved May 2, 2009 from www.lenovo.com/us/en/index.html.
16. Apple corporate web site, retrieved June 7, 2008 from www.apple.com/.
17. IKEA corporate web site, retrieved December 13, 2009 from www.ikea.com/.
18. "Presidential Campaign Memorabilia Exhibit Open at the Baylor Collections of Political Materials," Baylor University News, retrieved January 3, 2009 from www.baylor.edu/pr/news.php?action=story&story=49120.

19. Ibid.

20. "History and Heritage," Nike corporate web site, retrieved October 23, 2008 from http://web.archive.org/web/20071023034940/http://www.nike.com/nikebiz/nikebiz. jhtml?page=5&item=origin.

21. Intel corporate web site, retrieved September 12, 2008 from www.intel.com/pressroom/intel_ inside.htm.

22. Yelkur, R., Tomkovic, C. and Traczyk, P. "Super Bowl Advertising Effectiveness: Hollywood Finds the Games Golden," *Journal of Advertising Research,* March 2004, retrieved January 17, 2008 from http://journals.cambridge.org/download.php?file=%2FJAR%2FJAR44_ 01%2FS0021849904040085a.pdf&code=22c883372b2e623cb38b329bcd41b762.

23. Bajaj, V. and Edmonston, P., "ETrade Struggles to Avert Big Write-down as Shares Tumble," November 13, 2007, *International Herald Tribune,* retrieved November 15, 2007 from www.iht. com/articles/2007/11/13/business/etrade.php, cited in Davis, J. A., *The Olympic Games Effect,* © 2008 John Wiley & Sons (Asia) Pte Ltd, p. 173.

24. Davis, J. A. *The Olympic Games Effect: How Sports Marketing Builds Strong Brand,* © 2008 John Wiley & Sons (Asia) Pte Ltd, p. 173, which cites Berger, W. "Hot Spots!" retrieved December 14, 2007, from www.wired.com/wired/archive/8.02/commercials_pr.html.

25. American Marketing Association web site, retrieved August 24, 2008 from www.marketingpower. com/_layouts/Dictionary.aspx?dLetter=B.

26. U.S. Legal, retrieved February 11, 2009 from http://definitions.uslegal.com/b/brands- and-brand-names/.

27. "Global Business Law and Legal Definition," retrieved February 11, 2009 from http://definitions. uslegal.com/g/global-business/.

28. Aaker, D. A., *Building Strong Brands,* © 1996 David A. Aaker, Simon & Shuster UK Ltd., pp. 7–8.

29. Keller, K. L., *Strategic Brand Management: Building, Measuring and Managing Brand Equity,* © 2008 Pearson Education, Inc., pp. 2–3.

30. Schmitt, B. H., *Experiential Marketing,* © 1999 Bernd H. Schmitt, pp. 7–10.

31. Ibid. p. 21.

32. Source: retrieved May 17, 2008 from www.snopes.com/business/misxlate/ancestor.asp.

33. "Best Global Brands," retrieved December 21, 2008 from www.interbrand.com/best_global_ brands.aspx.

34. MAS Holdings corporate web site, retrieved May 11, 2008 from www.masholdings.com/, the author also visited the executive and toured factories for several days in 2005.

35. Based on ongoing research by John A. Davis. Reports on over 200 companies from around the world conducted from October 2000. Companies come from multiple industries. The primary focus of the research was to understand the attributes and associations that underlie brands, and identify the programs and processes undertaken to build brand value.

36. Davis, J., *Measuring Marketing: 103 Key Metrics Every Marketer Needs,* © 2006 John Wiley & Sons (Asia) Pte Ltd, pp. 252–259.

37. Benetton Group corporate web site, retrieved January 8, 2008 from http://press.benettongroup. com/ben_en/about/campaigns/list/.

38. TrendHunter Magazine, retrieved March 30, 2009 from www.trendhunter.com/photos/723.

39. Retrieved March 30, 2009 from www.trendhunter.com/trends/bloodvertising-red-cross-ad-for- blood-donation.

40. Best, R. J., *Market-Based Management: Strategies for Growing Customer Value and Profitability*, Pearson Education, Inc., 2005, 2004, 2000, 1997, pp. 220–223, cited in Davis, J., *Measuring Marketing: 103 Key Metrics Every Marketer Needs*, © 2007 John Wiley & Sons (Asia) Pte Ltd, pp. 236–240.

41. Interviews with Chip Conley in 2002, 2003 and 2008. Joie de Vivre corporate web site, retrieved December 12, 2008 from www.jdvhotels.com.

42. Meetings with the MAS Holdings executive team in fall 2005 in Colombo, Sri Lanka, MAS Holdings corporate web site retrieved September 21, 2009 from www.masholdings.com.

Brand Value

2

Topics

Preview

Why do companies aspire to build strong brands? Part of the answer lies in the value created and contributed by a well-known and respected brand. There are many factors that contribute to a brand's value. Measuring it is approached several ways. This is also a key challenge. While one might argue that value is attributable to a brand's tangible assets, such as goods produced for sale and inventories held, this does not account for *all* value as perceived by customers in particular and stakeholders overall. For example, strong brands can typically command a premium in the market, beyond that of lesser-known rivals, which creates a price value lift. Brands can also create value by being highly differentiated, spurring interest and demand from customers seeking uniqueness.

A brand's reputation affects the value associated with it—lower reputations garner less respect than higher reputations. As we will see there are differences in methodologies and philosophies. This complicates the pursuit of brand value measurement.

This book emphasizes the practices that help companies create strong brands and build sustainable value. In this chapter, we introduce ways to assess and measure brand value. Knowing how to measure a brand's value is vital to companies seeking ways to justify their investments in marketing activities. David Haigh, CEO of BrandFinance, a leading brand consultancy states, "63% of enterprise value is intangible."[1]

David Haigh's comment highlights the increasingly important role that intangible assets have in the total value of the firm. No longer is it sufficient to ascribe such unexplained value as *goodwill* on the balance sheet. Accounting rules for valuing intangibles have been updated around the world over the years, placing added importance on properly assessing their worth. This discussion is of paramount importance to brand building because management's strategic decisions will have a profound impact on corresponding organizational activities in support of growing the brand that, in turn, will affect intangible value.

Brand Equity and Brand Value Revisited

To begin, a point of clarification is in order. A minor controversy, or perhaps more accurately *confusion*, exists about the difference between brand equity and brand value. It is understandable given the profusion of theories and books offering alternative explanations. For the purposes of clarity, they are defined as follows:

- *Brand equity* describes stakeholder response in the form of an increase in customers, revenues, and margins than would otherwise be possible without marketing support to build awareness.
- *Brand value* represents the total value of the brand.

As one can readily surmise, complications still arise as there are numerous ways to interpret how best to measure brand value. But a simple example will help. While a company's customers, revenues, and profits are obviously vital statistics, they do not describe the entire value of the enterprise. For instance, prior to declaring bankruptcy in 2009, General Motors (GM)'s revenues were over US$200 billion. But its total market capitalization (total company value) had declined to less than US$20 billion. Revenues were high but investor support and company credibility were low, which affected its market capitalization. Brand value was a significant portion of this, and as evidenced by the low market capitalization, its brand value was low or even negative. Conversely, Apple's revenues were over US$32 billion in 2008 and its market capitalization was over US$100 billion.[2] According to Interbrand's 2008 Best Global Brands survey,[3] Apple's brand value was US$13.7 billion, representing over 40% of its revenues and over 13% of its market capitalization. Brand value, in essence, measures the total financial value of the brand, above and beyond the customers, revenues, and profits.

Throughout this book we will focus on brand value, whether that business is the entire company or an individual brand within. BrandFinance and Interbrand publish annual surveys of the world's best brands measured by brand value. The methodology they use is outlined in this chapter, as are other approaches. There is no single "best" approach to brand value but the approaches described in this chapter give a richer sense of the complexities and variables involved.

Brand Building to Create Brand Value

Building a successful brand means having a strategic brand-development plan that guides management thinking and actions. Brand value is created and enhanced through disciplined brand management practices. As a brand's reputation grows, so does its preference from customers. Consistently positive customer experiences with a brand further strengthen the customer's attachment to the brand. This brand attachment acts as a decision-making filter: when customers are asked to choose between the brand they know versus a new entrant offering a similar product, they are likely to select the brand they have grown to know. For this reason, a strong brand can be a competitive advantage.

However, brand building, including an earnest investment in developing profitable customer relationships, is not guaranteed and company management should be cautioned against thinking that once they have achieved a measure of brand success their work is done. Brand building must shift to brand management and enhancement if the initial work is to produce long-term success. Throughout the branding process, there are four factors that shape and determine a brand's ongoing value. They are given in Figure 2-1.

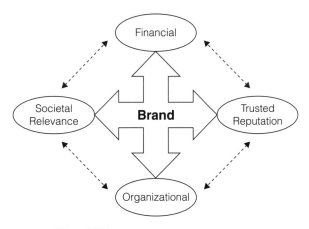

Figure 2-1 Dimensions of Brand Value

Dimensions of Brand Value

Examples are given for each value. In addition, Visa is illustrated in all four values because their over 20-year support of the Olympic Games provides a particularly rich example of how a focused brand-building effort can reap significant dividends across all areas of value.

Trusted Reputation

Trust between parties in any relationship is required for long-term success. When a company invests money and resources in building a brand, success is measured not just by financial return but by the trust invested by customers. This trust is reflected in the buyer's decision to select the brand over the competition. Trust is fundamental to economic success because customers are unlikely to depart with their money unless the product they receive in return is one they trust. Earning trust, both internally from employees and externally from customers, comes from management's efforts to provide the right combination of goods, services, and support that address relevant needs. Employees and customers gain a first-hand understanding of the company through internal practices and external offerings (in the form of goods and services) that prove or refute expectations that have been created by a myriad of influences in marketing communications, word of mouth, and past experiences. The net effect of these influences equates to the firm's reputation and answers the question "does the company deliver on its promises?"

Asking this question is not just an academic exercise and developing a trusted reputation does not happen overnight. Management must structure strategic planning, hiring, implementation, and customer-development practices with the expressed purpose of building trust inside and outside the firm. Traditional and new media tools, from broadcast and print to digital, offer marketers numerous avenues for communication that can be tailored to the interests of internal and external audiences. Successful brand building imposes an important responsibility on companies to communicate clearly with messages that reinforce their unique abilities while concurrently conveying the relevance of these abilities to their targeted audiences. Many of the factors that influence the development of trust are under management's control. Trust building is not limited to marketing communications approaches. Marketing management, of course, must devise coordinated and integrated programs (i.e. products, services, support, promotions, advertising, facilities, sales techniques . . .) that shape a positive experience for customers whenever they interact with the company. But there are many more variables to consider, so the complexity of building a trusted reputation has grown commensurately. At the same time, the Internet and wireless communications have placed more control in the hands of the market and away from companies, putting an added burden on companies to focus on alignment across all operations to minimize inconsistent delivery so that areas outside of management's direct control, such as consumer-led blogs and podcasts, are less prone to reputation-bashing messages. The benefit is that when trust is developed from multiple touchpoints (see below) in the customer's experience (pre-, during, and post-purchase phases), it becomes a more memorable and meaningful form of trust.

Touchpoints

The term "touchpoints" describes any point of contact related to the firm, whether tangible or intangible. Touchpoints affect people's perceptions of the firm, shaping their beliefs and confidence in the organization. Brand building is a complex undertaking because management has to ensure the highest quality with every touchpoint. The best touchpoints of a brand are relevant to customers and also resonate with them. Asking "are the touchpoints *relevant* to my customer's needs and, if so, do they *resonate* with them?" is essential to creating a positive brand experience. Not all touchpoints are either relevant to or resonant with customers. The front door of an office is unlikely to inspire customer fondness for the company, whereas products, services, and the people that deliver them will. "Relevant" products and services simply means that the offerings fill a specific need, and "resonance" means that the offerings connect with them emotionally and/or fit in with the customer's lifestyle.

Tangible Touchpoints

Tangible assets are physical representations of your brand. Examples include products, packaging, print advertising, store design and furnishings, and even people.

Intangible Touchpoints

Intangibles, by definition, cannot be physically touched. Instead, people *experience* them. Examples include services, atmosphere, ambience, and attitude. Intangible touchpoints can delight or disappoint consumers and two people may well interpret the same intangible touchpoint in entirely different ways. Successful brand building requires management to promote a culture in which employees are motivated to create an ongoing, positive experience for customers, which means employees have the flexibility to shape customer experiences individually, as long as the overall effort is consistent with the firm's brand strategy.

Chapter 11 describes how to create a touchpoints map, a valuable tool for understanding the many different points of contact between the brand and market.

EXAMPLE 2-1:

Visa

Since 1986, Visa's management has viewed sports as something valued and shared across cultures, bringing people together to celebrate competition and athletic achievement. By aligning the company closely with the Olympics (and Visa's other sports sponsorships—Paralympics, Futbol World Cup, and Rugby World Cup), Visa management believes that the halo effect from these renowned events would cast a favorable glow over Visa. The company has done far more than attach its name and logo to internationally recognized sports events. Visa becomes deeply involved in each community where an event occurs. The net benefit is that Visa has shifted its market position from a commodity product to market leader with a premier reputation. Not only did its market share increase 33% as shown above, but its rating as "best overall card" rose to 50%. The growth and solidifying of its reputation has been the result of a patient, long-term, strategic effort to position Visa as a reliable, convenient and vital contributor to the lifestyle of its customers, exemplified by its 23+ year relationship with the Olympic Games that will continue for several years more.[4]

Johnson & Johnson

Johnson & Johnson has been consistently recognized over the years as one of the most respected and trusted companies. In 2008, Johnson & Johnson was ranked #5 in the Ponemon Institute's annual ranking of the most trusted companies in the U.S.[5] In 2009 it was named "The Most Respected Company" by *Barron's* magazine[6] as well as "One of the Best Places to Work" by the Human Rights Campaign.[7] According to Interbrand's annual Best Global Brand Survey, their brand value has increased from US$2.5 billion in 2002 to $3.5 billion in 2008, a 40% rise during that time.[8]

Organizational

Organizational brand value describes the intangible benefits that all employees receive when company management describes long-term strategic direction clearly. As with having a Trusted Reputation, organizational value is a requirement for sustained success. Top companies that have built recognized global brands have management teams that are firm believers in inspiring their employees to understand and identify with customers. This is a departure from conventional business wisdom that focuses on persuading customers to buy products. For employees to identify with customers, they must first identify with their own organizations. Company leaders are responsible for making their companies special to employees. Celebrating the traditions that have made the firm successful over time and using past stories of success to inspire new generations of employees to add new chapters to the company's history are among the approaches management can use to connect more directly with their own employees. Employees that feel invested in the company and believe in the company's direction are more likely to be motivated to understand and empathize with customers, providing management with insights about customer needs. In turn, these insights can be turned into more relevant offerings that resonate with customers. When company leadership articulates a clear direction, then employees have an easier time understanding how they fit in and can contribute to the firm's long-term success. Company leaders have a corresponding responsibility to describe the long-term strategy in updated language that is consistent with the times in which they compete, yet also staying true to the personality characteristics for which the company is known. The strategic direction described by company leaders should implicitly recognize the investments made in attracting employee talent that reinforces the competencies for which the company is known, while explicitly reinforcing its reputation to the market.

EXAMPLE 2-2:

Apple

Steve Jobs' well-known emphasis on making "insanely great" products that fit in well with their customers' lifestyle has helped catapult the company from near bankruptcy in 1997 to the global leader in portable music, in addition to rebuilding their computer business to #3 (behind HP and Dell) in the U.S. with iconic products. Revenues, which were $7.1 billion, had climbed to $32.4 billion in 2008, and gross profits soared to $11.1 billion. Employees at Apple know they are working for a company driven by a larger purpose inspired by a singularly clear organizational value focused on making insanely great products. Such a clear focus translates into a culture that feels different inside, and employees both sense it and contribute to making it stronger. Apple's strong organizational value contributes to its reputation for both innovative products and a sense of mystique. This has made the premium attached to Apple especially lucrative, even though much of that premium is due to organizational intangibles. The net result: prior to the September 2008 financial crisis, Apple's market capitalization exceeded that of Hewlett Packard and Dell (August 2008: Apple = $143 billion; HP = $107 billion; Dell = $50 billion) even though both of them had substantially larger revenues (HP = $118.3 billion; Dell = $61.1 billion).[9]

Visa

Visa developed internal programs that involved employees in their Olympic sponsorship effort, from contests to win tickets to various Olympiads, to benefits provided by Visa's other corporate partners, from Disney to Taco Bell to Clearview Cinemas. These corporate relationships have associated Visa with other highly regarded brands, fostering internal confidence. Visa's success in winning the right to sponsor the World Cup in 2010 and 2014 provided another source of inspiration for employees, as do the company's efforts with the Paralympics and Rugby World Cup.[10]

Societal Relevance

Consumers and business leaders increasingly evaluate companies based on whether the companies themselves are good corporate citizens as reflected in any efforts to develop solutions to societal problems, including environmental, energy, education, healthcare, or humanitarian issues. We increasingly expect companies to be forces for good, beyond making quality products that earn a profit, by actively participating or investing in business practices that improve the quality of life overall. Societal relevance refers to value contributed by the company to society at large. There are two aspects:

- Individual value derived from acquiring products or services that reflect our own values and self-image and are relevant to our needs. This applies to people, who seek products that help define their identity and contribute to their self-worth, and businesses seeking products to address challenges that otherwise hinder competitive success.

- Societal value as demonstrated by the company's efforts to be genuinely involved with the communities it serves, whether they are local, national, or global.

Individual Value

Marketers are responsible for understanding the profiles of their target customers, be they consumers or businesses. The classic marketing customer identification framework known as *segmentation, targeting,* and *positioning* (see Chapter 9) is a helpful starting point as it assists marketers to understand that people buy things not just because they think they need them but because these goods reinforce their sense of identity. Marketers can add significant value to their customer analysis by researching the psychographic profiles of target customers. This information can guide clearer product design and marketing communications because marketers will know the factors that appeal more directly to these customers and satisfy relevant, even personal, desires. When consumers purchase well known branded goods, the purchase desire is often the result of familiarity born from past knowledge of and experience with the product, coupled with a sense of personal wellbeing that arises from having a recognized good with a clear image and reputation. Consumers gain a sense of identity from the way they see themselves and how others see them, providing a benefit in the form of self-esteem.

EXAMPLE 2-3:

Rolex

For example, Rolex has a well-known brand name in the premium watch market. While they are not the most expensive or exclusive watches in the world, Rolex has a premium image that defines luxury and success, and company management uses this image to appeal to a narrow target customer. The symbolic value of owning a Rolex suggests the owner is successful, wealthy, and has good taste—associations that are part of the appeal of owning a Rolex.[11]

Starbucks

For example, Starbucks is known for making high quality mass-produced coffee that has built a loyal customer following all over the world. But many customers would not continue buying Starbucks products if the company stopped selling fair-trade coffee.[12]

Nokia

Nokia has extensive involvement in local and global outreach through community projects such as corporate giving and volunteering on environmental issues, ethical supply-chain standards and human rights.[13] For example, in 2007 employees volunteered more than 32 000 hours in 32 countries for local communities. The company collaborates with governments and not-for-profit organizations to address youth-related social issues through its youth life skills and education.[14] Nokia has invested over 6 million in preschool care and education in rural China to establish 1200+ early childhood care and development centers benefitting more than 70 000 children.[15] Nokia also has joined forces with the international children's organization, Plan, to raise awareness of children's rights and tackle child poverty.[16]

Johnson & Johnson

Johnson & Johnson's societal relevance is well established. Over the years the company has supported significant causes as a component of their giving efforts, including Saving & Improving Lives, Building Healthcare Capacity and Preventing Diseases. Part of their building healthcare capacity effort includes support for nurses. "America's Nurses: They Dare to Care" was a campaign launched in 2002 to draw attention to the critical shortage of nurses in the U.S. by acknowledging the work of nurses and encouraging people to enter the profession. The campaign is a top corporate priority and reflects the company's Credo (see Chapter 5: Destiny). Johnson & Johnson was awarded "The Ron Brown Award for Corporate Leadership" by the White House for their work on the Campaign for Nursing's Future.[17]

In 2004, the company launched two successful programs—Together Rx Access™ Card Program and Partnership for Prescription Assistance. The Together Rx Access™ Card was jointly launched with nine other pharmaceutical firms to provide savings of 40% or more on prescription drugs and products to Americans lacking prescription drug coverage. The Partnership for Prescription Assistance, a voluntary collaboration between healthcare organizations and J&J, helped low-income and uninsured patients gain access to free or low-cost prescription medicines. Through these two programs, Johnson & Johnson upheld its responsibility in contributing to the society by meeting the challenges of making medical advancements accessible and affordable.[18]

Corporate Social Responsibility

For societal relevance to have actual meaning that contributes value, managers must develop programs that affirm the seriousness of the company's commitment to society at large, from charitable organizations to church groups to school programs to sports teams to environmental issues. Such efforts are labeled corporate social responsibility (CSR), although the term is sometimes regarded with cynicism as companies pretending to be concerned about society as a cover to hide their profit-driven ambitions. Corporate social responsibility has grown because people around the world are learning that many of the business practices of the past 100 years, while yielding growth and higher standards of living for many countries, have also led to significant social and health problems. Company leaders are paying closer attention to the CSR practices of their network of suppliers, distributors, and similar business partners, in addition to their own firms' efforts. Such efforts are becoming a far more important factor in determining successful business performance, since they contribute to while also extending well beyond basic financial results.[19]

EXAMPLE 2-4:

Mattel

Mattel was ranked #7 in the top "100 Best Corporate Citizens" in 2009 by CRO (Corporate Responsibility Officer) magazine,[20] which identifies companies that excel at serving a variety of stakeholders well. In 2007, Mattel released a Global Citizenship Report[21]—the first and only toy company to issue such a report, which included detailed information about the company's environmental and social performance. Chief executive Robert Eckert Mattel stated at the time that the company's values were not memorable or consistent with the company's culture or vision. They realized that "play" was a common theme, and reoriented their values accordingly: *play to grow; play together; play with passion; play fair.*[22]

Mattel takes an active role in improving the communities where it is located. For example, Mattel Children's Foundation, which was established in 1978, promotes the spirit of giving and encourages community involvement for all employees of Mattel worldwide. The programs included U.S. and international grant making, employee-matching gifts, scholarships and volunteer grants, toy donations, corporate contributions, partnerships and volunteerism.[23] Over 2000 employees have been involved in the Mattel Players volunteer program, where they volunteer in charitable activities in 45 locations and 21 countries around the world.[24]

Visa

Visa's Olympic sponsorship has provided over $120 million in support for Olympic teams and athletes around the world, including the U.S. gymnastics and U.S. track and field and Team Visa Europe (Summer and Winter teams), the U.S. ski and snowboard teams and the Canadian bobsled and skeleton teams. In previous years, Visa sponsored the Japanese ski jumping team and the Russian hockey team. Visa has also sponsored selected individual athletes in figure skating and snowboarding. Visa has also created a children's art program called "Visa Olympics of the Imagination." Launched in 1994, the program teaches children between the ages of 10–14 about the Olympic movement. Concurrently, the children are entered into an art competition, and selected winners have a chance to go to the Olympics, sponsored by Visa. According to company figures, more than 1 million children have competed, and 181 from 48 countries have attended the Games. The pictures from this program are a vibrant reminder of the power and imagery associated with the Olympics. Visa's "Olympics of the Imagination" illustrate nontraditional marketing (see Chapter 10), connecting children to the Olympics by channeling their energy and creativity for the purpose of conveying a hopeful image of the world, inspired by the possibility of actually attending the Games, yet also enabling Visa to use the resulting artwork to promote both the children's program and the company's support for the Olympics.

Equally important, Visa was the first global sponsor of the International Paralympic Committee and supports numerous national Paralympic sports federations. This effort included the first Paralympic web site, usable by people with hearing, sight, and other disabilities. Visa has actively and visibly supported and encouraged both fan and athlete involvement in the Paralympics. For example, Visa's support of the British Paralympic Association (BPA) sent over 300 athletes and staff to the 2004 Paralympic Games in Athens. The Athens Games saw Visa partner with regional Paralympic groups to encourage attendance by Visa customers. Visa also helped provide accessibility to the disabled that attended the 2004 Athens Paralympics.[25]

Financial

There are many methods for measuring financial contribution, including brand value. For brand value, the variables differ depending on the user's definition. (Is it a trademark? Is it goodwill? Is it a product? Is it the entire organization? Is it reputation?) Measuring brand value is both complex and imprecise because the calculation involves assumptions about tangible and intangible assets. Intangible assets are particularly challenging because determining a credible value for *leadership* or *confidence* is influenced by the judgment of professional analysts and even market perceptions overall. Marketers have numerous marketing tools they can use to attract and retain customers, from short-term promotions (i.e. price discounts for a limited period of time) to long-term awareness campaigns (i.e. national or global television ads that market a company's personality or lifestyle fit). Each can be measured with varying degrees of accuracy using methods illustrated throughout this book.

In 2008 Interbrand ranked Coca-Cola's brand value as the highest in the world at just over $65 billion, which was approximately 50% of Coca-Cola's total market capitalization of $125 billion at the time.[26] BrandFinance's methodology calculated Coca-Cola's brand value at more than $43 billion. Part of the $20 billion valuation difference is due to variations in methodologies employed by each firm. Both methods are useful, depending on the objectives sought by management in their measurement efforts.[27]

Measuring the financial value of most business activities provides management with results that indicate the success or failure of a given investment. Brand development is the combination of activities designed to produce a common understanding of the product or company and the associated reputation such that customers find enough value to inspire their purchase of products and/or services. When a brand's reputation changes, there is a corresponding change in measurable financial value, which then affects overall enterprise value. Marketers and senior managers are responsible for producing economic gain from their decisions and business activities to positively impact brand and enterprise value. To *extract* financial value from their activities means management must also *create* value by thinking then acting in support of activities that fully develop the firm's span of influence beyond financial results. In fact, financial results are the by-product of management's efforts to align resources and investments in a way that fully develops and exploits the firm's differentiated expertise.

EXAMPLE 2-5:

Visa

Visa financial and market performance has improved significantly over the years, particularly since it emphasized sports sponsorships as a key component of its brand building activities. Since 1986, Visa has sponsored the Olympic Games as a TOP Program sponsor (The Olympic Partner Program) initiating its Olympic sponsorship efforts in 1986. Visa's 2007 operating revenues were $5.84 billion and while figures are not available for 1986, one can surmise that revenues have grown.[28] The number of credit cards issued has grown from 137 million to over 1.7 billion and transactions volume (the total volume of payments and cash flowing through Visa payment services) has increased from $111 billion to $4.35 trillion. Between 2002 and 2009, the total number of transactions using Visa credit cards grew from 34 billion to over 46 billion. Visa's global market share increased 33% to 54% (MasterCard had a 29% share, American Express had 13% and Discover had 4% during this time). One of Visa's original reasons for sponsoring the Olympics in the mid-1980s was to increase awareness. As of the 2004 Olympic Games in Athens, Visa attained 87% consumer awareness, the highest level of awareness among all sponsors, indicating the power and strength of the Visa brand and the success of its Olympic sponsorship efforts. In March 2008, Visa changed from a private company to a public company, with the largest initial public offering (IPO) in U.S. history, valued at $17.9 billion. As of June 2009, Visa's market capitalization was $48.9 billion, which was eight times 2007 sales.[29]

Understanding and Measuring Brand Value

As a known brand comprises a significant portion of enterprise value, marketers have a responsibility to measure the contribution to total value that the brand adds. However, measuring brand value precisely is an elusive goal because there is no single best methodology. Instead, different approaches have been developed based on corporate objectives. Even with clear objectives, brand value measurement is subject to numerous variables and assumptions. This book is designed to provide useful tools and frameworks to help you understand the many ingredients that are mixed together to create a viable brand recipe.

Simplified Brand Valuation

MacInnis and Park Brand Equity Methodology [30]

Deborah MacInnis, Professor of Marketing at USC's Marshall School of Business, and C. Whan Park, the Joseph A. DeBell Professor of Marketing at USC's Marshall School of Business, describe brand equity "as the financial value of brand reflecting its efficiency in attracting and retaining customers." They describe a marketing accounting method similar to industrial accounting, but with marketing costs substituted for cost of goods sold. When marketing costs are subtracted from total revenues, a gross magnitude of brand value results, as Table 2-1 describes.

Calculating the return on marketing (brand value divided by marketing costs) helps determine the effectiveness of marketing investments made on behalf of the brand (see Table 2-2 and 2-3).

A brief look at companies A and B in example 1 shows they have identical brand values, but Company A has a higher return on marketing costs, a sign that Company A is more efficient with its marketing expenditures.

Table 2-1   Industrial and Marketing Accounting Systems

Industrial Accounting System	Marketing Accounting System
Total Revenues	Total Revenues
–Cost of goods sold	*–Total marketing costs*
=Operating Profit	=Magnitude of brand value
–Marketing expenses	*–Cost of goods sold*
=Contribution margin	=Contribution margin

Source: MacInnis, D. and Park, C.W., "Making the Most of Your Brand: Leveraging Brand Equity Through Branding Strategies", March 2004, retrieved June 2, 2008 from www.marketingprofs.com/4/macpark2.asp.

Table 2-2   Example 1 of Brand Valuation

Example 1	Firm A	Firm B
Total Revenues	$2.000,000	$3.000,000
–Total marketing costs	*–$1,000,000*	*–$2,000,000*
=Magnitude of brand value	=$1,000,000	=$1,000,000
Operating Margin	$1,000,000	$1,000,000
÷marketing costs	*÷$1,000,000*	*÷$2,000,000*
=Return on marketing costs	=1.0	=0.5

Source: MacInnis, D. and Park, C.W., "Making the Most of Your Brand: Leveraging Brand Equity Through Branding Strategies", March 2004, retrieved June 2, 2008 from www.marketingprofs.com/4/macpark2.asp.

Table 2-3   Example 2 of Brand Valuation

Example 2	Firm A	Firm B
Total Revenues	$2.000,000	$1,250,000
–Total marketing costs	*–$1.000.000*	*–$500,000*
=Magnitude of brand value	=$1,000,000	=$750,000
Operating Margin	$1,000,000	$750,000
÷marketing costs	*÷$1.000.000*	*÷$500.000*
=Return on marketing costs	=1.0	=1.5

Source: MacInnis, D. and Park, C.W., "Making the Most of Your Brand: Leveraging Brand Equity Through Branding Strategies", March 2004, retrieved June 2, 2008 from www.marketingprofs.com/4/macpark2.asp.

Example 2 shows that Company A has a larger brand value than Company B, but Company B has a better return on marketing costs. If this were to continue over time, Company B would eventually overtake Company A in brand value (assuming the other figures remain in the same relative proportions).

MacInnis and Park's basic brand value calculation is an initial pass at determining the magnitude of gross brand value. It is reasonable to assume that brand value would be attached to a company's marketing efficiency—companies with better marketing efficiency (higher ratio of brand value to marketing costs) should be rewarded with a higher brand value than companies with a lower marketing efficiency. The converse is likely to be true as well.

Finally, MacInnis and Park mention that this analysis is useful when evaluating the same brand in the same industry. But if the brand valuation objective is to compare your brand with that from a different industry, then the formula must be adjusted to reflect differing growth rates in each industry. The rationale is that growth-rate differences between industries can distort brand-to-brand comparisons because one industry may be growing overall and thereby lifting the value of all companies within (a simple example is the dot. com mania of the late 1990s), while a brand being compared from another industry may be affected by a slowdown in that industry (the U.S. auto industry, for example). In either case individual brand values are distorted by the larger industry forces. Therefore, adjusting the formula by adding growth rates would be useful:

$$\frac{Marketing\ efficiency \times total\ revenues}{1 + (1 + growth\ rate) \times marketing\ efficiency}$$

Formal Brand Valuation

BrandFinance Brand Valuation Methodology

BrandFinance's Brand Valuation[31]

BrandFinance, based in the U.K., is a global brand valuation consultancy. In its work, brand is defined as *trademark and associated intellectual property*. It argues that cost-based brand valuations are insufficient because the costs incurred building the brand have little relationship to the current value of a brand. Market-based brand valuation is also not adequate because directly comparative data between brands are hard to find and, furthermore, each brand's approach to building value is unique—a point that is emphasized throughout this book. The royalty relief method is one of the most common approaches because, as pointed out by BrandFinance:

> . . . if a brand has to be licensed from a third party brand owner, a royalty rate on turnover will be charged for the privilege of using the brand. By owning the brand such royalties are avoided. The royalty relief method involves estimating likely future sales and then applying an appropriate royalty rate to arrive at the income attributable to brand royalties in future years. The stream of notional brand royalty is discounted back to a net present value—the brand value."[32]

The royalty relief method has benefits for tax and financial-statement needs. However, more insightful analysis about how the brand actually creates value (and not just measuring it) is ideal. The economic use method serves this purpose because it brings together market data, including consumer research and competitor insights, with forecasted brand earnings. This helps value the brand by market segment and determine overall brand value. There are four analyses in BrandFinance's valuation methodology:

- financial forecasts;
- brand value added BVA®—analysis of the brand's contribution to demand;
- ßrandßeta® analysis—determination of the risk attached to future earnings;
- valuation and sensitivity analysis.

Ahead of the conducting the valuation, the segments to be valued must be determined so that comparable data that delineate customer segments and provide equivalent data on competitors are available. Once this is determined, the valuation process can begin.

Financial Forecasts
Financial data are gathered at the macro (market) and micro (firm) levels on the brand's customers, markets, products, and performance in recent years. Trends are determined, as are comparisons with competitors, to determine the brand's strengths and weaknesses.

Calculating Brand Value Added
Next, the brand's contribution to demand is determined by identifying key demand drivers using BVA®, which is derived from economic value added (EVA) and a combination of market data, company financial data and demand drivers. Demand drivers are derived from a combination of qualitative and quantitative research, along with management insight. Different factors affecting brand purchase are considered, such as product variety, the impact of competitor brands, the effect of different time periods, product quality and brand reputation.

ßrandßeta® Analysis
BrandFinance now determines the discount rate applying the following formulas. This step involves assessing the risk factor (beta) associated with the earnings using a tool called βrandβeta®:

$$\text{Discount rate} = \beta\text{rand}\beta\text{eta}^{®} \text{ adjusted cost of equity} \times (\text{proportion of equity funding})$$
$$+ \text{ cost of debt} \times (\text{proportion of debt funding})$$

$$\beta\text{rand}\beta\text{eta}^{®} \text{ adjusted cost of equity} = \text{risk free rate} + (\text{equity risk premium sector beta}$$
$$\times \beta\text{rand}\beta\text{eta}^{®})$$

βrandβeta® analysis incorporates the following 10 objective indicators of brand performance, shown in the general scoring template in Table 2-4.

Table 2-4   Brand Performance Scoring Table

Attribute	Score
Time in the market	0–10
Distribution	0–10
Market share	0–10
Market position	0–10
Sales growth rate	0–10
Price premium	0–10
Price elasticity	0–10
Marketing spend	0–10
Advertising awareness	0–10
Brand awareness	0–10
Total	0–100

Source: Haigh, D., *Brand Valuation: Managing and Leveraging Your Brand,* © 2000 Brand Finance plc., p. 16.

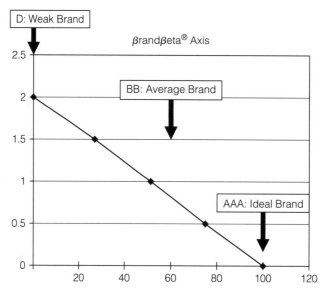

Figure 2-2   BrandBeta axis
Source: Haigh, D., *Brand Valuation: Managing and Leveraging Your Brand,* © 2000 Brand Finance plc., p. 16.

A score of 50 means the brand represents an average risk investment in the sector being studied. This equates to a βrandβeta® of 1, and the discount rate applied will be the average composite rate for the entire sector.[33]

Figure 2-2 displays the βrandβeta® risk factor for different cumulative attribute scores. Brands with lower scores have a higher risk.

Valuation and Sensitivity Analysis

Calculating net present value (NPV) is the last part of the analysis, determining the value of projected earnings for the brand over time. The spreadsheet in Table 2.5 shows the brand value.

A quick review reveals the sequence of calculations that resulted in value to Year 5 on the lower left. The base year is called Year 0, and the analysis runs out 5 years, to Year 5. Net sales are projected to increase from 500 in the base year to 650 in Year 5. Operating earnings are $75 in Year 0 increasing to 97.5 in Year 5. There is a 15% annual capital charge on tangible capital employed (i.e. 250 tangible capital employed in Year 0 × 15% = 37.5). This is subtracted from operating earnings, giving us the 37.5 earnings figure in Year 0, and the same calculation is performed for each subsequent year. The Brand Value Added (BVA) figure of 25% means that 25% of the brand's earnings are due to the intangible value of the brand in each of the 5 years. In Year 0, this amount is 9.4. A 33% tax rate on brand earnings each year is reflected in the row labeled "Tax" (BVA of 9.4 in Year 0 × 33% = 3.1, with the same calculation carried out through Year 5). Subtracting tax from BVA results in a post-tax BVA of 6.3 in Year 0 (again, with the same calculation performed for each of the subsequent years). The discount factor is the discount rate, determined in this instance to be 15% (the discount rate accounts for the diminishing value of money and assets over time). The Year 0 discount rate is 1, meaning the value of money in that initial year is at its maximum 100%. Thereafter, it declines in value 15% per year (hence the discount factor of 1.15 in Year 1, which is 1 = .15). In Year 2, the discount factor is 1.32 (1.15 × 0.15 = 0.17; 0.17 = 1.15 = 1.32) and so on. The discount rate is applied to the post-tax BVA in each year to determine discounted cash flow (DCF). So in Year 1, the DCF is 5.7 (6.5/1.15 = 5.7, and so on . . .). Totaling the DCF for all five years

Table 2-5   **Brand Value (Segmented)**

	Year 0	Year 1	Year 2	Year 3	Year 4	Year 5
Net Sales	500	**520**	**550**	**580**	**620**	**650**
Operating Earnings	75.0	78.0	82.5	87.0	93.0	97.5
Tangible Capital Employed	250	260	275	290	310	325
Charge for Capital @15%	37.5	39.0	41.3	43.5	46.5	48.8
Earnings	37.5	39.0	41.3	43.5	46.5	48.8
Brand Value Added @ 25%	9.4	9.8	10.3	10.9	11.6	12.2
Tax Rate	33%	33%	33%	33%	33%	33%
Tax	3.1	3.2	3.4	3.6	3.8	4.0
Post-tax BVA	6.3	**6.5**	**6.9**	**7.3**	**7.8**	**8.2**
Discount Rate	15%					
Discount Factor	1.0	1.15	1.32	1.52	1.75	2.01
Discounted Cashflow		**5.7**	**5.2**	**4.8**	**4.5**	**4.1**
Value to year 5	24.2					
Annuity	27.1					
Growth 0%						
Brand Value	51.3					

Haigh, D., *Brand Valuation: Managing and Leveraging Your Brand,* © 2000 Brand Finance plc, p. 17.

results in a value to Year 5 of 24.2. The 27.2 annuity figure accounts for the value of the brand's earnings beyond 5 years (in finance, this is called "in perpetuity," and it is merely an estimate since it is impossible to calculate this forever. A logical approach is to take the brand's lifespan out a few more years to estimate the annuity.) The cumulative total of the brand is 51.3 in Year 0.

Interbrand Brand Valuation Methodology [34]

Interbrand's Best Global Brands survey has been influential in raising awareness about the importance of brand value. Its proprietary methodology is based on economic use, which applies discounted cashflow analysis to long-term financial projections (typically 3–5 years).

Summary

When assessing brands publicly available financial data is used to project operating profits for a brand over the next five years, a capital charge is deducted and a 35% tax charge is applied, resulting in a figure called economic earnings. Next, Interbrand assesses a brand's strength to understand the impact of the brand on earnings. This assessment uses Interbrand's own methodology, scored using seven factors. Every investment and asset carries risk, and a brand is no different. Arguably, because of the influence of intangibles on brand value, a brand is particularly vulnerable to changes in business practices, product direction, and even public opinion. As such, a discount rate is determined and applied to the earnings figure to account for this risk.

Explanation

Interbrand's methodology uses well-known financial and accounting concepts and its own brand strength assessment, helping delineate between tangible product value and intangible brand value. In doing so, Interbrand provides some insight into less-understood but often equally important dimensions of a brand—the investment in marketing and the legal protections required to maintain brand integrity and intellectual property against competitors. Each of these dimensions influences the perception and, ultimately, the value of a brand. Since a brand is not, as already cautioned earlier, just a name or logo, Interbrand's methodology sheds light on the value of complex characteristics that create and sustain a brand. A five-step process is used:

1. *Market segmentation.* Define clear, nonoverlapping segments. The brand is then valued in each segment and the cumulative value of all segments equals the total brand value.
2. *Financial analysis.* Revenues and profits for each segment's brand intangibles are identified and forecast.
3. *Demand analysis.* Determine the drivers of demand for each of the company's brands and segments, then assess how much each driver is directly influenced by the brand.
4. *Competitive benchmarking.* Extensive review of the competitive position of the company's brands, including leadership, strengths and weaknesses, growth trends, legal protectability, geographic spread, and related items. This is done to determine the brand discount rate and the risk profile of its future expected earnings.

5. *Brand value calculation.* Defined as the net present value of the forecasted future brand earnings, discounted by the brand discount rate. The net present value takes into consideration both the forecast period and beyond, to model the brand's ability to continue generating quality future earnings.

As mentioned, an important component of Interbrand's approach assesses brand strength across seven factors (with corresponding weights):

1. *Leadership (25%).* Leadership reflects the brand's ability to set and/or guide the direction of a product category, market, or industry. Brands in leadership positions establish price, product quality, perception, and even expectations about future offerings. Consequently, brands in leadership positions are considered premier and can command premium product pricing and company value over lesser-known rivals.
2. *Stability (15%).* Perhaps this could also be termed "durability" and/or "resilience". In their influential 1994 book *Built to Last*, James C. Collins and Jerry I. Porras wrote about how, over years, even generations, a select group of companies had built enduring legacies of success. While some of the firms they profiled have either been eclipsed by other firms or their performance has wavered a bit, the fundamental concepts they describe set a reliable foundation for long-term success. Great brands must have long-term success and stability is a key factor as a result.
3. *Market (10%).* A brand's market is essentially the environmental and business context in which it operates. Many variables influence this, including type of industry (auto, education, consumer products, software). Each industry is directly driven by its own unique dynamics. The pace of product innovation in hotels is far slower than that of computers. The loyalty of customers is often more intense in sophisticated technologies than it is for hairspray. Of course, investment in time, resources, and money influences this type of loyalty, and not all indicators of loyalty mean that customers are necessarily happy. Nevertheless, market is a key factor in determining brand value.
4. *Geographic spread (25%).* Companies with established global operations often find it easier to introduce similar products in different regions and cultures as a result of market perception, consumer expectations, and general recognition of the brand. With this kind of operating scale, large multinational companies (MNCs) are usually more valuable than their region-specific counterparts, partly because the MNCs have developed capabilities that allow their products to be more easily accepted across diverse cultures.
5. *Trend (10%).* The concept of trend often carries with it connotations of the fickle, the fleeting, the ephemeral and, unfortunately at times, the insubstantial. Yet trends are either set or supported by consumers. Consumer embracement of new trends reflects changes in society and companies must pay attention if they wish to remain relevant. A strong brand must be relevant to consumers or it, too, will only be a fad.
6. *Support (10%).* From marketing communications to R&D, brands need a steady stream of care, maintenance, and investment. Much like people who need food and water to survive through good times and bad, brands must also receive nourishment from support, in good times and bad, to survive.

7. *Protection (5%).* Companies spend sizable amounts of money developing products, building identities, communicating to consumers, and developing their organizations to support the brand. Not protecting brand assets, like brand name, product, or other intellectual property, risks having competitors copy and thereby gain quick access to the market. Furthermore, investors expect companies to protect their brands since it directly affects both brand and investor value.

Interbrand regularly measures the market on behalf of companies and their brands through surveys and similar research in an effort to understand each of these factors as thoroughly and thoughtfully as possible. The results are scored using their own proprietary assessment and then applied to the earnings multiple. Much like assessing a company's risk profile in financial terms, Interbrand calculates a brand's return compared to low- and high-risk investments.

Interbrand's approach illustrates the complexity of valuing brands and the strategic importance a brand has on the overall value, perception, and performance of a company. David Aaker praises the Interbrand approach for its effort to put a financial value on the brand, but cautions, "The subjectivity of both the criteria and the assessment of the brands, however, makes the dimensions difficult to defend and affects the reliability of the resulting measures."[35]

Differences in Brand Value Results

Comparing the two methodologies reveals differences in valuation results. Table 2-6 summarizes the valuations of each firm's respective top 10 global brands from 2008. Note that this table reflects pre-September 2008 economic conditions. Brand valuation changes resulting from the full impact of the financial markets meltdown were not available when this book went to publication.

Table 2-6   Comparing BrandFinance and Interbrand Valuation Results 2008

BrandFinance's Top 10 Brands	BrandFinance Valuation 2008 In US billion $	Interbrand's Top 10 Brands	Interbrand Valuation 2008
Coca Cola	**45.441**	**Coca Cola**	**66.667**
Microsoft	**44.501**	**IBM**	**59.031**
Google	**43.085**	**Microsoft**	**59.007**
Wal-Mart	39.001	**GE**	**53.086**
IBM	**37.949**	**Nokia**	**35.942**
GE	**36.123**	Toyota	34.050
HSBC	**35.456**	Intel	31.261
Hewlett-Packard	34.109	McDonalds	31.049
Nokia	**33.116**	Disney	29.251
Citi	27.817	**Google**	**25.590**

Source: Data taken from two online soures: 1) BrandFinance® Global 500-Top 100 Update September 2008 p. 12, www.brandfinance.com/Uploads/pdfs/Top100UpdateReport.pdf; 2) Interbrand's "Best Global Brands 2008," www.interbrand.com/best_global_brands.aspx?year=2008&langid=1000. June 2, 2009

Highlighted in bold are the companies in common on both lists. Note that there are some significant differences between the two. Interestingly, Interbrand values Coca-Cola more than US$20 billion higher in brand value than BrandFinance, yet BrandFinance values Google nearly US$20 billion higher than Interbrand. Despite many of the similarities in their methodologies, there are significant differences in their respective approaches.

Which is better? The answer is "it depends." Each company incorporates many commonly accepted accounting and financial standards methodologies. Interbrand's brand strength assessment evaluates intangibles based on their ability to generate ongoing demand, a different approach from BrandFinance, which deducts a company's net tangible assets from total enterprise value. More simply, each firm accounts for intangibles differently. Since both methodologies are proprietary, we do not have full information on every aspect of their respective approaches. However, despite the methodological differences and corresponding variations in results, it is clear that brand value is a substantial portion of the total enterprise value.[36]

Consumer-Based Brand Equity

The brand equity definition at the beginning of this chapter says that brand equity is the value associated with the marketing activities that enhanced the overall offering such that a premium could be earned over the same offering if it were unbranded. This indicates that customers see and interpret brands different ways, giving brands meaning and validity. Customers have different levels of relationships with brands, depending on a range of factors. Young & Rubicam (Y&R) and Millward Brown each have a framework for understanding how customers relate to brands. Understanding this helps explain how brand value is enhanced over time.

The Young & Rubicam Brand Asset® Valuator

Y&R's Brand Asset® Valuator consists of four key elements:

- differentiation;
- relevance;
- esteem;
- knowledge.

Each element relates to consumers' beliefs about the brand. According to the Y&R model, *differentiation* refers to the brand's meaning and its uniqueness to the market. One can logically conclude that, without some level of differentiation, one firm and/or its products is no different from another, thus rendering any value from branding either a waste or unnecessary. *Relevance* describes how a brand fits a consumer's lifestyle, indicating that the company cares and is making products that are interesting and important to its customers. When a brand has higher differentiation than relevance, Y&R considers it a stronger brand, as relevance can be improved over time. If a brand has higher relevance than differentiation, there is risk that it is moving to a commodity position in the market. *Esteem* refers to the likability of the brand with consumers and their longer term preference for it. Having convinced consumers of both differentiation and relevance indicates they hold the brand in high esteem. However, people cannot hold a brand in high esteem without first knowing it exists, why it is unique, its quality, and how it relates to them. Finally, over time as consumers experience the brand they accumulate more and more *knowledge* about it. If esteem is stronger than knowledge, than a brand is better liked than known, whereas if it has stronger knowledge than esteem, then the brand is better known than liked, suggesting it has lost its special place with consumers.[37]

MillwardBrown BrandDynamics™ Pyramid

The Millward Brown BrandDynamics™ Pyramid shows how many consumers have a relationship with the brand at different stages. Loyalty increases as one moves up the pyramid. The relationship between the brand and its consumers is measured against the share of the consumer's wallet that the brand has. Share of Wallet is a concept that will be more thoroughly defined later in this book.

As you move up the pyramid, the consumer's relationship with the brand deepens. At the first stage, *presence* merely describes a general awareness, but little commitment to the brand. *Relevance* indicates that the consumer finds that the brand offers something of interest and may lead to an increased commitment. *Performance* indicates increased usage and growing confidence that the consumer finds the brand useful. *Advantage* implies that the consumer identifies more closely with the brand and that the brand offers some advantage that the consumer finds attractive over other brands in the category. *Bonding* describes the deepest relationship between the brand and the consumer, where the consumer is a committed user of the brand and will select that brand first when purchasing. It also implies that the consumer feels a strong affinity for the imagery the brand represents.

Since each step is sized according to the number of consumers in that stage, it stands to reason that, as a brand's relationship with its consumers intensifies, there are fewer

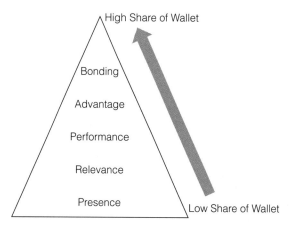

Figure 2-3 BrandDynamics™ Pyramid
Source: Millward Brown BrandDynamics™, www.millwardbrown.com.[January 11, 2009]

consumers who are at the top of the pyramid simply because not everyone who is aware at the bottom is likely to move up the pyramid to become highly bonded. Other brands and competitors will vie for their attention, creating a natural attrition of sorts. Ideally, a brand would like to see the number of consumers at the Bonding level as were originally at the Presence level, as this may well indicate that its marketing efforts to develop its customer base are working. (That is not the only conclusion one would reach, but it is certainly worthy of investigation.)

Measurement

This chapter presented several methodological approaches to measuring brand value. Here we present a customer-based measure of brand value to illustrate the impact a strong brand can have on customer interest and purchase.

Customer Brand Value

Metric
Customer brand value.[38]

Brand Value Benefits
This helps determine the approximate value of the average customer to the brand.

How
Penetration, buying rate, share of purchase, and gross margin are multiplied.

Formula

$$CBV = P \times BR \times SOP \times M$$

Where
CBV = customer brand value;
    P = penetration (percentage of the brand's users versus overall number of users in the category);
  BR = buying rate (the average number of units bought per customer during a specified period of time);
SOP = share of purchase (percentage of a brand's purchasers among its customers versus competitors);
   M = gross contribution margin;
   S_u = unit sales.

Knowing the average customer value of the brand can give guidance on future customer investments in product, marketing communication, or other offerings. Consider the Young & Rubicam and Millward Brown customer relationship frameworks. By understanding where customers are in their relationship to the brand, companies can more effectively target investments in a way that improves the customer's relationship with the brand and increases their purchases, which will have a direct impact on both brand equity and long-term brand value.

Summary

We began this chapter by discussing the importance that companies now attach to valuing brands, particularly intangible assets, because they represent significant strategic value that adds to the overall value of the enterprise. Two important concepts were defined: brand equity and brand value. Brand value is the main valuation approach in this book, and each of the subsequent chapters assumes that brand value is the key measurement benchmark in terms of a brand's financial contribution to the enterprise. The dimensions of brand value framework was introduced to illustrate the four key components of brand value: *societal, organizational, trusted reputation,* and *financial.* Brands contribute to society by providing offerings that benefit others. At the same time, society confers a certain amount of credibility on a brand for its efforts to contribute to the world through products and by working in the communities it serves. Corporate social responsibility (CSR) is becoming an increasingly important component of this. Organizational value is derived when stakeholders have a clear understanding of the brand, its meaning, and direction, which then guides individual behavior and support accordingly. When employees, for example, understand the direction, they have an easier time seeing how their work fits in and where they can best contribute. For many top brands, a sense of "cause" develops that motivates employee behavior and contributions. The value of a brand's trusted reputation is realized through loyalty, word of mouth support, and enhanced credibility as conferred by the market. In effect, brands are a sign of trust and growth is a sign that trust and goodwill are continuing to be engendered by the brand's activities, including people's experiences with the brand, its offerings, marketing communications, and other members of the value-chain. Financial value tells us the amount a brand contributes to the overall value of the enterprise, whether it is an individual product brand or a corporate brand. It is important to note that financial value is dependent on societal, organizational, and trusted reputation for it to have any meaning and relevance.

Companies are seeking ever more useful ways to determine the value of their assets. As brands are strategic assets, determining their contribution is of vital importance. It is also a complex undertaking with no single best method. However, there are several approaches that can help companies more effectively gauge the performance of their brands including the models from MacInnis and Park's, BrandFinance, and Interbrand. The customer's relationship with a brand is an important contributor to brand value. The Young & Rubicam Brand Asset® Evaluator offers a four-level hierarchy of effects that describe the shifting dynamic of a customer's relationship. The relative location of the customer on the hierarchy determines the strength and/or weaknesses of the brand. Millward Brown's BrandDynamics Pyramid describes five steps that customers climb as their relationship with a brand grows. As customers climb from presence, at the beginning, to bonding at the pinnacle, their commitment and share of wallet devoted to the brand increases. At the same time, the number of customers at each higher level decreases. Each level suggests an opportunity for the brand to change the nature of its relationship with the customer to keep it both dynamic and meaningful.

Discussion Questions

1. Why do you think the value of intangible assets has increased over the years? What factors are influencing this?
2. Select your favorite brand and list several of its attributes in each of the four areas of brand value: *organizational, trusted reputation,* and *financial.* Where does this brand create most of its value? Note: it will be tempting to merely focus on financial results. But keep in mind the actions that created those results.
3. Using the same framework from question 2, examine Coca-Cola, which was ranked in 2008 as the most valuable brand in the world by both BrandFinance and Interbrand (at two different valuations). At the time, Coca-Cola's market capitalization was approximately US$130–$140 billion. What would you say are the attributes that are part of its high intangible valuation?
4. Why is valuing intangibles difficult? Should valuing intangibles be secondary to valuing tangible assets? Why or why not?
5. How does customer-based equity contribute to an understanding of brand value?

Notes

1. Speech by David Haigh at BrandFinance Forum in Asia, March 2008, Singapore Management University.
2. Yahoo! Finance web site, retrieved June 12, 2009 from http://finance.yahoo.com/q?s=AAPL.
3. "Best Global Brands," Interbrand corporate web site, retrieved December 21, 2008 from www.interbrand.com/best_global_brands.aspx.
4. 1) Foster, G. and Chang, V., *Visa Sponsorship Marketing*, Case: SPM-5 p. 1–15, © 2003 Stanford University Graduate School of Business. 2) Read, M., "Visa IPO Could Be Largest in U.S. History," February 25, 2008, Associated Press, retrieved March 15, 2008 from http://biz.yahoo.com/ap/080225/visa_ipo.html. 3) Visa corporate information retrieved March 15, 2008

from www.corporate.visa.com/md/st/main.jsp. 4) Woolsey, B., "Credit Card Industry Facts and Personal Debt Statistics" (2006–7), retrieved March 17, 2008 from www.creditcards.com/statistics/credit-card-industry-facts-and-personal-debt-statistics.php. 5) "Top 10 IPOs by Deal Value," March 19, 2008, The Associated Press, retrieved March 24, 2008 from http://biz.yahoo.com/ap/080319/ipo_glance.html?.v=1. 6) Visa revenues retrieved June 4, 2009: http://finance.yahoo.com/q/ks?s=V.

5. Source: Ponemon Institute web site, retrieved December 12, 2009 from www.ponemon.org/local/upload/fckjail/generalcontent/16/file/008%20Most%20Trusted%20Companies%20for%20Privacy%20V%203.pdf.

6. "Respect: Here's How They Spell It," retrieved March 7, 2009 from http://online.barrons.com/article/SB123457681385686739.html.

7. "Best Places to Work 2009," Human Rights Campaign web site, retrieved June 1, 2009 from www.hrc.org/issues/workplace/11832.htm#Pharmaceuticals.

8. "Best Global Brands," Interbrand corporate web site, retrieved December 21, 2008 from www.interbrand.com/best_global_brands.aspx?year=2008&langid=1000.

9. Yahoo! Finance web site, retrieved March 6, 2009 from http://finance.yahoo.com/q?s=AAPL.

10. 1) Foster, G. and Chang, V., *Visa Sponsorship Marketing*, Case: SPM-5 p. 1–15, © 2003 Stanford University Graduate School of Business. 2) Read, M., "Visa IPO Could Be Largest in U.S. History," February 25, 2008, Associated Press, retrieved March 15, 2008 from http://biz.yahoo.com/ap/080225/visa_ipo.html. 3) Visa corporate information retrieved March 15, 2008 from www.corporate.visa.com/md/st/main.jsp. 4) Woolsey, B., "Credit Card Industry Facts and Personal Debt Statistics" (2006–7), retrieved March 17, 2008 from www.creditcards.com/statistics/credit-card-industry-facts-and-personal-debt-statistics.php. 5) "Top 10 IPOs by Deal Value," March 19, 2008, The Associated Press, retrieved March 24, 2008 from http://biz.yahoo.com/ap/080319/ipo_glance.html?.v=1. 6) Visa revenues retrieved June 4, 2009: http://finance.yahoo.com/q/ks?s=V.

11. 1) "The Rolex Company," Rolex corporate web site, retrieved July 24, 2009 from www.rolex.com/en/index.jsp#/en/xml/inside-rolex/rolex-company/index. 2) "A History of Rolex Watches," retrieved July 24 from www.swiss-luxury.net/rolex-history.html. 3) "Rolex-The Undisputed Leader of the Current Watch Phenomenon," retrieved July 24, 2008 from http://exquisite-watches.com/index.asp?ID=5&PageAction=Custom. 4) "A History of Rolex Watches," retrieved July 24, 2008 from http://repair-place.com/rolex_history.html.

12. "Starbucks, Fair Trade and Coffee Social Responsibility," retrieved October 28, 2009 from www.starbucks.com/aboutus/csr.asp.

13. Nokia Corporation, "Youth Development," Nokia corporate web site, retrieved December 29, 2008 from www.nokia.com/A4254327.

14. Nokia Corporation (November 5, 2007), "Nokia Provides Over EUR 6 million to China's Rural Children," Design Taxi, retrieved July 17, 2008, www.designtaxi.com/news.jsp?id=12948.

15. Ibid.

16. Nokia Corporation, "Youth Development," Nokia corporate web site, retrieved December 29, 2008 from www.nokia.com/A4254327.

17. 1) "Our Company, Awards and Recognition," Johnson & Johnson corporate web site, retrieved February 26, 2008 from www.jnj.com/our_company/awards/index.htm. 2) Johnson & Johnson Advertising, retrieved October 21, 2007 from www.jnj.com/our_company/advertising/index.htm.

18. Ibid.

19. Davis, J. A., *The Olympic Games Effect: How Sports Marketing Builds Strong Brands*, © 2008 John Wiley & Sons (Asia) Pte Ltd, pp. 166–173.

20. "Mattel Named One Of The '100 Best Corporate Citizens' For 2009," retrieved April 30, 2009 from www.mattel.com/about-us/corporate-responsibility.aspx.

21. Mattel, Inc. corporate web site, "Mattel About Us—Corporate Responsibility Report," retrieved June 17, 2008 from www.mattel.com/about-us/cr-csreport.aspx.

22. Ibid.

23. Mattel, Inc. *Mattel's Philanthropy*, retrieved June 17, 2009 from www.mattel.com/about-us/philanthropy/default.aspx.

24. Ibid.

25. Davis, J. A., *The Olympic Games Effect: How Sports Marketing Builds Strong Brands*, © 2008 John Wiley & Sons (Asia) Pte Ltd, pp. 166–173.

26. "Best Global Brands," retrieved December 21, 2008 from www.interbrand.com/best_global_brands.aspx.

27. 1) Speech by David Haigh at BrandFinance Forum in Asia, March 2008, Singapore Management University; "Top 100 Global Brands Scorecard." 2) Interbrand and BusinessWeek, August 6, 2007, retrieved December 21, 2008 from http://bwnt.businessweek.com/interactive_reports/top_brands/index.asp.

28. 1) Foster, G. and Chang, V., *Visa Sponsorship Marketing*, Case: SPM-5 p. 1–15, © 2003 Stanford University Graduate School of Business. 2) Read, M., "Visa IPO Could Be Largest in U.S. History," February 25, 2008, Associated Press, retrieved March 15, 2008 from http://biz.yahoo.com/ap/080225/visa_ipo.html. 3) Visa corporate information retrieved March 15, 2008 from www.corporate.visa.com/md/st/main.jsp. 4) Woolsey, B., "Credit Card Industry Facts and Personal Debt Statistics" (2006–7), retrieved March 17, 2008 from www.creditcards.com/statistics/credit-card-industry-facts-and-personal-debt-statistics.php. 5) "Top 10 IPOs by Deal Value," March 19, 2008, Associated Press, retrieved March 24, 2008 from http://biz.yahoo.com/ap/080319/ipo_glance.html?.v=1. 6) Visa revenues retrieved June 4, 2009 from http://finance.yahoo.com/q/ks?s=V.

29. Ibid.

30. MacInnis, D. and Park, C. W., "Making the Most of Your Brand: Leveraging Brand Equity Through Branding Strategies," March 2004, retrieved June 2, 2008 from www.marketingprofs.com/4/macpark2.asp.

31. 1) *BrandFinance's Brand Valuation: Measuring and Leveraging Your Brand*, May 2000, pp. 14–17. 2) BrandFinance250—*The Annual Report on the World's Most Valuable Brands*, April 2007. pp. 22–24. 3) BrandFinance250—*The Annual Report on the World's Most Valuable Brands*, April 2009, p. 37.

32. *Current Practice in Brand Valuation—A Gee Bulletin*, prepared by BrandFinance, June 2000 Brand Finance plc, p. 7.

33. Haigh, D., *Brand Valuation: Managing and Leveraging Your Brand*, © 2000 Brand Finance plc., p. 16.

34. 1) Interbrand corporate web site, retrieved December 21, 2008, www.interbrand.com/best_global_brands_methodology.aspx?langid=1000. 2) Keller, K. L., *Strategic Brand Management: Building, Measuring and Managing Brand Equity*, © 2008 Pearson Education, Inc., pp. 418–420. 3) Kapferer, J. N., *The New Strategic Brand Management*, © 2008 Les Editions d'Organisation, pp. 519–521.

35. Aaker, D. A., *Building Strong Brands*, © 1996 David A. Aaker; Simon & Shuster UK Ltd., p. 314.

36. 1) Synovate corporate web site, retrieved September, 2008 from www.synovate.com/changeagent/index.php/site/full_story/touching_on_the_intangible/. 2) "Top 100 Global Brands Hemorrhage $67B in Value" by Natalie Zmuda, September 22, 2008, *Advertising Age Magazine*, retrieved September 29, 2008 from www.brandfinance.com/Uploads/pdfs/Adage220908.pdf. 3) Interbrand's method for valuating the Best Global Brands, retrieved November 7, 2008 from www.interbrand.com/best_global_brands_methodology.aspx?langid=1000.

37. Young & Rubicam, retrieved February 11, 2009 from www.thebrandbubble.com/ explore (users must click on "us" and then the BAV link).

38. *Kellogg on Branding,* edited by Alice M. Tybout and Tim Calkins, © 2005 Alice M. Tybout and Tim Calkins, John Wiley & Sons, Ltd., pp. 256–257.

Brand Portfolios and Architecture

3

Topics

- Preview
- Brand Portfolios
- What is Brand Architecture?
  - Brand Relationship Spectrum
  - Brand Hierarchy
  - Brand Relationship Spectrum and Brand Hierarchy
- Building Brand Strength
  - Line Extensions
  - Stretching a Brand Vertically
  - Brand Extensions
  - Cobranding
- Associations
  - Focal
  - Superordinate
  - Subordinate
- Associations as Touchpoints
- Measurement
  - Brand Contribution and Review Analysis
- Summary
- Discussion Questions

Preview

Brand architecture is concerned with developing a structural approach to brand planning that guides the relationships between and among a company's branded properties. As we will see, brand architecture takes many forms, from company brands to individual brands within, and the choice of approach varies by company. There are no set rules governing the best approach for each industry. Indeed, many companies within the same industry use entirely different approaches to brand building, yet each may find success. The purpose of this chapter is to expose readers to a selection of better-known frameworks, discuss the pros and cons of each, and then allow individuals to determine an approach that works for them. More importantly, this chapter sets up the discussion of the new approach to brand building that dominates the rest of the book. The new approach, *Destiny, Distinction, Culture, Experiences,* will fill in gaps in existing theory and explain how top brands became successful. Suffice to say that even the new approach to brand building is not a panacea. But it does shed light on how companies must look at brand building, including shaking up existing practices.

Brand Portfolios

Consider brand portfolios as analogous to financial portfolios, which are a collection of investments designed to increase wealth. A brand portfolio is the firm's entire collection of brands, categories, and products and is organized in a way that facilitates resource allocation to each portfolio item to maximize brand value and customer satisfaction. Portfolio strategy helps management assess and develop the ideal brand structure. To begin, brands must be evaluated in the context of the firm's needs and expectations, along with brand contribution.

A 2004 article in the *McKinsey Quarterly* stated the crucial need for thoughtful and not mindless brand growth, by focusing on effective brand portfolio management. Often in the past growth has come through brand extensions that, as we will see in this chapter, have both positive and negative effects. Because brand extensions are typically an easier path to growth than launching entirely new products, brands have proliferated over the years creating complexity, confusion, and a more complicated management challenge. Companies like Procter & Gamble have become far more effective and successful by eliminating underperforming brands and focusing on high value performers. As the McKinsey authors argue, "How do such companies do so? In part by establishing clear roles, relationships, and boundaries for their brands and then, within these guidelines, giving individual brand managers plenty of scope, subject to oversight from one person who is responsible for the portfolio as a whole."[1]

An important insight from their article is one that mirrors findings from the research for this book: to develop brand success, customer *needs* must be clearly understood. Historically, companies think of their brands in terms of products and customer segments, leaving needs further down on the list of brand-building priorities. This is partly because understanding customer needs is complex as it deals with emotions and behaviors as well as functional/practical concerns. Needs are influenced by outside factors, such as word of mouth, and internal factors, such as self-expression, each statistically hard to analyze yet also known to be powerfully important in decision making. The McKinsey article makes several recommendations for making brand portfolios work:[2]

- understand each brand's contribution to the portfolio (market status, reputation, financial, organizational);
- determine if repositioning or restructuring will help underperformers. If not, divestment may be required;
- build strategies around leading brands;

- ensure portfolio plans are supportable internally;
- measure progress.

Implied in this effort is the need to develop a revised or even new brand portfolio plan as a consequence. Each decision on behalf of brands in the portfolio, whether investing more or divesting, will affect other brands in the portfolio and competitor decisions as well. Brand builders must be cognizant of these ramifications, planning different scenarios that help analyze possible outcomes.

An equally important issue coming out of the company research for this book is the need to eliminate or at least minimize clear duplication. This is easier said than done, particularly as brand portfolios grow in complexity. Nike, Adidas, New Balance, Asics, and Brooks all compete in the running product category. Each company has extensive product lines addressing various runner needs (pronation, support, cushioning . . .) and each product line has well-known individual brands. Furthermore, the products are offered at numerous price points, often with just a few dollars, if any, separating them. Procter & Gamble, Unilever, Kao, Nestlé, Kraft, Mars, and Danone have dozens of product categories in which multiple brands compete at similar price points with offerings that address similar needs. The question is determining when a brand duplicates (and may therefore cannibalize sales) or adds value. The decision will not always be clear, particularly as more data are introduced about customer buying preferences, behaviors, and outside influences (friends, media reports . . .). Often customers will have multiple, conflicting needs as well. Consequently, brand managers must regularly re-examine the performance of brands in their portfolios and re-evaluate criteria for judging performance. The complexity of this issue is illustrated by Figure 3-1, derived from one of Nestlé's family brands, Nescafe.

Imagine this chart expanded to include other family brands, individual brands, modifiers, and products across Nestlé's full range of offerings and one can quickly understand the complexity in managing brand strategies. To evaluate and better understand brand portfolios, several frameworks have been developed over the years, which help explain the labels used in Figure 3-1. We will now turn attention to these.

What is Brand Architecture?

Brand Architecture describes the structural organization and relationship of its brands. Just as architects design buildings to meet the needs of different businesses, marketers must design their brand, or brands, to address the unique needs and opportunities of customers in the marketplace. The reason brand architecture is useful for companies is because it helps sort, organize, and align the resources needed to support each brand while also helping outline the relationship among different brands (assuming a company has more than one brand). Brand architecture provides a framework for planning brand-building strategies for different customers and market needs. Investment and resource allocation decisions from product development, distribution channels, to marketing communication outlays can be more clearly outlined as well. Marketing and brand management research over the years has produced a number of frameworks for helping companies determine how

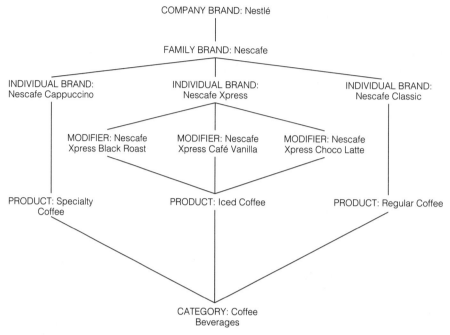

Figure 3-1   Brand Portfolio
Source: Derived from Nestlé web site, www.nestle.com/Brands/BrandsA-ZDetails.htm?LTR=N. Last accessed November 23, 2008.

to organize and build their brands and they provide helpful guidance for planning brand-building activities.

Let's look at three examples of brand architecture: the brand relationship spectrum; the brand hierarchy; and a blended approach that contains elements of the other two. For brands, the choice of architecture is not necessarily limited to the choice made, nor is it permanent. As we will see, brands are often found represented in more than one area. Indeed, one should not assume that one solution is better than another. The choice of where a brand fits in a given brand architecture depends on management's positioning, competitive conditions, brand growth objectives, and customer needs.

Brand Relationship Spectrum

David Aaker and Erich Joachimsthaler describe brands along a relationship spectrum, describing the different roles brands have depending on the overall brand strategy, as depicted in Figure 3-2.[3]

Branded House[4]

A branded house describes a single identity that encompasses all other products within. Also known as a master brand and/or umbrella approach (using the metaphor of an

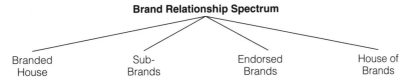

Figure 3-2 Brand Relationship Spectrum
Source: Based on Aaker, D. A. and Joachimsthaler, E., *Brand Leadership*, © 2000 David A. Aaker and Erich Joachimsthaler, The Free Press, p. 105.

umbrella covering a range of protected offerings underneath). Examples include: GE, CNN, Microsoft, HP, Intel, Harvard, Oracle, BMW, Virgin, and IBM.

Brand Strategy Implications[5]

Advantages   A branded house simplifies the investment required as a single identity is being marketed and, therefore, fewer if any additional resources need to be devoted to support multiple identities. Brand messages are likely to be streamlined, minimizing the need for multiple campaigns, which reduces the potential for conflict and increases the chances that the brand will be memorable. Stakeholders benefit because there is a single point of emphasis: employees know the brand and what it stands for, giving them a known and easy-to-describe identity; shareholders understand the basic marketing approach; and value-chain participants, like suppliers, also have an easier time understanding the brand. From an operational perspective, a single brand identity makes alignment easier to accomplish.

Disadvantages   The ability to appeal to diverse audiences is reduced since the positioning and communications efforts are focused on the master brand. Brand messages may get watered down, creating generic campaigns that are not very memorable. Creativity and risk taking may be hindered because only one brand is being marketed. The consequences of failure would be larger as a result because it could cascade more rapidly across business groups, casting a negative pall across the organization, even if other areas are performing well.

Sub-Brands[6]

Sub-brands are strong brands at a level below the master brand. Examples include: Nike's ACG (All Conditions Gear—both a sub-brand and category), Nike Sportswear, and Jordan; Lenovo's Thinkpad, Ideapad, and Valueline laptops; Apple's iPod, iPhone, and iMac; and Toyota's Prius, Landcruiser, Rav 4.

Brand Strategy Implications[7]

Advantages   Both give each other recognition and new associations that can help the market's understanding of the other. Sub-brands benefit from the strength of the master brand, while also creating potential new connections to customer groups not previously reached. The master brand also benefits because strong sub-brands can broaden customer choices and add dimension to the master brand's image. For management's long-term strategy, sub-brands can help grow market share, increase revenues and profits, supply new customers, and clarify competitive distinction and advantage over rivals. For employees, sub-brands help explain business direction, including the markets targeted, customer profiles within, enabling them to more easily understand how to organize resources to maximize company growth objectives. For distribution channels such as retailers, sub-brands add diversity to merchandise mix choices that can attract more customers and facilitate their own growth objectives. For value-chain participants, such as suppliers, sub-brands can inspire more focused component development, improving their relationship with the producer by making them a more useful and reliable partner. For investors, sub-brands suggest where market opportunities lie and diversify the company's revenue sources.

Disadvantages   Potentially adverse sales, profits, and image impact to the sub-brand if the master brand suffers a setback. Sub-brands can consume substantial resources, particularly at launch and rapid growth phases. Complexity and expense is added to marketing communications because the sub-brand needs to be explained and, if done so poorly, can confuse rather than enhance or modify the master brand. Furthermore, the master brand's overall message and image may be diluted as a consequence. Poor sub-brand performance can dent the image of the master brand. Distribution strategies will grow in complexity, adding to customer support costs, logistics complications, and risk of excess inventory markdowns further harming the brand image. Sub-brands can give competitors a singular point of attack that, if successful, can drive a wedge between the master brand and the market, casting doubt on the company's capabilities. Supplier challenges will increase, and the company is at a greater risk of poor product quality perceptions if supplier relationships are not carefully managed.

House of Brands[8]

A house of brands describes multiple strong brands housed in a de-emphasized, weak, or unknown corporate entity. Brands here have greater decision-making latitude, often operating as individual and/or separate entities with their own budgets and business plans. Examples include: Procter & Gamble (P&G); Apex Pal (a Singapore-based company with multiple restaurant brands); GM (in its heyday); and Kao Brands (a large Japanese consumer products company).

Brand Strategy Implications[9]

Advantages   Each brand can maximize impact on market or niches, shaping a sharp and distinctive image. Individual brands can be targeted to specific target markets and increasing connections to potentially important and influential new customers, resulting in new and varied revenue streams. Customer loyalty can be developed more fully with specific individual brands. Individual brands nurture marketing and branding expertise within, providing a wider range of opportunities to grow management talent and expose employees to unique business challenges vital to their long-term career growth. New brands can be created by the parent company within the same product category to add to its retail shelf-space, improving chances that their products will be purchased over less well distributed rivals. Marketing communications can refine each brand's personality, without concern for diluting or conflicting with a master brand's image. Market share in specific product categories can be increased when the brands within are totaled in aggregate. Retailer relationships can be deepened with a large selection of individual brands, satisfying different customer groups. Investors may find a series of strong individual brands an important portfolio diversification strategy that minimizes their investment risk.

Disadvantages Unlike a branded house, there is no umbrella coverage with a house of brands, therefore little or no leverage can be used with the parent company association. House-of-brands strategies are likely to be more expensive in aggregate, with each brand requiring substantial resources to support market development, from unique operations to inventory control to logistics to marketing communications to channels support to field sales. Moreover, funding from parent companies is not unlimited, so individual brands often have to vie for scarce resources, sometimes creating internal rivalries that can undermine operational effectiveness and team camaraderie. A house of brands makes creating unified customer loyalty at the corporate level harder and customer recruiting can often be more expensive in the aggregate, unless there is significant knowledge and database sharing internally between brands to reduce the potential for over-communication to customers. Multiple brands compete in different markets and product categories, each with unique business and economic characteristics that make management and financial oversight far more complex.

Endorsed Brands[10]

This describes independent brands, like a house of brands, which are overtly endorsed by a master brand, like a branded house. Examples include: Polo by Ralph Lauren; Home2 Suites by Hilton; most of Richard Branson's Virgin companies; and Grand Residences by Marriott.

Brand Strategy Implications[11]

Advantages This strategy provides credibility for the endorsed brand by closely aligning the master brand with the sub-brand in identity and marketing communications. This is particularly useful when launching a new brand because the master brand endorsement can raise visibility more quickly. Endorsed brands benefit from the master brand's reputation and associations. The endorser brand can use the association to more overtly appeal to new markets and demonstrate new capabilities, perhaps in an effort to make new product launches an increasingly important part of the company's strategy. Endorsed brands can help break into product categories where competitors are strong, using the endorser's overall strength and recognition to create buzz and attract customers.

Disadvantages The endorser must have a good reputation, particularly in the endorsee's product class. Endorsed brand strategies, like a house of brands, can be expensive to market because the endorsement needs to be explained and clearly positioned, otherwise the endorser risks dilution and creating competitive disadvantage in the product category.

The expense of repackaging and modified communications will increase, albeit temporarily, if the endorser eventually drops the association as the endorsed brand gains strength. Too many endorsed brands might also be a sign of weakness at the sub-brand level, sending a negative signal to customers and investors. The endorser brand may stretch its name and credibility too far by adding more endorsed brands, as opposed to decoupling from the sub-brands to minimize fallout should they fail.

Figure 3-3 summarizes highlights from the brand relationship spectrum.

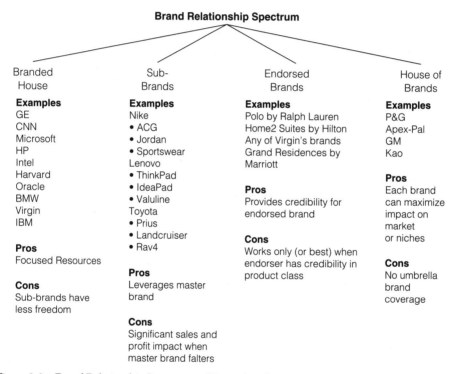

Figure 3-3   Brand Relationship Spectrum and Examples of Brands in Brand Relationship Spectrum
Source: Based on Aaker, D. A. And Joachimsthaler, E., *Brand Leadership,* © 2000 David A. Aaker and Erich Joachimsthaler, The Free Press, p. 105.

Overlap[12]

The astute student will note many examples of brands that fit in multiple categories: Nestlé is a branded house, evidenced by a well-known corporate brand name that also served as the name of its chocolate bar for years. Nestlé is also a house of brands, with individual brands like Perrier, Powerbar, Gerber, and Purina, each of which competes in a different product category. And Nestlé uses an endorsed brand strategy, with its Nestlé Crunch and Nestle Drumstick offerings. Mars' brands strategies are similar to Nestlé's, with a well-known name providing a branded house, yet the Mars name is also on the Mars Bar, an equally well-known sub-brand. It is also a house of brands, represented by its Pedigree pet food, Uncle Ben's Rice, and M & M's candies, all competing in entirely different product categories. Other companies whose branding strategies overlap include Nike, Adidas, Colgate, GE, Singapore Airlines, Unilever, Danone, LVMH, Johnson & Johnson, HP, and more. A review of Interbrand's Annual Best Global Brands survey will show many top brands that compete using multiple brand strategies.

Can such overlap work? Or does it lead to confusion and unnecessary expense, and contribute to diffusion of focus. Furthermore, can such an approach end up confusing the market and detracting from a company's growth opportunities? The answer, of course, is yes to all of these. But the practical reality for brands today is that multiple approaches are often justified in defense of pursuing new markets and customers, offsetting rival's strengths, and testing new ideas. Brand strategies should be pursued vigorously using carefully applied resources, but this should not become a prison. As the market responds, a brand may be better off by slightly shifting its strategy rather than rigid adherence to the brand framework. One of the most famous examples is Datsun, once a well-known car brand sold in North America, which dropped its name in favor of the parent company name Nissan. The rationale was clear: to simplify their global branding strategy. Conversely, Toyota added a brand with the launch of Lexus in the late 1980s in an effort to more effectively serve the mass and luxury markets. The luxury market, particularly in North America, did not perceive Toyota as a luxury brand name, hence the decision to create an entirely new brand. Acer, the Taiwanese PC brand, was better known as a manufacturer of well-known global brands before shifting strategy years ago to compete directly in the branded PC business. Marriott has shifted strategy over the years from a branded house to having hotels represented by each brand strategy: Marriott Hotels (branded house); Marriott ExecutiveStay (sub-brand); Townhouse by Marriott (endorsed brand); and Ritz-Carlton (house of brands). In Marriott's case, each hotel brand reflects highly targeted strategies to attract specific customer types and compete in known product categories. Campbell's Soup Company purchased Godiva Chocolatier in 1967, keeping the two brands separate. Then, Campbell's sold Godiva in 2005 to concentrate on its soup and snacks business to focus on healthy lifestyles. Godiva did not fit in this new strategy. Interestingly, Mars, Nestlé, and Hershey's are each devoting resources to research and new products emphasizing the healthier components of cocoa and chocolate-based products, which will undoubtedly give rise to new brand strategies in the future.[13]

Brand strategy is mistaken for uniformity, perceived and pursued by many companies as a rigid adherence to strict branding rules. But success is actually predicated on consistency, which affords brands greater flexibility to relate to different markets while also staying true to core brand principles and meanings. This cannot be overstated. Just as companies will suffer if their branding is fragmented and inconsistent, so too will they suffer if they pursue perfection and invariability.

Let's take a look at another branding approach, called *brand hierarchy*.

Brand Hierarchy[14]

Kevin Lane Keller describes brand hierarchy as a top to bottom (from general to narrow) arrangement of brands. It can be depicted as shown in Figure 3-4.

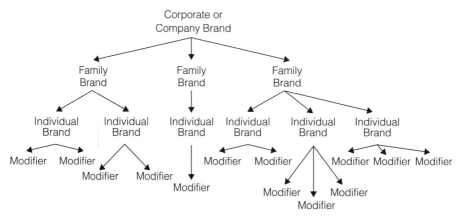

Figure 3-4   Brand Hierarchy
Source: Based on Keller, K. L., *Strategic Brand Management: Building, Measuring and Managing Brand Equity,* © 2008 Pearson Education, Inc. p. 446.

Corporate/Company Brand[15]

The corporate/company brand name describes the official legal entity. In one respect, this is similar to the branded house or master brand discussed in the brand relationship spectrum in which the corporate brand serves as the primary name for all businesses underneath the corporate umbrella, and many company brands use this approach (Nike, IKEA, Virgin, Apple, among others). Yet the corporate/company brand also applies to the house of brands as well, in which the corporate brand is plays a more behind-the-scenes role (Procter and Gamble, Apex-Pal . . .).

Brand Strategy Implications[16]

Advantages   The corporate/company brand is a convenient and often cost-effective way to leverage a single identity across multiple product categories. It may also help to enhance brand value more easily, because a single identity is representing all company interests and products. Doing this successfully is possible if the corporate name is consciously known and used as a differentiator and if the company has credibility in the different product categories. A single identity can help the market see the brand in a singular, more unified way, and it is likely that a more consistent brand image will be a by-product, assuming the brand maintains a positive reputation. Marketing communications will be easier for the most part since one entity is the subject of the communications. Plus, media-buying opportunities may have greater leverage under the single entity. Under former CEO Carly Fiorina, Hewlett Packard consolidated its brand marketing communications into a simpler approach that emphasized "HP" with the word "Invent" underneath. This recalled HP's historical legacy as a Silicon Valley pioneer, whose founders, William Hewlett and David Packard, had a reputation for invention and innovation, while also helping HP recapture some of those associations.[17] Any branding effort will conjure associations by customers in the market. A single corporate/company brand allows a wider range of associations to be attached to it. GE runs multiple businesses ranging from consumer products to aircraft engine manufacturing—consequently the market sees GE through a broader lens.[18] A corporate/company brand can help new market growth more easily assuming the brand has already built a known reputation in its existing markets. Some Western brands in China were highly sought by the growing ranks of middle-class and wealthy consumers in the first decade of the twenty-first century by virtue of their reputation alone, based on a single brand identity, including IKEA, Mercedes, and Louis Vitton.[19]

Disadvantages   Corporate/company brands where the name is not the primary brand (similar to a house of brands) are likely to have higher costs in support of each individual brand. Maintaining understandability and meaning with target audiences diminishes as a corporate/company brand adds new lines of business. If the corporate/company brand faces a crisis, there is greater risk to the rest of the organization and its various business units. The risk will vary from image degradation to financial decreases from customer concerns and/or attrition, and brand value declines. While corporate/company brands have the potential for a wider range of associations because they are not tied to a specific product or industry expertise, there is still risk of stretching the company past its areas of credibility, as far as the market is concerned. Therefore, any new business area has to be carefully weighed in the context of the company's overall reputation. While marketing communications may be simplified, the chance of building an overly general reputation is higher than with individual brands because the corporate/company brand must appeal to the interests of many different audiences. If a corporate/company brand has close, public relationships with outside events and/or other corporate partners, then any problems those entities have will negatively affect the company, whereas an individual brand can be deemphasized until problems are corrected, helping to contain any serious fallout.

Family Brand[20]

Family brands are identities that tie multiple product categories together. They may be tied to corporate brands (similar to a branded house), such as many Johnson & Johnson's baby products and BMW's sedans, but can also be separate (similar to a house of brands), such as Procter & Gamble's Gillette and Apex-Pal's Sakae restaurants.

Brand Strategy Implications[21]

Advantages   Family brands help keep different product categories united by a common theme. This can give the family brand more focused recognition and a more unique identity and range of touchpoints can be marketed. At the same time, the family brand has greater freedom to more fully develop its identity as a distinct personality within the company.

EXAMPLE 3-1:

Tied to Corporate

BMW is the corporate/company brand with several family brands underneath, designated by numbers: 1, 3, 5, 7 series passenger cars. Each family has features and characteristics that distinguish each series from the other. Johnson & Johnson's baby care products cover several product categories, including shampoo, powder, and oil.

Distinct from Corporate

Gillette is a family brand within Procter & Gamble that represents several men's product categories, including shaving, deodorant, and hair care. Each of these categories, while competitively unique, share connections with personal grooming and have many associations in common as a result. Sakae is a family brand within Apex-Pal (corporate/company brand), a restaurant company in Singapore. The Sakae brand carries across three different restaurant categories: sushi (Sakae Sushi), teppanyaki (Sakae Teppanyaki), beverages and finger foods (Sakae Izakaya), and home delivery (Sakae Delivery), united by a common connection to Japanese food. With both Gillette and Sakae, the corporate/company brands are less visible.

Disadvantages   For family brands tied to corporate, as product offerings broaden, links to the corporate brand become increasingly hard to leverage. If the corporate brand falters, the family brand may be at greater risk, even if it is performing well, simply by association with the troubled parent. Applying the corporate brand to a range of products can create confusion if each additional product category moves the company further away from its core business. Crafting distinct identities can become problematic as the range of products grows in size and investments in brand support increase as well.

Individual Brand [24]

Individual brands focus on a single product category (such as hair care products, or bleach, or entry-level family sedans), whereas a family brand ranges across several product categories.

Brand Strategy Implications [25]

Advantages   Individual brands enable companies to create a more direct connection to specific target audiences leveraging a common story told through imagery, marketing communications, and customer experiences. Companies with multiple individual brands, like Procter & Gamble, can use them as barriers to entry in different product categories, assuming the individual brands are strong with loyal customers, because retailers will want to carry brands that attract customers and sell well. The success of P&G's many different consumer brands essentially helps the company gain more retail shelf space over competitors. Toyota has numerous individual brands, including Camry, Corolla, and Prius, each with its own unique personality and accompanying associations catering to specific markets. Consumers associate Toyota cars and trucks with affordable quality and, especially with their hybrids, corporate responsibility as well.

EXAMPLE 3-2:

Tied to Corporate

Philip Morris, the tobacco products company, faced an increasingly negative press in the late 1990s and early 2000s, which was affecting nontobacco businesses at the time. The company created a new parent company, Altria, as a corporate/company brand to help reduce familiar associations with tobacco and provide a measure of protection for nontobacco businesses such as Ste. Michelle Wine Estates and Kraft General Foods (which was eventually spun off in 2007).[22]

Distinct from Corporate

When distinct from corporate, the opportunities to leverage the corporate name decrease, adding expense to supporting the brand. As a house of brands, in 2005, OSIM International, a healthy lifestyle products company based in Singapore, acquired Brookstone, a U.S. retailer of specialty lifestyle items with the Brookstone-branded products alongside other known brands across a range of product categories (electronics, exercise, gardening, bedroom). OSIM's massage chairs and related health products were distributed in Brookstone stores as well. The projected synergies, associations, and shared attributes did not achieve expectations. In early 2009, OSIM wrote down its investment in Brookstone to zero, with neither brand gaining the full benefits of the corporate/family branding potential at the time.[23]

Disadvantages Just as described with a house of brands, individual brands can be very expensive to support, especially as more individual brands and product variations are added. Customer confusion can increase as more brands are added. Cohesive, consistent brand building is harder with more brands to support, most likely necessitating individual budgets and P&Ls for each individual brand. This, too, increases the complexity of the organization, with more marketing and product management people required to oversee each individual brand, although many companies, particularly in consumer products, are shifting to category managers that are responsible for all brands within. Leveraging corporate tie-ins becomes challenging since new individual brands need to be explained clearly (if a strong brand is to be developed), which will undoubtedly force resources to be reallocated away from corporate branding.

Modifiers[26]

Modifiers are used to identify a specific version or model of an individual brand and/or product. Software companies often use version numbers to highlight the latest products. Automobile makers use modifiers to highlight unique differences between models with a common individual brand name. Consumer products companies will use modifiers for products with variations in ingredients and formulations.

Brand Strategy Implications[27]

Advantages   Modifiers describe differences in models of an individual brand. Saab automobiles has several models of cars within common individual and/or family brands (9-3 and 9-5 cars), using modifiers like Saab 9-3 Sport, Saab 9-3 Turbo, Saab 9-3 Sport-Combi, and 9-3 Convertible to emphasize feature differences. The Apple iPod brand offers iPod Touch, iPod Nano, and iPod Shuffle as modifiers, each with different capabilities and purposes, appealing to simple and sophisticated needs alike.

Disadvantages   The temptation to extend the brand using modifiers risks confusing the brand message. By offering so many variations of an individual brand, differences appear slight and become increasingly meaningless except to a very narrow subset of customers. With consumer products, customers may have trouble distinguishing "new and improved" from "super" or "all new" or "special" or any other superlative-laden modifier. The expense of supporting each version increases as well, with more money spent on trying to explain differences that may be sometimes marginal at best.

Figure 3-5 summarizes the brand hierarchy.

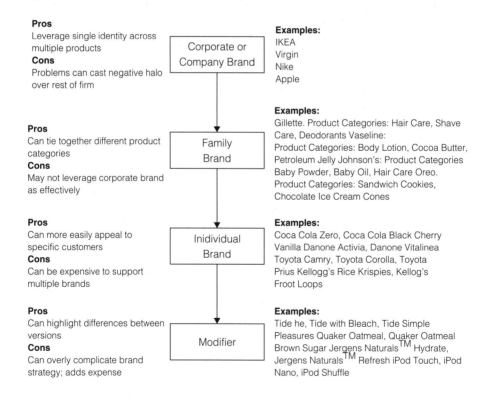

Figure 3-5   Brand Hierarchy
Source: Adapted from Keller, K. L., *Strategic Brand Management: Building, Measuring and Managing Brand Equity,* © 2008 Pearson Education, Inc., pp. 446–452.

Brand Relationship Spectrum and Brand Hierarchy

There are more similarities than differences between these two frameworks, but let's compare and clarify.

Similarities

Both frameworks work with the concept of a master or dominant brand. With the *brand relationship spectrum*, the branded house serves as the master brand strategy. In the *brand hierarchy*, both corporate/company brands and family brands can play the role of a master brand. A corporate/company brand that is strongly connected and visibly related to family brands is the same as a master brand. A strong family brand, on the other hand, emerges when the corporate/company brand is either weak or invisible.

The *brand relationship spectrum's* sub-brands, endorsed brands and a house of brands are similar, if not identical, to the *brand hierarchy's* family brands and individual brands. Each can describe a single brand name that either ranges across several product categories or is specific to a single category.

The *brand hierarchy's* modifiers can be found in any of the *brand relationship spectrum's* strategy choices, although it is most likely to be found at the individual sub-brand level.

Differences

However, a weak or invisible corporate/company brand would be more similar to a house of brands, in which case the family brand may become the master brand. The *brand hierarchy* modifiers are not directly accounted for in the *brand relationship spectrum* framework. Also, the *brand relationship spectrum's* sub-brands and endorsed brands are not readily apparent in the *brand hierarchy*. However, one can readily see how these two frameworks might actually blend together, using the hierarchy to explain brands below the branded house or house of brands levels.

Which is Better?

These frameworks are not mutually exclusive, rigid choices. There is a fair amount of leeway and maneuvering that occurs in the execution of brand strategies. A more important issue is how to ensure that the branding effort is consistently implemented and regularly reviewed for opportunities as well as areas of weakness. These approaches are designed to suggest different brand strategy choices and, as stated earlier, perhaps the best choice is recognizing how the two frameworks can work together to help build a well-structured brand strategy.

Building Brand Strength

Building a brand helps build a stronger business overall, whether applied to a company brand or individual product brand. In this regard, branding has far more potential to provide growth options for companies and needs fulfillment for customers. In weighing

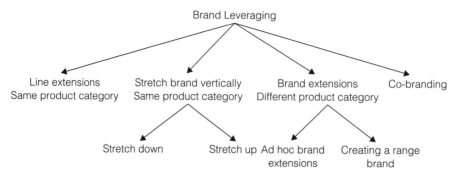

Figure 3-6   Brand Leveraging
Source: Adapted from Aaker, D. A., *Building Strong Brands*, © 1996 David A. Aaker and Simon & Shuster U.K. Ltd., p. 275.

opportunities, management must look beyond the brand strategy and toward any of several ways to leverage the brand to improve market share, expand the customer base, and solidify the brand's image and reputation. David Aaker discusses four primary ways brands can be leveraged.[28] They are:

- line extensions;
- vertical brand stretching;
- brand extensions;
- cobranding.

Vertical brand stretching and brand extensions can be further broken down into additional activities. They are represented graphically in Figure 3-6.

Line Extensions[29]

Products compete against rival offerings, typically within product categories. When an individual product spawns variations in the same product class, a product line is born. A line extension means taking an existing product, altering its attributes (such as new packaging, new ingredients and formulations, minor feature modifications, new sizes), then placing and/or distributing the newly extended product line to the customer. With many consumer products, placement occurs in retail stores and web sites that are either generalists (stocking a wide range of brands) or specialists (focusing on one product category, for example). The rationale for line extensions is to leverage familiarity with the existing product by creating different varieties of it. Most consumer products companies practice some form of line extension in their brand planning. Procter & Gamble, Nestlé, Unilever, Kellogg's, Danone, Kraft, Nike, Adidas, Kao, major automakers, and more, all have product lines born from a single product. Popularity is the usual catalyst for inspiring line extensions.

Brand Strategy Implications[30]

Advantages   Line extensions are one of the easiest ways to increase product sales, and companies have used this tactic for decades for growing their businesses. Line extensions can also be cost-effective because investments in tooling and design have been substantially made, with only minor changes required for the extended variations. For popular products, this can be a formidable barrier to competitors because retail buyers will want the security and comfort of the known product and its extensions over lesser known rivals. Line extensions are used to grow the customer base since the added varieties are intended to appeal to different needs, although some may be slight. They are also indicative of a product's popularity and signal management's confidence in it, as well as demonstrating strategic direction and emphasis (which affect competitor decisions, particularly when a dominant product extends its line further). A strong product line serves as a focal point for employees as well, rallying their support and acting as a magnet for fresh ideas in how to keep the product line fresh and relevant. Product line extensions also reinforce and expand on associations consumers have with the product, using the extensions as a visual and physical reminder of the product's presence. Marketing communications may also benefit since line extensions are easier to communicate than entirely new brands or products.

Unilever's Sunlight hand dishwashing liquid has several varieties in its product line: *Sunlight Standard Lemon, Sunlight Standard Green Tea and Lime, Sunlight Standard Lime, Sunlight Active Gel Lemon, Sunlight Active Gel Lime, Sunlight Active Gel Orange*, and *Sunlight Pouch* (Figure 3-7).

Volvo's S80 sedan comes in several varieties: *Volvo S80 3.2 (six-cylinder engine, front-wheel drive), Volvo S80 T6 AWD (Turbo engine with All Wheel Drive)*, and *Volvo S80 V8 AWD (eight-cylinder engine with All Wheel Drive)* (Figure 3-8).

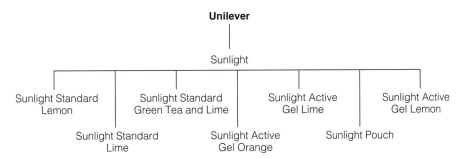

Figure 3-7   Unilever's Leverage of Sunlight Brand
Source: Retrieved April 21, 2009 from www.unilever.com/brands/homecarebrands/sunlight.aspx.

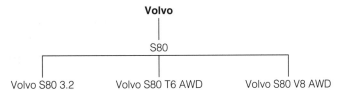

Figure 3-8   Volvo's Leverage of S80 Brand
Source: Retrieved April 21, 2009 from www.volvocars.com/us/models/s80/Pages/BuildYourS80.aspx.

Unilever and Volvo are not only extending the line to increase sales, but they are attempting to appeal to specific customer segments with interest in specific formulations and ingredient mixes (the ingredients in cars refers to engine and drive train variation).

Disadvantages   While line extensions are often cost effective in comparison with pure innovation around entirely new products, they are not free. Modifications to a core product still require investments in tooling and supplies, subtle changes in marketing communications, and specific added effort in sales management to convey why the extension makes sense and should be of interest to buyers (whether those buyers are retailers, dealers, or consumers). Insufficient volume can make the per unit cost higher and commensurate profitability lower. As a product line is extended, focus is increasingly diffused across more products. Each extension must therefore be meaningful enough to justify in terms of altered/enhanced performance and relevance to customers. Product cannibalization can be a substantial risk if a product line is overextended. Companies will justify such business strategies by arguing that self-cannibalization is better than having competitors do so. But this decision must be carefully considered because the financial impact of line extensions can negatively impact product line margins and even competitiveness at some point. Customers may grow weary of too many products being represented by a single product line in the market, seeking refuge in variety from rivals. Astute managers must pay attention to market signals, customer trends, and their own financial results. Brand value can be eroded by an overextended product line as a consequence, particularly for a branded house/corporate brand, since every addition to their product portfolio risks detracting from the company's known expertise and/or, at a minimum, eroding focus.

Stretching a Brand Vertically[31]

Stretching a brand vertically refers to increasing the brand's offerings in an existing product category, either at a different price point and/or into different levels of product complexity, for the purpose of reaching new customer audiences.

Brand Strategy Implications[32]

Advantages   The purpose of stretching a brand vertically is to capture more customers and increase market share by stretching downward, or higher value customers by stretching the brand upward. Brands have many associations and expectations attached to them, so the benefit of vertical stretching comes from taking advantage of these attributes, building upon them with expanded branded offerings, and capturing a larger share of business for the brand. This approach can also put competitors at a disadvantage because popular brands can leverage their name into different price levels, bringing the positive associations into the expanded offerings and leaving less room for rivals to gain a foothold. A downward stretch is designed to increase the customer base by providing simpler versions of established brands. An upward stretch can provide access to more upscale, premium markets and give the brand a more sophisticated, exclusive image that can generate more profitable business. Marketing communications can also be more effectively leveraged because the brand does not need to be explained—customers already know it and have associations attached to it.

Adidas offers a helpful example with its line of football shoes (soccer shoes, for U.S. fans). In 2009 the company had several branded product lines, including the F series, with the high-end F50i TUNIT at US$195, the F50i TUNIT Upper at US$85, the F30 i IN at US$85, the F50 TUNIT Comfort Classic at US$60, and the F10 i TRX TF at US$50. Each is designed to broaden the customer base with the F brand offered at different price points, appealing to unique customer needs by offering different features with each model.[33] Nike markets statement/premier level footwear in many sports along with "takedown" versions at lower, more affordable price points. Its men's tennis category features a line of shoes called "Courtballistec," ranging from the high-end Nike Air Max Courtballistec 1.3 for US$120, to the Nike Air Max Courtballistec 1.2 AF at US$82, to the Nike Air Courtballistec 1.1 at US$70, each with common visual design themes but distinguished by the type of upper and foot bed materials.[34]

Apple stretched its iPod brand upward when the iPod Touch was introduced, leveraging the touchscreen technology popularized by the iPhone for the benefit of iPod customers seeking greater functionality.

McDonalds is trying to stretch its brand upward by moving into the upscale coffee business to compete directly with Starbucks. At the same time, Starbucks is trying to stretch its brand downward by offering less expensive roasts and coffee blends, such as Pike's Place Roast, to mitigate against resurgent competitors like Dunkin' Donuts.

Disadvantages   Stretching the brand downward can dilute the brand's image by undermining any claims of exclusivity and/or state of the art status. Downward stretches can also signal to consumers that the brand may be changing strategy, which might invite a backlash in the form of reduced sales or the purchase of competitive offerings. This is especially true with loyal customers of brands because they often revere their favorite brands and want them to maintain the qualities and attributes that made them appealing in the first place.

Stretching the brand upward can be expensive because the additions will have increased complexity, requiring additional new tooling plus related support from suppliers, inventory, management, and new marketing communications. There may also be limits to how much a popular mass-market brand can be stretched upward before consumers begin to question if the brand has the credibility to compete at the premium level. When this occurs, the creation of a new brand may be in order, which invites significant new investments in operations, manufacturing, marketing, and even personnel.

The bottom line is that brand stretching requires careful thought if potential pitfalls are to be avoided and brand value can increase. For years, when Michael Jordan dominated basketball, Nike carefully managed the production of Air Jordan basketball shoes to ensure the market was not overly saturated, keeping supplies often far below demand. As the company believed, it was better to keep the brand's allure and prestigious image associated with the world's greatest player alive over time rather than pumping up sales for a year or two. Had this level of management oversight not occurred, there would have been an increased risk of oversupply, inventory markdowns, reduced customer appeal, and decreased brand value as well. Such a situation would also have cast a pall over Nike's other businesses, particularly because the Air Jordans were such a visible part of Nike's growth during the 1990s. To build off of Michael Jordan's success and the eponymously named shoe, yet avoid diluting the Air Jordan brand image, Nike introduced the Air Flight and Air Force basketball shoes in an effort to bring performance shoes in at a lower price point. Air Flights were for lighter, faster players and Air Forces were for bigger players pounding hard in and around the basket. This avoided many of the risks of brand stretching and helped Nike extend its lead in the basketball category.

Brand Extensions[35]

Brand extensions are used to expand the brand's presence into new product categories. This is especially useful if the brand has credibility in the new product categories. Aaker discusses two approaches to brand extensions: *ad hoc* and *range*.[36] *Ad hoc* extensions describe brands moving into multiple product categories and are harder to accomplish. It is rare to see a brand succeed across several unrelated categories (a software company is unlikely to have much credibility in the hotel business, and vice versa). More often than not, the new product categories will be in adjacent or compatible categories, which is what range brand extensions seek to do.

Brand Strategy Implications[37]

Advantages With *ad hoc* brand extensions, a primary benefit (if successful) is the introduction of the brand into entirely new product categories, refreshing the brand image and reinvigorating interest as well. *Ad hoc* extensions also convey versatility and can conceivably create new associations for the brand. Starbucks has pursued *ad hoc* brand extensions by moving beyond coffee beverages and beans into selected Starbucks branded merchandise (toys, kitchenware, books, and even magazine publishing at one point), Starbucks Entertainment (and its *Hear Music* label, which includes famous artists like Paul McCartney), and Starbucks Ice Cream.

Range brand extensions have the same benefits as *ad hoc* extensions, but in product categories more closely related to the brand's core business. Nintendo is an example of a range brand, with the brand in three product categories: consoles (Wii); portable players (DS); and software. All three are distinctly different competencies, yet they are compatible with the common theme of gaming. A range brand can link together distinct areas of a company under a more common identity. The brand will also have greater awareness since a wider range of segments will be exposed to the brand. Other examples of range brands include:

- Tylenol (Head & Body, Allergy & Sinus, Arthritis, Cold & Cough);
- Universal (Orlando, Production, DVD/Blu-Ray);
- Google (Web, Video, Maps, News, Gmail. Books, Images);
- Apple (iMacs, iPods, iPhones, iTunes, Apple Stores);
- Virgin (Atlantic, Games, Mobile, Books).

With both *ad hoc* and range brands, brand extensions attract new customers, may have a positive affect on market share, and can add interesting new associations with the brand that can strengthen its overall reputation in the marketplace.

Disadvantages Brand extensions risk associating the brand with product categories that confuse the brand's image and reputation, creating negative impressions and affecting brand value as a result. *Ad hoc* extensions are especially vulnerable to this phenomenon. Starbucks' rapid expansion was driven partly by massive investment in new stores worldwide and partly by *ad hoc* extensions, which took the brand beyond its known expertise. Having earned a reputation for making Starbucks a special destination over the years (Howard Schultz refers to Starbucks as the "third place" after home and work) distinguished by personalized service and superior coffee, the rapid growth and entry into new product categories reduced company focus on its core coffee business. In 2008, Starbucks announced that it would refocus on its core business and re-examine those businesses not directly related to their core.[38] This changed its entertainment strategy, turning over the management of its *Hear Music* Label to its partner in this venture, Concord Music. Even Apple faced early skepticism as it broadened its product range from computers to MP3 players to music downloads and then to 'phones. Their success with each new product class lent credibility to their efforts, grouping these product categories into a common "lifestyle" category. But such success requires financial depth, strong brand reputation, credibility, and a fair amount of brand self-confidence that can then be translated into thematically consistent messages. One can imagine the limits of range branding when pondering if Starbucks should expand into childcare or if Cathay Pacific should add microbreweries to their brand portfolios.

Range brand extensions can also be expensive to support, although not as costly as launching entirely new brands. Each new addition to the brand still requires a business plan with a long-term perspective on the value expected to be gained, combined with expert marketing communications and superb market execution to ensure the brand extensions enhance the brand's reputation and do not detract from it.

Cobranding[39]

Cobranding refers to two brands working together to create greater value and pursue growth opportunities they would not otherwise do as easily separately. While it may be as simple as copromotion activities, cobranding has much higher potential for growth when the partners collaborate either to produce a new product or improve an existing standard of some kind. Thus, growth opportunities would be either in the form of new products or new markets, or both. Cobranding can be among equals, or it can be a dominant brand paired with an ingredient brand (a brand that becomes part of a larger brand mix).

Brand Strategy Implications[40]

Advantages Companies cobrand to take advantage of each other's expertise, reduce market entry risk, keep costs under control, and reinvigorate their respective brands by the new associations the relationship brings and the new customers it might attract. Additional benefits include:

- reaching new markets and/or expansion into new channels;
- reduced new product launch/market entry risk;
- learning new competencies;

- collective marketing communications;
- more powerful combined identity;
- mutual credibility;
- new product innovation;
- shared resources.

Betty Crocker®, a popular food brand including baking products, cobrands with Hershey's on several different brownie mixes. Hershey's is an ingredient brand in the Betty Crocker® brownie mix. Both brands benefit from expanded associations—Betty Crocker® with its reputation for simple and easy baking products and Hershey's reputation as a recognized chocolate brand—based on their respective long-standing reputations and consumer followings. The Senseo Coffee Maker is the offspring of Douwe Egberts (a Dutch subsidiary of Sara Lee) and Philips. Virgin Mobile, one of Richard Branson's many brands in the Virgin Group, cobrands its service around the world with multiple partners.[41] In Australia, Virgin Mobile initially partnered with Optus (a well-known Australian telco owned by SingTel of Singapore, itself a large telecommunications brand) to offer mobile services. Subsequently, Optus acquired 100% of Virgin Mobile in Australia, keeping the Virgin brand name for marketing purposes in Australia. Apple markets its iPhone with Virgin Mobile in a cobranding relationship. And Optus also markets the Apple iPhone in another cobranding relationship. Optus gets the benefit of Virgin's and Apple's brand reputations, while Virgin and Apple get access to Optus's high quality telecommunications services. Visa® cobrands with numerous companies around the world, including Amazon. com where the two brands offer the Amazon.com Rewards Visa® Card.[42] Visa is the largest credit card in the world by market share and transaction volume and Amazon.com is an Internet pioneer and one of the most innovative online retailers in the world. Both gain benefits from being associated with their counterpart's attributes. Plus, their cobranding relationship simplifies online payment, making it easy for customers to use both services. Customers also earn reward points that can be redeemed with a number of other recognized brands, including Hertz, BP, Marriott, and British Airways.

Disadvantages Cobranding presents challenges to both firms because of different operating models, different corporate cultures and potentially different financial objectives. These are significant management issues. Each brand's respective success is based on a unique path taken, including differing cultural values, management control, employee freedom, social fabric and more. Each of these can become an obstacle to a smooth cobranding effort, derailing what might otherwise be a powerful combination with high potential. The key is for the cobranders to firmly outline expectations for the relationship, including details on what both brands will provide, how they will cooperate, who the key personnel involved are, how they will measure results, and an agreed upon formula for termination should the relationship turn sour. If one of the partners in the relationship falters or faces a crisis, it can have a magnifying effect on the other partner, eroding brand reputations and associated brand value as a consequence. Even successful cobranding may not always be favorably viewed by all customer segments. Some customers may be loyal to a competitor of one of the cobranders, tarnishing their relationship with the other. The cobranding between Kmart stores and Martha Stewart faced two serious challenges in the early 2000s, with Kmart's 2002 bankruptcy filing and Martha Stewart's conviction and subsequent jail sentence in 2004 for insider trading. Both brands struggled, exacerbated by the taint associated with their respective challenges.[43] Starting in 2006 AIG became a key sponsor and cobranding partner with Manchester United, the famed English Premier League football club, gaining great exposure with the company name prominently displayed on the players' jerseys. AIG's near collapse in 2008 during the financial crisis, and subsequent $150 billion[44] U.S. government bailout compelled the company to announce in early 2009 that it would not renew its agreement upon expiration in 2010.[45] While AIG continued to work on reorganizing its business, Manchester United went on to win the 2009 English Premier League title. In this instance the cobranding did not work out, but there was no apparent sustained harm to Manchester United's on-field performance or the support of its fans. Nevertheless, the cobranding challenge for a few months highlighted the risks such high visibility relationships can have.

Despite the challenges, leveraging the brand to create growth opportunities is a proven way to build strong brands and enhance brand value. The pivotal challenge is determining when leveraging a brand has gone too far or, ideally, anticipating in advance the cutoff point between leverage and over-leverage. Part of management's responsibility is proactively weighing growth options and staying disciplined in their implementation, resisting the temptation to leverage the brand rapidly when it is hot, otherwise the result may be a rapidly declining brand that harms future growth prospects and does damage to the brand's long-term reputation.

We can quickly see how the various frameworks discussed so far are important planning tools, yet they do not comprehensively address all brand-building issues, nor were they designed to achieve this. How do top brands then build sustained success? This is what the rest of this textbook discusses with the introduction of the *Destiny, Distinction, Culture, Experiences* model for successful brand building.

Associations

As a brand develops and gains acceptance in the market, it stirs emotions, provokes thoughts, and connects with people's imaginations. These various associations directly and indirectly affect customer behavior, triggering their desire to purchase. As scientific as that sequence sounds, the process is far more complex and loaded with obstacles, distractions, and other competing inputs that affect buyer behavior. The task for brand builders is determining which associations should be nurtured, a decision-making process that is typically influenced by a combination of facts, judgment, and outside influences. The precise composition changes by customer and situation, so certainty is rare. To mitigate against poor decisions, however, brand builders can prepare by researching their target customers, evaluating market conditions, assessing competitor strengths and weaknesses, and reviewing their own capabilities.

This information gathering never stops and will always be a part of brand development, causing strategies to be modified and new tactics introduced in order to improve their chances for success.

The information gathering should help highlight existing perceptions of the brand and any associations customers have. James C. Anderson and Gregory S. Carpenter state that associations fall into three categories: *focal*, *superordinate*, and *subordinate*.[46]

Focal

These are the clearest and most common associations with a brand. Customers link focal associations most closely together with direct benefits. Nordstrom, the U.S. department store chain, is known for great service. Visa is associated with purchasing freedom and convenience. Blackberry is associated with always-connected business users and, perversely, a form of professional addiction (many users refer to their devices as "crackberries," tongues firmly planted in their cheeks).[47] Ferrari is linked to powerful, fast, and expensive sports cars. Bali is a relaxing, tropical getaway.

Superordinate

Superordinate associations are less direct, more emotional, and more powerful. Lifestyle, expressive (self-image, self-worth), and fulfillment are examples of superordinate associations. People feel special and successful when wearing a Rolex watch. Reading *The Economist* magazine makes one feel intelligent. Watching a tennis Grand Slam final gets one excited to play tennis. McKinsey, the global consultancy, is seen as a trusted advisor to senior executives of the world's leading companies. Buying a residence in London's Belgravia neighborhood conjures notions that a person is part of a prestigious, elite sector of society.

Subordinate

Subordinate associations are less important. Simple images, shapes, words, colors, and sounds are typical examples. Many brand logos have familiar designs that distinguish their offerings. Coca-Cola uses its distinctive white wave graphic against a red background on Coke packaging. Mercedes Benz has its ubiquitous three-point star inside a circle as its primary emblem and identifier. Leo Arnaud's composition "Bugler's Dream" is associated with The Olympic Games and the Olympic flag is recognized by its colorful five rings.

Associations as Touchpoints

As discussed elsewhere in this book, touchpoints are where brands and customers intersect. As such, any association with a brand is theoretically a touchpoint, even though many associations are intangible and cannot literally be touched. Memories, emotions, product use, recommendations, marketing communications, service experiences, management speeches, analyst reviews are all examples of touchpoints and each brings to mind a wide range of associations, good and bad, that affect the perceptions of a brand.

For brands, managing touchpoints and creating associations are among the most important value-building activities, yet they are also hard to control since customer perceptions and associations are triggered by innumerable stimuli and connections, well beyond the scope of any brand-building effort. Despite the challenges, identifying the brand's touchpoints and related associations should be part of every brand manager's responsibilities. Indeed, other senior managers should be directly involved as well, since their respective responsibilities undoubtedly affect the company's operations and ability to deliver on brand promises to the market. Chapter 11 discusses how to assess touchpoints.

Measurement

Each framework is comprised of numerous subpoints, so a single measurement does not adequately help marketers. A useful device is the Brand Contribution and Review Analysis, derived from the author's research.

Brand Contribution and Review Analysis

Metric
Brand Contribution and Review Analysis.

Brand Architecture Benefits
Helps determine each brand's tangible and intangible contributions to the overall portfolio. As a consequence, investment decisions, resource allocation, repositioning, and even divestments can be more easily determined.

How
A diagnostic tool comprised of financial and nonfinancial criteria.

Formula
There is no formula. Instead, the following tool provides management with a snapshot review of each brand's contribution, whether it is a corporate or individual brand:

Financial (annual)

Revenues (attributed to the brand)	$_____
Subtract Brand-Specific Marketing Costs	$_____
Gross Brand Contribution	$_____

- -

Brand contribution as % of firm's total revenues	_____%
Brand contribution as % of firm's total profits	_____%
Brand contribution as % of firm's total customers	_____%
Brand market share	_____%

- -

Brand value increase/decrease	$_____ & %_____

- -

(Continued)

Brand	1 = poor 5 = excellent
Market awareness	1 2 3 4 5
Contribution to company reputation	1 2 3 4 5
Reputation with customers	1 2 3 4 5
Reputation with suppliers	1 2 3 4 5
Reputation with employees	1 2 3 4 5
Ability to extend/stretch	1 2 3 4 5
Clear differentiation	1 2 3 4 5

Product	1 = poor 5 = excellent
Quality	1 2 3 4 5
Reliability	1 2 3 4 5
Relevance to customers	1 2 3 4 5
Clear connection to product category	1 2 3 4 5
Addresses specific needs	1 2 3 4 5
Compares favorably to competitors	1 2 3 4 5

Brand Management	Yes	No
Strong team	___	___
Good decision making	___	___
Realistic business plans	___	___
Proactive	___	___
Profitable business	___	___
*improved over prior years?	___	___
Handles crises well	___	___
Flexible	___	___
Communicative	___	___
Measures results	___	___
Good internal reputation	___	___
Good industry reputation	___	___
Retraining needed	___	___

*explain briefly_____

Strategic	Yes	No
Good growth prospects	___	___
*Revenues	___	___
*Profits	___	___
*Customers	___	___
Favorable economic conditions	___	___
Advances firm's strategic objectives	___	___
Relevant to brand's market segments	___	___
Favorable market trends	___	___
Overlap with firm's other brands	___	___
*Is this a problem?	___	___
Growth potential in new geographies	___	___
Growth potential to new customer segments	___	___

Customer	*Gain?*	*Loss?*
Number of customers	——	——
Market share	——	——
New segments	——	——
Revenues per customer	——	——
Profits per customer	——	——
Share of customer wallet	——	——
Needs fulfilled	——	——

Market	*High*	*Low*
Growth potential	——	——
Competitive threats	——	——
Supplier strength	——	——
Regulatory restrictions	——	——
Environmental concerns	——	——
Socio-cultural benefits	——	——

Marketing	*Yes*	*No*
+		
Receiving appropriate advertising support	——	——
Influential customers	——	——
Consistent marketing communications	——	——
Clear brand message	——	——
–		
Unplanned additional sales force effort	——	——
Uneven channel support	——	——
Confusing and/or overlapping offerings	——	——
Product quality problems	——	——
Unreliable suppliers	——	——
Unexpected competitor moves	——	——
Company press	——	——
Industry press	——	——
Customer support and satisfaction	——	——
Word of mouth	——	——

Corporate	*Yes*	*No*
Overt senior management support	——	——
External corporate crises/challenges	——	——
Shareholder support	——	——
Employee turnover	——	——
Internal operations challenges	——	——
Budget support for growth plans	——	——

Impact on Brand Architecture

Beyond determining resource allocation, this tool can facilitate strategic planning, including relationships among and between brands. Management can also gain a stronger sense of which brands are capturing customer attention and if that implies changing trends and/or investment opportunities. Positive responses should be explored further for opportunities to exploit. Negative responses should lead to additional investigation to determine severity.

Summary

This chapter introduced frameworks for brand portfolios, brand architecture, and brand growth. Brand portfolios contain the entire set of brand assets within the company. They are similar to financial portfolios: the best performing assets are nurtured to enhance value and corporate performance. Underperformers are then evaluated for potential to improve or for elimination from the portfolio. Brand architecture provides structural guidelines for building brand relationships within the overall portfolio. We reviewed the *brand relationship spectrum* and *brand hierarchy* as two useful approaches to organizing brands. The brand relationship spectrum defined and demonstrated four strategic approaches: *branded house, sub-brands, endorsed brands,* and *house of brands.* The brand hierarchy framework introduced us to *corporate/company brands, family brands, individual brands,* and *modifiers.* Each approach has benefits as well as risks to brand building. Note that both approaches have areas of overlap (such as a branded house and corporate/family brands) and yet, even when combined, the approaches do not completely address all branding needs and conditions. Instead, they are more effective as one of the starting points in brand planning.

This chapter also discussed brand growth, specifically in the context of product extensions, vertical brand stretching, brand extensions, and cobranding. Brand growth options are often considered "low hanging fruit" because they are among the easiest choices management can make to increase growth quickly, as opposed to launching entirely new brands, which can take considerable effort and significant organizational resources by comparison. But brand-growth options come with risk as well. Overdependence on them can lead brands to be extended into categories and/or markets in which they have little expertise or credibility. Too many brand extensions can become a significant drain on resources and also dilute brand reputations. Innovation may suffer as attention is more focused on existing brands and not R&D. Brand-growth choices can also cause management to short-circuit the planning process, including updating customer needs research, to grow quickly. The downside is that long-term potential may actually suffer if brands ignore changes in customer needs, particularly by thinking that once a brand is established it will always remain relevant.

Finally, this chapter introduced brand associations and touchpoints as essential factors in determining brand strength. Brands evoke a range of responses and reactions from customers and a key management task is finding ways to develop the right associations and touchpoints that give the brand a favorable reputation. Associations range from focal (the most common associations, including key direct benefits), to superordinate (the most powerful associations that fulfill vital needs, including indirect emotional cues and self-expressive benefits), to subordinate (lowest level associations that offer little customer benefit beyond basic recognition, including familiar brand colors and logos). As we will learn throughout this book, successful brand building creates a competitive advantage and associations are one of the most important by-products of brand investments. Almost every activity undertaken on behalf of the brand, whether internal or external, will eventually create an association in the customer's mind. This association will be positive, negative, or of little consequence. For brands, the objective is to create as many positive associations as possible.

Discussion Questions

1. What is the purpose of brand portfolios?
2. How do brand architectures work? What is their role in the brand portfolio?
3. Select two brands that are product category competitors. Create a table that compares them using the following criteria:
   a. Products by price point.
   b. Likely target audience by product.
   c. Likely target need fulfilled by product.
   d. Stronger than competitor?
4. Is IBM a branded house? Or a family brand? Or an individual brand? Discuss.
5. What is the purpose of a modifier? Is its role major or minor in brand building? Explain.
6. Pick one of the brands from question 2 above. Has their growth come from product extensions, vertical stretching, brand extensions, or cobranding?
7. What are the challenges of stretching a brand upward? Downward?
8. What are the challenges in cobranding?
9. What associations come to mind when you think of mobile phones from Nokia? Motorola? Apple?
10. What are the differences? Are those differences important? Why?

Notes

1. Carlotti, S. J. Jr., Coe, M. E., Perrey, J., "Making Brand Portfolios Work," *The McKinsey Quarterly*, 2004, 4, p. 3.
2. Ibid., pp. 31–35.

3. Aaker, D. A. and Joachimsthaler, E., *Brand Leadership*, © 2000 David A. Aaker and Erich Joachimsthaler, The Free Press, pp. 105–115.

4. Ibid., pp. 118–123.

5. 1) Aaker, D. A. and Joachimsthaler, E., *Brand Leadership*, © 2000 David A. Aaker and Erich Joachimsthaler, The Free Press, pp. 105–115. 2) Keller, K. L., *Strategic Brand Management: Building, Measuring and Managing Brand Equity*, © 2008 Pearson Education, Inc., pp. 433–436. 3) Kapferer, J. N., *The New Strategic Brand Management-Creating and Sustaining Brand Equity Long Term*, 4th edition, © Les Editions d'Organisation, 2008, pp. 361–371. 4) Davis, J. A., *The Olympic Games Effect: How Sports Marketing Builds Strong Brands*, © 2008 John Wiley & Sons (Asia) Pte Ltd, p. 241.

6. Aaker, D. A. and Joachimsthaler, E., *Brand Leadership*, © 2000 David A. Aaker and Erich Joachimsthaler, The Free Press, pp. 115–118.

7. 1) Aaker, D. A. and Joachimsthaler, E., *Brand Leadership*, © 2000 David A. Aaker and Erich Joachimsthaler, The Free Press, pp. 105–115. 2) Keller, K. L., *Strategic Brand Management: Building, Measuring and Managing Brand Equity*, © 2008 Pearson Education, Inc., pp. 433–436. 3) Kapferer, J. N., *The New Strategic Brand Management-Creating and Sustaining Brand Equity Long Term*, 4th edition, © Les Editions d'Organisation, 2008, pp. 361–371. 4) Davis, J. A., *The Olympic Games Effect: How Sports Marketing Builds Strong Brands*, © 2008 John Wiley & Sons (Asia) Pte Ltd, p. 241.

8. Aaker, D. A. and Joachimsthaler, E., *Brand Leadership*, © 2000 David A. Aaker and Erich Joachimsthaler, The Free Press, pp. 106–110.

9. 1) Aaker, D. A. and Joachimsthaler, E. *Brand Leadership*. © 2000 David A. Aaker and Erich Joachimsthaler, The Free Press, pp. 105–115. 2) Keller, K. L., *Strategic Brand Management: Building, Measuring and Managing Brand Equity*, © 2008 Pearson Education, Inc., pp. 433–436. 3) Kapferer, J. N., *The New Strategic Brand Management-Creating and Sustaining Brand Equity Long Term*. 4th edition, © Les Editions d'Organisation, 2008, pp. 361–371. 4) Davis, J. A., *The Olympic Games Effect: How Sports Marketing Builds Strong Brands*, © 2008 John Wiley & Sons (Asia) Pte Ltd, p. 241.

10. Aaker, D. A. and Joachimsthaler, E., *Brand Leadership*, © 2000 David A. Aaker and Erich Joachimsthaler, The Free Press, pp. 110–114.

11. 1) Aaker, D. A. and Joachimsthaler, E., *Brand Leadership*, © 2000 David A. Aaker and Erich Joachimsthaler, The Free Press, pp. 105–115. 2) Keller, K. L., *Strategic Brand Management: Building, Measuring and Managing Brand Equity*, © 2008 Pearson Education, Inc., pp. 433–436. 3) Kapferer, J. N., *The New Strategic Brand Management—Creating and Sustaining Brand Equity Long Term*, 4th edition, © Les Editions d'Organisation, 2008, pp. 361–371. 4) Davis, J. A., *The Olympic Games Effect: How Sports Marketing Builds Strong Brands*, © 2008 John Wiley & Sons (Asia) Pte Ltd, p. 241.

12. Ibid.

13. 1) "Campbell Soup Sells Godiva for $850 Million," New York Times DealBook edited by Andrew Ross Sorkin, December 20, 2007, retrieved September 12, 2008 from http://dealbook.blogs.ny-times.com/2007/12/20/campbell-soup-sells-godiva-for-850-million/. 2) "Health Chocolate a Dream Come True?" Associated Press, February 20, 2006, retrieved September 10, 2008 from www.msnbc.msn.com/id/11453538/. 3) Willmer, K., "Nestlé Campaigns for Benefits of Dark Chocolate," retrieved September 4, 2007 from www.confectionerynews.com/The-Big-Picture/Nestle-recasts-its-Black-Magic-recipes. 4) Hershey's corporate web site, "Products: Antioxidants", retrieved November 20, 2008 from www.hersheys.com/nutrition/antioxidants.asp.

14. Keller, K. L., *Strategic Brand Management: Building, Measuring and Managing Brand Equity*, © 2008 Pearson Education, Inc., p. 446.

15. Ibid., pp. 446–447.

16. 1) Aaker, D. A. and Joachimsthaler, E., *Brand Leadership*, © 2000 David A. Aaker and Erich Joachimsthaler, The Free Press, pp. 105–115. 2) Keller, K. L., *Strategic Brand Management: Building, Measuring and Managing Brand Equity*, © 2008 Pearson Education, Inc., pp. 433–436. 3) Kapferer, J. N., *The New Strategic Brand Management—Creating and Sustaining Brand Equity Long Term*, 4th edition, © Les Editions d'Organisation, 2008, pp. 361–371. 4) Davis, J. A., *The Olympic Games Effect: How Sports Marketing Builds Strong Brands*, © 2008 John Wiley & Sons (Asia) Pte Ltd, p. 241.

17. 1) Hewlett Packard corporate web site—HP Invent, retrieved September 21, 2008 from www.hpinvent.com/hpinfo/abouthp/histnfacts/timeline/main4.swf. 2) Fiorina, C., "Invent/Reinvent: Strategic Imperatives for the Internet Era," 2000 World Congress in Information Technology, Taipei, Taiwan. June 12, 2000, retrieved September 21, 2008 from www.hp.com/hpinfo/execteam/speeches/fiorina/ceo_invent_reinvent.html.

18. Silverstein, B., "Older and Wiser: How Brands Stand the Test of Time," BrandChannel.com, retrieved December 11, 2008 from www.brandchannel.com/features_effect.asp?pf_id=421.

19. 1) "Rich Chinese are Partial to Foreign Brands," *China Daily*, February 21, 2008, retrieved May 11, 2008 from www.china.org.cn/english/environment/243403.htm. 2) "The Young Urban Chinese Consumer," *China International Business*, May 11, 2009, retrieved May 22, 2009 from www.cibmagazine.com.cn/Features/Focus.asp?id=908&the_young_urban_chinese_consumer.html. 3) St. Maurice, I. and Süssmuth-Dyckerhoff, H. T. "What's New With the Chinese Consumer?" *McKinsey Quarterly*, September 2008, retrieved October 9, 2008 from www.mckinseyquarterly.com/Whats_new_with_the_Chinese_consumer_2218.

20. Keller, K. L., *Strategic Brand Management: Building, Measuring and Managing Brand Equity*, © 2008 Pearson Education, Inc., p. 447.

21. 1) Aaker, D. A. and Joachimsthaler, E., *Brand Leadership*, © 2000 David A. Aaker and Erich Joachimsthaler, The Free Press, pp. 105–115. 2) Keller, K. L., *Strategic Brand Management: Building, Measuring and Managing Brand Equity*, © 2008 Pearson Education, Inc., pp. 433–436. 3) Kapferer, J. N., *The New Strategic Brand Management—Creating and Sustaining Brand Equity Long Term*, 4th edition, © Les Editions d'Organisation, 2008, pp. 361–371. 4) Davis, J. A., *The Olympic Games Effect: How Sports Marketing Builds Strong Brands*, © 2008 John Wiley & Sons (Asia) Pte Ltd, p. 241.

22. "Kraft Spin-Off (Completed)," January 31, 2007, Altria corporate web site, retrieved May 19, 2008 from www.altria.com/investors/2_2_2_kraftspinoff.asp.

23. 1) Tay, M., "Osim Writes Off US Investment," February 18, 2009, *The Straits Times*, www.straitstimes.com/Breaking%2BNews/Singapore/Story/STIStory_339995.html. OSIM corporate web site, retrieved May 2, 2009 from http://osim.listedcompany.com/financials.html.

24. Keller, K. L., *Strategic Brand Management: Building, Measuring and Managing Brand Equity*, © 2008 Pearson Education, Inc., p. 451.

25. 1) Aaker, D. A. and Joachimsthaler, E., *Brand Leadership*, © 2000 David A. Aaker and Erich Joachimsthaler, The Free Press, pp. 105–115. 2) Keller, K. L., *Strategic Brand Management: Building, Measuring and Managing Brand Equity*, © 2008 Pearson Education, Inc., pp. 433–436. 3) Kapferer, J. N., *The New Strategic Brand Management-Creating and Sustaining Brand Equity Long Term*, 4th edition. © Les Editions d'Organisation, 2008, pp. 361–371. 4) Davis, J. A., *The Olympic Games Effect: How Sports Marketing Builds Strong Brands*, © 2008 John Wiley & Sons (Asia) Pte Ltd, p. 241.

26. Keller, K. L., *Strategic Brand Management: Building, Measuring and Managing Brand Equity*, © 2008 Pearson Education, Inc., p. 451.

27. 1) Aaker, D. A. and Joachimsthaler, E., *Brand Leadership*, © 2000 David A. Aaker and Erich Joachimsthaler, The Free Press, pp. 105–115. 2) Keller, K. L., *Strategic Brand Management: Building, Measuring and Managing Brand Equity*, © 2008 Pearson Education, Inc., pp. 433–436. 3) Kapferer, J. N., *The New Strategic Brand Management-Creating and Sustaining Brand Equity Long Term*, 4th edition, © Les Editions d'Organisation, 2008, pp. 361–371. 4) Davis, J. A., *The Olympic Games Effect: How Sports Marketing Builds Strong Brands*, © 2008 John Wiley & Sons (Asia) Pte Ltd, p. 241.

28. Aaker, D. A. *Building Strong Brands*, © 1996 David A. Aaker; Simon & Schuster UK Limited p. 275.

29. Ibid., pp. 275–277.

30. 1) Aaker, D. A. and Joachimsthaler, E., *Brand Leadership*, © 2000 David A. Aaker and Erich Joachimsthaler, The Free Press, pp. 105–115. 2) Keller, K. L., *Strategic Brand Management: Building, Measuring and Managing Brand Equity*, © 2008 Pearson Education, Inc., pp. 433–436. 3) Kapferer, J. N., *The New Strategic Brand Management–Creating and Sustaining Brand Equity Long Term*, 4th edition, © Les Editions d'Organisation, 2008, pp. 361–371. 4) Davis, J. A., *Olympic Games Effect: How Sports Marketing Builds Strong Brands*, © 2008 John Wiley & Sons (Asia) Pte Ltd, p. 241.

31. Aaker, D. A., *Building Strong Brands*, © 1996 David A. Aaker, Simon & Schuster UK Ltd., pp. 278–291.

32. 1) Aaker, D. A. and Joachimsthaler, E., *Brand Leadership*, © 2000 David A. Aaker and Erich Joachimsthaler, The Free Press, pp. 105–115. 2) Keller, K. L., *Strategic Brand Management: Building, Measuring and Managing Brand Equity*, © 2008 Pearson Education, Inc., pp. 433–436. 3) Kapferer, J. N., *The New Strategic Brand Management–Creating and Sustaining Brand Equity Long Term*, 4th edition, © Les Editions d'Organisation, 2008, pp. 361–371. 4) Davis, J. A., *The Olympic Games Effect: How Sports Marketing Builds Strong Brands*, © 2008 John Wiley & Sons (Asia) Pte Ltd, p. 241.

33. Adidas corporate web site, retrieved May 30, 2009 from www.shopadidas.com/family/index.jsp?categoryId=2012802&cp=2019627.2039609.2039613.

34. Nike corporate web site, retrieved May 28, 2009 from http://store.nike.com/index.jsp?sitesrc=USLP&country=US&lang_locale=en_US#l=shop,pwp,c-1+100701/hf-10002+4294967109+12001/t-Men's_Tennis_Shoes.

35. Aaker, D. A., *Building Strong Brands*, © 1996 David A. Aaker, Simon & Schuster U.K. Limited, pp. 291–298.

36. Ibid., pp. 292–298.

37. 1) Aaker, D. A and Joachimsthaler, E., *Brand Leadership*, © 2000 David A. Aaker and Erich Joachimsthaler, The Free Press, pp. 105–115. 2) Keller, K. L., *Strategic Brand Management: Building, Measuring and Managing Brand Equity*, © 2008 Pearson Education, Inc., pp. 433–436. 3) Kapferer, J. N., *The New Strategic Brand Management—Creating and Sustaining Brand Equity Long Term*, 4th edition, © Les Editions d'Organisation, 2008, pp. 361–371. 4) Davis, J. A., *The Olympic Games Effect: How Sports Marketing Builds Strong Brands*, © 2008 John Wiley & Sons (Asia) Pte Ltd, p. 241.

38. "Howard Schultz's Memo," BusinessWeek online, January 7, 2008, retrieved March 27, 2009 from www.businessweek.com/bwdaily/dnflash/content/jan2008/db2008017_860745.htm.

39. Aaker, D. A., *Building Strong Brands*, © 1996 David A. Aaker, Simon & Schuster UK Ltd., pp. 298–301.

40. 1) Aaker, D. A. and Joachimsthaler, E., *Brand Leadership*, © 2000 David A. Aaker and Erich Joachimsthaler, The Free Press, pp. 105–115. 2) Keller, K. L., *Strategic Brand Management: Building, Measuring and Managing Brand Equity*, © 2008 Pearson Education, Inc., pp. 433–436. 3) Kapferer, J. N., *The New Strategic Brand Management–Creating and Sustaining Brand Equity Long Term*, 4th edition, © Les Editions d'Organisation, 2008, pp. 361–371. 4) Davis, J. A., *The Olympic Games Effect: How Sports Marketing Builds Strong Brands*, © 2008 John Wiley & Sons (Asia) Pte Ltd, p. 241.

41. Source: "Media and Mobile," Virgin corporate web site, retrieved July 5, 2009 from www.Virgin.com/media-and-mobile/telecommunications/.

42. Source: Amazon.com web site, retrieved February 17, 2009 from www.amazon.com/gp/help/customer/display.html?nodeId=13845911.

43. 1) Crawford, K., "Martha: I Cheated No One," July 20, 2004, CNNMoney, retrieved July 14, 2008 from http://money.cnn.com/2004/07/16/news/newsmakers/martha_sentencing/. 2) "Kmart Files Chapter 11," January 22, 2002, CNNMoney, retrieved July 14, 2008 from http://money.cnn.com/2002/01/22/companies/kmart/.

44. Pleven, L., Karnitschnig, M. and Soloman, D. "U.S. Revamps Bailout of AIG," March 2, 2009, Wall Street Journal online, retrieved March 15, 2009 from http://online.wsj.com/article/SB123589399651003021.html.

45. "AIG Says It Will Not Renew Manchester United Shirt Sponsor Deal," January 21, 2009, Street & Smith's SportsBusiness Daily, retrieved February 15, 2009 from www.sportsbusinessdaily.com/article/127086.

46. Anderson, J. C. and Carpenter, G. S., "Brand Strategy for Business Markets," Chapter 9 in *Kellogg on Branding*, edited by Alice M. Tybout and Tim Calkins, © 2005 Alice M. Tybout and Tim Calkins, John Wiley & Sons, Inc., pp. 181–183.

47. 1) Langfitt, F., "'Blackberry or Crackberry' A PDA Culture War," January 12, 2005, NPR (National Public Radio), retrieved March 2, 2008 from www.npr.org/templates/story/story.php?storyId=4279486. 2) Crackberry.com, retrieved March 3, 2008 from http://crackberry.com/.

Part II

New Brand Frameworks

The New Brand Building Framework: Destiny-Distinction-Culture-Experiences (DDCE)

4

Topics

- Preview
- New Brand Framework
  - Understanding the Big Picture
  - Brand Framework Elements
- Using the DDCE Framework
- Relationship to Brand Value, Customer Equity, Purpose Brands
- Measurement
  - Market Share
  - Relative Market Share
  - Brand Development Index
  - Category Development Index
  - Customer Lifetime Value
- Summary
- Discussion Questions

Preview

The subtitle of this book is "how branding creates value." Chapter 2 introduced several approaches for measuring brand value and also pointed out that there are differences in the ways that brand value is defined and measured. More broadly, the reason for building brands is to create value for all stakeholders: employees, management, shareholders, suppliers, customers, strategic partners and value-chain providers. As we will learn in this chapter, the relationship between brands and customers is particularly important because that is where the core economic value is most visible. In this regard, brand value, customer equity, and brand purpose are often, but not always, closely linked. More specifically, successful brand building is about making the brand meaningful to customers by understanding the job that customers need done (or the problem they want solved), designing solutions that address this, then employing a range of marketing tactics designed to bring the customer and the brand together. A brand-building challenge is that not all customers see the brand the same way nor have the same needs, so focusing on brand building ahead of customer development risks leading the company to produce products that have little relevance to their target audiences. Conversely, focusing brand building around customer equity risks ignoring competitor responses and may underemphasize the intangible benefits associated with a stronger brand focus.

Another complicating factor is deciding the proper brand architecture, as discussed in Chapter 3. This explained important brand-building questions, such as: "Is the brand a branded house, like GE, in which every major division with the company is labeled as 'GE (name of business)' and is therefore subsumed under a common identity; or is it a house of brands, like Procter & Gamble, in which dozens of well-known individual brands are managed within product categories (and P&G essentially remains invisible to the consumer)?" Before determining which brand architecture is used, we must first apply the brand definition from Chapter 1 to a new planning framework that encompasses both the internal and external dimensions of a brand. This framework applies to all brand types, from corporate to product. The key distinction is the level of complexity required to build the brand. For example, a global brand like GE is a vast, complex entity, with thousands of employees, products, offices, and associated business activities. GE's success depends on numerous internal operating and external competitive factors, particularly whether the GE corporate brand has meaning and significance for employees. At the same time, a small product brand's success, such as Sakae Sushi (a restaurant chain based in Singapore), also depends on the same factors, especially a clear understanding of the brand. As you will learn, GE can benefit from the new brand framework introduced in this chapter, as can a smaller product brand like Sakae Sushi. We will now turn our attention in this chapter to a new brand framework with four elements called *Destiny-Distinction-Culture-Experiences,* which describes key brand-building activities, providing a blueprint to help brand planning and decision-making. The subsequent six chapters will discuss each of the four elements in depth. Chapter 5 will focus on the importance of identifying, understanding, and using the brand's *Destiny* to guide its long-term direction. Chapter 6 will discuss the importance of brand *Distinction,* how to develop and nurture it, and how it acts to position the brand in the marketplace. Chapter 7 is dedicated to understanding and developing brand *Culture* which, as the term implies, suggests that successful brands have a set of mores and practices that animate the work environment and ultimately support the external delivery of the brand. Chapters 8–10 discuss brand *Experiences,* which are the many ways brands can relate to the marketplace and their customers within.

New Brand Framework

Understanding the Big Picture

Chapter 2 showed that brand value is recognized four ways: *financial, trusted reputation, societal relevance, and organizational,* and incorporating these into brand-building strategies and activities will create a more well-rounded brand. The annual business planning cycle is not a static exercise involving one-time marketing tactics. The process of brand building never stops. Brand building requires continual adjustment, fine tuning, and sometimes even significant strategic and tactical changes to ensure that the brand stays relevant. Such shifting may seem counterintuitive at first because companies, and managers in particular, often mistake the focus on brand building as simply a scientific methodology to which rigid adherence is paramount. Much of the research and literature on successful brand building concerns the tactical execution, primarily through marketing communications vehicles. However, such a narrow focus captures only the very tail end of brand building. In practice, successful brand building emphasizes relentless and varied approaches to creating a differentiated position in the minds of customers—differentiation that eventually inspires consumers to purchase the firm's products and or/services ("offerings"). Creating a differentiated position means brands must be both relevant to and resonant with target customers. Relevance means that the firm's offerings are appropriate to the needs of customers and resonant means that the offerings evoke favorable imagery and emotions. To help brand planning, this chapter will introduce the new brand framework that is the core of this book, with subsequent sections and chapters devoted to detailed descriptions of each brand element. As was once famously said, "luck favors the prepared mind." Brand success favors those who are prepared, and part of preparation is learning and understanding the proverbial "big picture" of the firm's brand, as seen by the brand's stakeholders.

Brand Framework Elements

In years past, branding was primarily an externally focused set of marketing communication activities consisting of advertising, selling, public relations, and promotion (including price discounts, bundled offerings such as "two-for-one" offers, giveaways, and samples). Having a customer focus often meant relentlessly directing brand messages toward a target audience (such as consumer product companies' emphasis on housewives in the U.S. in the 1950s and 1960s), hoping to inspire purchase. These communications were one way, because consumers could not respond directly (unless it was a direct response ad, such as a direct mail offer or a televised phone number asking consumers to call within a limited time to receive a special deal).

Companies, consumers, and marketing have changed significantly since those times. Successful brands are now the result of a complex set of plans directed both inside and outside the firm. Research has shown that companies with strong brands have developed reputations for understanding their customers, delivering relevant products, promoting reliable value-chain collaboration, while also simultaneously building the strength and competencies inside their own organization. Successful brands are born from a clear sense of direction that articulates what makes the brand and/or company unique, attracts employees that are both talented and devoted to the company's efforts, and shapes customer relationships with the firm. Four main elements, shown in Figure 4-1, guide brand planning and implementation. These four elements, when properly pursued, add substantial long-term value to companies, their brands, and their stakeholders. The remainder of this book describes each element in detail, providing guidance through the brand-building process.

Let's turn our attention to an overview of the four elements:

Figure 4-1　New Brand Framework

Destiny

Dictionary definitions state that Destiny is the hidden power that controls the future. In the context of brands, Destiny answers the question "why is the brand here?" and, as such, suggests that larger, longer term, and more far-reaching factors are at work. Destiny describes the collective ambitions and aspirations for the brand, serving as a guide for overall brand planning and implementation. Equally important, Destiny acts as a motivating force for employees, helping them to better understand how their work contributes to the long-term success of the brand. Destiny can also be described as the DNA of the brand—essentially the unique combination of traits and values that give the brand meaning and a reason to exist. In this context, Destiny guides decision-making and inspires profitable financial results for the brand.

Progress toward achieving the brand's Destiny requires a regular review of its position in the business world and society, including its reputation, in order to identify and refine the brand's unique and distinctive traits. The brand's Destiny must also be regularly communicated to all employees using a variety of informal and formal marketing methods.

In this latter regard, Destiny serves as an internal guide for understanding the brand, meant for all employees, and is not an external advertising campaign or slogan. Destiny cannot be easily created in brainstorming sessions, although in the absence of a clear Destiny, those responsible for the brand can and should meet regularly to discuss and identify the characteristics that would ultimately serve as the brand's destiny. Destiny is not the product of a one or two hour meeting. Instead, Destiny evolves over time as the brand's reputation grows.

Destiny can be conveyed using a brand mantra, vision, or mission statement. Kevin Keller describes brand mantras as a "three to five word phrase that captures the irrefutable essence or spirit of the brand positioning."[1] Here, the distinction between Destiny and brand mantras must be understood. Whereas Destiny is an all-encompassing description of the firm's meaning

Table 4-1 Brand Destiny Examples

Company or Organization	Destiny
Real Madrid FC (Spain)	To have respected players known for championship caliber futbol.
	Explanation: Florentino Perez, President of Real Madrid from 2000–2006, stated that the spirit of the club for more than a century was embodied by the idea of being both a champion and a gentleman. Since its founding in 1902, Real Madrid has become one of the most successful sports clubs in history, rivaling Manchester United for the most valuable futbol club in the world.
	Brand mantra: *A champion and a gentleman*
Singapore Airlines (Singapore)	To concentrate on customer needs by providing exceptional in-flight service.
	Explanation: Since its founding in 1972, Singapore Airlines has focused its strategy around superior customer service, rationalizing that any competitor can copy their planes and uniforms, but the practices of the organization cannot be copied as they are embedded deep into the founding principles of the company.
	Brand mantra: *Superior customer service*
Hewlett Packard (U.S.)	To distinguish itself by how the company treats employees and customers, thereby contributing to improving society.
	Explanation: Most companies focus on revenue growth. Bill Hewlett and Dave Packard believed that HP's success would be the result of an emphasis on people and profits. But HP believed that taking great care of its employees would lead to better results for their customers, who would then pay more for HP's offerings.
	Brand mantra: *Make technical contributions for advancement of science and welfare of humanity*

Sources: Brand Destiny examples.[2] John A. Davis brand research, 2000–2009. Concept of brand mantras adapted from Keller, K. and Lane, K., *Strategic Brand Management-Building, Measuring, and Managing Brand Equity,* © 2008 Pearson Prentice Hall, pp. 121–124.

and ultimate ambition directed internally and designed to animate employee performance, planning, and direction, a brand mantra distills the Destiny into a simplified message. Brand mantras are created once the brand's Destiny is clearly understood. The reason for this sequence is important: developing a brand mantra without a clear sense of Destiny risks turning this vital brand-building element into an exercise in sloganeering, devoid of substantial meaning or any connection to a larger vision. Brand mantras, vision, or mission statements are shorthand devices to help describe externally what people inside the firm already understand. While the specific wording of these may change over time to reflect terms appropriate to the business context, the underlying Destiny itself remains the same. Table 4-1 highlights examples of Destiny, with Keller's concept of brand mantras incorporated within.

Distinction

Distinction describes how and why the brand is differentiated from competitors and, therefore, of special interest to the marketplace. Distinction is directly influenced by the company's Destiny. An important point to remember is that while Distinction describes the thinking and planning in support of creating a unique brand, stakeholders and, in particular, customers determine whether the brand is *actually* differentiated. If customers recognize why the brand is different and, just as importantly, relevant to their needs, then the brand owns a potentially valuable place in the customer's mind. No amount of cleverly worded marketing messages can convince customers that the brand is truly different unless that difference is clearly understood by customers. Therefore, the never-ending task in brand building is determining what is needed so the brand is differentiated and relevant, especially as perceived by customers. Table 4-2 shows examples of Brand Distinction.

Table 4-2   Brand Distinction Examples

Company	Distinction
Infosys (India)	Become global brand shifting up from low-cost outsourcing to high value strategic consulting
	Explanation: Infosys was initially known as a low-cost provider of software coding. As its business grew globally, Infosys wanted to win more customer deals, so the company began to reposition toward high value strategic consulting.
Four Seasons (Canada)	Specialize within the hospitality industry by offering only experiences of exceptional quality.
	Explanation: Isadore Sharp founded Four Seasons Hotels in 1960 on the principle that travelers wanted the best service 24 hours a day, which led to Four Seasons' legendary golden rule that says to treat others as we would want them to treat us.
Lenovo (China)	"One-Two Punch" Brand Strategy • Masterbrand: Lenovo • Product Brand: Thinkpad
	Explanation: This product-led brand strategy emphasizes building a global brand name by leveraging the known innovative reputation of the former IBM PC division it acquired in 2005. Subsequently, Lenovo has won numerous industry awards for innovation and has increased its PC market share worldwide.

Sources: Mutiple sources. John A. Davis brand research 2000–2009. See endnotes for details.[3]

Culture

As we saw in Chapter 2, *organization* is one of the four brand values because having a clearly articulated brand helps employees inside the company to understand better how their work contributes to the success of the firm and align their work efforts accordingly. When employee alignment occurs, brands are able to more effectively deliver on the promises they make to customers, which will positively impact revenues and profits and lead to higher financial value for the brand.

It is important to understand the use of the term "Culture" when brand building because it describes the customs, behaviors, and practices (often unwritten) of an organization. Culture conveys a rich set of relationships and traditions about the organization that inspire the people within. In this context, brand building has important internal implications for the ongoing success of the firm. A well-known brand, built from a clear understanding of its Destiny and Distinction, serves as a magnet for attracting the best talent, which, in turn, helps sustain and build the company's culture—a culture whose members have to fulfill the brand's promise to the market. A useful exercise to illustrate the importance of culture in brand building is to ask a firm's employees to select a well-known brand and describe any associations they attach to it. For example, if one were to select Apple and ask colleagues to describe its culture, responses might include: "creative," "innovative," "colorful," and "dynamic." More often than not, one's colleagues are not likely to have worked at Apple before, yet they have a reasonably clear understanding of the company's culture. This knowledge is the result of Apple cultivating a specific image, based on its Distinction (to make "insanely great"[4] products) that is supported by a long-standing reputation and clever marketing communications, and verified by tens of millions of customers around the world. We can observe Apple and many other global brands and identify the qualities that we associate with them. To casual observers, a brand's success may appear to be the consequence of clever marketing communications. But the secret to building a successful brand culture that yields ongoing success and a positive reputation is to begin at the beginning, well before an advertising campaign is even considered. Every new employee represents an opportunity to build and/or change the culture. Company traditions must be shared from one generation to the next, just as societies in each country do. Brands must be marketed internally first since internal understanding and support is vital to delivering on the market's expectations. Table 4-3 highlights three examples of Brand Culture.

Experiences

The concept of "Experiences" encompasses everything that the customer sees and associates in connection with the brand, and is where a trusted reputation (one of the four brand values from Chapter 2) is either confirmed or denied. Value is created when customers buy the brand, and value to the customer is created when the brand delivers on the promises made by the marketing efforts. (Value is also created when the brand's

Table 4-3   Brand Culture Examples

Company	Culture
MAS Holdings (Sri Lanka)	MAS, based in Sri Lanka, is a US$700 million apparel manufacturer with 45 000 employees. Their customers include: Victoria's Secret, Speedo International, Nike. More than 80% of their manufacturing employees are women. MAS's culture-building practices include *Women Go Beyond (WGB),* a program that recognizes the achievements of top female employees for their work both in the company and the community, which can lead to promotion. WGB has been recognized by the UN's Global Impact and hailed by the global press as a progressive and successful people program. MAS's customers work with MAS partly because their employees are motivated, talented, and produce superior quality, by-products of the *Women Go Beyond* program. While MAS is not a globally known B2C brand, they are a well-known B2B brand.
NetApp (U.S.)	NetApp, based in the U.S., is a US$3.3 billion company with over 7000 employees, specializes in storage and date management solutions. They were ranked #1 in Fortune Magazine's 2009 annual "100 Best Companies to Work For" survey, *"...NetApp early on ditched a travel policy a dozen-pages long in favor of this maxim: 'We are a frugal company. But don't show up dog-tired to save a few bucks. Use your common sense.' Rather than business plans, many units write 'future histories,' imagining where their business will be a year or two out."* NetApp's unique approach people, travel, and work has succeeded in building a company recognized not just for their superior products, but for their distinctive culture.
ConSol (Germany)	ConSol, based in Germany, is a 19.5 million high-end software and IT consulting. Their corporate culture is founded on 3 principles: equal opportunity; work–life balance; and transparency. They have been awarded 'Best Workplaces in Europe' in 2008 and Germany's Best Employer in 2009 (4th year in a row) by Great Places to Work Institute. They also received the Bavarian Advancement of Women Prize in 2008. These achievements ensure ConSol attracts the best talent so that ConSol can deliver on their promises to customers.

Sources: Mutiple sources. John A. Davis brand research 2000–2009. See endnotes for details.[5]

other stakeholders—such as suppliers, distributors, shareholders—view the brand favorably and increase their support for it accordingly. Suppliers, for example, may offer special terms to the brand due to its higher status and recognition. Distributors might allocate more inventory space or promotion resources to support the brand and shareholders may increase their holdings if they believe the brand represents long-term value and growth.)

Experiential marketing, as this is also known, is a concerted effort to surround customers with a variety of touchpoints that enhance and improve their enjoyment of the brand. Integrated marketing communications, which will be discussed later in Chapter 10, is an important component in delivering positive customer experiences. Integrated marketing describes the coordination of various marketing communication tools (PR, print and broadcast advertising, trade shows) into a consistent overall theme. With the advent of the Internet, followed by mobile media and digital technology, brands can be communicated in numerous ways that communicate not just one way, as with print or broadcast advertising, but engage customers through digital tools, such as social media (Facebook, LinkedIn, MySpace).

Focusing on creating brand experiences has an important implication: every part of the company and its value-chain relationships is potentially a touchpoint that can affect the customer's perception of the brand, either positively or negatively. As such, brand building is an enormously complex task due to the challenge of determining the right combination of touchpoints that create the best possible customer experience. This is further complicated by the differences across customer segments and corresponding needs, necessitating different approaches to developing customer experiences that produce positive results – see Table 4-4.

Table 4-4   **Brand Experience Examples**

Company	Experiences
Apple (U.S.)	Apple, based in the U.S., is a global leader in innovative consumer products, from computers to software to music players to cell phones. 2008 revenues were US$32.4 billion. A key to Apple's success has been its ability to deliver superior experiences for customers by reinforcing the company's innovative image through multiple touchpoints, including: inviting retail environments, well-designed products, simple and emotional advertising, work of mouth generated by Apple's own customers, highly anticipated product launches, and even Steve Jobs' flair for drama and suspense that creates an aura of uniqueness around the Apple brand.

(Continued)

Table 4-4 (Continued)

Company	Experiences
Virgin Atlantic (U.K.)	Virgin Atlantic, based in the UK, is an international air carrier owned by Richard Branson (51%) and Singapore Airlines (49%). In 2008, its revenues were £2.3 billion, with profits of £60.9 million. The airline, like most Richard Branson ventures, has a quirky personality that is known worldwide, particularly for its unique service and product features that distinguish it from most other airlines, including: a bar in upper class; in-flight massages; limousine service; unrivaled airport lounges; and provocative advertising. Each of these touchpoints surrounds Virgin's customers with highly personalized services that are unlike those of rival air carriers.
Sakae Sushi (Singapore)	Sakae Sushi is part of Apex-Pal, founded by Douglas Foo and based in Singapore. It is one of the most successful sushi chains in Asia, with more than 70 restaurants and 2007 revenues of approximately S$67 million (Apex-Pal's 2007 revenues were S$83.8 million and Sakae Sushi is 80% of total revenues). Sakae sushi has several advantages that create a great experience: understandable menus with high quality sushi at affordable prices; visually inviting restaurants that are particularly well-suited for families; multiple, convenient locations; and a patented food delivery service in each restaurant (a conveyer belt system that passes by each table).

Sources: Mutiple sources. John A. Davis brand research 2000–2009. See endnotes for details.[6]

Using the DDCE Framework

Here are two applications of the DDCE framework: a successful regional boutique hotel brand—Joie de Vivre Hotels—and EMC, a global B2B information storage company.

EXAMPLE 4-1:

Example: Joie de Vivre Hotels[7]

Joie de Vivre Hotels is based in San Francisco, California. Founded by CEO Chip Conley in 1987, the company has grown to become the largest independent hotelier in California with 35 hotels and the second largest boutique hotelier in the U.S. The company's performance has been excellent, with revenues exceeding US$250, a 75% occupancy rate, an average room rate of approximately US$175

per night, and the luxury to support their own in-house philanthropic program called "Joie de Vivre Gives", in which each hotel donates a minimum of $200 per year per room to worthy organizations in their neighboring community. This success originates from Joie de Vivre's "unique approach to business, as represented by the Joie de Vivre Heart" (www.jdvhotels.com/about/our_heart, last accessed May2, 2007) which is based on four principles:

- creating a unique corporate culture;
- building an enthusiastic staff;
- developing strong customer loyalty;
- maintaining a profitable and sustainable business.

Destiny

Joie de Vivre's Destiny is captured by a simple idea: creating dreams to celebrate the joy of life. This influences everything the company does. Joie de Vivre's brand mantra is "Create joy," and all 3500 employees are given wristbands with this mantra on them. Chip Conley, Joie de Vivre's Founder/CEO, believes that the company's success is partly due to being a *meaning-driven* business, as defined in his book *PEAK: How Great Companies Get Their Mojo from Maslow*. Chip stresses that employee loyalty is fostered by inspiring a sense of calling to something larger than the job, such as a cause, and this gives the business *meaning*. To illustrate, Chip and his executives helped the company's housekeepers clean rooms. The executives were struck by the strong sense of community the housekeepers shared and how that fostered a team spirit. Part of what motivated this camaraderie was the thrill housekeepers experienced whenever guests complimented them on their service. Chip and his executives then conducted a brief test, asking some of the housekeepers to do a "half-assed" job for a couple of days. He didn't want the housekeepers to ruin the rooms, but just not be as detailed, neat or tidy. After the two days, Chip asked the housekeepers how they felt and they were not as happy because the guests were not as complimentary. The housekeepers wanted to return to the sense of community and mutual support for doing a superior job on their rooms because they could then gain a sense of group satisfaction for a job well done and regain the positive feedback from the guests. Meaning, for the housekeepers, was more than just cleaning a room, it was doing so supported the others on their team and led to compliments from guests, which created a more positive work environment.

Distinction

Each hotel is distinctively themed, often influenced by a niche magazine, reflecting the company's emphasis on a *destination-driven* marketing strategy. For example, the Hotel Phoenix is a rock-and-roll hotel. Hotel Rex reflects the literary and art traditions of decades past. The Hotel Del Sol is themed after California beach houses. Joie de Vivre's individualistic, lifestyle approach to their hotels is contrary to more conventional hotel business models that seek to replicate facility designs from one location for the sake of consistency for guests.

Joie de Vivre's service is also highly differentiated, emphasizing employee-driven decision-making, which empowers staff to address guest needs immediately without conferring with supervisors and managers first.

Culture

Joie de Vivre's employees must be confident to succeed because they are expected to make decisions that are in the best interests of guests. This means the company looks for a certain kind of individual who is comfortable making on-the-spot decisions.

Employees participate in an annual "work climate" survey that seeks their opinions about what it is like to work at Joie de Vivre, what is done well, and what can be improved. All employees discuss the results at follow-up meetings, involving them directly in efforts to make Joie de Vivre a better place to work every year. The company was rated second in the "Bay Area Best Places to Work" survey. Regular meetings between front office and back office staff help with the coordination of guest policies and procedures. The company fosters an entrepreneurial culture, reflected by four programs: *Joy of Life Guides, JdV University, Dreammaker,* and *Cultural Ambassadors.*

Joy of Life Guides

These are guides for each hotel's guests, written by employees and based on their own experiences, sharing both conventional and lesser-known recommendations about things to see and do. These guides introduce guests to those things that "locals" do and love.

Joie de Vivre University

Employees benefit from and can teach in unique career development programs, including "Boutique Hotels: The Past, Present and Future of our Stylish Industry" and "How to be a Black Belt Manager."

Dreammaker

The Dreammaker program encouraged Joie de Vivre employees to fulfill guests' dreams by taking the initiative to satisfy unusual requests wherever possible. The Joie de Vivre web site illustrates with this example:

While calling to confirm his late check-in at the Hotel Del Sol in San Francisco, Mr. Herbert mentioned how upset he was to miss the Oklahoma basketball game. Andrew at the front desk took the initiative to tape the game. Upon check-in, Mr. Herbert found a video of the game, a six-pack of beer, and a note reading, "Enjoy the game from the staff at the Del Sol!"

Cultural Ambassadors

Cultural ambassadors are rising stars at each hotel, whose are empowered to keep the culture of each hotel alive and dynamic, consistent with each hotel's unique personality. This helps ensure that every aspect of the guest's experience is consistent with Joie de Vivre's Destiny of creating dreams to celebrate the joy of life. Employee benefit from unique career development programs offered by the company, including "Boutique Hotels: The Past, Present and Future of our Stylish Industry" and "How to be a Black Belt Manager."

Experiences

Joie de Vivre's guest experience is driven by a simple notion: *inspire all five senses in the first five minutes.* This idea is the equivalent of three-dimensional branding, whereby a customer's senses are the target and each hotel environment is the medium, creating a highly engaging experience. The company appeals to customer *psychographics* (attributes such as lifestyle, personality, values, attitudes and interests), as opposed to demographics. Psychographics reveal common connections between otherwise uncommon groups of people. For example, an 85-year-old woman may share the same interest in jazz as a 20-year-old male college student. Demographics would not reveal such subtle commonalities. Understanding these characteristics is crucial to Joie de Vivre's success because this knowledge inspires employees to conduct themselves in accordance with the unique expectations of their guests.

Joie de Vivre uses the aforementioned cultural ambassadors to pay close attention to the atmosphere at each hotel. In addition, Joie de Vivre uses split second surveys to capture a snapshot insight into the guest's experience, and more conventional guest comment cards as well.

EXAMPLE 4-2:

Example: EMC[8]

EMC is a B2B technology company based in Massachusetts and a global leader with expertise in information storage. Revenues in 2008 were nearly $15 billion and its operations grew an additional 17% in 2008, despite the worst economy since the Great Depression.

Destiny

At EMC's core is a recognized expertise in information and data storage and this reason to exist has not changed. As business and technology have evolved, so too has EMC's refinement of its Destiny. From 1991–2002 EMC was widely known as the *storage company*, using mostly hardware to store data from business customers around the world. From 2002–2005 EMC expanded the message into s*torage and information*, a logical adaptation given the company's historical emphasis as an expert in storing information. Since 2005, EMC has refined their Destiny further around the theme of *information infrastructure* to reflect the continued rapid changes of businesses today requiring not just storage and information, but transforming that information into useful intelligence.

Distinction

Since 2005, EMC has focused its brand building efforts on creating the new "information infrastructure" category to reflect the changing needs of its business customers. An important point here has been the company's emphasis on solidifying this as a legitimate new business category. To that end, *information infrastructure* is not a trademark name, allowing it to become more easily adopted by the market.

Culture

EMC has a reputation for quality, resulting from constant investment in talent and in rewarding a culture that creates sustained value. Internal communication and branding is an important catalyst in this effort, keeping employees around the world. Hiring the right talent is expected. EMC then ensures the talent understands the objectives, goals, and offerings of the company through a variety of communications efforts:

- *Management communication and internal branding.* Every EMC executive and business leader around the world has repeatedly emphasized that EMC's goal is to be the world leader in information infrastructure. This goal has been repeated both internally to employees globally in every operation and externally to the market, particularly at industry conferences and with technology analysts. Additionally, the company relentlessly uses annual customer event, EMC World, kick-off meetings, management retreats, and local office meetings to hammer home its Destiny and Brand Strategy.
- *Total customer experience focus.* EMC gives all EMC employees the opportunity to recognize and be recognized for contributions to the total customer experience—EMC's commitment consistently to exceed customers' expectations for quality, service, innovation, and interaction.

About TCE

The Total Customer Experience actually begins and ends with talking with our customers. This program gives us the opportunity to broaden the conversation we have with our customers, making certain that we are working as partners to help solve their business problems. And it is a competitive differentiator for us.

It's true that TCE is about product, process, and data. But at the end of the day, TCE is about you, it's about me, it's about building a strong relationship with our customers, and it's about furthering our company culture—culture that puts our customers first to ensure that their experience with EMC is as positive and pleasant as it can possibly be.

Experiences

To reinforce the new brand strategy, EMC is using several tools, including: corporate brand message, product acquisition and expansion, sports sponsorships, analyst reviews, customers, CSR (corporate social responsibility), and information heritage.

- *Corporate brand message.* EMC's slogan, "Where Information Lives," conveys the essence of EMC's brand promise and hints at the information infrastructure category it is promoting.
- *Product acquisition and expansion.* EMC has purchased over 35 companies in recent years in an effort to realize its information infrastructure ambition, including VMWare in 2003 (which provides software that enables different operating systems to run simultaneously on a common server, thereby facilitating corporate information integration) and Iomega (a well known consumer storage brand). EMC has shifted its business from an 80% focus on hardware 20 years ago to 50% emphasis on software, which offers customers a more diverse and relevant set of products used in supporting the Information Infrastructure company focus.
- *Sports sponsorships.* EMC wants to be where its customers are, which is one reason why it has long supported and sponsored sports, including the Boston Red Sox Major League Baseball team, cobranding with leading NFL football clubs (including the New England Patriots), rugby, and F1 racing. Sports provide a large audience for reinforcing brand awareness and many of its customers are also sponsors and/or fans of these and other sports. With the Boston Red Sox, EMC announced in 2008 that it is the first company in the more than 100-year history of the team to have its logo on the sleeve of every player's jersey. The Red Sox have two Japanese players on the team and since Japan also has a major fan base for baseball, the Red Sox ran promotions in Japan in 2008 that EMC helped sponsor, further raising the company's visibility. EMC is putting NFL logos on IOMEGA drives that are sold in consumer markets, associating its products with the NFL in the process. EMC sponsors the Hong Kong Sevens Rugby, one of the largest rugby tournaments in the world. EMC helps sponsor the Panasonic F1 racing team, getting visible placement on the racing suits of the drivers and the mirrors of the cars. Each of these sponsorships enables EMC to reach a large, diverse business and consumer audience.
- *Analyst reviews.* Part of a technology company's credibility comes from independent analysts that evaluate and review technology solutions, looking for genuine differentiation and value. EMC updates technology industry analysts regularly each year with their newest solutions. Gartner, one of the most respected technology analysts in the world, picked up and now uses "information infrastructure" as a business category it tracks, lending credibility to EMC's efforts in this area.
- *Customers.* EMC works with organizations around the world, in every industry, in the public and private sectors, and of every size, from startups to the Fortune Global 500. Their customers include banks and other financial services firms, manufacturers, healthcare and life-sciences organizations, Internet service and telecommunications providers, airlines and transportation companies, educational institutions, and public-sector agencies. EMC also provides technology, products, and services to consumers in more than 100 countries. Their customers provide credible testimonials for EMC's offerings, and EMC uses customers from more than 100 countries around the world to help promote them in that customer's home country.

- *Corporate social responsibility.* EMC has been deeply committed for years in a variety of philanthropic endeavors, including: community involvement; education, information heritage, underprivileged children, and more. These efforts give the company a more human face and the broad range of programs get widespread employee involvement, an important indicator of the company's seriousness in this area. In the Asia Pacific region, for example, EMC is dedicated to supporting the education of underprivileged boys and especially girls at the School of Hope located in the slums of Bangalore, India. In Cambodia, EMC supports house building and water well projects that lift families out of abject poverty, providing them the shelter and irrigation needed to live on and farm the land.
- *Information heritage.* From EMC's web site (http://www.emc.com/leadership/digital-universe/information-heritage-trust.htm, last accessed March 24, 2009): "The EMC Information Heritage Initiative recognizes organizations and individuals leading the way to protect and preserve the world's information heritage. EMC and its partners in this philanthropic and commercial initiative believe that information should be preserved, protected, and made globally accessible in digital form."

Helping Preserve the Irreplaceable

This initiative makes historical documents and cultural artifacts readily accessible—for research and education—via the Internet. EMC and initiative partners work with diverse organizations throughout the world to protect valuable information and improve access to international treasures.

In addition to the investments made by initiative partners, EMC provides financial assistance, in-kind donations, and proven expertise. These contributions complement EMC's other corporate philanthropy programs.

EMC also relies on a global field sales and channel account manager force to work with customers and partners every day, consistently sharing the same set of brand messages and solutions that emphasize the information infrastructure expertise for which the company is known.

Relationship to Brand Value, Customer Equity, Purpose Brands

The start of this chapter briefly discussed the marketing issues associated with a brand value, customer equity, or a purpose brand focus. (A purpose brand is one in which the product is designed to do a specific job. Federal Express is a purpose brand because it is designed to deliver packages from point A to point B as quickly, accurately, and affordably as possible. This will be discussed further below.)[9] Roland Rust, Valarie Zeithaml, and Katherine Lemon state that brand building should be in the service of growing customer equity.[10] The reason this is important is because customers are the ones determining if a brand is attractive and worth buying or not, not marketers or marketing communications. Putting customers at the center of the company's brand building will help create strong customer equity that, in turn, should lead to strong brand equity. But if brands are emphasized over customer, then the potential for creating offerings that are not relevant or attractive increases. Witness the struggles of U.S. automakers in recent years, which tended to favor reinforcing core brands instead of understanding customers and their increasing preference for well-made and distinctive imports. Conversely, if customers decide they like a brand, then they will purchase it and, if the brand stays relevant over time, they will keep doing so for many years. As Rust *et al.* state:

> … for firms to be successful over time, their focus must switch to maximizing customer lifetime value—that is, the net profit a company accrues from transactions with a given customer during the time that the customer has a relationship with the company … companies must focus on *customer equity* (the sum of the lifetime values of all the firm's customers across all the firm's brands) rather than *brand equity*.[11]

Rust, R. T., Zeithaml, V. A. and Lemon, K. N., "Customer-Centered Brand Management," R0409H, *Harvard Business Review*, September 2004, pp. 3–5.

The end of this chapter will discuss ways to measure customer lifetime value to help reinforce the concept. For now, it is important to understand the potential relationship between customer equity and brand equity. The challenge for companies is determining how to succeed in each of the four elements so that the collective effort creates a stronger brand that all stakeholders believe in, versus focusing only on one or two areas (such as brand strategy or experiences—the most common brand-building areas), which can lead management to develop tactics in pursuit of short-term goals at the expense of a less cohesive and consistent brand over the long term.

In their article "Marketing Malpractice," Clayton M. Christensen, Scott Cook, and Taddy Hall argue that traditional customer segmentation can lead marketers to producing products and/or features without knowing if customers will actually find them beneficial:

> The problem is that customers don't conform their desires to match those of the average consumer in their demographic segment. When marketers design a product to address the needs of a typical customer in a demographically defined segment, therefore, they cannot know whether any specific individual will buy the product— they can only express a likelihood of purchase in probabilistic terms.[12]

Christensen, C. M., Cook, S. and Hall, T. "Marketing Malpractice-The Cause and the Cure," R0512D, *Harvard Business Review*, December, 2005, p. 2.

Christensen *et al.* recommend that firms simplify their brand-building approaches to attracting customers by taking the customers' point of view—"they just need to get things done."[13] Their view is that brand builders mistakenly believe that if you understand the customer, you will understand the job that customers want done. Yet the likelihood of this occurring is quite low. When the job is understood and corresponding solutions are developed, then customers essentially hire companies/products to do the jobs for them. "We call the brand of a product that is tightly associated with the job for which it is meant to be hired a *purpose brand*."[14]

Clearly, brand building is complex and does not easily lend itself to a singular approach, which is why we state that brands are the entire organization as seen through the eyes of stakeholders.

This textbook is based on research of more than 200 companies around the world, many of which were global brands, and others that were niche and/or local brands. As a result, we take the point of view that a strong brand is the entire organization as seen through the eyes of stakeholders (customers, employees, suppliers, distributors, shareholders …). In other words, the market determines the ultimate value of the brand. If brand value were to be the sole focus of the business strategy, then the subtler needs associated with different customer groups might be missed because resources would be used to push the brand into new growth opportunities. If customer equity were the focus then brands might not be as responsive to competitive moves since most of their effort would be spent on serving specific customer needs. If purpose brands were the focus, then innovation might suffer since resources would be concentrated on designing a narrow set of features to address a specific job, which would reduce time and resources dedicated to "out-of-the-box" solutions.

For planning purposes, each DDCE element may be viewed as possessing a distinct identity because this will focus attention on its unique components. However, the practical demands of managers in business do not always recognize artificial planning boundaries, particularly when a customer has a problem. They simply want it fixed, and this demand compels companies to prepare their employees to handle customer needs readily, without waiting for the organizational approvals built into each firm's structure. Customers rarely care about chains of command, unless their problem remains unresolved, in which case customers may demand to "speak to a supervisor." Such an occurrence implies a breakdown in the customer-orientation of the brand owner and should spark quick management action to prevent this from happening in the future. As implied, while these four elements have distinct identities, they interact continually, affecting a company's relationship with the marketplace. In this sense, each element is already being pursued in the normal course of the firm's business activities (even though the brand framework's terminology may not be used) and the work within is constantly evolving at the same time.

Therefore, while focusing brand building on each element's components, knowing that each element operates in concert with others should inspire broader thinking about how the *total brand* is perceived by all stakeholders. Brands are rarely built successfully on the basis of just one or two brand framework elements. While a company may produce a high quality brand, this should not mislead management into believing that the organization is capable of properly delivering the brand to the market, and supporting it with memorable experiences. Recognizing that each element interacts with the others fluidly will infuse brand planning with a more accurate sense of the interdependencies inside and outside the company that shape the brand's reputation. There are no starts, stops, magic doors, or singular formulas that dictate the exact steps needed to build brands. Part of branding success is the result of a combination of exceptional competence, research, flexibility, ongoing questioning of the established order, planning, and serendipity.

Measurement

The introduction of the DDCE framework shows that building a strong brand involves the entire organization and not just marketing communications. This chapter provided the strategic view of a brand and subsequent chapters will discuss each of the framework's elements in detail. There are several measures that can be used to guide the brand-building strategy which are discussed in this section. While this is not a comprehensive list, it does provide guidance on important and common strategic measures that serve as helpful tools in brand building. They are:

- market share;
- relative market share;
- brand development index;
- category development index;
- customer lifetime value.

Market share and relative market share are important for assessing the brand's position in the market compared to competitors, with relative market share describing how a brand is performing relative to its biggest competitor. The brand development index and category development index work together to help identify strong and weak customer segments, albeit from two different perspectives: the brand itself and the category in which the brand competes. Customer lifetime value helps determine both the long-term value associated with loyal customers and the maximum costs to acquire those customers. All five of these measures provide strategic insight into the performance of the brand.

Market Share

Metric
Market share.[15]

Overall Brand Performance Benefits
Gauges how well a company is doing against the market's competitors, as a percentage of total market revenues or units.

How
Market share is derived by dividing the company's unit sales or revenues by total market unit sales or revenues.

Formula

$$M_{it} = \frac{S_{it}}{\sum S_{it}}$$

Where
M_i = company i's market share in time t expressed in percentage terms;
S_i = sales of company i in time t (in units or dollars);
ΣS_t = Sum of all sales in time t (in units or dollars).

Impact on Overall Brand Performance

Market share helps management understand the success of its efforts to penetrate the market relative to its competitors, an indicator of the success of its brand strategy. A rising market share is generally a good sign, although it is subject to several qualifications. The company's market share (in units) may have risen because the company lowered its price substantially and may now be losing profits. Or its share may have risen because the product category is aging and smarter firms are quickly abandoning the category, leaving the crumbs to this firm. The data used to measure market share will likely come from several sources. The brand's finance or accounting departments should have up-to-date information on company sales provided from sales management or distribution operations. Total sales in the market will come from several outside sources, including industry trade reports, consulting firms, market research specialists and even business magazines. Data from multiple sources should be compared because of differences in data-collection time periods, precision of measurement criteria, reporting time periods, and the collection methodology.

Analyzing market share in-depth can also help identify the sources of the brand's market share performance. If market share gains were made over a specified period of time, were they ahead of plan or behind plan? Is this increased share sustainable? If market share declined, what were the factors that may have caused this? Competitor innovation? Competitor pricing? Customer dissatisfaction? Changing customer preferences?

Market share is typically used in several planning areas. As a business planning metric, senior management may set a market share target for a forthcoming time period (typically 1–2 years) for the company overall. Marketers would typically include the market share figures when discussing strategies and objectives in the marketing plan and in their internal efforts to build support from other departments. If marketing managers are responsible for a specific product, product line, or product category, then individual market share goals may also be set for each specific product, in addition to overall company objectives.

Relative Market Share

Metric
Relative market share[16]

Brand Performance Benefits
The purpose is to compare the brand's market share against that of its closest competitor.

How

The brand's market share is divided by that of is closest competitor.

Formula

$$\text{Relative market share (I)}(\%) = \frac{\textit{brand's market share } (\$)}{\textit{largest competitor's market share}}$$

Impact on Brand Performance

Relative market share provides insight on how a brand or specific product is performing versus its key competitor in a specific brand or product category. Brands with a larger share vis-à-vis its main competitor may also command higher profits and/or a premium position. Understanding this relative comparison can help refine brand-building investments.

Brand Development Index

Metric

Brand Development Index (BDI).[17]

Brand Performance Benefits

Identifies strong and weak customer segments by measuring a brand's performance within a particular segment in comparison to its performance across the entire market.

How

The brand's sales to a group or a segment of customers are divided by the total households in that group. This is then divided by the result of total brand sales divided by total households in the market.

Formula

$$\text{Brand development index} = \frac{\textit{brand sales to group} \div \textit{households in group}}{\textit{total brand sales} \div \textit{total households}}$$

Impact on Brand Performance

The brand development index describes which customer segments represent the highest sales per capita in comparison to the market overall. Sales per capita might be higher in the brand's home market versus the market at large, and the BDI can help prove or disprove this. The result can identify customer segments where the brand has the greatest potential.

Category Development Index

Metric

Category Development Index (CDI).[18]

Brand Performance Benefits
The CDI measures the strength of a particular category to a select segment relative to its performance in the market overall.

How
The category's sales to a group or a segment of customers are divided by the total households in that group. This is then divided by the result of total category sales divided by total households in the market.

Formula

$$\text{Category Development Index} = \frac{category\ sales\ to\ group \div households\ in\ group}{total\ category\ sales \div total\ households}$$

Impact on Brand Performance
The impact is similar to that of the BDI, except for categories, not brands. Categories cover a wide range: hair care, fruit, soft drinks, basketball footwear, social media, luxury vacations, and more. Knowing the relative performance of a category may inspire changes in brand-building activities to more effectively support that category.

Customer Lifetime Value

Metric
Customer lifetime value (CLTV).

Brand Performance Benefits
Customer lifetime value identifies the value of a customer relationship based on the present value of future cash flows expected from this customer. There are several approaches to CLTV. Two will be highlighted here.

Approach 1[19]

How
Estimate the dollar value (typically, the flow of profits) of a customer's long-term relationship with a company. This measures how much a customer is worth while remaining a loyal purchaser of a company's products and also determines a value for new customers referred by existing customers, accentuating the added value to the relationship developed with the referring customer. Retention is a primary objective. However, this approach does not factor in cross or up-selling opportunities, focusing instead on new customer referrals.

Formula

$$\text{CLTV} = [(M - C) \times (P \times Y) - A + (A \times N)] \times F$$

Where
  M = average amount of money spent per purchase;
  C = average costs to service each purchase;

P = number of purchases per year;
Y = number of years managers expect to keep this customer;
A = new-customer acquisition cost;
N = number of new customers referred by original customer;
F = customer adjustment factor for the period of time being evaluated.

Allen Weiss, founder and publisher of Marketingprofs.com, describes F, the customer adjustment factor, as follows:

> ... (F) captures changes in a customer's behavior over time. If you estimate that the customer will increase the money spent per visit over time (because you estimate you will increase their loyalty), then put in a higher number—say, 1.4. If you estimate that customer will decrease spending over time, put in a lower number—say, 9. This is obviously a subjective estimate.
> www.marketingprofs.com/5/weiss7.asp

Therefore, 1.0 is considered steady state, so no correction is needed. The subjective nature of the correction factor reveals the importance of including both qualitative and quantitative measures in the customer analysis. Next, the terms are grouped into individual equations.

M − C = the average gross profit per customer visit;
P × Y = total number of visits over the customer's lifetime;
A × N = the amount of money saved by the customer's referral.

Approach 2[20]

How
This approach divides the percentage customer retention rate by one plus the percentage discount rate minus the percentage retention rate. This is then multiplied by the dollar margin.

Formula

$$\text{CLTV (\$)} = \text{margin (\$)} \times \frac{\textit{retention rate}\,(\%)}{1 + \textit{discount rate}\,(\%) - \textit{retention rate}\,(\%)}$$

Impact on Brand Performance
There is potentially sizable long-term value represented by nurturing loyal customers. The result of the CLTV calculation may well influence the development of marketing programs designed to build customer retention and loyalty. Assuming the CLTV result is positive, then it reinforces why businesses should try to develop long-term relationships rather than short-term or, worse, one-time purchase gains. The calculations also help guide the amount to be spent on customer acquisition.

Summary

This chapter began with an overview of the new brand building blocks, DDCE (*Destiny-Distinction-Culture-Experiences*) required to build strong brands today, highlighting that brand success depends on interaction and coordination among the four brand building blocks rather than a separate, discrete emphasis on individual areas of the company. The DDCE framework gives a proper, organization-wide perspective on brand building and its impact on the entire firm, illustrating why brands must be understood in the context of an overall system and not just a set of individual activities. Seen this way, one can understand the heightened role brand building plays in developing long-term value for all stakeholders. Subsequent Sections of this textbook will address specific details of the planning activities in each of the four brand framework elements. Following the discussion questions, we will turn our attention to an in-depth discussion of each of the four elements.

Discussion Questions

1. Motorola and Sony are two well-known global brands that have faced challenges to their businesses in recent years. What would you say their respective Destinies are? How have these Destinies possibly influenced their performance? How can senior management leverage each firm's known expertise to improve the performance of these firms?
2. Which firms have a well-differentiated Brand Strategy? What stands out about their brand that supports your assertion?
3. Select a brand you know well. How would you describe its Culture?
4. Discuss your most recent hotel stay. What was the experience like? In answering this, identify both the tangible and intangible factors that contributed to your stay.

Notes

1. Keller, K. L., *Strategic Brand Management-Building, Measuring, and Managing Brand Equity*, © 2008 Pearson Prentice Hall, pp. 121–124.
2. 1) Research projects conducted by students at Singapore Management University for term projects in their strategic brand management course between 2004 and 2008. 2) "Trophies Tell Story of Madrid's Decline," *Guardian*, retrieved November 1, 2009 from www.guardian.co.uk/sport/blog/2009/mar/10/real-madrid-champions-league-failure. 3) Pae, P., "Singapore Airlines Will Tuck You Into Bed—for $10 000," October 30, 2006, *Los Angeles Times*, retrieved October 22, 2007 from http://articles.latimes.com/2006/oct/30/business/fi-singapore30. 4) "Airline Bans A380 Mile-high Club," October 31, 2007, BBCNews, retrieved December 12, 2007 from http://news.bbc.co.uk/2/hi/7071620.stm. 5) HP corporate web site, retrieved January 14, 2008 from www.hp.com/hpinfo/abouthp/histnfacts/. 6) Jacobson, D., "Founding Fathers,", *Stanford Magazine*, retrieved January 24, 2008 from www.stanfordalumni.org/news/magazine/1998/julaug/articles/founding_fathers/founding_fathers.html.

3. 1) Research projects conducted by students at Singapore Management University for their strategic brand management course between 2004 and 2008. 2) Padmini, M and Desai, V., "Infosys: The Challenge of Global Branding," pp. 1–2, Case: 950A01, Richard Ivey School of Business, © 2005 Ivey Management Services. 3) Four Seaons Hotels, Inc., retrieved April 7, 2008 from www.fundinguniverse.com/company-histories/Four-Seasons-Hotels-Inc-Company-History.html. 4) Martin, R. L. "Creating the Four Seasons Difference," January 23, 2008, retrieved March 17, 2008 from www.businessweek.com/innovate/content/jan2008/id20080122_671354.htm. 5) Four Seasons corporate information retrieved multiple times between 2006 and 2009, www.fourseasons.com/about_us/company_information.html. 6) Based on two meetings with David Shaw, Director of Brand/Asia Pacific for Lenovo: the first was a speech that he gave at the BrandFinance Forum in Asia, March 2008, held at Singapore Management University; and the second was a meeting with David Shaw on April 17, 2008.

4. Jobs , S., "The Next Insanely Great Thing," in *Wired* magazine (February 1996), retrieved May 2006, www.wired.com/wired/archive/4.02/jobs_pr.html.

5. 1) Research projects conducted by students at Singapore Management University for their strategic brand management course between 2004 and 2008. 2) MAS Holdings corporate information retrieved May 11, 2008 from www.masholdings.com/. 3) The author also visited with MAS Holdings' executive team and toured their factories for several days in 2005. 4) *Fortune* magazine http://money.cnn.com/magazines/fortune/bestcompanies/2009/snapshots/1.html, retrieved February 2009. 5) MAS Holdings' recognition as a "best place to work" discussed at www.greatplacetowork-europe.com/best/list-eu.htm. 6) "100 Best Places to Work 2009," retrieved March 3, 2009 from http://money.cnn.com/magazines/fortune/bestcompanies/2009/snapshots/1.html. 6) Tansey, B., "Fortune Names NetApp Best Place to Work," January 23, 2009, *San Francisco Chronicle,* retrieved February 19, 2009 from www.sfgate.com/cgi-bin/article.cgi?f=/c/a/2009/01/23/BUQB15FEON.DTL. 7) "Best Workplaces in Germany," retrieved May 17, 2009 from www.greatplacetowork.com/best/list-de.htm. 8) ConSol corporate information retrieved January 2009 from www.consol.com/company/awards/.

6. 1) Research projects conducted by students at Singapore Management University for their strategic brand management course between 2004 and 2008. 2) "Sakae Sushi: Looking Beyond Singapore's Shores," research completed December 2006, updated December 2008, pp. 1–4. 3) "The Apple Core: What Makes it the Brand Today," research completed November 2007. 4) "Creative Technology: Fighting Back," with Apple as the comparison company, research completed April 2006, pp. 4–7. 5) Dyson, C. J., "Virgin Atlantic Experienced," April 1, 2002, retrieved November 17, 2007 from www.brandchannel.com/features_webwatch.asp?ww_id=66. 6) Martindale, N., "Virgin Atlantic's HR in Practice: High-flying Management," August 20, 2007, retrieved January 11, 2008 from www.personneltoday.com/articles/2007/08/20/41937/virgin-atlantics-hr-in-practice-high-flying-management.html.

7. Information courtesy of interviews and emails with Chip Conley. Additional information was obtained from Chip's books: *Peak: How Great Companies Get Their Mojo From Maslow,* © 2007 Jossey-Bass. *The Rebel Rules: Daring to be Yourself in Business,* © 2001 Fireside. Joie de Vivre's web site provides a thorough overview of the company's history, success, and business practices. Visit www.jdvhotels.com.

8. Information supplied by Steven Leonard, President of EMC Asia Pacific and Japan, in a speech that he delivered at Singapore Management University in February 2009, and Becky diSorbo, Director of Communications and PR for EMC Asia Pacific and Japan. Supplemented by EMC corporate web site: www.emc.com, retrieved October 2008–February 2009.

9. Christensen, C. M., Cook, S. and Hall, T. "Marketing Malpractice-The Cause and the Cure," R0512D, *Harvard Business Review,* December, 2005, pp. 4–6.

10. Rust, R. T., Zeithaml, V. A. and Lemon, K. N., "Customer-Centered Brand Management," R0409H, *Harvard Business Review,* September 2004, pp. 3–5.

11. Ibid., pp. 9–11.

12. Christensen, C. M., Cook, S. and Hall, T. "Marketing Malpractice-The Cause and the Cure," R0512D, *Harvard Business Review,* December, 2005, p. 2.

13. Ibid.

14. Ibid., p. 5.

15. Davis, J., *Measuring Marketing: 103 Key Metrics Every Marketer Needs,* © 2007 John Wiley & Sons, pp. 71–73.

16. Farris, P. W., Bendle, N. T., Pfeifer, P. E., Reibstein, D. J., *Marketing Metrics: 50+ Metrics Every Executive Should Master,* © 2006 Pearson Education, pp. 19–20.

17. Ibid., pp. 23–25.

18. Ibid.

19. Davis, J., *Measuring Marketing: 103 Key Metrics Every Marketer Needs,* © 2007 John Wiley & Sons, pp. 117–122.

20. Farris, P. W., Bendle, N. T., Pfeifer, P. E. and Reibstein, D. J., *Marketing Metrics: 50+ Metrics Every Executive Should Master,* © 2006 Pearson Education, pp. 143–148.

Brand Destiny

5

Topics

- Preview
- Destiny
- Four Subcomponents of Successful Brand Destiny
  - Ultimate Dream
  - Creating Value
  - Values
  - Personality
- Measurement
  - Destiny Diagnostic
- Summary
- Discussion Questions

Preview

As children, we dream about what we want to be some day, imagining our lives at some distant point in the future. Attached to this are aspirations and goals that are refined over time, guiding us toward our dream. Underlying this are our core values, convictions, and principles that we hold dear. As we grow older, our dreams may change, but we still harbor a sense of "what could be." This same experience holds true for top brands as well, with the brand's caretakers (whether they are founders, owners, or managers) envisioning the future on behalf of the brand. In considering the brand's future, a crucial requirement, indeed a primary requirement, is to know and understand the brand's Destiny because this touches upon every other aspect of the brand and every decision made for the brand. The dictionary defines Destiny as the hidden power believed to control what will happen in the future. In less ominous terms and applied to business, Destiny describes management's aspirations for the future of the brand. Their efforts to describe their future serve, in effect, as a form of directive control over strategic decisions, guiding the company's long-term course. Unfortunately, many companies ignore or underserve this important concept, partly because business expectations today demand instant answers and immediate results. As a consequence, consideration of deeper issues like Destiny is deferred to some later date, if it takes place at all.

But ignoring examination of the firm's Destiny is akin to living for the moment, never planning ahead or considering the ramifications of one's actions. In business, such behavior is destructive to sustained growth, value enhancement, and societal contribution. How can a firm develop expertise, a reputation, or appeal to customers if it is not clear about its own Destiny? The answer is it can't. This book puts significant emphasis on the importance of Destiny and on companies gaining deep insight into their Destiny, precisely because doing so creates a path toward long-term growth and value. Brands with an explicit understanding of their Destiny create competitive advantage over rivals. Destiny helps drive distinction, and it helps make a brand more memorable in the eyes of both employees and the public. Decades of marketing and brand research have provided us with known and accepted frameworks for brand management. Many of these are discussed in this book as well. But a crucial difference is that successful brands today look far beyond conventional branding practices to pursue their own path. This journey begins with understanding their Destiny.

Destiny

Why does a company exist, beyond the need to make money? If revenues and profits were the only drivers then companies could sell anything. But successful branding requires a company's leadership to focus its energy and thinking around a specific, compelling vision, then organizing every activity and effort to develop expertise that inspires organizational direction and fulfills long-term ambitions. Understanding a company's Destiny helps develop clear branding practices that are genuine and authentic, reflecting the company's personality and skills. While strategies and tactics will change over time because of competitive conditions, brand destiny generally remains constant, providing a compass heading for a company's development.

Destiny is an expansive concept that describes the core characteristics of the brand and/ or company and answers thematic questions related to corporate philosophy, "*Why* is the organization here?" and "What is the organization's personality? '*Who*' is this organization?" Destiny is analogous to the reason for the organization to exist, as discussed by Collins and Porras in *Built to Last*.[1] However, destiny encompasses not just the organization's *raison d'être* but also its soul. Destiny is an important area for an organization to understand for a few simple reasons: if a company does not know why it is here, then it is unlikely to know where it can go, what it can do, and which opportunities it should exploit. Articulating and understanding Destiny is necessary for organizations because its absence means that there is no clear sense of what the company stands for or its direction. Without a clear self-definition, there is little chance of developing recognized expertise. Companies that do not understand their destiny risk becoming faceless to the market and their message would lack clarity (because there would be little understanding of what is necessary to communicate).[2] Interestingly, not-for-profit organizations such as nongovernmental organizations (NGOs) often have a clearer sense of their Destiny than their for-profit counterparts. Part of this is because they have an unambiguous cause they are pursuing (eradication of disease; helping the under-privileged; fighting global hunger; improving the environment) and their efforts gain a great deal of sympathy and support from the public. They have a crystal clear destination, in other words. Most companies do not garner sympathy or support (unless tragedy has struck) but many do build strong brands and develop loyal customer relationships as part of their success. Those that succeed put significant effort into understanding their Destiny, identifying their equivalent of a cause.

Four Subcomponents of Successful Brand Destiny

Destiny is comprised of four components, shown in Figure 5-1.

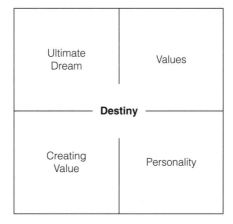

Figure 5-1   Components of Destiny

Let's look at all four areas and see how they relate to building brands and creative competitive advantage.

Ultimate Dream

The ultimate dream is the ideal description of success for the brand if the company could perfectly control its offerings and markets. It is a timeless understanding of the brand's enduring contribution. Such an undertaking is daunting, but the galvanizing idea behind the ultimate dream serves as an animating catalyst for all employees, from entry level to senior management. Ultimate dreams are about anticipating the unknown and *imagining ahead*. This involves leaps of faith. In order to imagine ahead, brands must explore uncertainty. This may sound sloppy and disconnected from the rigors of business planning, which encourages hard facts and reams of data, but such exploration actually encourages leaders to deal with uncertainty and brainstorm various scenarios.

In 1961, President Kennedy said that the U.S. would put a man on the moon by the end of the decade. No existing evidence suggested if this was realistic. There were many challenges of deep space flight that were unknown and unexplored by the very basic (by comparison) space flights of that time. Kennedy did not know how to make it happen. But describing the dream set in motion a focused research effort to bring the dream to reality.

A division of Harris Corporation, a large international communications and IT company, believed it needed a fresh perspective in order to improve growth and competitive positioning. The division embarked on an intensive effort with senior managers and senior field personnel to *imagine* a more successful future, beyond their normal planning approach. Using innovative scenario planning and brainstorming sessions, the management team devised entirely new practices and solutions combinations, resulting in a $425 million sales increase, well above forecast.[3] In their particular market, Harris is considered a highly reputable brand and innovative leader.

There are two sub-components of the ultimate dream as shown in Figure 5-2:

- aspiration;
- vision.

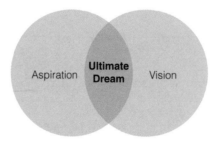

Figure 5-2   Subcomponents of Ultimate Dream

Aspiration

Brands that weave their way deep into the interests of their customers typically have a competitive advantage over unbranded or less sophisticated brands. Having a clear aspiration creates a more penetrating bond that makes those customers feel a stronger sense of ownership over the brand, partly because the company's own devotion and commitment permeates the organization. Level 5 brands are typically characterized by aspirational qualities, evidenced in leadership activities, operational practices, and customer-oriented relationship development. Aspiration means the brand has hopes for achieving something great in the future.

Aspiration is comprised of the following factors:

Beliefs

Beliefs are at the core of aspiration. To use a simple analogy, beliefs are the company's compass, always guiding it toward true north. Vision, on the other hand, is the global positioning system, providing more specific guidance on the various routes available to reach true north. Beliefs are the principles that the organization holds to be true, evidenced by management's continued references to their company's view of the world. Beliefs are also the spiritual underpinning of strong brands. Each of the top brands studied had a culture of managers and employees that shared an instinctive sense of organizational beliefs, and these beliefs served as decision-making guides. There is no set of the top three or four beliefs, nor any prescribed criteria for determining their beliefs. Instead, beliefs evolve over time as a company grows, shaped by its own business practices. Beliefs include an inherent sense that the company is there ultimately to contribute for the benefit of society, beyond accumulating profits. In fact, profit making results from good, ethical business practices. Beliefs are rooted deep inside the organization and reflect its self-confidence. Of course, financial success boosts company confidence in good times, but in bad times, beliefs keep confidence high as well because legions of employees and managers understand that they would "get through this together". As Benjamin Franklin, one of the U.S.'s Founding Fathers stated, "We must all hang together, or assuredly we shall all hang separately."[4]

The strongest brands studied held a similar sense of collective wisdom, even camaraderie. They had trust and faith that the organization could withstand challenges and prevail in making good choices.

For example, Nike *as an organization* believes that sports and fitness improve individuals and society. The company does not have hard-and-fast rules for what constitutes sports and fitness, other than their oft-stated moniker "If you have a body, you are an athlete."[5]

This concept is in contrast to common definitions that imply athletes are intense competitors wanting to win at all costs. Certainly, this is true for a subset of athletes. But Nike's belief is that sports and fitness cover a wide range of activities, defined by the participant. One can infer that physical disabilities do not prevent participation in sport and fitness. Instead, they merely change the type of sport and fitness pursued. Inherent in this idea is an overriding, optimistic set of beliefs that minimizes limitations and maximizes possibilities for people to achieve their aspirations. The same is true for other top brands: guided by an innate optimism, they set their sights on overcoming obstacles to create better solutions that benefit people and businesses.

Ambition

Ambition transforms beliefs into actions. Understanding the ultimate dream requires some organizational soul searching to uncover the hot buttons that will trigger desire and ambition. There is a certain internal resolve shared amongst employees that says "we will find a way to persevere." Typically, companies that have endured to develop successful brands have adapted to changing times yet adhered to timeless principles. This adaptation reflects the collective determination, led by senior management, to encourage, cajole, and push the organization, through objectives and incentives, to achieve a common goal or set of goals. Employees within provide their own reinforcing mechanisms through innumerable techniques, from team incentives and self-policing ("you don't want to let the team down") to image ("my work will be reflected in product quality, which leads to better perception in the market, which in turn makes me proud to be part of a recognized, successful firm").

The top brands have a corporate psyche that motivates people to apply effort, through hard work and sheer determination, to achieve success.

Vision

The American Marketing Associations states that vision is

> A guiding theme that articulates the nature of the business and its intentions for the future. These intentions are based on how management believes the environment will unfold and what the business can and should be in the future. A vision has the following characteristics: (1) informed—grounded in a solid understanding of the business and the forces shaping the future, (2) shared—created through collaboration, (3) competitive—creates an obsession with winning throughout the organization, and (4) enabling—empowers individuals to make meaningful decisions about strategies and tactics.[6]

Vision lays out the direction for the next 5–10 years or so, in pursuit of the ultimate dream. It is influenced by existing business conditions and trends, helping management craft a long-term direction. Visions are informed by articulated conditions, meaning that projections are predicated on what is currently known. Visions are concerned with *looking* ahead and seeing the likely places the brand can and should go. Visions are seen by stakeholders as almost a requirement for understanding the direction of a business and brand because it indicates whether company leadership has a plan for defining its competitive edge.

Brand Vision Path

A top athlete may harbor the ultimate dream of winning an Olympic Gold Medal, but her vision for achieving it spells out her general direction and anticipated path for getting there. The vision path includes several steps as shown in Figure 5-3:

1. Define why the ultimate dream is important to the organization
2. Work collaboratively to craft a viable vision
3. Evaluate the vision in the context of the competitive environment and the brand's long-term needs
4. Assign responsibility for the vision
5. Communicate the vision relentlessly
6. Conduct periodic reviews.

1. *Define why the ultimate dream is important to the organization.* The ultimate dream is the organization's *raison d'être*, and vision describes how company leadership sees this playing out. This is not meant to suggest that every top brand had specific social causes or missions to which the company contributed (although that is true with some brands, such Ben and Jerry's Ice Cream or The Body Shop). Many companies produce goods and services designed to improve the quality of life, even if they are not directly contributing to a social cause. Their ultimate dream itself is their cause, providing a powerful

Figure 5-3 Brand Vision Path

attraction to employees from entry level to senior management. Since organizations are comprised of people with differing motivations appealing to these varied interests can be challenging. "Head, heart, hands"[7] is a technique designed to appeal to each of these motivations and was often used by top brands to galvanize widespread support for the brand's vision. "Head" is the intellectual description of the vision. "Heart" represents emotional interests, enabling employees to internalize their commitment to the brand's vision, and "Hands" refer to activation and implementation—the actual work required to fulfill the vision. Company leaders must be able to clearly describe the brand's vision in a way that captures the organization's head, heart, and hands. This often involved using different illustrations and metaphors to help people understand the overall picture. In the early 1990s, Pepsi President and CEO Craig Weatherup foresaw significant challenges to earnings growth if the company did not radically change. Over the preceding years, the company had acquired most of its independent bottlers, dramatically increasing the number of customers it directly serviced (since it now had the bottlers' hundreds of thousands of business customers as well). Based on internal research, he believed that the company had to change its culture. For years, Pepsi rewarded individual performers, people who catered to top management. With the newly acquired bottling operations, the company needed to be more customer focused. After months of discussion and planning, a comprehensive new strategy was launched that included a significant reorganization and accompanying new human resource policies. The challenge was how to get widespread buy-in from employees. The solution depended, in part, on Weatherup's use of the head, heart, hands concept to convey the importance of the changes to Pepsi's future. The ensuing implementation helped Pepsi's growth and profitability for the next several years.[8]

2. *Work collaboratively to craft a viable vision.* The strength of a brand over time will be based on the input of many influential people inside the organization. The genesis of a brand's vision may begin with a single person, such as an entrepreneur or a business unit manager but bringing it to life and having it resonate with the rest of

the organization will require collaboration with other decision makers to gain their expertise and input. Other managers may identify weaknesses that need clarification, or they may have insights into other factors from the market and/or customers that can help shape and refine the mission. Furthermore, collaboration invests others in ownership of the vision, which aids in making it more important and tangible for them. In developing a vision, the people involved should do so with minimal outside distractions so that the issues can be fully debated. Ideally, this would be done away from the corporate office. This has the added benefit of providing alternative surroundings that can stimulate new ideas that might otherwise be inhibited.

3. *Evaluate the vision in the context of the competitive environment and the brand's long-term needs.* Is the vision viable? Does it take advantage of known gaps and needs? Or does it logically anticipate latent needs? Getting organizational buy-in about the vision is important for setting the foundation upon which the brand will be built. The vision, however, needs to be fine-tuned in the context of the competitive environment and conditions in which it competes. Practical considerations will always influence the vision since financial necessity and market expectations will err toward the known. It is unhelpful to have a grand ultimate dream about being the world leader in transportation, yet have a vision that says the firm will create travel at the speed of light in two or three years. It would be deemed impractical and delusional. Most people and organizations can imagine a future in which interstellar travel at the speed of light is possible, most likely beyond their lifetime, yet at the same time using that ambition as a motivator to create a vision about what is achievable and also serves to advance the state of the art. As many brands indicated in the research, consumers are "paying" them to innovate. For years, Nike had a group of product visionaries called the APE group. Advanced Product Engineers (APE) were responsible for thinking about products several years or more out, even if they were not commercially viable in the present day. Their task was to imagine what those products would be like, what materials would be needed, and how to one day make it practical. While it was a small group inside the company and represented only a fraction of the company's overall investment in R&D, its very existence served as a catalyst of sorts for employees, knowing that a specialist group was doing its utmost to stay on and beyond the leading edge.

4. *Assign responsibility for the vision.* Assigning responsibility for the vision is the collective responsibility of the entire organization, and senior management leads the way. However, the CEO is ultimately the individual held accountable for the firm's overall success. Therefore, he or she must get buy-in for the vision from all senior management team members, typically before the rest of the organization is enrolled. Vigorous debate can and often does occur, as should be expected. In fact, a vision must reflect the ambitions and aspirations of those inside the company. Perhaps surprisingly, not everyone's opinion counts, however, because companies have employees with varying degrees of commitment to the company. Getting some input, from those most devoted to the company, is better than getting everyone's input, where disloyal or even poisonous personalities can negatively color opinions. But the bottom line is that once the vision is fully vetted, the CEO is the person who must ensure the vision is carried out. As such, the CEO has the ability to reward or penalize senior managers based on their

ability to carry out the vision. The next tier of management below the senior level is also responsible for their portion of carrying out the vision, as is each subsequent level below, each given incentives according to its department's needs in relationship to fulfilling the vision.

5. *Communicate the vision relentlessly.* The basic premise behind a successful vision is getting buy-in for it across the organization. This is quite literally an ongoing communications effort, using both formal and informal mechanisms to inform and seek input from employees. Companies have become more sophisticated and sensitive in the methods for reaching out to their own employees, an effort once thought of as less important compared to appealing to customers. Now, of course, organizational competitiveness and brand success are predicated on having informed employees working across departments in an integrated fashion throughout the company. Just as marketing communications are used for informing the marketplace about the brand, they are equally important in reaching out to employees. But marketing communications alone are insufficient and, just like the growing skepticism today's consumers have about advertising messages, employees share similar concerns. To remedy this, senior management needs to get personally involved in communicating the vision of their brands. There are many ways for senior management to share the vision:

- company-wide meetings;
- regional and local office meetings;
- informal, townhall-style meetings characterized by question and answer sessions with direct input from employees;
- online forums, such as company blogs, for sharing information.

Each of these is important for launching new initiatives and discussing important strategic issues such as vision. However, brands are not built by having a cleverly worded mission communicated once or twice via large-scale meetings. Managers from the CEO on down are responsible for repeating the vision, showing how their division or department plans fit in, and seeking ongoing input from employees both about the overall direction of the brand and the specific activities undertaken to support it.

6. *Conduct periodic reviews.* Referring to the old adage, "what gets measured gets done," the plans developed to implement the vision must be reviewed regularly. While a vision is typically a general articulation of management's view of the future, it sets in motion activities across the organization in support of achieving the vision. Those activities must be measured in some form or fashion to help gauge if they are helping the organization achieve its goals. Adjustments can then be made along the path toward fulfilling the vision and, ultimately, getting closer to achieving the ultimate dream. Reviews should be a combination of formal and informal. Formal reviews should be at important calendar milestones, such as quarterly, requiring managers to report on their progress. Informal reviews can occur at any time, and can be as innocuous as a casual "how are things going?" update in the hallway. For formal and informal reviews to succeed, the organization must have a culture in which direct and open communication is encouraged so that good news and bad news can be discussed.

Creating Value

The concept of *creating value* is not directly about making money, although that is certainly a by-product of creating value. Instead, it refers to the *contribution and impact* that the brand seeks to make, and the *competencies and skills* required to get there. Keep in mind that Destiny considers why the brand exists at all, providing a philosophical grounding that gives meaning to the brand and the work needed to make it successful.

Contribution and Impact

Successful brands have a strong sense of how they are to contribute to improving life for customers, industries, and even society. This may be as mundane as a niche all-natural biodegradable soap brand contributing to help people stay healthy and clean while minimizing the environmental impact of the suds and associated residue from usage. The more carefully management considers contribution and impact, the greater is the likelihood the brand will fulfill its promises to the market—and to employees for that matter. Brands need to remember that customers buy value, not goods.

Why should firms be concerned with contribution and impact? The short answer is because the rest of the organization takes its operating cues from having a clear sense of their Destiny, which must encourage more than an intangible sense of what the brand could ultimately be. Defining the contribution and impact provides employees with an understanding of the expectations underlying the overall pursuit of the Destiny. Identifying contribution and impact gives a more tangible foundation for determining strategies and actions.

Contribution can be defined in several ways:

• What advances does the brand hope to make?
• Does this give new business opportunities to the brand, competitors, market, all?
• Does it enrich customers' lives? Reduce anxiety or stress? Extend enjoyment?
• What recognition would provide credibility?
• What problem(s) should the brand solve?
• How will the brand extend its success to other markets?

Impact is concerned with the influence the brand will have over time, and can be looked at as follows:

• Who will benefit from this and how?
• Where will the impact be noticed?
• How will this affect market share?
• How will competitors respond?
• Can the firm support rapid growth if the impact is strong?
• Will the affect on financials be small or large?

Competencies and Skills

Competencies and skills describe the strengths and unique abilities that the brand wants to develop. Strengths refer to disciplines like accounting, marketing, sales, and manufacturing, whereas unique abilities place added emphasis on developing a specific expertise in an area, or set of areas. For example, while Disney is strong in multiple disciplines like many top global brands, one of their unique abilities is creative expansion: turning a simple idea like a cartoon character into a range of products and services that last for decades. Competencies and skills ought to be consistent with the overall Destiny if the brand is to maximize its potential and minimize confusion with its customers and the market overall. Furthermore, competencies and skills directly influence the brand culture, since achieving the Destiny will require the ingenuity and talent of people across the organization working in concert with one another to achieve something great. The plan for building the brand's culture will come directly from the Destiny and, specifically, from the brand's understanding of how it creates value. Google succeeds in the search business because the company has a clear sense of the culture they want to build and the talent needed to populate it.

Contribution, impact, competencies, and skills can be more easily identified by having a clear understanding of how value is created. Anjan Thakor at Olin Business School at Washington University, along with Jeff DeGraff, Robert Quinn, and Kim Cameron of University of Michigan's Business School, researched how organizations create value, captured in their *Competing Values Framework*.[9]

- *Control.* Creating value is defined by operational efficiency, risk reduction, and cost control effectiveness.
- *Compete.* Here, creating value concerns the ability to rapidly respond to changes in the marketplace through external programs like customer satisfaction, M&A activity, and divestitures.
- *Create.* Value is added here via new product and program investment, rapid prototyping, innovation, pursuit of new markets. Similar to the Ansoff Matrix's New Products/New Markets quadrant (see Chapter 6), the risk here is significantly higher.
- *Collaborate.* Value creation is realized through culture-building activities that enhance critical skills and competencies, more effectively retain employees, and foster team collaboration.

The authors argue that the competing values framework gives companies strategic guidance by identifying strong and weak value-creating areas of the organization. This serves as an insightful diagnostic, helping where appropriate strategic investments can be made to improve the firm's overall value creating ability.

Having a clear sense of creating value also helps brands to determine their values and define and develop their personality, as we will now see.

Values

Values are the unshakable core principles at the very center of the organization. They influence company direction and define the codes of conduct that are acceptable within the culture. There is an important distinction that needs to be made here. The top brands typically do not begin with strategy when weighing growth options and brand development. Instead, they focus on building values, which in turn inspires the development of the culture. In considering culture, top brands then think about the kinds of people they want. Common questions are: "Who will fit in our culture? Who will thrive in our environment? Who will contribute, be inspired, and inspiring?" Note also that these relate directly to how the firm creates value and works toward its ultimate dream. Nowhere at this stage has strategy been directly developed or researched. This is not meant to suggest that strategy is unimportant. But it is meant to underscore the importance of having the right beliefs, long-term dreams, and value-creating perspective *before* a strategy can be properly developed. Otherwise, a strategy may stall before it begins if these other elements are not known first. One cannot have a brilliant strategy executed by the wrong people or an organization with contrary long-term ambitions. The inherent conflict would quickly surface and suffocate any strategic plans.

Living the Values

A word of caution is warranted here. Many companies trot out values, displayed in corporate literature, web sites, and employee handbooks. Those values are fine, and as learned in the research for this book, were shared among thousands of organizations around the world. Integrity, honesty, authenticity, caring, customer-focus, putting people first, employees are our most important assets, and more, are all familiar values and admirable in intent. But the cautionary note is that listing these values and *living* the values are two different things. This means values must be inculcated into the culture at the individual employee level and this must be done authentically, without a trace of artifice. One can readily surmise that doing this is easier if working with a potential new hire than an established employee with bad habits. As will be discussed in Chapter 7, creating a brand culture requires not just hiring people for their competencies and skills but making sure that they exhibit the kind of behaviors appropriate for the culture, work well in group environments, and contribute to the social atmosphere of the firm. In other words, they must fit in with the overall culture and not just have a basic set of required skills.

For brands, the task of understanding and living the organization's values means that management must find ways to reinforce the values everyday. Earlier in this chapter we discussed the importance of internal communication as it pertained to vision. Of course, internal communication is vital to support and reinforce values as well. But more is needed. The top brands embed values into a wide range of routines, from new hire criteria, to compensation reviews, to job performance, to promotions and more. Nike espouses *authentic athletic performance* in every corner of the company, from the first day on the job to new product launches, to industry analyst meetings, to employee retirement. Meetings touch on the implications of authentic athletic performance as it pertains to business decisions being considered. The idea of *authenticity* is deeply rooted in the psyche of Nike employees, arising from the company's history of making shoes for top athletes. Few frivolous products are ever considered let alone commercialized. Tracking the growth trajectory of Nike and Reebok since 1990 shows dramatic growth for Nike during that time whereas Reebok grew little if at all. Research shows that part of the answer may be because of Nike's relentless focus on authentic athletic performance, essentially making products that help top athletes perform their best. Reebok certainly had its share of success, particularly in women's fitness. But Nike's core values never varied, and this was most visibly evident in their advertising, where "Just Do It" has been a cornerstone slogan since 1988. Reebok, on the other hand, was more focused on identifying new trends and popularity, resulting in 11 different slogans during that same span of time. Reebok's challenges were best summarized by Herbert Hainer, CEO of Adidas, which acquired Reebok in 2005 for US$3.8 billion:[10]

"The Reebok brand didn't have any direction at all," acknowledged Adidas Group Chairman and CEO Herbert Hainer during a rare interview recently at Reebok's Canton, Mass., headquarters. "Consumers didn't know what the brand stands for: Is it a hip-hop brand or a football brand or a women's brand or a licensed brand?"[11]

The lack of consistent core values was visible to the market as well:

"I didn't believe they [Adidas] picked up anything especially complementary when the deal happened and I've seen no reason to change my mind," said Sports Authority founder and former Chairman and CEO Jack Smith. "Sports are about authenticity, and their roots are a fashion and women aerobics brand. That's what they need to get back to."[12]

How has Adidas envisioned Reebok fitting into their offerings?

"Reebok says have fun with sports, whatever you are running," Hainer said. "Adidas says if you want to win a marathon, you have to wear Adi shoes."[13]

His statement reflects a stark contrast in both brands: Reebok values appear to be centered around fun and the latest opportunity, whereas Adidas is focused on authenticity, much like Nike. Some of Nike's values were tested in the 1990s when they were scrutinized for labor practices at contracted factories overseas (primarily in Asia) and for waste resulting from old pairs of Nike shoes sitting in landfills. Rather than ignore the criticism, or distract with PR about their latest products, Nike addressed these issues, reshaping their relationships with manufacturers to include better working conditions, and creating a new environmental initiative called "Regrind" that ground up discarded products and used the resulting material in all-weather surfaces for sports events and commercial buildings. These two efforts helped Nike turn around its societal image to a far more positive one. Plus, employees were directly involved in each initiative, fostering a strong sense of ownership that connected people to the core values of the company.

Johnson & Johnson is one of the oldest pharmaceutical companies in the world, and a recognized brand. The company's credo is famous. As it states: "Put simply, Our Credo challenges us to put the needs and well-being of the people we serve first."[14]

The credo is reinforced in every decision each day and serves as a guiding compass, moral imperative, and business success driver. This was exemplified during the 1982 Tylenol crisis during which capsules were found to contain cyanide, causing seven deaths. Johnson & Johnson issued a recall of all 31 million bottles in the market valued at over $200 million, even though the poisoning had been limited to Chicago and none of the production facilities themselves had been compromised.[15] Johnson & Johnson put the safety of its customers first, helping the company regain trust and demonstrating that the values described in the credo are taken quite seriously inside the company.

Just as the market sees these values on display everyday, so too do employees, whose professional beliefs are partly based on the values of the company where they work. Nancy McGraw, of the Aspen Institute's Business and Society Programs, and Lisa Fabish, with Booz Allen Hamilton, state that for employees to take company values seriously, there must be alignment between the values and the firm's management practices.[16] Anything short of that and the value statements are not likely to have much credibility. One can surmise that company leaders in such organizations would be viewed less credibly as well. Their recommendations are consistent with the research findings for this book. In effect, employees will adhere to company values if several conditions hold true:

- They believe that senior management has integrity, simply demonstrated by practicing what they preach.
- In addition to walking the talk, employees must believe that there is also integrity in the performance evaluation system. They must have belief based on experience that the performance criteria by which they are judged are inherently fair.
- They believe that the corporate culture supports values-based performance and that unethical behavior will not be tolerated.
- The company and/or brand has a reputation for a values-based operating philosophy that delivers on promises made, and this is infused in all touchpoints, from employees to products to marketing communications.
- There is general trust that the organization will be transparent in its practices, including repairing and addressing deficiencies in living up to their values.

Interestingly, there is a great deal of corporate success that is dependent on the values component of brand Destiny, yet it is one of the least tangible areas of the company. Accountability for actions goes well beyond producing high quality products at a fair price. It comes down to whether a company's reputation is genuine and has integrity, or not.

MAS Holdings, the Sri Lankan apparel manufacturer referenced elsewhere in this book, prides itself on being highly responsible toward its employees, more than 80% of which are female. Their web site states that people are their greatest asset, a key corporate value claim. And they back it up by reinforcing recognition and reward policies to performance, including their renowned "Women Go Beyond" program (see Chapter 7 for more details on MAS Holdings), which has given management opportunities to deserving female workers in a traditional male society.[17]

Nokia emphasizes four core values: customer satisfaction, respect for the individual, achievement, and continuous learning.[18] An annual meeting called Nokia Way highlights the values in action. Employees worldwide are brought together to brainstorm about Nokia's priorities, using the results to help refine the company's vision.[19] The Nokia Way meetings directly discuss Nokia's values, organizational competencies, and operating practices involving many employees directly. The effort reinforces their respect for the individual. The by-product of this effort is broader "ownership" of key topics, enabling faster acceptance of decisions so the process of getting new ideas to market is accelerated. Continuous learning is exemplied by Nokia's managers, who update each other on market performance, then return to their offices to share these findings with other staff, quickly transforming insight into action.[20]

Personality

Personality describes the brand's distinctive character. The fundamental rationale for developing the brand's personality is to raise its visibility. Every company has a personality, but the challenge is making it valuable in helping define the identity and image of the brand. Many companies are bland, with dull, or vague personalities, whereas others cultivate a strong personality in an effort to highlight differentiation. Many well-known brands have clear personalities as far as customers are concerned, even if those descriptions are relatively simplistic.

With an identifiable personality, brands can take on a deeper and more expansive meaning for customers, making them more compelling and even giving them a more *human* quality. This helps customers relate more directly and personally to brands. Part of Rolex's appeal is its status and personality as a brand representing class, privilege, and distinction. Its customers have an affinity for these qualities, and associate the brand's personality with their own sense of identity. For years, Southwest Airlines has cultivated a personality centered around fun. Passengers knew that they were not getting full service and had to pay extra for virtually everything beyond the price of the ticket but they willingly accepted this bargain because

Table 5-1   Company Personality Associations

Company	Personality
IKEA	Innovative, Genuine
Apple	Creative, Cool
Singapore Airlines	Caring, Thoughtful
Nike	Aggressive, Athletic, Contrarian
Toyota	Reliable, Stable
SAP	Disciplined, High Quality
Nintendo	Fun, Imaginative
Marlboro	Rugged, Masculine, Cowboy
Dell	Practical, Professional
Harley Davidson	Individualistic, Freedom, Rebel
Mercedes	Elegant, Successful
Four Seasons	Cultured, Sophisticated, Relaxed
The Body Shop	Socially-Conscious, Responsible

the fares were lower and the airline went out of its way to make flying quirky and humorous by telling stories, jokes, and reading the safety instructions in unconventional ways.

Personality consists of several subcomponents, which are similar to criteria ascribed to individuals. Within each of these are individual traits that add dimension to the personality. Many overlap and, of course, there are numerous other traits not listed:

- actions;
- intellect;
- emotions;
- instincts;
- authenticity.

Actions

Personalities are multidimensional. People can be described by their activity level, such as energetic or lethargic. So, too, can brands. Many consumer products brands regularly launch new products, sponsor sports events, advertise on TV and social media, and are generally seen and heard in multiple places. Their level of activity can be considered high. Other brands are more conservative, choosing activity that is measured, considered, and more slowly paced. Consumers sense this. During the dot.com era of the late 1990s, start-up software companies had the aura that they launched a nonstop stream of new offerings every few months or even weeks, gaining a personality around speed and novelty. In contrast, Boeing and Airbus were far slower in the pace of entirely new products launched. Their personalities were decidedly less energetic, leaning more toward reliable, if slow.

A selection of *action* traits:

- fast;
- slow;
- aggressive;
- relaxed;
- passive;
- assertive;
- dynamic;
- tenacious;
- persistent.

Intellect

Brands can appear to be thoughtful and pensive. Or, in contrast, they can be simple. IBM and GE both have reputations for nurturing *thinking* leaders inside their organizations and their brand images lean toward being professional and cerebral. Their personalities are, in effect, deep and complex, no doubt reflecting in part the size and complexity of their organizations. Google straddles intellect with humor. Co-founder Sergey Brin was asked to describe Google's personality in a few words, to which he replied, "trustworthy, powerful, easy-to-use, fast, friendly."[21] Google's VP of Marketing, David Lawee, said the brand is about "trust, humility, responsibility, innovation, user focus, and being quirky."[22] In his book, *Planet Google*, *New York Times* columnist Randall Stross said "the company enjoys a public image that associates its brand with experimentation and innovation."[23]

By comparison, Donald Trump and his various enterprises are associated with simpler themes, characterized by brash statements, bold claims, and vivid imagery. His projects are always "the biggest" or "the best." His TV show *The Apprentice* simplified the politics and social fabric of corporate offices, and his books espouse simple solutions (such as *think big* and *never give up*) to business challenges.

A selection of *intellect* traits and characteristics:

- expertise;
- smart/intelligent;
- thoughtful;
- pragmatic;
- creative/innovative;
- humorous/funny/witty;
- clever;
- reasoned;
- simple;
- clear;
- complex;
- empathetic;
- fair/balanced;
- courageous;
- opinionated;
- perseverance.

Emotions

The emotional qualities of a brand can be expressed through feelings-based devices, such as vivid imagery, evocative language, and imaginative storytelling. Emotion may share traits with the other subcomponents. We know that a person's actions suggest they are relaxed, and we can easily see that person reacting emotionally calm in stressful situations. Many leading brands rely on emotion to capture the public's imagination, through both overt and subtle means. Car companies like BMW and Audi, show the thrill of driving their cars. VW evokes fun. Sports teams highlight excitement, energy and competitive rivalry to stoke fan enthusiasm.

A selection of *emotions* traits and characteristics:

- loving;
- happy;
- fun;
- sad;
- serious;
- safe/stable;
- energetic;

- spirited;
- strong;
- weak;
- quiet;
- loud;
- enthusiastic;
- warm;
- nurturing;
- personal;
- cold;
- impersonal.

Instincts

Instinct describes and/or implies a unique ability that influences actions, intellect, and emotions. Microsoft once ran an ad campaign with the tagline "Where do you want to go today?" connecting to people's need and desire to explore (as it relates to information). Service firms, like hotels and consultancies, advertise their competence and distinctive ability to take great care of their customers' special needs.

A selection of *instincts* traits and characteristics:

- gift;
- flair;
- talent;
- facility;
- innate ability;
- skill;
- knack;
- competency;
- intuition;
- need;
- insight;
- aptitude.

Authenticity

Brands, like people, tend to be viewed and judged on whether others perceive them as genuine. In the case of brands, authenticity refers to practices undertaken that appear and are consistent with the brand's known qualities, values, and core identity. Carlsberg has long been considered one of the leading European beers, with a proud brewing tradition that dates to 1847. Since the early 1970s, their tagline "Probably the Best Beer in the World" is suggestive but not boastful, using a touch of humility to convey its authenticity (since brash claims of superiority are often perceived as insincere and inflated). The company has been an active sponsor of European football clubs, UEFA, and the FIFA World Cup, a sport with passionate fans devoted to their teams, thereby connecting the brand to fans at highly emotional events with storied traditions. Being inauthentic can also be used, particularly with humor, to convey authenticity. Alaska Airlines ran a very successful ad campaign for years that pilloried its competitors, without mentioning them by name, in a series of exaggerated portrayals of the negative aspects of typical air travel (crowded seating, rude flight attendants, terrible food, unruly passengers).

A selection of *authenticity* traits and characteristics:

- sincerity;
- genuine;
- real;
- valid;
- bonafide;
- valid;
- truth;
- trusted;
- belief;
- faith;
- certainty;
- reliable;
- responsible.

Beyond helping define and distinguish a brand overall, a well-defined personality helps the company and customers in other ways. For the company, a distinctive personality acts as a magnet for attracting talent, and a filter for weeding out those that do not fit in. This will be discussed in detail in Chapter 7, but for the moment consider IBM, with a reputation for comprehensive business solutions, particularly in IT. IBM has been a successful company for decades, albeit with a tough period in the early to mid-1990s when there was talk of the company breaking apart. Its personality can be described as serious and professional. On occasion, whimsy and humor have been used to convey a more "with it" brand personality. But the company's overall persona attracts particular types of professionals. Wildly creative artistic types are unlikely to find the company appealing whereas business-minded professionals would find the company attractive. Or consider IKEA, the Swedish home furnishings brand, with its Scandinavian design, colorful and humorous ads, conveying a vibrant and creative personality. Beneath this exterior lies a disciplined operating model, yet its business strengths mesh well with its creative flair. People with an open, engaging, and playful attitude (along with superb design sensibilities) would undoubtedly find IKEA inviting.

For customers, a brand's personality can help them express their individual identities. Customers find that Apple's iconoclastic image appeals to their individualistic nature. Luxury customers flock to LVMH's many different luxury brands because they connote quality, reflect their own exclusive tastes, and exude high status.

Brands can also use their personality and reputations to help align and position with society at large. Energy companies like Shell and BP increasingly focus on alternative energy research, mirroring the global climate and environmental challenges facing the planet. Some would consider these efforts insincere, even too little too late, given the significant negative impact energy companies have had on the environment over the decades. But others recognize that there is intellectual talent and curiosity at these companies that can be redeployed toward solving vexing energy challenges. Automakers are under tremendous pressure to manufacture more efficient, lower emissions cars. Hybrid cars are increasing in number and demand around the world. New car companies, like Tesla[24] seek to set entirely new standards for energy and environmental responsibility by producing all-battery electric cars. Fair trade is a global social movement that supports and promotes sustainability of goods from developing countries around the world, in an effort to give producers in these markets a strong competitive foundation versus more established companies from developed markets. When brands agree to market fair trade goods, they are repositioning their brand, whether slightly or significantly, in an effort to be more closely aligned with society's needs.

Measurement

Destiny provides a conceptual understanding of the brand, its roots and its meaning. It is a philosophical standard that, as an intangible, can be challenging to grasp. Temptation will motivate people to discuss and solve the easier aspects of business, such as tangibles and/or how to sell more widgets tomorrow, since Destiny is open to some interpretation and may seem removed from making daily business decisions. Precision is not a deciding factor in understanding Destiny. When people discuss art, for example, a wide range of opinions ensues based on what they see and the precise description of the artwork (it has paint, is on a canvas, people are featured, it hangs on a wall) is secondary to their interpretations of its meaningfulness to them. With Destiny, a brand may be a physical product and/or a known name but the interpretation of its meaning to employees animates the discussion and helps to uncover the brand's larger significance. This, in turn, ultimately affects how the company makes decisions that enable the business to prosper. The Destiny Diagnostic below helps provoke discussion that will lead to a better understanding of a brand's Destiny.

Destiny Diagnostic

Metric
Destiny diagnostic.[25]

Brand Destiny Benefits
Destiny analysis is challenging because it considers intangible, even philosophical factors, which are subject to interpretation. The extent to which concurrence exists across the company determines whether the Destiny is truly understood. Highlights where the brand destiny is strongest and weakest, helping identify areas that need attention for strengthening the overall destiny.

How
Diagnostic questions in each area of Destiny.

Formula

There is no formula. Instead, the following questions guide the analysis:

Ultimate Dream

Aspiration

1. Why does the company exist?
2. Can you identify and describe the brand's aspiration for the future?
3. What is management's view of the world?
4. What is the brand resolved to accomplish?
5. Is there truly a collective will to succeed?

Vision

1. What is the firm's direction for the next few years?
2. Is it obvious why the vision is important to the success of the brand?
3. Does the organization work collaboratively to achieve the vision?
4. Is the vision practical and viable given the competitive environment?
5. Is it clear who is responsible for the vision?
6. Has the vision been communicated? Is it clearly understood? Can it be easily described to others?

Creating Value

Contribution and Impact (from questions earlier in the chapter)

1. What advances does the brand hope to make?
2. Does this give new business opportunities to the brand, competitors, market, all?
3. Does it enrich customers' lives? Reduce anxiety or stress? Extend enjoyment?
4. What recognition would provide credibility?
5. What problem(s) should the brand solve?
6. How will the brand extend its success to other markets?
7. Who will benefit from this and how?
8. Where will the impact be noticed?
9. How will this affect market share?
10. How will competitors respond?
11. Can the firm support rapid growth if the impact is strong?
12. Will the effect on financials be small or large?

Competencies and Skills

1. What is the brand's expertise?
2. Is this consciously weaved into culture-building practices?
3. Evaluate the firm's abilities, on a 1 to 5 scale (1 = poor, 5 = excellent) in its ability to *create, compete, control, and collaborate.*
4. Are these core skills and assets in the firm? Or is it situational? Or can they be improved?

Values

1. Can you identify and describe the organization's values?

2. What evidence exists that these values are deeply embedded, or not, in the culture?
3. Does the CEO and senior management espouse the values directly?
4. Is senior management perceived as credible advocates of the values?
5. Are the organizations practices transparent?
6. Does the organization have a strong values-based reputation?

Personality

1. Can you describe the brand's personality?
2. Is it distinctive? To employees? To customers? To other stakeholders?
3. List the traits associated with each subcomponent (actual traits, not wishful thinking): *actions, intellect, emotions, instincts, authenticity.*
4. Are these traits consistent with perceptions in the public and internally?
5. Are the traits positive? Negative? How would you change or improve negative ones?

Impact on Brand Destiny

Having an in-depth discussion and review of Destiny will take time and cannot be accomplished in the course of a single brainstorming meeting. Senior management must take the lead and devote the time to fully analyzing their Destiny if they want to develop a strong and sustainable brand. A strong Destiny will directly and significantly affect the other key areas of brand success: Distinction, Culture, and Experiences.

Summary

Several important concepts were introduced in this chapter and they directly affect the long-term direction and potential for a brand. First, Destiny was introduced as an entity's reason to exist, giving brand-building efforts a destination. As such, Destiny plays a vital role in shaping management decision-making, brand distinction, culture development and the experiences customers ultimately have. Destiny has a direct impact on how the company aligns resources as well as brand management tactical decisions. When regions, divisions, and departments know the Destiny, then differences due to geographic and cultural distances shrink, enabling the development of the brand to occur more consistently across markets.

A key point is that a firm's Destiny is both complex and intangible, which can frustrate those seeking quick answers and simple solutions. A simple mission statement and/or slogan is not a sufficient descriptor of a Destiny, any more than the clothes people wear are descriptive of their entire personalities. In fact, the creation of brand slogans and mission statements is much harder when there is a poor understanding of the Destiny. For management, this may well feel uncomfortable because understanding one's Destiny implies a bit of corporate soul searching and philosophical reflection on behalf of the brand, activities not often associated with the image of the hard-charging executive armed with spread sheets, acquisition targets, and quarterly performance pressures. But the absence of this self-study puts the brand at a competitive disadvantage, which, ultimately, will affect the very real business results management seeks.

We learned that there are four components that comprise Destiny. The hard work of understanding Destiny is contained in each of the four components. Senior management should spend a great deal of time on defining and describing their Destiny because innumerable actions and decisions will flow directly from this as a result. It is a distant endpoint that succeeding generations of company leaders will always work toward.

The *ultimate dream* describes the brand's aspirations and vision for the future. This implies a sense of collective ambition, which can serve as a cultural motivator that energizes employees to work toward a common goal. The vision clarifies the direction for the next several years, spelling out more specific objectives. Succeeding generations of management will also revisit the ultimate dream to ensure that their decisions are consistent with it. Johnson & Johnson's famous credo puts "the needs and well-being of the people we serve *first*" (their emphasis)[26] and this has guided decisions and business practices for over a century.

Creating value provides guidance by helping identify what the brand will be known for, what its expertise is, and what will make it distinctive. For a brand to succeed, its contribution and impact must also be actively discussed and planned. Such an effort will force senior management to consider what will distinguish them from other competitors and how the market will perceive this distinction. Look at almost any top brand that has been successful for years and one can readily identify how it creates value. Apple makes iconic lifestyle products that are well designed, easy to use, and of superior quality. Mercedes builds high-end luxury cars with superb quality and an image of exclusivity. Carlsberg makes a range of award winning beers that facilitate one's social lifestyle, particularly as it relates to sports.

Values are the core principles that guide behavior and the organization's sense of right and wrong. These, too, are fundamental to having a Destiny that is motivating and credible. Values must be lived to be meaningful—they can't just be posted on a web site or on company banners. People inside the organization must see the values in action everyday. The CEO and senior management must be active representatives of the values as well, walking the talk. Nordstrom, a well-known upscale U.S. department store chain, has a longstanding reputation for adhering to a strict set of values about what the company stands for. This includes caring for people, demonstrated by its award-winning customer service and an employee environment that supports entrepreneurial behavior for the benefit of customers. Employees are empowered to make decisions, on the spot, to take care of the customer's needs. They reinforce this by ensuring diversity in hiring practices and even supplier recruiting. This is reinforced by a rewards and benefits package that is aligned with the values that the company espouses.[27]

Personality explains the brand's unique character and identity. Brand personality is important because one that is well defined and understood can be a competitive advantage over less distinctive rivals. Virgin Group, founded and headed by Richard Branson, has infused each of its businesses with a quirky, energetic zeal that separates each business from its respective rivals.[28]

In closing, consider the old sailing ship without a compass or a sextant: it would be directionless and would never reach its envisioned destination, unless it was terribly lucky. It is more than likely that the journey would be a disaster. The same is true for brands. Without a Destiny, there is no guiding understanding about their business, expertise, distinctiveness, or their principles. Eventually, employees would sense the disarray and move on. Too much good can come out of a serious analysis of Destiny for companies and their management to ignore.

Discussion Questions

1. Choose a brand. Between now and next class, do research to help you understand this brand's Destiny and then describe it. Use each of the four components of *ultimate dream*, *creating value*, *values*, and *personality*.
2. Choose the brand's competitor and conduct the same analysis. What key differences do you notice? Are these significant? Why or why not?
3. What are the challenges in understanding a brand's Destiny? How would you go about overcoming those challenges?
4. Who is responsible for the brand's Destiny?
5. Why is it important for the organization to understand its Destiny? How does Destiny affect the brand's success?
6. Compare the personalities between the following pairs of competitors: Coke and Pepsi; Mercedes and BMW; Singapore Airlines and Virgin Atlantic; Apple and Sony. Are the differences between pairs important? Why? How do you think that affects their brand-building choices?

Notes

1. Collins, J. and Porras, J. I., *Built to Last—Successful Habits of Visionary Companies*, © 1994 Harper Business, pp. 76–78.
2. Davis, J., *Measuring Marketing: 103 Key Metrics Every Marketer Needs*, © 2007 John Wiley & Sons, pp. xii–xiv.
3. Comments by Steve Scott, Vice President, Harris Corporation, Los Angeles, California. Based on work conducted at Harris in 2002 and 2003.
4. Isaacson, W., *Benjamin Franklin: An American Life*, © 2004 Simon & Schuster, pp. 325–349.
5. Nike web site, "History," retrieved November 11, 2008 from www.nikebiz.com/company_overview/.
6. American Marketing Association web site, retrieved October 1, 2008 from www.marketing-power.com/_layouts/Dictionary.aspx?dLetter=V.
7. Keller, K. L., *Strategic Brand Management—Building, Measuring, and Managing Brand Equity*, © 2008 Pearson Prentice Hall, pp. 452–453.

8. "Craig Weatherup: Learning from Success and Failure," Knowledge@W.P. Carey, May 23, 2007, retrieved July 18, 2008 from http://knowledge.wpcarey.asu.edu/article.cfm?articleid=1425. "Thank You, Craig Weatherup," retrieved March 12, 2008 from www.pbg.com/investor/2002_Annual/thankyou.html.

9. Gary, L., "Can You Create More Value?" *Harvard Management Update*, August 2004, © 2004 Harvard Business School Publishing.

10. 1) Research projects conducted by students at Singapore Management University for their strategic brand management course between 2004 and 2008. 2) "Adidas Sports Marketing," research completed March 2009. 2) Lefton, T., "Reebok's Shine Dims Post Adidas Deal," April 16, 2009, retrieved May 7, 2009 from http://boston.bizjournals.com/boston/stories/2009/04/13/daily41.html.

11. See www.sportsbusinessjournal.com/article/62189.

12. Ibid.

13. Ibid.

14. 1) Research projects conducted by students at Singapore Management University for their strategic brand management course between 2004 and 2008. 2) "Johnson & Johnson: A Case Study," research completed November 2007, updated July 2008. 3) Johnson & Johnson, "Our Credo Values," retrieved April 3, 2008 from www.jnj.com/connect/about-jnj/jnj-credo/.

15. Multiple sources: Pryor, C., "The Masters of Disaster," July 31, 2006, BusinessWeek, retrieved November 29, 2008 from www.businessweek.com/bwdaily/dnflash/content/jul2006/db20060731_864858.htm?chan=search. Jia Lynn Yang. "Getting a Handle on a Scandal," May 22, 2007, *Fortune Magazine*, retrieved September 5, 2008 from http://money.cnn.com/magazines/fortune/fortune_archive/2007/05/28/100033741/index.htm.

16. McGaw, N. and Fabish, L., "Put Your Values to Work," *Harvard Management Update*, January 2006, © 2004 Harvard Business School Publishing.

17. 1) "MAS Holdings: Championing Women's Empowerment in the Apparel Sector," March 2007, retrieved April 17, 2008 from www.enewsbuilder.net/globalcompact/e_article000776336.cfm. 2) Research projects conducted by students at Singapore Management University for their strategic brand management course between 2004 and 2008. 3) www.masholdings.com/ retrieved May 11, 2008. 4) The author also visited with the executive and toured factories for several days in 2005. 5) Esbenshade, J., "Monitoring Sweatshops: Workers, Consumers, and the Global Apparel Industry," Temple University Press, 2004.

18. 1) Research projects conducted by students at Singapore Management University for their strategic brand management course between 2004 and 2008. 2) "Nokia," research completed November 2007, updated November 2008. 3) Masalin, L., March, 2003, "Nokia Leads Change Through Continuous Learning," *Academy of Management Learning and Education*, 2(1), pp. 68–72, retrieved November 6, 2007, from Business Source Premier database.

19. Ibid. See also Fox, J., May 1, 2000, Nokia's Secret Code, *Fortune*, 141(9), pp. 160–174, retrieved December 1, 2008 from http://money.cnn.com/magazines/fortune/fortune_archive/2000/05/01/278948/index.htm.

20. Ibid. See also Nokia Corporation, "Structure, Nokia Corporation," retrieved November 4, 2007 from www.nokia.com/A4126325.

21. 1) Research projects conducted by students at Singapore Management University for their strategic brand management course between 2004 and 2008. 2) "Google Report 2008," research completed November 2008—source cited is Taylor, C. P., 2002, "The Little Engine that Could: in an Era where Word of mouth Marketing Cannot be Understated, the Duo Behind Google

Leveraged A High-Quality Product To Capture Users' Hearts," Brandweek, 14 October 2002, available from OneSource: http://globalbb.onesource.com.libproxy.smu.edu.sg/sharedscripts/text/getarticle.asp?id=RDS_03564124. 3) "Happiness and the Art of Information," March 6, 2006, retrieved February 28, 2009 from www.businessweek.com/innovate/content/mar2006/id20060306_579621.htm.

22. Ibid. See also "Google Annual Report—Risk Factors," retrieved November 11, 2008 from investor.google.com/proxy.html.

23. Ibid. See also, Stross, R., 2008, *Planet Google: One Company's Audacious Plan To Organize Everything We Know,* Pocket U.S.

24. Tesla Motors is a new car company offering all-electric cars. The CEO is a former cofounder of PayPal. The company is attempting to set a new standard for environmentally responsible cars that also perform well. Their product line features a Roadster and a sedan, both well designed (trade reports). For more information, visit: www.teslamotors.com/.

25. Derived from the research projects of the author in conjunction with students from Singapore Management University between 2004 and 2008.

26. 1) Research projects conducted by students at Singapore Management University for their strategic brand management course between 2004 and 2008. 2) "Johnson & Johnson: A Case Study," research completed November 2007, updated July 2008. 3) Johnson & Johnson, "Our Credo Values," retrieved April 3, 2008 from www.jnj.com/connect/about-jnj/jnj-credo/.

27. 1) "Nordstrom—Great Service For Over 100 Years, Best Company For 25 Years," Great Place to Work Institute, retrieved May 22, 2008 from www.greatplacetowork.com/best/100best-2009/100best2009-nordstrom.php. 2) Imperato, G., "New Channels, Old Values," December 19, 2007, *Fast Company Magazine,* retrieved February 3, 2008 from www.fastcompany.com/magazine/39/fastfunction.html. 3) Mulady, K., "100 Years of Nordstrom," June 25, 2001, *Seattle Post Intelligencer,* retrieved November 2, 2008 from www.seattlepi.com/business/28731_nordstrom25.shtml.

28. 1) "Because He's Game for Anything. In fact, Everything," *Inc. Magazine,* retrieved August 13, 2008 from www.inc.com/magazine/20050401/26-branson.html/. 2) "The Importance of Being Richard Branson," January 12, 2005, retrieved August 7, 2008 from http://knowledge.wharton.upenn.edu/article.cfm?articleid=1109.

Brand Distinction

6

Topics

Preview

Brand distinction describes where the brand is headed, what makes it different from the competition, why it should matter to the company and customers, and ultimately how it will grow. Whether competing at the local or global level, companies face competitors everyday. Seeking competitive advantage is a vital driver of brand strategy because a strong brand is imbued with associations about quality, usefulness, image, reputation, and meaning. A strong brand stands out from its competitors, carving a distinctive set of qualities that inspires customer loyalty, serves as a competitive benchmark, drives financial growth, and enhances long-term brand value. The presence of numerous competitors brings consumer choice and the task for marketers is to stand out from the others—to create a *differentiated* position that highlights why an offering is unique. Differentiation is a quality that customers must recognize and confer upon the offering. At the same time, a brand's differentiation needs to be *relevant* to customers if they are to be persuaded to purchase. Relevance means that the offering satisfies and is appropriate to the customer's needs. Differentiation and relevance help distinguish an offering. Ideally, with many products, whether B2C or B2B, this relevant differentiation must *resonate* with consumers as well, stirring an emotional response that helps make a product meaningful, affects how a consumer feels about the offering, and thereby creates an intangible attraction beyond the satisfaction of basic needs.

As markets mature and the competitive space grows more crowded, brands often shift from a specialty toward a commodity position, blurring the differentiated advantages that once clearly stood out. Brands must find ways to return to a specialty position. Apple performed this return to a specialty position superbly when Steve Jobs returned as the company's CEO in 1997. By culling the product line, refocusing on iconic design and ease of use, and then emphasizing innovation that fit with consumer lifestyles, Apple recaptured a specialty position in its markets, entered new markets with new products, and delivered superior performance as a result. Let's look at the components that help companies develop a distinctive and memorable brand.

Brand Distinction's Role in the Firm

Chapter 1 defined brand as the *entire organization as seen through the eyes of stakeholders*. This means that for today's companies, the brand and the company are not separate but one and the same. Part of management's job in any company today is to create value in any of several ways:

- building a positive reputation in the market;
- inspiring employees to achieve great things;
- developing offerings that customers wish to buy;
- through trusted relationships with other companies;
- producing financial returns that benefit shareholders;
- contributing meaningfully to society.

Brand building is the responsibility of the entire organization, not just a marketing-specific task. As such, Distinction guides the company's overall direction and is directly linked to the core capabilities of the firm. Emphasizing Distinction influences every operating activity within the organization as well.

Four Subcomponents of Successful Brand Distinction

Chapter 3's discussion of brand architecture introduced the four factors responsible for brand success. Whether developing a single umbrella brand strategy or a strategy for multiple brands, the same planning logic applies—marketers must pay attention to each of the four components. As Figure 6-1 shows, there are four sub-components of Distinction: *Heritage, Goals, Context,* and *Positioning.*

We will first turn our attention to *internal* influences.

Figure 6-1   Components of Distinction

Heritage

Part of the task of planning brand Distinction requires recognition and understanding of the company's *internal context* because this will ultimately affect how a company chooses to go to market. Each company has a unique set of customers, traditions, and practices that exert varying degrees of influence on the brand strategy chosen. Decision-making is likely to reflect historical precedent combined with current market needs and expectations. To illustrate, the managers in a firm with a conservative product reputation are unlikely to decide in favor of a bold, high-risk innovation as such a choice would be uncharacteristic and might lead to market confusion about the brand. Such confusion could dilute the brand reputation and reduce brand value. Knowing their firm's Heritage will guide brand planners to make choices that are more likely to gain internal support and, ultimately, lead to market growth because customers will anticipate and expect the company to do things a certain way. To better understand Heritage, consider the areas in Figure 6-2.

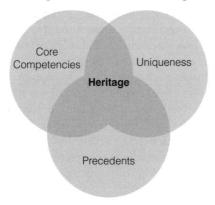

Figure 6-2   Subcomponents of Heritage

Uniqueness

Innumerable influences contribute to making any company distinctive in the eyes of the market. The task is to identify the brand's known reputation *in general*. For example, Singapore Airlines' (SIA) success is the result of many factors, including: friendly staff, state-of-the art products (aircraft, audio/visual on demand, seat designs), nontraditional aircraft leasing policies, the Singapore Girl, exotic associations with Singapore, good food (for airlines), nonstop flights to far-flung destinations (from Singapore to New York, for example), reliable baggage handling, on-time flights and more. But when considering how the public perceives SIA, superb service is commonly cited as a primary feature that distinguishes the airline from all others. Arguably, the other factors mentioned can be considered extensions of SIA's emphasis on superb service. The annual World Airline Awards gave SIA the Airline of the Year Award for 2008, the third time the airline won the award in 10 years. The award is based on surveys of 15 million passengers around the world conducted between August 2007 and June 2008. The survey asks passengers detailed questions about their travel experience in three categories: Ground/Airport; Onboard: Product; and Onboard: Staff Service.[1] As of the time of writing, SIA finished second in 2009 to Cathay Pacific Airlines, another three-time winner. SIA also received the OAG (Official Airline Guide) Airline of the Year award in 2008, the sixth time they have received this distinction since the award's inception in 1982, more than any other airline.[2] SIA won Best International Airline in both premium and economy seating in the 2008 Zagat Airline Survey, ranking number one in food, service, and comfort as well. This was the ninth year in a row that SIA led this survey.[3] *Fortune* magazine regularly selects SIA in their annual "World's Most Admired Companies" survey.[4] The Singapore Airlines web site provides details on the hundreds of awards that they have won over the last 10 years.[5]

Precedents

Each generation of management inherits expectations and practices that influence how the decision-making process occurs and what the types of decisions are. Most managers will recognize such inheritance in the form of the internal dialog found in formal and informal meetings. While these dialogs are rarely formalized in a written set of guidelines, those within the organization understand them. The words "we do things a certain way" or "that's not how we do things around here" are examples of this. Thus, as marketers contemplate their brand strategy, they must first consider whether their ideas are consistent with the brand's Heritage and past decision-making practices of the firm. A word of caution here: paying heed to past practice is not the same as rigid uniformity. Instead, paying attention to Heritage is a way to ensure that the branding ideas are not wildly out of character with the firm's known reputation. There will always be instances when a departure from past practice is needed. Indeed, this is imperative if a company wishes to remain vital. The challenge is determining when a significant change in a brand's distinctiveness can be justified without harming the overall reputation of the firm.

EXAMPLE 6-1:

Grupo Modelo

Grupo Modelo, founded in 1925, is a beer producer and distributor based in Mexico. Corona is the company's flagship brand. Over the years the company has built a distinctive portfolio of Mexican beers through a combination of acquisitions, vertical integration, and organic growth. Their marketing celebrates the beauty of Mexico, its beaches, having fun, and the good life. Staying focused on being an authentic Mexican beer company has guided the company's business practices for nearly 100 years (Anheuser Busch has a 50% noncontrolling interest).[6]

Acquisitions

In 1935, the company bought Victoria, "the oldest and most traditional beer brand in the history of the country"[7] as well as Cerveceria Toluca y Mexico. In the 1950s and 1960s, they acquired Cervecería Estrella and Cervecería del Pacífico. The centerpiece of their strategy was to purchase beer brands with strong and loyal followings in Mexico's different regions. For example, Pacifico which they acquired in 1954, was particularly popular on Mexico's North Pacific Coast.[8] Their history of acquiring strategically popular Mexican beer brands has been a vital part of their brand Heritage.

Vertical Integration

Nearly 100% of the raw material (boxes, bottles, caps, transport equipment) used in production and packaging comes from tightly integrated internal suppliers. Grupo has also acquired additional supply and service firms, including National Glass Factory (1968), Barley and Malt (1979) and Inamex of Malt and Barley (1981).[9]

Organic Growth

Organic growth has been funded by internal cash flow, keeping debt low, even with the many acquisitions over the years. Through the construction and expansion of breweries, such as Cervecería Modelo de Guadalajara (1964) and Compañia Cervecera del Trópico (1984), Grupo Modelo has increased its production significantly, from 10 million liters in 1925 to 51 million hectoliters in 2004.[10] Each of Grupo Modelo's efforts reflects an ongoing commitment to investing in Mexico and in celebrating Mexican Heritage.

Core Competencies

Many companies share common core competencies (customer service, timely delivery, design), but to create true Distinction involves a serious consideration of the competencies that are unique to the firm. For example, most hotels provide customer service in the form of reservations and check-in/out efficiency. But Four Seasons Hotels has a long-standing reputation for superior service that consistently distinguishes it from other leading hotel brands, even at the premium end of the market. Like Singapore Airlines, Four Seasons has won numerous awards over the years and is consistently recognized as the best hotel chain in the world. Many organizations deliver letters and packages. But FedEx has carved a reputation for precise, time-guaranteed delivery, further supported by superior customer-friendly tracking systems. The 2009 *Fortune* magazine survey ranked FedEx as the number one most admired company in the world in the delivery industry. They have been ranked first or second every year since 2006.[11] A number of consumer electronics companies claim superb design capabilities. But Apple has found a way to blend design with artistic flair, ease of use, and ability to meet consumer lifestyle needs that has enabled them to develop a recognized reputation for distinctive, high quality offerings.

Considering these issues is more than an academic exercise. To make this useful, the following questions should be asked to kick-off the Distinction planning process.

Heritage Questions

- What makes the company special?
- What have been the company's historical decision-making tendencies?
- What are our distinct core competencies that contribute to making the company special?

Brainstorm these questions and then isolate the factors that succinctly address each question, using this as a guide for further delving into attributes that create Distinction. These questions involve some corporate "soul searching" to reveal the answers, and senior management should be prepared for a lack of precision in this analysis. The key at this stage is to dig deep into the company's past to find the ingredients that, when mixed together, create the company's unique approach to business. Doing this is more than an academic exercise: it provides useful ammunition for defending and supporting brand-building plans, conveying the qualities that have historically made the company successful and using those to continue the traditions into the future.

Context

The task of developing brand distinction needs to be done with management acknowledging and understanding the business conditions in which their brand competes. Developing a strategy devoid of the competitive situation puts the brand-planning efforts at risk of missing important opportunities, insufficient differentiation, and/or irrelevancy. Brand planning must therefore take into account the overall market situation in which the brand operates. While variations on gathering market context data did vary by company, the common categories researched were analogous to the 5 Cs, a familiar marketing framework that is helpful for understanding the overall market situation, providing a useful organizational tool in early brand-planning stages. This level of strategic planning is necessary at this early stage of brand building because it steers early decisions on the factors that will help create Distinction and competitive advantage over time. The 5 Cs are:

- Customers;
- Company;
- Competitors;
- Collaborators;
- Conditions.

Customers

Building strong brands requires marketers to gain a deep understanding of their customers, whether they are consumers or business buyers, answering the question "what customer needs should we serve"? This includes learning as much as possible about the following customer characteristics: interests, needs, wants, demographics, behaviors, decision-making criteria, and purchase and usage patterns. The result will be a clearer understanding of opportunities and how to develop relevant products that resonate with customers.

Company

Assessing the firm's strengths and weaknesses will help answer the question "what unique skills do we have for addressing customer needs?" This includes assessing the firm's unique competencies because this will determine whether a customer opportunity can be successfully exploited by the firm's existing capabilities, or if new skills are required and, if so, whether it is sensible to invest in new skills given the market opportunities.

Competitors

Few brands compete in a vacuum. Rivals exist in almost every industry and sector of society. Researching "who competes with us?" will provide an invaluable understanding of competitors' capabilities, including what they do well and where they are weak. Competitors come in many forms, from price to product to attribute to benefits to lifestyle impact (and more), so the marketer needs to decide what the competitive factors are that target customers understand. An innovative new offering being introduced for the first time presents a different brand strategy planning challenge (i.e. how do I create awareness and build a positive reputation for my new product?) than a product competing in a mature market (i.e. should I compete on price, value-added components, or some other set of attributes?). Ideally, gaining a deep understanding of past competitor behavior can help determine future responses. Finally, knowing competitors motivates planning on developing differentiated solutions that are relevant to customer needs and captures their imagination.

Collaborators

Many companies lack the total resources required to satisfy customer needs. Collaborator analysis answers the questions "who should we engage to help us, why would they want to work with us, and how should we motivate them?" Working with other companies with complementary offerings and/or capabilities can strengthen solutions for more effectively addressing customer needs while also contributing to new knowledge. A review of the value-chain, beyond firm-level activities like marketing/sales and operations, including suppliers and distribution networks, will provide a more comprehensive understanding of the many factors that ultimately affect the solution the customer receives and their corresponding satisfaction.

Conditions

Studying environmental factors (political, economic, socio-cultural, and technological) can reveal underlying causes of market change and affect the success of subsequent brand-building activities. Political factors to weigh include whether the government in that area (whether a small town or a country) is stable and if they might be supporters or detractors in the company's efforts to expand its brand presence into their area. Economic considerations include knowing if the economy is growing, stagnating, or declining (at the consumer and business levels). Socio-cultural elements describe the mores, customs, and traditions of the target audience in the area the marketer wishes to enter and whether those are compatible with the brand's reputation. Technological issues include whether the business infrastructure is set-up in a way that makes it easy for the company to build its presence (logistics, shipping routes, distribution centers, IT sophistication, communications). Understanding general market trends, such as shifting business and consumer preferences, interest rate changes, business investment shifts, and regulatory changes that might affect the company's own offerings and those of the industry in which it competes will help position brands more effectively. Disruptions can and do regularly occur, from political events (new government leadership, for example) to economic (the September 2008 financial market meltdown) to cultural (citizens in China protesting Starbucks' outlet in the Forbidden City) to technological (digital and mobile technologies that change the way consumers communicate).

Given rapid changes in marketing since the 1990s, the 5 Cs may appear to some as lacking another key C: Communication—"what is our message and how will we reach target customers?" With the advent of digital tools, new media, and nontraditional marketing (see Chapter 10), brands have a much wider variety of ways to communicate with target markets, and customers have innumerable forums for sharing opinions about brands. Despite the risk of overcommunication, a bigger risk is poor communication, so considering communication from a strategic vantage point is an important responsibility at a much earlier planning stage than ever before.

While some of the Cs may not perfectly fit all management information needs, gathering and organizing data about the general environment is a smart way to begin understanding the market and any potential opportunities within.

Brand Lifecycle

The classic product lifecycle as shown in Figure 6-3 is a helpful framework for examining the brand planning needs of the company in pursuit of Distinction. In this instance we substitute "brand" for "product." Recall that, as offerings change from being new and unique to being common, the market itself changes as well. As a brand gains traction at the introduction stage, growth begins to accelerate. Growth signals to competitors that a market opportunity exists and they therefore develop their own offerings. As even more competitors with similar offerings enter, they push the market away from a specialty position toward commodity and growth slows correspondingly, signaling a more mature market. Eventually, the decision whether to extract value by disinvesting in the product and shifting resources to other, newer offerings (from video to DVD or digital, for example), or to reinvest in adding value to the product, perhaps because it is vital piece of the consumer's life (computer operating systems, for example), will need to be evaluated.

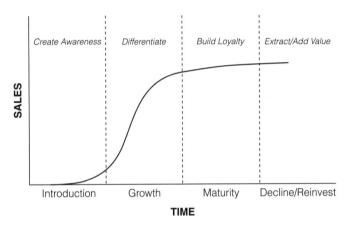

Figure 6-3   Brand Lifecycle

A common and ongoing tension that brands confront is how to retain a specialty position over time when market momentum is simultaneously pushing toward commodity offerings. Attempting to shift from a commodity to a specialty position is known as the *bent arrow theory of marketing*, shown in Figure 6-4.

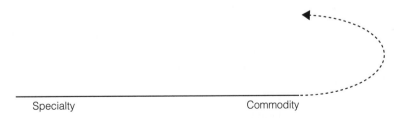

Figure 6-4   Bent Arrow Marketing (returning to a distinctive specialty position)
Source: Davis, R. T., *Marketing in Emerging Companies,* © 1984 Perseus Books.

The savvy competitor seeks to distinguish its offerings by focusing on value-added enhancements and innovation in order to recapture a specialty status, command premium profits and, thus, differentiate its offerings once again. This is illustrated by Figure 6-5, which shows how brand Distinction adapts when bent arrow marketing efforts are applied to the lifecycle.

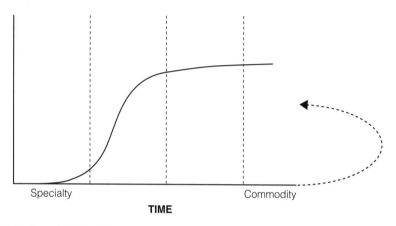

Figure 6-5   Brand Distinction

An important point here is that while a brand's Distinction will adapt over time to reflect market conditions, the core values and DNA of the brand remain the same. Movie studios did not stop making movies when consumer preference shifted from video to DVD and/or online delivery. In fact, the technology change of this shift ushered in a new era of expanded revenue streams for studios as they could provide not just the original movie but supplemental offerings such as deleted scenes, interviews, and even information on movie-related merchandise tie-ins. Microsoft did not abandon the Windows operating system when open source and other competitors gained momentum. Instead, they modified the product to accommodate many of the changes customers found valuable in competing operating systems.

In summary, doing the research to gain a better understanding of the Context helps pinpoint gaps and opportunities for improving the brand. Of course, knowing the Context and responding with relevant offerings are often complex and competing issues. General Motors (GM) has witnessed a steady and, in recent years, devastating decline in market share since the 1970s. At the same time, Japanese and European car manufacturers exploited gaps in GM's brand strategy by developing strong product offerings in highly differentiated areas (affordable quality with Japanese cars and performance-based luxury with many European auto brands). GM responded with inconsistent product lines, unclear brand personalities, and product quality that were perceived as below that of international competitors. For much of the time since the 1970s, GM struggled to consistently define its brand reputation, a challenge that caused further erosion in their market share and led the company into bankruptcy in mid-2009.[12]

Context Questions
1. Is our market growing, stagnating, or declining?
   a. Which of the four time periods are we likely in: introduction, growth, maturity, or decline/reinvestment?
2. What are our competitors' strengths and weaknesses?
3. Is our product on the specialty or commodity end of the lifecycle?
4. Assuming it is on the commodity end, is it possible to recapture a specialty position?

Goals

Setting a goal of building a reputable brand is a useful philosophical start, but far more detailed coordination and planning is required. Brand building involves a wide range of activities in marketing, and across the company, directly and indirectly influenced by marketing. At their simplest, goals succinctly describe intended future brand-building results. A keen awareness of the brand's Heritage aids in developing distinctive goals, which are a necessary prerequisite for successful *internal planning,* if proper cross-functional alignment in support of marketing programs is to be achieved. Goals can be categorized using several approaches, but often the most effective is to consider a sequence of goals: short-term, medium-term, and long-term, as illustrated by Figure 6-6.

Figure 6-6 Goals Timeline

- *Short-term goals.* Because of their timing, short-term goals are usually the most achievable. In business planning, short-term goals are usually less than a year and often set to be reached within a few weeks or a couple of months.
- *Medium-term goals.* Medium-term goals are the stepping-stone toward longer term objectives, covering the period between the end of the short-term goal to the start of the long-term goal, which can be anywhere from a couple of months to a year or two.
- *Long-term goals.* Long-term goals might include several related subgoals, including: distribution, unit sales, market share, revenues, profits, and brand value increases.

Table 6-1   Goals Planning

	Customer	Product	Marketing Communications	Financial
Short-term (<1 yr)	Research new customers Identify new retail channel partners	Develop new product plan for new customer target Source materials and manufacturing Produce sample products/demos Test product	Develop communications brief RFP to 3–5 marketing agencies Select agency of record Agency produces full creative and media plan Test market creative ideas	Invest $250 K in research and product planning Get senior management buy-in
Medium-term (1–2 yrs)	Secure distribution with top 3 accounts in target market Review progress with field sales	Plan production run of 500 000 units Review progress with production team and suppliers	Roll-out initial media blitz in target market Adjust campaign based on response Review progress with agency	3%–5% of revenues from new customers Review progress with senior management
Long-term (>2 years)	Expand to new geographies and top 10 accounts Review progress with field sales	Expand production to 1 500 000 units on first product Add 1–2 product extensions in product line Review progress with product team and suppliers	Expand media plan to new geographies Adapt to fit media type (digital, traditional) Review progress with agency	Market share of target customer increases 8% Brand value increase of 5% Review progress with senior management

Table 6-1 illustrates short-, medium-, and long-term strategic planning goals in four areas: *customer, product, marketing communications, and financial.* These areas are not exhaustive and one can conceivably justify strategic goals in service, support and value-chain requirements as well. The key is that goals are developed and used as a way to ensure proper organizational alignment, including the approximate timetable implications. Such planning will eventually directly affect the specific tactics chosen, as will be discussed in Chapters 8–10 about Experiences.

Growth Strategies

The exact structure of setting strategic goals will depend on each company's particular needs and the goals can even be quite specific, such as an increase in market share over three years. Typically, as Table 6-1 illustrates, growth goals are usually among the main areas of focus in brand planning, whether they are short term, medium term or long

	Current Markets	New Markets
Current Products	A **Market Penetration** Increase market share Increase product usage	C **Product Development** Add product features New generation products
New Products	B **Market Development** Expand geographically Attract new segments	D **Diversification** Related Unrelated

Figure 6-7   Growth Choices
Source: Ansoff, H. I., "Strategies for Diversification," *Harvard Business Review*, 35(2), September–October, 1957.

term. Growth goals will be established for current and new products in current and new markets, and the Ansoff matrix, shown in Figure 6-7, is a planning framework analyzing various brand strategy needs. The matrix is a useful way to think about and plan different brand-building initiatives, particularly those in large companies with complex brand and product offerings, although most companies will find it beneficial. Each of the four boxes represents a different growth choice and the implications for other marketing activities will become apparent later on in Chapters 8–10 on brand Experiences. For now, the emphasis is on evaluating different pathways for growth rather than explicit detail on the tactics used. Marketing tactics deployed without a sense of where they will take the company may increase short-term sales but the long-term brand value is likely to be undermined. Working through quadrants can help refine and even isolate how the brand can be Distinctive within each growth choice. In other words, there are no restrictions on where differentiation and Distinction occurs in the quadrants. Instead, Distinction will be answered by asking "how?" will the brand stand out?

Quadrant A: Market Penetration

Market penetration means brand-planning focuses on increasing sales with current products in current markets. There are two ways to accomplish this:

1. *Increase market share.* This requires taking share and customers away from competitors. The company management must have a clear understanding of their strengths and competitor vulnerabilities if competitors' customers are to be convinced to switch. This includes knowing what customers perceive as your brand's uniqueness and finding ways to highlight this to attract competitor customers (assuming this uniqueness is something they value. Keep in mind that these customers have been purchasing

the competitor's offerings, so switching may not be an easy decision, unless it is purely price-based, in which case there is a different problem—the brand is seen as an undifferentiated commodity.)

2. *Increase product usage.* This means existing customers buy more of the company's products. Company management must have detailed customer profiles and a clear understanding of corresponding needs if the customers are to be persuaded to buy more. Increasing product usage as a growth strategy has to also be consistent with the brand's image. Companies do sometimes produce a limited number of products to enhance the perceived exclusivity. Having customers purchase more may cause the product to seem less special, reducing its prestige and affecting brand value, so embarking on this growth path requires careful planning to ensure brand integrity remains.

Quadrant B: Market Development

Growth here is based on finding new markets for current products. This is accomplished two ways:

1. *Expanding geographically.* Management must select new locations (region, country), preferably where the customers are similar to the firm's existing customers in existing markets. New geographies create new logistical and operational challenges, including possible language and culture differences. Brands must be prepared to adjust to changes in customer demand and communications issues, during launch, as interest grows, and as the market matures. Known brands that have succeeded in one market are not guaranteed success in a new market, particularly when language and cultural practices are vastly different. Even associations the brand's core customers have may be different, if they exist at all, in a new market, so brand building is even more complicated because customer education must occur.

2. *Identifying new segments.* New segments can be in existing or new geographies, requiring more extensive knowledge of different customer groups and their associated characteristics. New segments can be in existing or new geographies. If the segment(s) are in existing geographies, then management must focus on making the products relevant to the new segments. If the segments are in new geographies, then product relevance in the cultural and language context must be emphasized. Ideally, preference should be on those segments with some overlap to existing segments in order to leverage on past customer investments. However, entirely new segment options should be evaluated as a means of achieving growth, implying additional research will be needed to fully understand the potential of each new segment.

Quadrant C: Product Development

This brand growth strategy focuses on selling new or improved products to current markets. There are two ways to do this:

1. *Add product features.* Marketing and/or R&D emphasizes improving existing products to appeal to existing customers to increase their purchases. Growth can also be achieved through relevant product improvements. Customer research will help

identify which changes offer the best value while reinforcing the overall brand image. Minor/incremental changes by leveraging the brand, as discussed in Chapter 3, offer a relatively simple answer to growth needs. "New and Improved, with (name of new ingredient) . . ." is a familiar tactic used to highlight product updates. For the change to succeed, customers must recognize the update as credible and useful to them. A clever marketing communications campaign may boost short-term purchases but if the new features are deemed insignificant, then long-term benefits are unlikely and there is even a real risk of a brand value reduction and a decline in reputation.

2. *New generation of products.* Marketing and/or R&D develops new products, based on their updated research of existing customers. New products face even greater expectations than feature additions. The new offerings must be compelling enough so existing customers either supplement their current product purchases or replace them with the new product.

With both new product features and a new generation of products, senior management is committing to a more complex and expensive product strategy because money will be spent on R&D, suppliers, materials, and then communicating the product development changes to existing and/or competitor customers (to increase share) while also implementing the other facets of the brand strategy.

Quadrant D: Diversification

Choosing diversification means that growth is expected to come from developing entirely new products for entirely new markets. There are two ways:

1. *Related.* This means the company pursues new products sold to new markets but within the same industry. In this case, consideration must be given to not diluting or eroding the company's current brand position or detracting from other marketing efforts. This is akin to launching a new company, so it is a significant undertaking unto itself.
2. *Unrelated.* This is pure pioneering work in both new products and new markets. It is the highest risk growth choice of all and, as such, requires extraordinary dedication and resources (financial, people, energy, time) in order to succeed. Given the existing demands to support the company's other brands and marketing activities, this growth choice requires enormous resources.

Pursuing diversification carries the highest risk because growth success here means attempting something entirely new and possibly out of the company's "comfort zone." Therefore, management will be tempted to concentrate on quadrants A, B, or C as those leverage existing knowledge and experience, and can be more easily linked to the known brand reputation.

A simplified selection of Nike's offerings in Figure 6-8 illustrates how they might fit in the Ansoff matrix.[13]

For the sake of simplicity, just a few examples are shown. In Quadrant A are Nike's existing product categories. These are familiar to customers in most markets and have been the cornerstone of the company's growth and reputation over the years. Customers in these markets continue to expect these offerings. In Quadrant B are examples of Nike's innovation: Air and Zoom Air are innovations in midsole cushioning; Nike ID

	Current Markets	New Markets
Current Products	A **Market Penetration** Existing product categories: running, basketball, tennis	B **Product Development** Air, Zoom Air, Nike ID, Nike+
New Products	C **Market Development** Customers seeking self-expression (Nike ID), new countries and cultures	D **Diversification** Related: Hurley, Converse, Umbro Unrelated: Cole-Haan

Figure 6-8   Growth Choices Illustration—Nike

allows consumers to customize their products and Nike+ features new products and tools for improving training techniques. Quadrant C describes Nike ID's customers who, one might surmise, are self-expressive and seek to be in control of their own product designs; and any new countries and corresponding cultures help grow new markets. Quadrant D shows a few of Nike's acquisitions. The most closely related in this group is Converse, as a well-known athletic shoe brand. Hurley and Umbro are in different apparel businesses—surf and (non-U.S.) football, respectively. Cole-Haan was acquired in 1988 and is an upscale footwear company.[14] Each of these quadrants illustrates different growth paths for Nike.

The Ansoff matrix can also serve as a planning tool for different marketing tactics in support of each specific growth objective, as will be discussed in depth in Chapters 8–10. Brand strategy is rarely as simple as selecting one of Ansoff's growth choices and focusing there alone. Successful brand development often involves multiple products and brands (from the corporate umbrella brand to individual products and sub-brands), so a company like Nike has the luxury of pursuing several growth strategies in different markets simultaneously, depending on the characteristics and needs of each market and Nike's own ability to adapt.

In developing their strategic goals, marketers should consider these questions:

General Strategic Goals Questions

1. Are our goals realistic?
   a. Short-term
   b. Medium-term
   c. Long-term
2. Do our goals match our brand development needs?
3. If we achieve the goals in 3–5 years, how will the brand have changed?

From there, the following questions will help marketers in their growth planning:

Growth Options (Ansoff Matrix) Questions

Market penetration:

1. Is it reasonable to expect that we can gain a higher share of our customer' wallet?
2. Are the competitors' customers dissatisfied in a way that gives us an opportunity to gain their business if we market to them properly?
3. What additional investment in resources is required to gain share or increase usage?

Market development

1. Is geographic expansion logistically feasible?
2. Do we need to adapt our marketing efforts to new market conditions? If so, how significant are the changes and how will they affect our brand reputation?
3. Will serving the new segments be easier, the same, or harder than our current segments? Depending on your answer, how do we deliver on the new segment's expectations?

Product development

1. Are the new features/products likely to be seen as relevant to customers?
2. Will the new features/products resonate with customers? How do you know?
3. How will you market the new features/products while ensuring the brand's reputation and image are consistent?

Diversification

1. Why is pursuing new products and new markets the best growth strategy?
2. Are there competitor incumbents? If so, how do you plan to displace them?
3. How will diversification support the company's brand strategy and growth objectives?

Of course, planning the growth choices and corresponding marketing tactics must be considered along with risks as well as how to measure success.

Brand Distinction as Inspiration

There are also conditions when a more general strategic goal is designed to inspire renewed vigor by employees to achieve something great. As elusive and even ambiguous as that sounds, such goals can imbue a sense of purpose in an organization that a specific financial target cannot. In *Built to Last*, authors Jim Collins and Jerry Porras discussed a concept called Big Hairy Audacious Goals (BHAGs).[15] One example they highlight is that of Stanford University in the U.S., which set a BHAG in the 1940s to become the "Harvard of the West." This inspirational goal set in motion a myriad of activities designed to build the university's reputation over the long term. In subsequent decades, the university pursued ambitious endowment development, invested in new curricula, expanded its research funding from private and public sources, recruited leading faculty from around the world, invested in state-of-the-art facilities, and set stringent admissions criteria to ensure the very best (and well-rounded) students were selected. Stanford has since transformed itself from being a very good regional university in the U.S. to being recognized as one of the world's leading research universities. Such simple direction setting can often yield profound changes because it rallies employees around a cause and not just a financial outcome, serving as a galvanizing force that inspires long-term brand strategy planning.

With internal influences now examined, let us look at external factors that affect Distinction.

Positioning

To be successful, positioning must reflect the marketer's understanding of the target market, provide a frame of reference (how the brand compares to other brands in the same category), and articulate the customer value proposition (which reinforces why the product is both similar to yet differentiated from competitor offerings). The focus now is on the value created by a strong brand position.

David Aaker states that a clear brand identity and position creates value several ways:

- it provides meaning and focus for the organization;
- it guides and enhances brand strategy;
- it provides extension options;
- it improves brand memorability;
- the bottom line provides a value proposition.

Let's look at each of Aaker's brand position benefits.

- *Provides meaning and focus for the organization.* The concept of Destiny guides the direction of the firm, the people, and the processes within. A clear Destiny is easily understood by all inside, enabling people to see where and how they contribute to the company's success. One can easily understand why the employees at any of Interbrand's Best Global Brands companies find those companies inspiring—each serves as a source of inspiration, with past traditions and successes adding a sense of allure and importance to everyone's work.
- *Guides and enhances brand strategy.* As Aaker points out, when employees clearly understand the brand, their decision-making and planning on behalf of the brand can be better organized and implemented. A brand's known personality and reputation serves as a set of guidelines for how the brand is presented to the market through messages, advertising, PR, product development, pricing, field sales, and channel selection.
- *Provides extension options.* As discussed in Chapter 3, an extension describes when a company leverages a known identity to promote a new offering. Extensions can either be product extensions or brand extensions and the choices management makes will have a direct impact on brand value, customer loyalty, corporate performance, and competitor response. The key is that an extension is a relatively simple and effective method for growing a brand, when exercised responsibly and avoiding the temptation to over-extend, because the core brand's popularity casts a positive halo across related

new products and even the rest of the company. At some point, customers will question extensions if the addition is not distinctive enough or if they perceive it as beyond the brand's known credibility and expertise, which can negatively affect the brand's image and customer goodwill. Conversely, considered extensions can facilitate competitive advantage by blocking, or certainly inhibiting, competitor entry. Extensions can also give a brand richer and more complex associations that enhance overall market strength.

- *Improves brand memorability.* Interestingly, a quick review of Interbrand's Best Global Brands Survey and the BrandFinance 250 list reminds us why top brands are so valuable: each of the companies has a memorable identity and a variety of qualities that the market associates with each brand. Identities are most often in the form of logos, which serve as a symbol of the brand. Associations can be both formal and informal. Formal associations include direct linkages to other companies (suppliers, cobrands, partners), locations (such as retail, country, or channels), people (such as iconic CEOs, celebrity endorsers, mascots), and events (sports, music, art). Informal associations are often intangible references, such as a company's reputation for innovation (Apple, Nike, IKEA), social consciousness (Body Shop, Ben and Jerry's, Toyota Prius), or customer focus (FedEx, Nordstrom, Singapore Airlines). Brand identities and associations reinforce the brand's position and remind the market about the qualities for which the brand stands.

- *The bottom line provides a value proposition.* Brands have a rich array of associations that connect to stakeholders, other businesses, and even society. Value for the brand is added directly through the sale of products and increase in brand value. For customers, value is added by the solution and/or comfort the brand provides. Value-chain participants benefit as the economic benefits of the brand's growth stimulates demand of supplies and related materials used in creating the brand. Shareholders gain benefit from the increase in value of the stock holdings. Employees gain value from the notoriety and respect of working for a recognized and successful brand. This chain of effects creates relationship value as well, with each of these variables connected either directly, or indirectly quite closely. For society, a brand adds value through the social good created from employment and offering choice. Plus, a brand gives voice to status and self-expression, affirming people's images of themselves and/or their organizations.

A useful diagnostic tool for determining whether brand-positioning efforts are likely to be effective over the long term is as follows.

Positioning Questions
Give the brand meaning

1. Is our differentiation understood internally throughout the entire organization?
2. Does our position serve as a general source of inspiration?
3. Is our value proposition clear?

Inspire and Strengthen the Brand

1. Does our differentiation clearly help focus attention on appropriate internal operating activities that are consistent with the meaning and personality of our brand(s)?

2. Does our position suggest the kinds of external business partnerships needed to ensure brand integrity and differentiation?
3. Is it clear which kinds of marketing and brand-building activities are best suited for maintaining brand uniqueness?
   a. What is the risk that improper marketing program choices might devalue or harm the brand's position?

Advance Brand Addition and Protect Growth

1. Does the position suggest a clear set of do's and don'ts for growing the brand?
2. Are the line and product category extensions achievable?
   a. Are the extensions likely to be profitable?
   b. Will the extensions block or hinder competitors?
   c. If so, will the brand's uniqueness remain, or is there risk of diluting the brand's long-term image?

Boost Brand Recognition

1. Are the brand's associated identities memorable?
   a. Logos?
   b. Slogans?
   c. Imagery?
   d. Extended relationships (partners, suppliers…)?
2. Do they conjure positive or negative associations with customers?
3. Are the brand's partners knowledgeable of the brand's reputation?

Brand Worth and Usefulness

1. Does the position signal to value-chain participants how they are expected to add value?
2. Is the brand considered reputable and helpful to society?
3. Does the position clarify how the brand fits into the company's overall financial and growth goals?

Measurement

As strategic planning activity, developing Distinction is a rigorous research and analytical effort. At the same time, the temptation to overly plan and analyze brand strategy can distract and/or delay companies from actually going to market, missing important opportunities as a result. It is simply not tenable to plan every conceivable strategic choice in perfect detail. Instead, the pursuit of Distinction should crystallize management thinking around a core set of plans that clearly describe how the company will create valuable brand differentiation.

Since distinction also deals with long-term expectations, often more abstract than tangible, precise measures are not always as important as setting broad-based objectives that provide longer term guidance. The company can assess progress toward the objectives over the short, medium and long term in pursuit of creating Distinction. Measuring sales over a specified period of time provides basic insight into the brand's progress. Reaching revenue targets is certainly helpful. But more importantly, understanding the context of the overall market situation will ensure that a distinctive point of view can be identified during brand planning. Three measures, in particular, are useful in the brand strategy stage:

- market growth;
- share of wallet;
- market penetration.

Market Growth

Metric
Market growth.[16]

Distinction Benefits
Determines if the overall market offers attractive growth opportunities. Serves as an indicator of dynamics in the marketplace and the potential for the brand to make a positive impact.

How
Market growth is determined by measuring the total sales in the target market and then comparing this figure to the sales changes in preceding time periods (typically years).

Formula

$$G_m = \frac{R_I}{R_L}$$

Where
G_m = percentage market growth;
R_I = market dollars/units increase this year;
R_L = market dollars/units last year.

Impact on Distinction
Knowing the market growth rate can provide marketer's insight into the future potential for their businesses (although there is no guarantee that historical growth rates will continue into the future). Market data can be easily obtained from industry trade publications, independent market-research firms, product analysts, reputable business magazines, government reports, and trade associations.

Marketers must measure their own companies' growth first, for two reasons: first, to see what the growth trend has been over the past few years and determine whether their current pace is above or below the recent historical average and, second, to compare their business's growth to that of the competition.

Market growth can serve as a good indicator of dynamics in the marketplace. It provides guidance on the market's potential (the total number of customers in the target market segment), the level of customer penetration (how many customers have entered the market) and the rate of customer entry (how quickly new customers enter the market).

Share of Wallet/Share of Customer

Metric
Share of Wallet/Share of Customer.[17]

Distinction Benefits
Share of wallet provides insight into a brand's success with its customers by measuring the level of commitment customers have to the brand as a percentage of that customer's total purchases of products of that type.

How
The brand's sales to the customer are divided by the sum of all customer spending.

Formula

$$S_i = \frac{S_{it}}{\sum Mi_t}$$

Where
S_i = share of customer i (in percentage terms);
S_{it} = brand sales to customer i in time t (in units or dollars);
$\sum M_t$ = sum of all customer spending in the category in time t (in units or dollars).

Impact on Brand Strategy
While market share measures an individual company's share of total market sales, share of customer analyzes it at the individual customer account level, measuring the percentage share of the total dollars for a brand or product. It can be a useful guide in assessing success at persuading a customer to purchase a larger share of the brand's products over the competition's. Share of customer can even be a valuable measure for assessing the performance of individual sales representatives because it is a partial indicator of how successful they are in developing their customer relationships.

Share of customer results can be a driver of customer relationship programs designed to improve brand loyalty, yet they are also an early indicator of brand or product problems if there is a decline in average per customer purchases over time or if the customer increases purchases of the competitor's products. Finally, share of customer is useful when meeting with senior management as it provides insight into specific customers, their value and potential.

Market Penetration

Metric
Market penetration.[18]

Distinction Benefits
Measuring market penetration helps marketers determine whether acquiring a competitor's customers, or attracting new customers to the product category, is best for the brand strategy.

How
Measures number of people that buy a brand or product one or more times during a specified period of time divided by the total target market population.

Formula

There are several market penetration formulas, each for a specific type of market measure:

Market Penetration

$$M_p = \frac{C_c}{T_p}$$

Where
M_p = market penetration (%);
C_c = number of customers who have purchased a product in the category;
T_p = total market population.

Brand Penetration

$$B_p = \frac{C_b}{T_p}$$

Where
B_p = brand penetration (%);
C_b = number of customers who have purchased the brand;
T_p = total market population.

Penetration Share

$$P_s = \frac{B_p}{M_p}$$

Where
P_s = penetration share (%);
B_p = brand penetration (%);
M_p = market penetration (%).
  or

$$P_s = \frac{C_b}{C_c}$$

Where
P_s = penetration share (%);
C_b = number of customers who have purchased the brand;
C_c = number of customers that have purchased a product in the category.

Impact on Distinction

The market penetration metrics guide the marketer's decision toward either taking customers from their competitors or focusing on growing the category by attracting new customers. If taking share from customers is successful, it suggests that the competitors are weak and/or unresponsive to customer needs, with either result indicating that the marketer's company is perceived more favorably (and just needs a marketing communications boost or price adjustment to convince customers to switch). If growing the category by attracting new customers is successful, then the marketer's brand may have some previously unknown or untapped appeal that can be further leveraged into added customer growth, helping the brand gain yet more market share.

Summary

Distinction is the part of the brand-planning framework concerned with *differentiation* and *brand growth choices*. In developing Distinction, particular emphasis should be placed on four components: *Heritage, Context, Goals,* and *Positioning.* Heritage includes considering the firm's historical decision-making when determining the brand's future direction. Context refers to the competitors against which brands compete and the market context, or conditions, that may affect developing Distinction. Goals are the guiding expectations of where the brand should be in the short-, medium- and long-term time horizons. The Ansoff matrix guides growth choices among current and new products and markets, helping further shape and refine the brand toward long-term greater value. Positioning helps the brand by developing memorable offerings that have a unique place in the customer's mind. Once a unique position is owned, product and brand extensions can be evaluated. Each extension decision must always be considered relative to the impact it will have on overall brand value and reputation. Developing Distinction includes reviewing and evaluating themes vital to long-term brand success discussed throughout this book: *relevance* and *resonance.* An offering may be different, but if that difference is not relevant to the target customer, then there is little or no benefit to the brand. Assuming the product meets customer needs, analyze if it is then important for the product to resonate with the customer at an emotional level and, if so, how to establish this bond. As with any critical business planning process, assessment tools are needed to help measure results. Market share, market growth, share of requirements, and market penetration are among the helpful tools for measuring Distinction.

Discussion Questions

1. Visit the web site for BMW www.bmw.com, paying particular attention to the investor relations section and postings of management conference slides. Based on what you read, how would you describe their *strategic Heritage, strategic Goals, strategic Environment,* and *strategic Positioning?*

2. Assume you are the brand manager responsible for IKEA's growth choices. How would you fill in the Ansoff matrix quadrants? Why did you make the choices you did?

3. Describe Apple's iTunes Strategic Position. What ways could you extend iTunes, either as a line or category extension (or both)? How would your decision impact the brand? What target markets would you go after with your extensions? Why?

4. Choose three well-known brands in different industries and their respective closest competitor. Describe what makes each well-known brand differentiated. Are those differences relevant and do they resonate with customers? Explain your reasoning using examples.

Notes

1. "World Airline Awards: Survey Methodology," retrieved January 28, 2009 from www.worldairlineawards.com/main/mthds.htm. Updated July 7, 2009.

2. "Singapore Crowned Best Airline for Sixth Time, Singapore Changi wins Best Airport, at the 26th OAG Airline Industry Awards," June 4, 2008, retrieved January 28, 2009 from www.oag.com/oagcorporate/pressreleases/08+winners+of+the+oag+airline+industry+awards.html.

3. "The 2008 Zagat Airline Survey," November 24, 2008, retrieved January 28, 2009 from www.zagat.com/Blog/Detail.aspx?SNP=NBOB&SCID=42&BLGID=16424.

4. "World's Most Admired Companies," *Fortune* magazine, retrieved January 28, 2009 from http://money.cnn.com/magazines/fortune/mostadmired/2009/snapshots/8155.html.

5. "Our Achievements," Singapore Airlines corporate web site, retrieved February 24, 2009 from www.singaporeair.com/saa/en_UK/content/company_info/news/achievements.jsp.

6. 1) Research projects conducted by students at Singapore Management University for their strategic brand management course between 2004 and 2008. 2) "Grupo Modelo," research completed November 2007 and updated February 2009. 3) Irusta, M. A. L., April 23, 2007, "Grupo Modelo at the Beginning of the XXI Century," case study, retrieved February 7, 2009, from www.ifama.org/conferences/2007Conference/SymposiumPapers_files/1060_Case.pdf. 4) "History," retrieved February 2, 2008 from www.gmodelo.com.mx/index-1_en.asp?go=historia.

7. Ibid.

8. Ibid. See also, "Beer—Mexico," *Euromonitor International*, June, 2007, retrieved September 13, 2007, from Global Market Information Database, p. 6.

9. Ibid.

10. Ibid.

11. "World's Most Admired Companies," *Fortune* magazine, retrieved April 16, 2009 from http://money.cnn.com/magazines/fortune/mostadmired/2009/index.html.

12. 1) Isidore, C. "GM Bankruptcy: End of an Era," June 2, 2009, *Fortune* magazine and CNNMoney.com, retrieved June 9, 2009 from http://money.cnn.com/2009/06/01/news/companies/gm_bankruptcy/. 2) Sandler, L., Scinta, C., Voris, B. van and Green, G., "GM Files Bankruptcy to Spin Off More Competitive Firm (Update1)," June 1, 2009, retrieved June 8 from www.

bloomberg.com/apps/news?pid=20601087&sid=aA1LQFDhqkJ0. 3) Isidore, C., "Will the GM Bankruptcy Work?" June 2, 2009. *Fortune* magazine and CNNMoney.com, retrieved June 9, 2009 from "What if GM *Did* Go Bankrupt ..." December 12, 2005. *BusinessWeek*, retrieved July 17, 2009 from www.businessweek.com/magazine/content/05_50/b3963114.htm. 4) Levine, M. S. "Why Bankruptcy Is the Best Option for GM," November 17, 2008, *The Wall Street Journal*, retrieved December 1, 2008 from http://online.wsj.com/article/SB122688631448632421.html.

13. 1) "Nike History & Heritage," Nike corporate web site, retrieved September 30, 2008 from www.nikebiz.com/company_overview/history/1950s.html. 2) Kalin, S., "Nike's Sneaker Net Speeds Global Info Sharing," August 5, 1999, CNN.com, retrieved October 11, 2007 from http://edition.cnn.com/TECH/computing/9908/05/nike.ent.idg/index.html. 3) "Redesigned Nike Website Debuts," August 21, 2008, Nike corporate web site, retrieved September 16, 2008 from http://invest.nike.com/phoenix.zhtml?c=100529&p=irol-newsArticle&ID=1189364& highlight=. 4) "Nike Expands Sustainable Design Into All Shoe Types," October 29, 2008, SustainableBusiness.com, retrieved December 2, 2008 from www.sustainablebusiness.com/index.cfm/go/news.display/id/17039. 5) "Will the New Nike-iPod Sport Kit Hit the Ground Running, or Hit the Wall?" July 26, 2006, Knowledge@Wharton, retrieved May 27, 2008 from http://knowledge.wharton.upenn.edu/article.cfm?articleid=1527. 6) Walters, H., "Nike's New Downmarket Strategy," February 27, 2007, *BusinessWeek*, retrieved May 27, 2008 from www.businessweek.com/innovate/content/feb2007/id20070227_004086.htm.

14. "Company News; Cole-Haan to Nike for $ 80 Million," April 26, 1988, *New York Times*, retrieved September 28, 2008 from www.nytimes.com/1988/04/26/business/company-news-cole-haan-to-nike-for-80-million.html.

15. Collins, J. and Porras, J. I., *Built to Last-Successful Habits of Visionary Companies*, © 1994 Harper Business, pp. 90–114.

16. 1) "Because He's Game for Anything. In Fact, Everything," Inc. Magazine, retrieved August 13, 2008 from www.inc.com/magazine/20050401/26-branson.html/. 2) "The Importance of Being Richard Branson," January 12, 2005, retrieved August 7, 2008 from http://knowledge.wharton.upenn.edu/article.cfm?articleid=1109.

17. Davis, J., *Measuring Marketing: 103 Key Metrics Every Marketer Needs*, © 2006 John Wiley & Sons (Asia) Pte Ltd, pp. 92–94.

18. Farris, P. W., Bendle, N. T., Pfeifer, P. E. and Reibstein, D. J., *Marketing Metrics: 50+ Metrics Every Executive Should Master*, p. 26, © 2006 Pearson Education, Inc.

Brand Culture

7

Topics

Preview

We have shown how the Destiny of a brand leads to brand strategies that are distinctive—company leaders and employees want the brand to succeed and feel a sense of responsibility for reflecting the values and heritage of the organization. The thinking and planning of a brand, its meaning, and where it is heading must be decided by the people within. As obvious as that sounds, the differences across top brands are startling. This chapter focuses on the ingredients of a strong brand culture. Other than the basics of hiring the "right people" and paying them competitively, each top brand set about building an utterly unique culture.

Even within the same industry, no two competitors were exact replicas, or had the same internal practices (other than the normal legal requirements to which every company adheres in its home country). Business schools teach students about processes, predictability, scaling, and efficiency, among other topics, which are all important. However, the issues and challenges surrounding culture building, decision-making in the absence of complete information, and leading are equally if not more important. They are also inherently more challenging because of the unknown variables. How will that person react? Why is that group responding differently? How are these kinds of situations handled? These are examples of the tough questions that confront people in their jobs every day. A healthy, vibrant culture is vital for creating an atmosphere in which employees thrive and do not underperform.

The external strength and reputation top brands enjoy is built on a strong internal foundation. Top brands do not view the market's view of their brand as unrelated to employee hiring, cultural practices, or ongoing training. On the contrary, those activities and more *distinguished* top brands from all other companies. The nurturing of a corporate culture deeply imbued with the company's sense of Destiny and history, along with the recognition that developing the next generation of leaders and brand builders across the organization is paramount to having a successful brand as recognized by all stakeholders. Each top brand sought certain qualities in its people and then set about populating its organizations accordingly. The culture-building effort is not a lesson in uniformity. It is a prescription for vitality that inspires progress and innovation, where everyone within feels like they are contributing meaningfully to the success of the brand, supported by ongoing internal branding, training, skills development, and general collaboration working toward a valuable future.

Brand Culture

Many companies devote their marketing budgets to external brand building by investing in advertising and marketing communications campaigns targeted to specific audiences. This external focus is intended to attract profitable, long-term, loyal customers and is a vital ingredient in brand development.

However, before success in attracting customers happens, companies must build their brand *internally* with their own employees first. As Shelly Lazarus, Chairman of Ogilvy & Mather Worldwide (one of the world's leading branding agencies), pointed out when asked about the importance of internal branding, "They are absolutely critical. If the people who work in a company don't understand what the brand is, if they can't articulate what the brand's all about, then who can?"[1]

However, successful internal branding requires more than a general understanding of the brand. Every point of contact can potentially affect how consumers relate to brands, which means that marketing is not solely responsible for ensuring customer satisfaction.

Operations, sales, customer service and support, design, and even accounting can all enhance or harm this relationship. Brand value will be affected as well, since a good portion of what customers value beyond the products they buy are the implied promises, including trust, which come with a well-known brand and those promises determine whether a company can command a premium and/or a differentiated position in the market vis-à-vis competitors. Internal branding is an important mechanism for turning employees into big believers and supporters of their own brand. The combination of internal and external branding should produce a positive image from generating support and buzz for the company.

When branding results are below expectations, a common management tendency is to blame the choice and/or implementation of external marketing communications tactics designed to reach customers. This may well be true. But another common yet more easily overlooked factor is related to the people responsible for the branding activities. This is not to suggest that marketers, or even other employees, should be replaced when brand building falls short, as they may be exceptionally talented people. But the underperformance may be due to inattentive management efforts to build a strong culture.

In this chapter, we will look at Brand Culture and internal branding from two perspectives: nonmarketers and marketers. For nonmarketers, the days are gone when they could focus just on their area of expertise, irrespective of the related impact of their activities on the rest of the organization. Since companies have recognized that branding is more than a marketing communications activity, the emphasis is on aligning each employee's work with the larger strategic direction of the company. In essence, people have an increasingly hard time hiding in functional silos. Instead, employees are either directly or indirectly working to enhance the value of their contribution so that the company's collective effort enhances the overall value of the brand. Every action has a potential impact on the brand, and the onus is on employees and management to ask "is what I am doing going to contribute to improving our overall brand effort?"

Marketers must recognize that their role has changed as well. No longer responsible for external marketing, they must market internally with the same effort and intensity. This means that marketers must recognize the differences between the company's internal audience and the customers outside in the market. Both audiences must understand and appreciate the brand. But the internal audience must feel as if it is part of something special and that its work is important to the market's ultimate acceptance of the brand. Whereas externally the reward for customers is that they obtain a high-quality offering that is relevant to their needs and adds intangible value to their life, internally the reward for employees is in knowing that their company is respected and even admired, qualities that can add significant psychological value to their work. Furthermore, like external branding, successful internal branding creates a *buzz* that builds and reinforces support from employees, enhancing the connection they feel to the company.

Indeed, companies are finding that external branding success is a by-product of their devotion to internal branding.

EXAMPLE 7-1:

Nike

When new employees join Nike, among their activities in their first few days is a two-day company orientation session. This is Nike's chance to tell the company's story, from its founding as Blue Ribbon Sports in the late 1960s, to becoming Nike in 1972, and to the innumerable achievements of the athletes who have worn Nike products. The orientation is akin to a motivational session with inspiring images of great athletes as well as the heartbreak that accompanies loss filling new employees with the emotional side of sport, and Nike's role in it. New employees learn about Nike's history of product innovation, from the Waffle outsole to Nike Air, to Zoom Air, and many other athletic innovations, all designed to support athletes during rigorous training and competition. As the orientation leaders tell new hires, Nike is consumed with the needs of athletes, and linking innovative products with them. As Phil Knight, Nike's founder and Chairman once said, "Nobody roots for a product." But when that product is linked to an athlete that fans follow, the product takes on a whole new meaning. Consumers of products become fans of Nike at that point. After orientation, Nike employees receive ongoing updates on their athletes, new product launches, event sponsorships, and creative media campaigns, all tied together to inspire employee support. In addition, four times each year all employees are invited to company-wide meetings to learn about the latest product launches and corporate updates. Employees celebrating 10 years with the company are invited to the Decathlete's Dinner. The result is that thousands of employees are well-informed about the company's direction, told through a variety of methods, from formal management presentations, to athlete visits, to sales meetings, to thousands of informal meetings and internal communications continually. An equally important benefit is that Nike employees feel more connected to the activities of the company and become more devoted advocates of their brand. In effect, they believe that their work has meaning, which creates a more positive and engaged corporate culture.[2]

Of course, the purpose of internal branding is not just to make employees feel good, but to translate that positive atmosphere into activities that produce great products and continue building on the brand's historical legacy of success while also creating substantial value for all stakeholders. Internal branding, done well, helps reinforce and build the company's culture. The term *culture* is important for several reasons. For years, businesses have used more clinical terms like human resources or personnel when thinking about the development and uses of human capital. In contrast, the term "culture" conveys the richness that defines organizations, whether social or professional. Culture immediately conjures images of customs, mores, and traditions. Companies have cultures, just as countries do, and employees increasingly seek work with organizations that fit their values and lifestyle, not just meeting basic living requirements such as fair compensation and benefits. To build a successful brand means companies must understand and develop their own corporate culture because the people within are ultimately responsible for delivering on the promises made to the market (promises that are typically in the form of marketing communications that indicate what a product can do and why people should buy it). Furthermore, a strong and well-defined corporate culture serves another purpose: it functions as both a filter and magnet for attracting the right talent.

Consider two well-known global companies that are also iconic brands: Apple and Louis Vuitton Möet Hennessy (LVMH). They also have substantial brand values: LVMH US$21.6 billion; Apple US$13.7 billion.[3] Apple's reputation for creative innovation and superb product design attracts a specific type of person and personality. One can imagine a conservative, risk-averse person finding Apple less than appealing. The benefit to Apple, and any company with a clear corporate personality and culture, is that candidates for jobs tend to self-select prior to the final application decision, basing their choice on whether they believe they would fit in with Apple's culture and known reputation. The same is true for LVMH, with its well-established reputation as a premier provider of luxury products catering to very select, high-end consumers. Louis Vuitton Möet Hennessy has a reputation as a sophisticated company that understands prestige and the intangible benefits that accompany an exclusive lifestyle.[4] As such, prospective employees would need to fit into LVMH's talent profile. As their web site states, they are looking for pragmatic, entrepreneurial people with a creative flair, a love of luxury, and an appreciation for international experiences. Louis Vuitton Möet Hennessy is not suggesting that one must be wealthy to work there, but one must understand and appreciate the mindset of the luxury market. The qualitative dimensions sought by LVMH are important because they want to ensure that prospective employees fit within the context and social fabric of the company's unique corporate culture. One cannot just be superb at numbers crunching, for example, without having respect and admiration for the subtleties that distinguish luxury products from other offerings.

Brand Management and Senior Management

Brands are usually handled, of course, by brand management teams. For decades, brand management has been taught in business schools from a consumer products perspective, although its practice is applicable in industrial settings as well. There is no single brand management organizational design that is ideal. Indeed, what works well for Procter & Gamble does not necessarily work for Nike, or Nestlé, or BMW. Each company develops its own brand management structure based on its own needs and competencies and, over time, their brand management organizations may change. Procter & Gamble shifted away from brand management to category management, as discussed earlier in this textbook. Nike has changed as well, from product line management to marketing managers to category managers, over the past 20 years. However each company chooses to organize its brand management, there are several functions within that should be considered (again, depending on the company). These are not necessarily job titles or individual people, although particularly in larger companies they could be. But often, members of brand management teams are responsible for multiple marketing-related activities. They include:

- *Category management.* Responsibility for several planning, strategic direction, and implementation of brands/products in same category (such as hair care, portable music players, cereals). This may include profit and loss (P&L) responsibility for all brands/products in a category, as well as market share improvement, brand value enhancement, and overall performance gains for the company.
- *Brand management.* Responsible for the planning, strategic direction, and implementation of a specific brand and its product line, plus possible P&L responsibility. Examples include: Nike Air Jordan, Unilever's Sunlight Dishwashing Liquid, Kao's Kanebo cosmetics, and Mars' Pedigree pet food.
- *Marketing management.* Responsible for the customer-facing marketing activities in support of the brand, including marketing strategy, marketing communication planning, media planning, marketing research.
- *Marketing communications.* This sometimes comes under the marketing management responsibilities. Activities include: development of marketing message, advertising agency management, media buying, corporate identity development (brand logos, slogans, trademarks), corporate presentations. May be responsible for tracking and measuring marketing communications programs, as well as public relations and even crisis management.
- *Marketing research.* Marketing people that research customer (consumer and B2B) behaviors and preferences so that marketing positioning and messages can be tailored to the appropriate customer audience. Researchers use both quantitative and qualitative techniques, as well as ethnographic and experimental studies. Market researchers may also be responsible for broader information gathering on competitors, markets, countries, regions, global issues, and numerous measurement tools.
- *Product management.* Responsible for product line direction, planning, and development. This includes planning statement level (high end, premium) to mid-point to entry level and corresponding prices. May work with development (also known as sourcing and/or operations management) in identifying appropriate materials and ingredients for each product in the product line.

Aside from these marketing-specific responsibilities, those responsible for brand management will need to coordinate their activities with other functions/departments inside the company, from operations to delivery, to accounting, to sales to customer service/support. The role of brand management team leaders is to persuade other departments to support the brand management effort, from the moment a brand is added or enhanced, through the concept design and development, to market delivery and follow-up. Furthermore, brand management teams must also persuade senior management, including the company's CEO and chief marketing officer (if they have one, or perhaps the vice-president of marketing), to support, approve, and fund the brand's market plans for the next planning and budget cycle. This effort is often one of the most challenging aspects of marketing jobs since staff have to convince others in the company of the merits of their plans, well before any new products or marketing communications are created. But there is far more to building a strong and successful brand culture than the formation and structure of brand management teams. In fact, true brand culture success requires all employees to think and act beyond their functional mandate and senior management has to lead this effort. From their leadership down, senior management must consider the entire company as a large-scale brand-development effort. Every personnel decision must be viewed from the context of how a person can best contribute to the overall company and its culture. Do new hires fit in? How can existing employees be motivated to contribute more actively on behalf of the brand? In this regard, brand becomes the responsibility of every department in the sense that each activity ultimately affects the customer's perception of the company, therefore each employee within every department is part of the larger brand effort. This is not to suggest that each department must now structure itself as a brand management or marketing team would. Instead, managers throughout the company must thoughtfully consider how a new employee adds value beyond their education, technical skills, and past experiences. Do they understand the brand and what it stands for? Does it excite them? When viewed through this larger lens, the narrow focus on specific skills, while still important, must be considered alongside the larger needs of the brand. The next section discusses the four criteria required for building a successful brand culture.

Four Subcomponents of Successful Brand Cultures

Research on dozens of global brands for this book identified a consistent set of four criteria successful brands use for building and developing a culture and shown in Figure 7-1.

The work top brands put forth to develop their cultures is ceaseless. While every company uses unique practices, the four ingredients discussed in this chapter are themes common to the best practices of the very top brands. Culture affects and is influenced by internal branding and it also directly affects behaviors and tactics. Within, there are formal and informal culture-building activities centered around the development of individuals and organizations within the company. Internal branding is an important activity for communicating to employees about new products, marketing campaigns, corporate initiatives, business partner activities, and much more. In essence, anything that can affect how a

Figure 7-1   Components of Culture

brand is perceived in the market needs to be clearly understood within the company so that employees not only know what is being told and promised to the market but also how their work affects the company's ability to deliver. In this sense, internal branding *influences* culture. Logically, assuming employees are receiving clear communication about the company's products and customer activities, then their own behaviors will more easily be aligned toward satisfying customer needs, even if some of the employees are not directly working with customers (such as internal staff who support customer-facing functions). At the same time, the tactics used (marketing programs, pricing, customer service activities, and more) will be the result of the understanding and expectations conveyed by the internal branding efforts.

Developing a strong culture implies a strong degree of integration. This is where brands can get into trouble, despite the best of intentions. As powerful as the desire is to have a strong culture that is aligned and integrated, if compensation systems continue to reward departmental silos, then integration will never be fully realized. Companies must address compensation and reward systems so that truly integrated cultures can flourish.

Ongoing training also distinguishes top brands, with investments in company-specific leadership and advancement programs, cultural practices, to more generic skills enhancement.

EXAMPLE 7-2:

Hermès

Hermès, the French family-owned luxury goods company, "seeks to cultivate a well-rounded set of values among its employees in a family-style environment."[4] These are introduced through training programs and instilled via ongoing internal communications, control policies, and procedures.

Programs include Ateliers de l'imaginaire (Workshops of the Imagination) in which employees meet to discuss and discover new ideas while forging stronger bonds with one another. Ateliers de Pantin is an employee party celebrating Hermès' dedication to art, craftsmanship, and architecture. There is an active intranet site called Toile H, *Hermès intranet* site, in which people share news about company life and developments. These various efforts reinforce Hermès' culture.[5]

Competencies

We will first examine the role of *competencies* in shaping brand culture. Competencies are the *formal* criteria (minimum qualifications) that organizations seek in every *individual*. Any serious effort to recruit the best talent requires that individuals have a select set of formal skills and competencies, determined by each company's unique needs and related expertise. It is worth recalling the importance of Destiny and Brand Strategy here, because they directly influence a company's preference for specific abilities in the people they hire. While marketers are unlikely to be responsible for most nonmarketing hiring decisions, they are responsible for ensuring those they do hire and develop in their discipline have the best possible skills for their position. Corporate culture development, of course, extends beyond hiring great marketing talent that can convey the brand internally and externally.

Managers across the organization have an equal responsibility to fill their organizations with the very best. This is easy to say and far harder to execute on a day-to-day basis. But an important starting point is determining if an employee candidate has the core competencies and skills sought by the company. In particular, these include requisite education levels and previous professional experiences, because these are often the minimum entry requirement for any new employee, just as many universities require minimum grades and test scores before admissibility can even be considered in full.

To illustrate, consider the faculty selection process at a university. While each university differs somewhat in its faculty needs, there are numerous criteria that are considered critical minimums for tenure-track candidates at leading universities. These include a strong preference for an earned doctorate and a publishing track record (preferably in premier academic journals that are peer-reviewed, known as "A-level journals"). Meeting these minimums does not guarantee one will be hired, but they ensure that a reasonably high standard of preparation is met before a candidate can even be considered.

Software companies expect their engineers to have formal training in coding and, often, other engineering and mathematical disciplines before being worthy of serious consideration.

Senior-level field sales people must have a relevant background in selling to a variety of customers, from individual to corporate, as well as small to very large and complex deals before even being called in for the first interview.

Marketing managers should have a solid understanding of marketing fundamentals, such as a grounding in marketing's many academic frameworks (4 Ps/Marketing Mix; Customer Development, including Segmentation/Targeting/Positioning; Pricing), plus verifiable experience participating in and/or leading marketing teams, usually in industries related to the job sought.

Competencies are, in effect, the minimum cost of entry into an organization. Yet that should not suggest that minimum standards should be set low. Indeed, part of the success of top brands is that they often set aggressive standards for talent. A review of most job requirements today from online job boards around the world (including Monster.com, hotjobs.com, Korn Ferry, Brassring.com, LinkedIn, and many more) describes the qualifications sought in their ideal candidate, saying that those that do not meet the minimum should not reply. Company management, not just marketers, should ask the following questions when considering competencies, keeping brand building firmly in mind throughout:

- What is the position description and how does it fit in our company?
- What specific expertise do we possess in our company?
- Does this job strengthen us in this area of expertise? How?
- What objective skills should our ideal employees have (by job/function/department . . .)?
- What is the minimum education we seek?

- Should the person have strong interpersonal skills?
- Is international experience required?
- Is travel required?
- Are multiple language skills required?
- What job-specific experiences are needed?
- What is the minimum number of years of experience sought?

EXAMPLE 7-3:

Johnson & Johnson

Johnson & Johnson's recruitment and retention practices have received widespread recognition. Johnson & Johnson rates leadership and communication skills as the two most important characteristics for new hires.[6] In 2006, the company spent an average of US$6000 per new employee on training—a significant amount within the pharmaceutical industry.[7] In *BusinessWeek*'s ranking of Best Places to Launch a Career, J&J was ranked 24th in 2007.[8]

In 2009 the company was the tenth most popular company for post-graduation employment by *Fortune* magazine.[9] Johnson & Johnson runs voluntary mentorship programs at each of its different operating companies in place of a standardized mentorship program. Its decentralized structure supports knowledge exchange of business practices and encourages a culture of integrity and personal responsibility. Employees are appraised twice a year and assessed on customer satisfaction, organization skills, and efficiency.

Behaviors

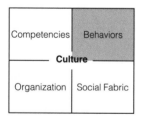

The formal side of individual culture building centered on the competencies and qualifications organizations establish as minimum criteria. Beyond the technical skills and training are the desired behaviors sought in *individual* employees, from entry to senior executive. Behaviors, by their very nature, are imprecise and highly qualitative, hence their designation as *informal*. However, the inherent subjectivity of behaviors should not dissuade brand builders from focusing on it as a key factor in the development of the company's culture.

The Five Ambassadors[10]

There are numerous studies of talented people and the attributes they share. The brand research that underlies this book included a review of the behaviors of top performers. Alternatively, another way to look at this is by using the concept of *brand you*, meaning each person inside a company is, technically, trying to build their own brand reputation through their work and professionalism. The aggregation of the individual employee brands, assuming they are built with an eye toward their respective contributions on behalf of the company's long-term strategy, should add up to a consistent external brand that delivers on the promises that the company makes to the market.

The reason for understanding the behaviors of top performers was that their contributions were deemed influential externally to customers and internally as organizational opinion leaders, the combination of which affects the development of the brand's culture. Assuming that developing a strong corporate culture is desirable, then it stands to reason that understanding the behaviors of top performers in successful global brands might shed additional light on how companies can harness these behaviors, adapted to each national culture of course, for the purpose of enhancing their overall brand reputation and value. Common behavioral patterns emerged and were consequently categorized into five areas called *the five ambassadors*, highlighted in Figure 7-2.

The term *ambassador* is important because it conveys that a person is a good representative of the organization. Each of the five ambassadors is a behavior that creates favorable results for practitioners. However, one must be careful about the term "practitioner": while the top performers worked hard to achieve success, they were not mechanical or canned in their work. The top performer did not think to himself or herself, "Now I must act like a *resource ambassador*." Indeed, the behaviors do not occur sequentially, nor are they job titles. Rather, the five ambassadors were practiced enough over time that they were automatic and rarely conscious, becoming a fluid set of behaviors exhibited by the top performers at different times of their job, depending on the specific business conditions they faced at the time, that ultimately convinced the other party of the merits of the top performer's point of view. Typically, these behaviors were most prominent when the individual was selling a product, service, or idea—activities that fit neatly into conventional paradigms about marketing and sales roles. With marketing and sales important activities in brand building, the five ambassadors take on added relevance. The five ambassador behaviors were also exhibited internally when the top performers were seeking assistance (funding, budget increase, project help) from another department. The five ambassadors are:

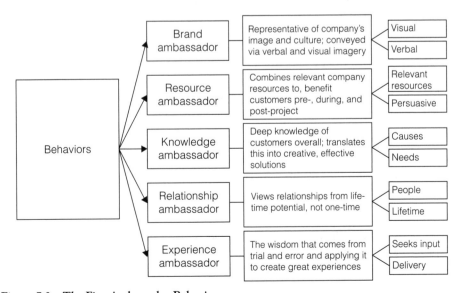

Figure 7-2   **The Five Ambassador Behaviors**

Brand Ambassador

This describes the top performer's efforts to represent and present his or her company, product, or department to another person or group (customer, vendor, or another internal department), using visual and verbal imagery. Visual imagery is self-explanatory: top performers are adept at using relevant visual examples to complement their presentation, making it memorable and connecting the audience to the initiative being presented. Verbal imagery deals with the words used to paint verbal pictures, and is vital to successful brand building. Verbal ability takes a significant effort for people to master, because it depends on knowledge of the target audience, their needs, one's own company and offerings, and an understanding of cultural differences (when working with international audiences). Part of verbal imagery is being adept at explaining something clearly. Many business people use vocabulary familiar to their functional discipline and industry, yet when they meet with those outside those areas a more common language is needed to ensure that understanding is achieved.

Resource Ambassador

The term "resource ambassador" describes the top performer's understanding of his or her own company. This is not merely a surface level awareness of the company's products, but an in-depth understanding of its organization: the most influential people, how different departments contribute, and which resources would be most appealing and relevant to the buying or receiving party. In this regard, top performers serve as active influencers and networkers, deploying the company's various resources in ways that benefit customers *and* grow the company's business profitably. It is often exhibited as an explicit description of which departments or functions were part of the solution being sold. For example, in the enterprise software industry, a product sale is far more than just the software. It includes engineering support, customer service, warranties, consulting, and more. Once the sale is made, the customer requires that the product works and functions as specified and, if not, wants to know what remedies are available. Top performers understand this and, in the presales effort, they work hard to describe these various resources to convince the customer that the company supports its products and to differentiate themselves from competing products. Part of resource ambassador behavior is persuasiveness. Marketing staff can use their knowledge of their own organization in persuading the other party of the full benefits received by the solution being offered. Persuasiveness also means a personal ability to use reasoning that convinces others. This complements the verbal imagery described in the brand ambassador role. The key point is that the resource ambassador behaviors connect a company to the customer beyond the core product purchase by extending the product definition to include the areas that support it. As a result, the customer develops confidence that the company will support the products it sells.

Knowledge Ambassador

Knowledge ambassador behavior helps customers understand the larger market context in which they compete and why the seller's products are an integral piece of their success. When behaving as a knowledge ambassador, top performers describe market conditions and trends to help customers understand the causes and factors that could affect their business and why the offering is ideally suited to address their business needs. Furthermore, top performers frequently update their market knowledge and communicate this to their customers, serving as an advocate for both the customer and their own company. In this context, top performers behave and function more as consultants, providing contextual knowledge to internal and external customers to help them with their final decision.

Relationship Ambassador

As implied, the relationship ambassador behavior describes how top performers relate to their target audiences and, more specifically, how they develop relationships with their key customer audiences. They implicitly believe that business success comes when people are treated like *people* and not numbers, or a deal to be won, or slot fillers. They look at business relationships as a long-term opportunity, not a one-time transaction. Not all business relationships will be valuable over the long term but the philosophical bias toward long-term gain compels top performers to seek multiple ways to make the relationship genuinely rewarding. Conversely, when business people see another party as a one-time gain, less attractive qualities (such as urgency, impatience, steep discounting) emerge that can often undermine the brand's reputation and financial strength. Therefore, top performers must have a deep understanding of their customers, whether internal or external. This includes familiarity with the other party's business overall and the individuals responsible within, including who they are, what they like and dislike, what their interests are, what and why they have bought before. The relationship ambassador behavior continues even when a transaction and/or an agreement has been completed, with top performers maintaining contact and continuing to build the relationship, even when there is no obvious immediate economic or professional gain. The top performer wants to be the first person the customer thinks of when it comes time to purchase again.

Experience Ambassador

The experience ambassador behavior has two components: the first relates to longevity and the wisdom that comes from trial and error. Each of the top performers had a minimum of 10 years' professional experience, which suggests that they were identified as top performers because they were able to succeed over many years, and not just for a few months or a year or two. This success was illustrated by their willingness to seek regular input from colleagues, indicating a high degree of self-confidence, while also serving as a fallibility model, suggesting that they were able to admit mistakes in an effort to create a climate of psychological safety that encouraged fellow employees, whether junior or senior, to more openly contribute without fear for their jobs; the second component describes the experiences the top performers deliver to their customers (whether those customers are external or internal). Top performers made working with them worthwhile, creating memorable and trusted conditions that facilitated business success.

EXAMPLE 7-4:

Yum Brands

Yum! Brands, Inc. is the largest restaurant company in the world with over 36 000 restaurants in 110 countries and 1 million employees. Their restaurant brands include KFC, Pizza Hut, Taco Bell, and Long John Silver's. With so many employees, hiring is a challenge, but the company's restaurants are well-organized systems with consistent standards and training throughout, based on each restaurant brand's core expertise, so new employees generally adapt quickly and well into the culture of the company.[11]

David Novak, Chairman and CEO of Yum Brands, sees employees needing more than just classic business skills to succeed:

> Everybody is looking for ambition, passion, the ability to inspire. I think the thing that I have found in the highest-potential people, and the people who can have the most impact in your organization, is that they're avid learners. Are they continually trying to better themselves? Are they continuing to look outside for ideas that will help them grow the business? The other question I ask myself is, would I want my daughter to work for this person?
>
> If I couldn't convince myself that I could learn from this person or be inspired by them, then I won't hire them.[12]

Brand value at Pizza Hut has declined over the years, from nearly US$6 billion in 2001 to just over US$4 billion in 2008. KFC has seen its brand value grow during that time from US$5.2 billion to US$5.5 billion. System-wide revenues increased from US$9.5 billion in 2006 to US$11.28 billion in 2008. Pizza Hut has been adapting to shifting consumer tastes toward healthier fare, a transition that will continue. KFC has revamped many of its offerings over the years, de-emphasizing fried chicken in favor of grilled offerings and expanding its offerings to accommodate breakfasts and portable meals for people on the go.[13]

Xerox

Xerox is well regarded as a document management technology and services leader. Since 2001, brand value has increased from US$6 billion to nearly US$6.4 billion, a 6% increase. Revenues increased from US$16 billion to US$17.6 billion during that time. In the early part of the 2000s, Xerox underwent a major turnaround, from a US$300 million loss in 2002 to a US$1 billion profit in 2006. CEO Anne Mulcahy is credited with leading the turnaround effort. In discussing employee hiring, she described the qualities that she believes are most important:[14]

> They have more to do with behavior and culture than they do with competence and expertise. Generally speaking, the people you talk to have the competence and expertise. That's how they got to the interview. So then

> the most important aspect is whether it's a good fit . . . It's a little bit of a test. Have they done their homework? Do they understand the place? Do they aspire to the kind of value system and culture we have here? I've learned that it's probably the biggest success or failure indication, as well, about whether people are a good fit with the culture.[15]

> The notion of a good fit goes beyond hiring for competence and toward hiring for attitude, which is where the five ambassadors are particularly important. Part of the efforts to revive Xerox involved changing the culture toward being more adaptable, a quality that is not easy to discern in a single interview, but can be gleaned from discussions with teammates, customers and previous business situations. As Mulcahy said:

> Part of it's from their experience. I think seeing how much breadth someone's had, and their appetite for not just vertical career ladders, but their appetite for what I call the horizontal experiences, where it wasn't always just about a title or the next layer up. And that there was this desire to learn new things, to kind of grab onto things that were maybe even somewhat nontraditional.[16]

Overall, the five ambassadors are a seamless pattern of behaviors exhibited by top performers. Rather than approaching each business relationship with a methodical, rigid plan outlining their behavior, the top performers combine spontaneity with thoughtful planning to achieve their objectives. They are instrumental to brand building success because they affect individuals and groups internally, and customers externally.

Organizational Behavior Questions

Extensive research attention has been given to the assessment of talent and the evaluation of desirable characteristics in employees over the years and students are encouraged to visit the organizational behavior literature for an in-depth understanding of this area. The following questions are quite useful for a brand culture-building perspective in assessing the capabilities of new hires and emerging top performers.

Brand Ambassador

1. What is the employee doing to whet the appetite of target customers and increase their desire to want the offering or accept the proposal?
   a. What is the content of the message used?
   b. How is it conveyed?
2. Is the message relevant to the target customer?
   a. Why would the customer find this helpful in evaluating the solution?
   b. Does it describe why the offering/solution fulfills needs?
   c. Does it convey the benefits of working with the company?
3. Does the message help convey the brand's reputation?
   a. How do customers respond to the employee's effort?

     b. How do they feel?

     c. Does the message help tell the company's story in a way that provides credibility and reinforces expertise?

4. Is the message easy to remember?

     a. Visually?

     b. Verbally?

     c. Does it convey the top 1–3 key points that customers *must* remember?

Resource Ambassador

1. Does the employee know the company's capabilities?

     a. Is the formal organizational structure known?

     b. Are responsibilities of each department known by the people on the customer team?

     c. Are the strengths and weakness known?

2. Does the employee understand what motivates the other party?

     a. Is the employee tying customer needs, company objectives, and individual tactics together to create value for all?

3. Are key deliverables and milestones planned and understood within the company and by the customer?

Relationship Ambassador

1. What do employees know about the customer/target audience?

     a. Is it general, or detailed?

     b. Do they know the customer's unique characteristics?

     c. Do they actively consider other points of view?

2. Is the employee's orientation long-term or short-term?

3. Is the employee's demeanor professional? Judgmental? Confrontational?

     a. Do they treat others with respect?

4. Does the employee convey understanding and sensitivity toward each target audience's personality type?

5. Are commitments followed through in a timely fashion?

Knowledge Ambassador

1. What is their knowledge of their own products and support?

2. What is the level of personal knowledge they have of the target audience (important family events, personality types, professional anniversaries)?

3. How is their knowledge of the customer/target audience's business?

     a. Do they know and understand the customer's business problems/needs?

     b. Does the employee know the customer's competitors?

     c. Are the buying influences inside the customer's company known?

     d. Do they know the customer's customer and business trends?

4. Do they know and understand the customer's business problems/needs?

5. Does the employee have a good understanding of national or global business trends?
   a. Are they familiar with international trade conditions that might affect the customer?
   b. Are they aware of regulatory, governmental, legal, financial, technical, or social trends that might impact the customer's business?
   c. Do they know growth markets/opportunities that could benefit the customer?

Experience Ambassador

1. Does the employee demonstrate the ability to share key lessons with colleagues?
2. Does the employee invite input and feedback?
3. Does the employee strive for results at both the individual and team levels?
4. Does the employee have a reputation for thinking about, understanding, and implementing a total customer *experience*?
   a. Are customer needs understood and reviewed throughout the relationship?
   b. Are resources properly identified and assigned based on customer needs?
   c. Are any service or related response gaps identified?
   d. Is role playing, if appropriate, used with the customer team prior to working directly with the customer?
5. Does the employee solve problems, not point fingers?
   a. Do members of the team become involved in identifying, recommending, and solving problems?

Organization

Continuing with *formal* aspects of culture building, let's look at the role of organization. Since "organization" suggest more than one person, this ingredient is designated as *group*. Organization encompasses both the formal organizational structure in a company (hierarchies, reporting lines, job titles), and teams within (department, cross-departmental). As companies grow, organizational structures mature and departments are added and expanded. Departments, such as marketing, R&D, sales, and finance, are collections of individuals with functional expertise (silos, as many managers call them). Within departments, expertise may still vary. For example, a global brand's marketing department may include vertical experts in market research, marketing communications, customer development, marketing strategy, and product marketing. Furthermore, such companies usually duplicate part of their marketing organization in different offices around the world simply because it is too large a responsibility for one group in the home country to manage everything. At the same time, a corporate marketing department is usually the central decision-making body for issues related to marketing strategy and global brand direction. Each individual country's marketing group would then take the corporate-level direction and adapt it to local conditions, which means that local marketing experts, versed in the unique business conditions and cultures of that country, may be needed. Similar kinds of functional expertise variations occur in most large company departments and are then partially replicated in offices around the world.

Cross-functional teams are also frequently used. These differ from functional departments because teams may need a variety of skills to address a specific need. For example, customer-centric teams could include: lead account manager (in charge of keeping that customer happy), sales, operations, logistics, support, and delivery. Senior management may create internal teams and designate people from different departments to tackle an important issue (such as improving process efficiency; getting involved with corporate social responsibility initiatives; developing training programs; or even brainstorming new ideas).

Matrix organizations offer another variation on organizational structure. Here, employees may report directly into their vertical department leader and indirectly (perhaps because of a team project on which they are working outside the department) have reporting relationships with managers in other departments and even other geographies.[17]

David Aaker points out that Procter & Gamble's (P&G) organizational approach to brand management has adapted over the years to constantly changing external business conditions, as well as to its internal decision-making needs. In the 1980s, P&G shifted from a product silo structure, with individual brand managers, to a category management approach. The category manager took on responsibility for all the brands within a given category. In the 1990s the company's 11 categories were run by a global category team chaired by an Executive Vice President (EVP) who was the *de facto* global category manager. The EVPs had four regional category managers reporting to them, each of whom was responsible for that product category in their particular region. This individual also had a line job (meaning profit-and-loss responsibility for a specific business). In the 2000s, P&G gave the global category manager even greater authority over the global category in order to speed up the decision-making process.[18]

The variations on formal group structures are many and it is beyond the scope of this book to discuss them in depth. But the important point is that organizational structures have a profound influence on the culture of the company by prescribing reporting formalities, interdepartmental relationships, and internal protocols. Unquestionably, these formalities shape part of the company's culture, which can and does ultimately affect how the company delivers on market expectations. While "organization" is not a new concept, tying it more directly to brand building, rather than decoupling internal operations from external brand building, can and does have a positive effect on long-term brand value.

Top performing teams and departments succeed because they have a clear understanding of their responsibility and the roles of team members. At the same time, teams must have a leader who sets the direction for the team. For most companies, brand building is still the purview of marketing, which is led by a senior executive, increasingly known as *chief marketing officer* (CMO), although vice-president of marketing is a common marketing leadership title as well. For CMOs to be effective, they must have visible CEO and senior management support and sufficient authority to make and act on major decisions that affect the brand-building effort. Senior management must help to break through functional silos and organizational barriers to create a smoother path to brand-building success. To succeed, CMOs cannot operate alone because their jobs require ongoing interaction with their executive colleagues and coordinating activities among the various departments in support of the company's branding efforts. Companies must pay close attention to how they communicate the CMO's role, from the CEO on down. Chief marketing officers must use a significant part of their time educating people internally about the benefits, risks, and role of marketing in the corporate brand-building effort. This is important because marketing is so often viewed as purely tactical, using basic price discounts and advertising approaches to boost business. The reality is far different, with marketing a set of strategic and tactical plans designed to build brand value at several levels: corporate, category, and product. These plans will work best if they are closely coordinated with other departments and if those departments are aware of the contribution made by marketing. The CMO leads the overall marketing effort by describing direction and establishing strategic objectives, with marketing management the next level down in the organization responsible for making more detailed plans for their respective regions and/or product categories, which are in alignment with the CMO's overall plan. The marketing managers find themselves frequently leading and working in cross-functional teams in which team members must carry out brand-building plans yet do not report directly to the marketing managers. Enforcing action with vague authority is a regular and ongoing challenge for marketing managers and CMO's everywhere. Yet there is little question that brand building will be handicapped if marketing is not clearly understood as a vital function inside the company. Senior management starting with the CEO, must publicly affirm the importance of the CMO and their role as guardian of the brand.

Whether within marketing's functional structure or in support of other team-based activities, there are certain factors that set successful teams apart from others, illustrated by Figure 7-3.[19]

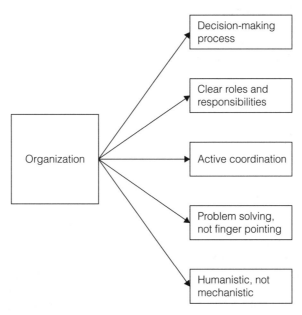

Figure 7-3   Organization Success Factors

For the sake of clarity and consistency, departments are defined as functional areas of expertise with vertical reporting lines (marketing, finance, HR, customer service) and teams are defined as cross-functional organisms designed to work on a specific issue or need (customer account management, category management, internal process teams). Departments are generally easier to structure and organize than teams, with clear lines of authority because most companies have some variation on the executive/management/nonmanagement hierarchy. There are, of course, many variations on these themes but our intent is to discuss success factors for organizations where people work together, rather than the specific merits of different organizational approaches.

Decision-Making Process

Successful organizations breed a decision-making culture at every level. This is not to suggest that lower performing companies always suffer from the inability to make decisions, although one can understand why this might be true. Instead, successful brand cultures consciously develop a decision-making *process* that works for them. Nike evolved in the 2000s from a product-driven business model, to a consumer-focused model organized around category management. Category managers lead cross-functional teams of managers from design and development. Interestingly, each of these functional managers reports through both their vertical bosses as well as into their horizontal category teams. Coordination in decision-making is paramount to avoid confusion and delays. Decision-making is aided by deadlines that are fixed every product season, and category teams know that they must have products ready for retail delivery by a certain launch date. Working backwards from this date, the category teams have several pre-launch deadlines that occur in sequence until the products are delivered to retailers. These deadlines include: product design briefs, preliminary designs, models, materials sourcing, preliminary line reviews, final product line reviews, sales meeting samples, and retail delivery. A similar planning sequence occurs with the marketing communications that are created to support key categories and statement products within. Category teams know they cannot miss a deadline without severe consequences, which imposes a disciplined decision-making process that every team follows. There is enough latitude in this process to allow for internal debate and discussion, enabling team members to refine the product line throughout the process.

Clear Roles and Responsibilities

Roles and responsibilities are conferred on the team itself as well as on the individual members within. Key questions that must be addressed with any team are: why is it here; and what is its purpose? This must be understood before team members are selected. With team members, roles and responsibilities can be related to job title but often are not. In classic command-and-control hierarchies, the CEO gives orders to the Vice Presidents, who then command the Managers, who then tell the staff what to do. It is clear who does what. But in many organizations, including many discussed throughout this book, job title does not always equate with authority, particularly *when team members come together for a specific project*. In this instance, teams may consist of like-rank managers from different departments, in which case authority can be vested in the department primarily responsible for the project outcome. On the other hand, team authority may be determined by the team members themselves in the early stages of sorting out their work. Irrespective of the team structure, everyone must have a clear understanding of their reason for being on the team and their potential contribution and, at some point, a team leader must be determined. Finally, senior management must also be clear in their expectations of the project *and* what compensation or other rewards are to be extended to team members for their effort and results. Without senior management support, many cross-functional teams quickly fail since there is no obvious incentive or purpose for the project.

Active Coordination

Closely related to the decision-making process and roles/responsibilities are the coordination mechanisms that occur among and between team members. Coordination describes the level of specificity, deeper and more detailed than roles and responsibilities, which prescribes how and when team members will collaborate, how the work progress will be tracked, and how team members will be notified when any aspect of the project is off schedule. This often involves a combination of formal and informal discussions, determined by the team itself. For software companies, project roadmaps, which schedule the various stages of a product's development from concept to commercialization, assign highly detailed requirements to every team member, including "milestone" dates. In between formal meetings, teams use collaborative software tools that enable any team member from anywhere in the world to update their individual contributions for the rest of the team to see. Progress can be easily and visually tracked. Slowdowns and delays are immediately apparent to other team members, which is important because many software projects require engineers to write code in a particular sequence before it moves onto the next engineer.

Problem Solving, Not Finger Pointing

The CEO of a large insurance company that had been consistently ranked as one of Fortune Magazine's "Best Places to Work" once said that the secret to their success is a team-based culture in which everyone is expected to solve problems and not point fingers. As often as this sentiment is heard and discussed in management circles, it is harder to practice. Assigning blame may help a person deflect criticism but the problem itself remains. Teams driven by an ambitious goal, with a clear purpose, known rewards for contributions made, and dynamic interaction among team members, are almost naturally inclined to a problem-solving mindset. Active coordination allows team members to know how their fellow teammates are proceeding and, since they are working toward a common objective, are willing to help when someone needs it. Ongoing problems are dealt with at the team level and/or between the individual and the team leader privately, enabling the team's focus to remain on finishing their work. Problem-solving cultures tend to be more positive as well, whereas finger pointing serves as a poison that undermines teams and, ultimately as it spreads, organizations.

Humanistic, Not Mechanistic

Successful teams are collections of talented people, selected because they are the right people for the particular issue being addressed. A great deal of thought should and does go into developing a team, just as it does to build a highly competent functional department. Team members are talented people with their own ambitions, desires, and perhaps even reservations about being on the team. Senior management must treat teams accordingly and not as a group of unknown slot-fillers akin to a number or a machine. The people on the team need to know that their work is being evaluated and is considered valuable, and that their individual selection was purposeful (as opposed to assigning someone to a project because management didn't know what else to do with them).

EXAMPLE 7-5:

Grupo Modelo

Grupo Modelo (see Chapter 6 for more information) organizes its beer business into 10 divisions, with each division responsible for its own part of the beer product process, allowing the company to control the quality of their beer production. The challenge is how to achieve efficiency and coordination across each of these divisions. To facilitate communications and coordination each division reports directly to the headquarters, Diblo, the primary holding company for Modelo's businesses.[20] Within Diblo, the executive board is the decision-making authority and each board member is in charge of a specific area of the business, and in turn reports directly to the CEO, Carlos Fernández. Such vertical integration assists in maintaining an efficient communication channel with its various divisions. CEO Fernández has worked with the company for 13 years, rising from junior management before assuming the post of CEO in 1997. His tenure has given him significant first-hand experience operating within the company, helping understand the operational differences and challenges of each division.[21] Part of the corporate culture and human resources philosophy is a strong commitment to recruiting and training top employees, highlighted by a campaign to recruit the best students from Mexican universities. Modelo also sends its brewing masters to top universities to learn the latest brewing techniques, in an ongoing effort to maintain the quality of its beer through knowledge accumulation and subsequent transfer to succeeding generations of management.[22] High performance teams are also used throughout to improve the company. To reinforce their ambitions, Grupo Modelo launched a "blue-band policy" in which each employee was given a blue wristband with the message "winning is the only option" serving as a perennial source of motivation.[23] Reflecting his personal belief in essentially walking the talk, CEO Fernández wears the same blue band worn by every Grupo Modelo employee.[24]

Questions to ask when reviewing the organizational aspects of brand culture building include:

1. Is our formal organizational structure well suited to reinforcing our brand reputation and development?
   a. If not, what should be changed?
2. Are the reporting practices conducive to supporting decisions on behalf of building the brand?
   a. If not, how can they be improved without undermining necessary responsibilities?
3. Who "owns" the brand-building effort? Marketing? The chief marketing officer? Somebody else? No one?
   a. Identify the known leaders in this effort.
   b. Do the brand builders have sufficient resources and related corporate support (financial, senior management buy-in, and visible support)?
4. How do our various departments align with and support our brand-building efforts?
5. What could we improve organizationally that would have a lasting and positive impact on our brand(s)? Be specific and include potential implications.
6. Is senior management an active proponent and supporter of brand building?
7. Do departments understand their roles in supporting brand objectives?
8. Look at each of the five organizational success factors. Review your teams and departments and assess how effective they are in each area.

Social Fabric

Social fabric describes the unwritten, *informal* communications that permeate every organization and create the social atmosphere that guides community and *group* behavior. The proverbial conversations around the water cooler, in the hallways, in between meetings, and during breaks are when and where a company's social fabric comes to life. Social fabric serves as an informal governor of proper etiquette, behavior, and decision-making inside a company and, at a macro level, is where the heart of the company's personality exists and is lived by each employee everyday. Social fabric is also influenced and guided by opinion leaders and similar influencers inside the company. Sometimes these individuals do not have formal title authority but they have informal influence over other individuals and groups that is often as powerful and effective in getting the business of the company accomplished. Interestingly, unstructured and subjective social fabric is often where a company's reputation, beyond its known expertise, is grounded. When we think of companies, a mental image automatically arises. While this includes a familiar product, logo, or well-known slogan, the company's personality resurfaces as well. Chapter 5 discussed *personality* in the context of the company's Destiny, which is essentially a strategic understanding of the brand, similar to how people describe another person's personality (conservative, innovative, quick, methodical). Social fabric describes the human interactions that both shape and add depth to the personality. In other words, Virgin can be described overall as a vibrant, colorful company. But the thousands of daily, informal conversations and group behaviors (social fabric) within both shape and are influenced by this personality, just as an individual's personality both influences and is the result of innumerable personal decisions, behaviors, and interactions. Two companies can be described as *creative* and yet have two entirely different social fabrics that engender each firm's creativity. Using another metaphor to help instill the concept of social fabric, consider an actual textile fabric, such as silk. Upon observation, silk feels smooth—the equivalent of its personality as described by Destiny. A closer examination reveals the type and quality of fiber, and the tightness and intricacy of the weave, which are analogous to the social fabric. Both Destiny and Culture are aspects of the brand's personality. Whereas one is based on broad descriptors, the other is based on the detailed textures and ingredients that give rise to the descriptors.

A company's social fabric can be better understood by examining these issues:

1. How would the company's social atmosphere be described (rigid, loose, creative, practical, friendly, serious)?
2. Are informal conversations encouraged?
3. Who are the opinion leaders and key influencers inside the company?
4. What are the main ingredients in the company's culture that shape its personality?
5. Are the answers to each of these questions consistent with the firm's overall personality? Why or why not?

EXAMPLE 7-6:

IKEA

IKEA has built a reputation for hiring assertive individuals, with a positive attitude towards their work, which founder Ingvar Kamprad proudly describes as "'Why?' Sayers"—people who are naturally curious and are not afraid to ask questions. Employees are encouraged to take the initiative and challenge established patterns by proposing solutions for improving the company. The company's well-known informal culture includes using only first names and forbids management to wear ties. Titles and status are de-emphasized in favor of group support and camaraderie. Kamprad himself has no priority parking when visiting IKEA's many stores. Remarking on the impact of his leadership on IKEA's culture, he once said. "If there is such a thing as good leadership, it is to give a good example. I have to do so for all the IKEA employees."

He is also a firm believer in trying out new ideas for the sake of helping customers and improving IKEA's stores: "Only those who are asleep make no mistakes."

IKEA's brand value has risen from US$6 billion in 2001 to US$10.9 billion in 2008, an 81% increase.[25]

Internal Branding

Building a brand culture involves identifying the right people and creating organizational mechanisms that promote a combination of strong individual behaviors and team-based capabilities that support and reflect the overall values and reputation of the brand. But there is more to do to build a brand culture: the brand must be completely understood internally. In essence, the brand must be brought to life for employees, making the company more than just a place to do work and earn a living. Employees must believe that the work they are doing is worthwhile. This does not mean that every day must be exciting and fun. But employees must see the connection between their work and the company's reputation and results, just as athletes know when their efforts contribute to the team's victory. The benefit is that employees develop an emotional bond with the company that transcends the more rudimentary work/pay dynamic, which can give rise to greater effort and commitment toward supporting the brand.

Marketers, and senior management, must recognize that internal marketing is far more than describing the latest marketing campaign. Such an approach is a one-way message that is passively received by the audience. Just as this book emphasizes the importance of creating a brand *experience* for customers, employees must be part of their own internal brand experience. To make any internal branding effort more credible with employees and, as a result, garnering broader and deeper support, senior management (including the CEO) must explicitly endorse and regularly support the internal branding programs. Internal branding can succeed without overt CEO support but the effort takes on far less importance because the lack of public interest from senior management suggests indifference. Of course, dictums from on high, while helpful, can be far more powerful if employees themselves are directly involved is aspects of internal branding.

Five Es of Internal Branding

Several important findings came out of the research for this book with regard to successful internal branding. Called the "5 Es", each "E" is a component of the internal branding process.

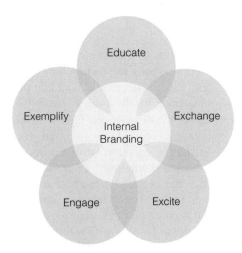

Figure 7-4 Internal Branding

Educate

The first step in any internal branding campaign is analogous to the launch of a new product: create awareness. With customers, part of awareness building involves educating them about the product. The same concept applies to internal branding. Educating employees about the brand, or a new branding initiative, is the first step to gaining their acceptance, although this stage is too early for them to endorse and embrace it wholeheartedly. When students take a new course in school, the instructor does not tell them everything in one day. Instead, the students are given important information in stages to help them construct their own understanding of the topic—this helps them absorb the material more thoughtfully. For internal branding, connecting employees to the brand and its heritage is part of the education process, just as those same things are crucial to connecting to customers.

One method that worked well at a number of top brands was relaying information in a storylike fashion. Not in the sense of a tall tale or fantasy world but in the more symbolic meaning that the company is on a multi-chapter adventure and the internal branding is another way of helping the story develop. This approach is useful in making any internal branding more personal and less corporate, or "slick." In a literal sense, some companies even have people responsible for keeping the company's history and traditions alive, adding to the legends that have made the company famous over time. Their role is that of storyteller, working with new employees during orientation and speaking to existing employees during important company events and presentations. The storyteller role is found throughout history and used by various civilizations as a means to convey tales of great sacrifice, challenge, and achievement. Storytellers were also, literally, chroniclers of their times. Pindar was a poet in Ancient Greek times. Among his interests was writing odes to the Ancient Olympic Games, which celebrated accomplishment, told of tragedy, and warned of grave consequences for the ill behaved. Today's brand storytellers keep track of the ongoing developments and innovations that continue the company's success, and it is a useful approach for educating employees.

Exchange

While the education stage sets the basis for understanding, exchange means inviting employees to share their ideas. Since the internal branding process is still in the early stage, one should not expect a groundswell of input, partly because some people don't like to be put on the spot. Part of the success with the exchange stage is providing alternative avenues for idea exchange to occur. From townhall meetings, to one on one, to email, to suggestion boxes—all can be effective without intimidating people. The important point of exchange is to transition employees from the education phase to the early participation phase where they can begin to actually shape and influence the internal branding. It is crucial, however, to do this well by encouraging exchange gently, in a way that makes employees feel as if they are part of something special and not being "sold" or coerced. If a company's culture is not familiar with internal marketing, the first attempts will feel stifled and awkward. But pursued with good intentions and transparent explanations, internal confidence will increase and skepticism will diminish. Just as having a clear

Destiny helps employees understand their company's larger "cause" and how they fit in, internal branding helps employees even more by reminding them not just how they fit in but how they contribute, giving meaning to their work. Any internal branding must be done in ways consistent with the company's values, personality, and heritage. Employees will know whether an internal campaign smacks of insincerity or whether it reinforces the true values of the company.

Excite

Companies that market externally attract customers. Companies that market internally *win over* employees. An absence of marketing will kill a product, no matter how good, and the same is true internally. So just like any customer-facing campaign, the "secret" to internal branding success is to be visible and interesting, otherwise no one will know what to expect, let alone care. Employees are already aware of the internal branding and some are informally exchanging ideas, so now the opportunity is to bring the internal branding campaign to life in a more multidimensional way. This effort should incorporate a sense of adventure and imagination. Show employees that they are participants, not observers. To excite and inspire employees use all the tools possible to help spread the internal branding effort (without falling prey to overcommunication or, worse, loud/noisy/attention-getting communication). The benefit is that internal marketing efforts ensure that everyone is "on the same page" and is not surprised by advertising, promotions, and customer requests seeking more information. Of course, by exciting employees through a thoughtful marketing campaign directed to them, they are also seeing and experiencing their own brand in new ways . . . the essence of brand experience.

A division of Transamerica (now owned by Aegon, the Dutch insurance giant) called Transamerica Intellitech (which specialized in real estate data and information), was undergoing a multiyear rebranding effort that included a name change, acquisitions, new products, and new marketing communications. Employees throughout the company were asked what they would need to improve their jobs in support of the company's rebranding. The resulting feedback led to the development of a company intranet site that described all new products, marketing, and customer data, making it easier for employees fully to understand the various rebranding initiatives of the company. A good portion of the information, data, and marketing communications on the site came directly from employees, involving them directly in this effort and creating a sense of ownership that enable the intranet to grow organically with ongoing employee-drive updates.

Engage

Engaging involves employees in directly working on projects in support of the internal branding, beyond exchanging ideas. This does not have to be pure marketing-related involvement in the traditional sense. Engagement can also be through contributions made to new products, or new processes, or hiring new people, or speaking at a conference, each of which contributes to making the brand stronger. Joie de Vivre Hotels conducts annual internal surveys of their employees to gauge their enjoyment of the work. The results are discussed with all employees internally at offsite meetings in which they work together in teams to find ways to improve their Joie de Vivre experience so that the brand comes to life for them.

Exemplify

After the *thinking* (education and exchange) and *doing* (excite and engage), there is the *living*, meaning the demonstration by all employees of their deep commitment and understanding of the special place where they work. This is exemplified through improvements in quality, new ideas generated, coworker enthusiasm, customer appreciation, and market/societal recognition. Every time an employee demonstrates the values and quality of the brand, that employee is helping build brand value internally and externally. Superlative efforts should be recognized and rewarded by senior management. Over time, employees will become familiar with internal awards, further enhancing their meaning and value while reinforcing the esteem and respect accorded those that win recognition.

Managing the Brand Throughout the Company

Building a global brand has strengths and challenges from a management and company culture perspective. Strengths include:

- consistent brand image;
- common marketing plans and activities;
- leverage budgets effectively.

Challenges commonly fall into the PEST framework:

- political;
- economic;
- socio-cultural;
- technological.

The combination of strengths and challenges in every market will affect how a company plans, develops, and implements its brand strategy. Let's look more closely.

Strengths

Consistent Brand Image

By focusing on a single, clear brand image, companies can ensure a more consistent and streamlined approach to managing all aspects of the brand because resources are allocated to a specific set of needs. A clear brand image means that the brand has the same, well-understood reputation everywhere. Nokia has established a global leadership position as the number one mobile phone brand, despite the success of competing products from Apple and Blackberry. Nokia's success is attributed to a relentless focus on mobile communications, quality, and innovation.[26]

Common Marketing Plans and Activities

Having a clear brand image helps management align marketing processes and develop specific marketing programs that communicate the brand's attributes to each market in which it competes. Such a standard approach ensures relative consistency because every company office will use the same basic marketing programs in its own country. Rolex, the largest luxury watch brand in the world, has common marketing plans and activities in every market, based on a central theme of luxury, hand craftsmanship, and association with celebrities and elite athletes.[27]

Leverage Budgets Effectively

With a universal brand strategy and common marketing plans, management can more effectively allocate financial resources, which can then be more easily leveraged because marketing activities will be concentrated around common brand themes. This may also simplify the choice of marketing measures marketers use to evaluate the success of their various marketing programs. IKEA has built a global brand based on well designed, affordable, and disposable furniture. IKEA product designs must be easy to ship in the smallest possible flat packages so that shipping costs and inventory storage are kept to a minimum for all of its stores. IKEA focuses its marketing on creating positive in-store experiences for customers with ready-to-go product availability, restaurants, and kids' centers, all designed to keep families engaged and encourage more time spent shopping. IKEA keeps more traditional marketing expenditures in advertising and promotion to a minimum as well. The end result is positive word of mouth generated by customers.[28]

Challenges

Any company intent on building a consistent brand operating in multiple countries confronts challenges owing to differences in culture, labor practices, political stability, economic progress, legal and regulatory structures, and technological adoption. Each of these challenges makes the development of a consistent global brand tricky and, despite the desire for simplicity, complex to implement for organizational and logistical reasons.

When companies are smaller, managing and communicating the brand's meaning, product updates, and marketing messages to other employees is more controllable than with larger, geographically dispersed corporations. While a company may have a known identity and reputation, translating it successfully across cultures requires thorough marketing planning, just as a new product launch requires planning that reflects a deep understanding of each customer audience in different markets so that corresponding adjustments in marketing programs can be made to ensure wider acceptance. Language issues and cultural differences, particularly around lifestyles, may prevent a brand's marketing message from having the same impact as it does in its home market, compelling marketing management to tailor its message to fit the needs of different countries better. Yet any adjustment also means a possible departure from brand consistency and adds to the complexity of execution because even the basic creation of marketing communications tools will require more resources to accommodate the needs of different markets, let alone different media buying and consumer behavior preferences.

Internally, challenges to developing brand consistency are also inevitable. Employees, from entry to CEO, may understand intellectually what the brand stands for but may interpret it differently in their specific circumstances. Brand execution may vary in different markets as a result. This can be compounded by organizational boundaries. Some companies are more decentralized than others, which makes brand-related coordination an even bigger challenge as operations away from headquarters located in different countries will not always feel they have to march to HQ's orders because, they may argue, their country situation is unique and requires a different business approach. While this may produce local success, it also risks fragmenting the brand's meaning and reputation. There are several methods for minimizing brand fragmentation, especially in larger, complex organizations (although small to mid-size companies would find these useful as well):

1. Get regular, overt, public CEO and senior management support.
2. Assign senior executives to vertical and horizontal roles.
3. Plan for an internal branding budget that provides for creative communications.
4. Develop an internal communications and information dissemination process.
5. Use company events to revisit brand issues and update on new programs.
6. Regularly measure so that progress and performance are always known.

- *Get regular, overt, public CEO and senior management support.* Strong, obvious support from senior management is one of the keys to ensuring that branding challenges are overcome, both internally and externally. There is always internal tension in organizations between different departments, which can be quite healthy and is not always destructive. Nevertheless, greater credibility is conferred on any department that has the clear support of the CEO. When a CEO hires a new CMO (as SAP, the German enterprise software firm, did in 1999 when the CEO at the time hired Sony's former Playstation marketer), it strongly suggests to the rest of the company the importance of marketing's role in the enterprise.[29]
- *Assign senior executives to vertical and horizontal roles.* When a manager has only vertical responsibilities, they naturally focus on maximizing the performance of their own product line. Such a structure may produce strong financial results for each product line but each will also act more independently of the others, which can fragment a brand. But when an executive has both vertical (i.e. product line) and horizontal (i.e. across categories) responsibilities, it can create a larger organizational understanding of the various demands each brand or product category has and compels business leaders to think more openly about how to facilitate a more cohesive brand reputation. Procter & Gamble does this, with senior executives in charge of both vertical businesses and broader categories. In P&G's case, this improves decision-making speed and effectiveness.[30]
- *Plan for an internal branding budget that provides for creative communications.* No amount of customer communications will succeed if a company, its products, and its

employees fail to deliver on expectations. Delivery failure is partly caused by poorly designed internal communications, poor internal education, and poor engagement with employees. Internal branding can be a significant help but it requires as much ingenuity and varied communication tools as external branding, which means it also requires that more money is allocated for it. Alternatively, if additional funds are not available, marketing has a responsibility to think more creatively about how to communicate internally.

- *Develop an internal communications and information dissemination process.* Brand consistency is supported by a clear process for communicating and sharing information, both formally and informally. When employees have known company events to attend, it can serve as a motivating reward, assuming the company has done its job well with creative communications and building a reputation for great products. Nike communicates constantly to its employees around the world through four annual meetings, regional meetings, regular training, local workshops, department meetings, off-site gatherings and more. Additionally, Nike's corporate headquarters in Beaverton, Oregon is a living celebration of sports and fitness, with each building named after a famous Nike athlete, and wide variety of sports facilities on campus for employee use, ranging from tennis courts to a fitness center, indoor basketball court, swimming pool, and miles of running trails.[31]

- *Use company events to revisit brand issues and update on new programs.* From large to small, company gatherings provide another point of communication to repeat key messages and inform of updates and changes. Management should be cautious to avoid inundating employees with too much information—as with any marketing communication, too much can be bad. Instead, designing communication that fits the occasion and does not mindlessly trot out the same message can serve as a productive way to reinforce key themes. REI is a retailer of outdoor recreation products (including tents, backpacking gear, mountain bikes, kayaks). Its corporate culture is devoted to taking care of the environment and having a passion for the outdoors. Employees regularly go on outings together, as well as longer adventures. The events serve as team-bonding opportunities, chances to use and discuss company products, and learn about the latest updates in the company's direction.[32]

- *Regularly measure so that progress and performance are always known.* Internal branding must produce results to be successful, just as external branding does. However, the challenge is determining what measures to use because much of the internal branding effort is intended to inspire greater commitment and belief in the company, as opposed to generating sales. Surveys and brand audits can help companies evaluate the success of their programs, as the MAS Holdings example will illustrate shortly. Longer term surveys designed to measure financial performance gains tied to internal programs can be useful, but the programs have to be deployed over many years to have any measurable impact, so patience will be required. Nevertheless, interim goals can be developed that give directional indications of internal branding success.[33]

Managing a brand internally offers many of the same strengths and challenges as it does when reaching external customer markets.

Brand Culture Interactivity

The four components of brand culture, *competencies*, *organization*, *behaviors*, and *social fabric* are not isolated or independent from each other. Hiring competent people will not necessarily lead to the development of a well-structured and effective organization, just as practicing the behaviors of top individual performers will not always lead to a positive and productive social dynamic. Instead, the overall sense of *culture* comes from the ongoing interplay and interactivity across and among the four components. This interplay is not orchestrated, at least not in the scripted formal sense. Yet successful brand cultures do perform like professional orchestras. In an orchestra, musicians must be competent with their respective instrument while also performing in an organized fashion, as guided by the musical score and conductor. At the same time, individuals must be among the very best in their field and behave with confidence while also directly connected to and sensitive to the social dynamic between and among musicians. Random solos would undermine the collective musical effort, just as renegade company performers might impair the company's ability to maintain a consistent, quality reputation. But at the same time, both successful orchestras and brands allow enough individual interpretation (through solo performances and individual initiative) that enhances and distinguishes the overall organization. This interplay can be seen in innumerable ways, depending on which company one examines. MAS Holdings, the apparel manufacturer from Sri Lanka mentioned briefly in Chapter 5, provides a useful illustration.

EXAMPLE 7-7:

MAS Holdings[34]

MAS Holdings started in 1987 and is an apparel manufacturer headquartered in Colombo, Sri Lanka. Founded by three brothers, Mahesh, Ajay, and Sharad Amalean, the company had 45 000 employees, 30 manufacturing facilities, and sales of US$700 million in 2008. Its corporate clients are a *Who's Who* of the world's leading brands, including Nike, Speedo, Reebok, Victoria's Secret, Adidas, The Gap, and Marks & Spencer. From its founding, the three brothers were determined to make MAS different by treating all employees with dignity because they believed it was the right thing to do. While they did not plan it, their efforts began changing the reputation of manufacturing companies from "sweatshops" to beacons of corporate social responsibility. They developed consistently high standards for the treatment of employees (more than 80% of whom are women), working conditions, benefits, and career opportunities. Manufacturing operations are located in or near local towns so that workers can live at home rather than a company-supplied dormitory. Onsite, the facilities are air conditioned, well lit, with free meals during working shifts. The company provides transportation to and from the facilities.

Culture

All MAS working conditions meet standards set by the UN Global Impact. In 2003, the company launched Women Go Beyond, a program designed to celebrate the achievements of their female workers. The program focuses on three areas of their female employees' lives:

- Personal care and motivation of employees—which emphasizes the employees' work quality and addresses issues like "are they doing good work while demonstrating care and concern for their responsibilities and for their fellow workers?"
- The community surrounding MAS—which focuses on the local villages and families near each MAS facility, answering "are they good community citizens?"
- Society as a whole—which deals with, in essence, "are they demonstrating care and concern for the larger, common good?"

Women Go Beyond is geared to promoting the advancement of women's careers. In addition to the areas mentioned above, MAS Holdings provided annual training in job and leadership skills, as well as work/life-balance issues. Female employees were recognized each quarter and from those winners an annual Women Go Beyond winner was selected. Particularly noteworthy is the selection process for the Women Go Beyond winners: their fellow employees, not senior management, nominate them. They are then interviewed by a diverse range of people, from the corporate board to local celebrities to women's rights activists.

To market the program and winners, MAS hired a local marketing agency to produce brochures and posters. A large awards ceremony is held at a local convention center, which includes entertainment from each of the manufacturing facilities, with the awards given out by leading pillars of Sri Lankan society. The end result is that the Women Go Beyond program serves to recognize and reward remarkable female employees while also acting as an aspirational tool for other workers and a unique culture-building catalyst.

Women Go Beyond costs MAS US$50,000 per year to support.

Results

Women Go Beyond has gained favorable reviews in the market. MAS Holdings has received numerous international awards and recognition. The American Apparel and Footwear Association gave MAS the Excellence in Corporate Social Responsibility for Women's Issues award. The United Nations (UN) recognized Women Go Beyond as a recognized "good practice." In 2006, 616 Women Go Beyond programs were run for nonmanagement employees at MAS's various facilities, with each employee seeing an average of 4.2 exposures per program. This translates into a sizable number of exposures to this program and made Women Go Beyond synonymous with success and achievement at MAS Holdings. More importantly, 71% of employees in 2006 said that the program made a significant difference in their lives. This increased to 85% in 2007. MAS senior management conducted a survey of its directors and managers in 2006 in which 63% stated that they perceived the program favorably and that it had made a positive impact on their lives. This rose to 82% in 2007.

Externally, MAS's key customers agreed that ethical sourcing was vital for their own reputation, so they looked to MAS's efforts as significant and positive. Each customer gave Women Go Beyond very high ratings because it set standards for the apparel manufacturing industry and for the proper treatment of employees within. In 2006, MAS launched a new program that emphasizes environmental sustainability, called "Eco Go Beyond," targeted to teenagers in school. The Eco Go Beyond program has taught sustainability to 15 000 teens in 30 schools near MAS's various manufacturing facilities. The Gap also started its own program called "Gap Go Beyond" in which they conduct community outreach workshops to female entrepreneurs in the communities near MAS facilities. The specific financial gains resulting from Women Go Beyond are still unknown.

Measurement

Measuring human performance is subject to numerous variables that mean that objective precision is not always feasible. It is particularly challenging to measure behaviors with precision. Instead, 360-degree evaluations with subordinates, supervisors, colleagues, and even customers can paint a more complete behavioral picture. Each company should devise its own measures based on the culture-building objectives that it has for its brand and the corresponding performance targets set by senior management. Nevertheless, there are some measures that, at a strategic level, can indicate whether the company's culture-building efforts are paying off. Of course, these can be modified for functional and departmental-level needs, depending on each company's situation. We will look at:

- recruiting;
- sales/profits per employee;
- turnover rate.

Recruiting

Metric
Recruiting.[35]

Brand Culture Benefits
Helps gauge how many applicants are required to fill key positions, assisting management in determining recruiting effectiveness.

How
The recruiting measure uses hiring trends in prior years to project the likely number of candidates required for the current hiring needs.

Formula

$$R = \frac{H}{S \times A}$$

Where
R = recruiting;

H = new hires required;
S = percentage of recruits selected;
A = percentage who accept.

Impact on Brand Culture

Recruiting is an important activity in building brand culture, for obvious reasons, and management must carefully plan the time and people resources required to do an effective job. No matter how large the organization, recruiting requires a keen sense of the following:

- the company's culture;
- the employee personalities that would fit the company's culture;
- the skills of recruits sought;
- a clear hiring process for the recruit, which is explained upfront;
- a thoughtful description of the job;
- a set of interview questions designed to identify the best possible candidates for the company;
- the professional will to stick to the company's overall recruiting standards and not settle on talent less qualified than needed.

Sales/Profits per Employee

Metric

Sales/profits per employee (SPPE).[36]

Brand Culture Benefits

SPPE determines the financial contribution in terms of revenues and/or profits per employee, which helps management understand how productive employees are.

How

Total sales, total profits, and total number of full-time employees are the three simple variables required.

Formula

$$SPPE = \frac{S \; or \; P}{E}$$

Where
SPPE = sales/profit per employee;
S = total sales;
P = total profits;
E = total number of full-time employees.

Impact on Brand Culture

Sales/profits per employee is important because it measures productivity by showing the amount generated (either revenues or profits) per employee. A lower figure is an indication that either the company is over-staffed or under-productive with its employees and that, therefore, ways must be found to improve. Training might prove to be a worthwhile investment, for example—or perhaps new computer systems are needed that make operations and customer support more efficient, which can ultimately enable employees to take better care of customers.

A company's sales are likely to be somewhat cyclical during the course of the year, with certain times of the year stronger (from a revenue standpoint) than others. This will affect the SPPE figure differently at each change in the business cycle. For example, various holiday seasons are often the busiest times of the year in different countries around the world, and a sizable percentage of brand sales are generated during those times. SPPE numbers are stronger during these times as a result, which can distort the overall productivity picture for a company.

SPPE may also be misleading if industry averages are used as performance benchmarks because competitors, while offering similar products, may have very different business models and cost structures. Therefore, marketers and company managers need to consider SPPE in the context of their capabilities and asset utilization first, before comparing it to the competition. However, if a company's SPPE is dramatically different from industry norms, especially if all companies offer similar products, then it would be prudent to examine the reasons behind the differences more closely as this may suggest that longer term challenges need correcting to remain competitive.

Turnover Rate

Metric
Turnover rate.[37]

Brand Culture Benefits
Employee turnover is expensive for any company, so management has every incentive to reduce turnover (assuming that most employees are ones they wish to keep). Employees that work together regularly, over time, can become effective teams and problem solvers, just as sports teams anchored by a core group of experienced performers can lead teams to long-term success. Of course, poor performers can and should be weeded out. But assuming the recruiting and selection process is sound, then the company should be hiring the best possible talent, so any departures can disrupt performance and cost money because new people have to be hired, trained, and integrated into the culture.

How
To measure turnover requires two metrics: number of annual departures and the total number of employees.

Formula
The turnover rate calculates the number of salesperson departures relative to the total sales force size, multiplied by 100 (to convert it to a percentage):

$$TR = \frac{D}{E} \times 100$$

Where
TR = turnover rate;
D = number of employee departures annually;
E = total number of employees (annual average).

Impact on Brand Culture
Turnover is inevitable as organizations change. The turnover rate should be reviewed in light of the company's strategic objectives to determine if the results are "acceptable." Industry and competitor comparisons may be part of any company's turnover review but caution is encouraged as these statistics are based on averages and may offer little practical guidance given each company's unique circumstances. A low turnover percentage may sound great from the HR and expense perspectives but it may also signal that a company is overly generous with its compensation, loose with its performance standards, or that management has a hard time identifying and replacing underperforming people.

Turnover is comprised of several components:

- death;
- involuntary departure (termination);
- voluntary departure (recruitment by another company);
- retirement;
- internal transfer.

Death, of course, is a form of involuntary departure. As the least controllable factor, it should not be a key management concern. Termination results from poor performance, poor employee/company fit, illegal or unethical employee behavior, or job loss due to company-wide cutbacks. Management can minimize turnover from termination if their recruiting and candidate selection criteria are clear, the interview process involves managers and colleagues from several departments, and a thorough background check is conducted. Voluntary departure may be within management's control if they are familiar with their employees and can identify sources of dissatisfaction before they grow into problems. Management may decide to respond by improving financial compensation, promoting staff, changing responsibilities, or offering other nonfinancial benefits (more days of paid vacation, for example). Any of these decisions will be weighted against the potential future value expected from the top performers that might otherwise depart. Retirement is less likely to be a significant challenge for savvy management because they will have anticipated replacing those retiring for months or even years, allowing time to recruit new employees and for succession planning. However, early retirement may occasionally surprise management, perhaps due to personal reasons from the employee. In each of these instances, management must decide whether replacement is warranted or if the departing person's responsibilities can be reassigned to other employees in the company.

Other Measures
Chapter 10 discusses more marketing communication-specific measures that are more commonly used for external campaigns yet, with minor tweaks to account for variation in media and audience, can be equally useful in assessing the success of internal branding.

Summary

This chapter emphasized a far more organizational approach to brand value enhancement by discussing the merits of building a strong brand culture. Brand culture is both a marketing and nonmarketing area of focus for any company seeking to build a brand. Brands today are far more than an external marketing communications campaign. Brands must be strong on the inside as well, if the promises made to the market are to be kept. Before internal branding, which is similar in many ways to external marketing, can be developed, companies must think about the components that create strong brand cultures. Brand management teams are an important ingredient within brand cultures in that they guide the business aspects of revenue generating offerings. Management also needs to consider how employees in every area of the company contribute to creating a strong brand culture. In this chapter, we learned about four areas that create strong cultures:

- *Competencies* (Formal Individual): qualification minimums sought in all new hires;
- *Organization* (Formal Group); organizational structure and teams;
- *Behaviors* (Informal Individual): what top performers do and how they behave;
- *Social Fabric* (Informal Group): the unwritten social norms that govern internal interactions.

Once the components of successful brand cultures are understood, management can organize its internal brand-building efforts accordingly, from people decisions to programs that help people understand, genuinely embrace, and live the brand. The emphasis on these four components is a departure for most brand management textbooks because they deal primarily with brand positioning, product management, and marketing communications. In addition to those areas, however, managers must recognize that nothing substantial will happen without an organization run by talented people who believe in the brand. This requires more than a passing mention of people management issues, hence the depth pursued in this chapter.

Discussion Questions

1. What is marketing's role in brand culture development?
2. What should senior management do to encourage a more brand-focused culture?
3. Review the latest Interbrand survey of the Best Global Brands (www.interbrand.com). Select three brands that you believe you know particularly well and describe their corporate culture. What are the qualities you associate with these companies and how would those affect their culture?
4. Discuss what the social fabric might be like. Why do you say this? Support your answer.

5. Using these same three companies, identify the competencies they are likely to seek in their employees.

6. Pick one of the companies and do further research to learn how the company is organized. What are the advantages and disadvantages of their structure? Is their structure consistent with their brand image? How are their brand management teams structured? What would you change, if anything?

7. Identify a well-known top manager (this can be a nonmarketing person) who is covered regularly in the business press and do some background research on him/her. Given what you learn, discuss how he or she compares to the five ambassadors behaviors. Where are they strongest? Weakest? Why? What can they do to improve or is it important that they improve?

8. What are the key strengths and challenges in managing brands throughout a company? What else would you add and why?

9. Review the MAS Holdings example at the end of the chapter. How would you evaluate the financial impact of the Women Go Beyond program? Would brand value be affected? If so, how? If clear linkages between this program and financial gain cannot be made, should the program be abandoned? Why or why not? How can MAS link the program to clear financial outcomes?

10. Aside from the measures described in this chapter, what other tools would you use to assess brand culture and corresponding company performance? Why?

Notes

1. Baldoni, J., *Great Communication Secrets of Great Leaders*, © 2003 McGraw-Hill, p. 64.

2. "100 Best Companies to Work For," *Fortune* magazine, February 4, 2008, retrieved August 11, 2008 from http://money.cnn.com/magazines/fortune/bestcompanies/2008/snapshots/82.html.

3. 1) Research projects conducted by students at Singapore Management University for their strategic brand management course between 2004 and 2008. 2) "Moet Hennessy and the LVMH Brand," research completed November 2007, updated November 2008. 3) Helm, B., "Best Global Brands," September 18, 2008, retrieved October 3, 2008 from two sources: www.businessweek.com/magazine/content/08_39/b4101052097769.htm?chan=magazine+channel_special+report and www.interbrand.com/best_global_brands.aspx?langid=1000. 4) Bradshaw, D., "LVMH," March 21, 2002, retrieved April 6, 2008 from http://specials.ft.com/businesseducation/march2002/FT3LWNSR2ZC.html.

4. 1) Research projects conducted by students at Singapore Management University for their strategic brand management course between 2004 and 2008. 2) "Hermès Strategic Brand Management," November 2008, Hermès' Annual Report 2007, Executive Management report, p. 26.

5. Ibid. See also "Profits Up at Luxury Group Hermes," March 19, 2009, BBCNews, retrieved May 4, 2009 from http://news.bbc.co.uk/2/hi/business/7952666.stm. Friedman, V., "Hermes May Pose as New Luxury Model," June 10, 2005, *Financial Times*, retrieved February 2, 2009 from http://articles.latimes.com/2005/jan/10/business/ft-hermes10.

6. 1) Research projects conducted by students at Singapore Management University for their strategic brand management course between 2004 and 2008. 2) "Johnson & Johnson: A Case Study," research completed November 2007, updated July 2008. 3) "2007 Best Places to Launch a Career," September 13, 2007, retrieved July 28, 2008 from www.businessweek.com/careers/bplc/2007/24.htm.

7. Ibid. See also, "Best Places to Launch a Career," Johnson & Johnson corporate web site, retrieved August 17, 2008 from www.businessweek.com/careers/bplc/2007/24.htm.

8. Ibid. Updated data retrieved February 2, 2009 from http://bwnt.businessweek.com/interactive_reports/career_launch_2008/index.asp?sortCol=rank_2007&sortOrder=2&pageNum=1&resultNum=50.

9. Ibid. See also, "Top 100 MBA Employers," *Fortune* magazine and CNNMoney.com, retrieved May 6, 2009 from http://money.cnn.com/magazines/fortune/mba100/2009/full_list/.

10. The five ambassadors are based on qualitative research of top performers (not necessarily by title) selected by senior management, then evaluated based on observed behaviors with stakeholders (customers, colleagues, shareholders, value-chain participants). The research began with interviews of CEOs and entrepreneurs of Fortune 1000 and leading entrepreneurs across several industries: entertainment, software, airlines, consumer products, manufacturing, and healthcare to identify qualities of company leaders. This led to the identification of the qualities of top performers inside corresponding organizations and has since been further developed through discussions with CEOs of companies in Asia and Europe, feedback about top sales performers in multiple industries, and university research of over 150 companies in the U.S., Europe, and Asia since 2001.

11. "Yum Brands!" Yum Brands Company web site, retrieved April 7, 2009, from www.yum.com/company/default.asp.

12. "At Yum Brands, Rewards for Good Work," Adam Bryant, *New York Times*, July 11, 2009, pp. 1–2, retrieved July 11, 2009 from www.nytimes.com/2009/07/12/business/12corner.html?_r=1&scp=2&sq=corner%20office&st=cse.

13. "Best Global Brands," Interbrand web site, retrieved July 12, 2009 from www.interbrand.com/best_global_brands.aspx?year=2008&langid=1000.

14. 1) "About Xerox," retrieved May 15, 2009 from www.xerox.com/go/xrx/portal/STServlet?projectID=ST_About_Xerox&pageID=Landing&Xcntry=USA&Xlang=en_US. 2) Bryant, A., "The Keeper of That Tapping Pen," March 21, 2009, *New York Times*, retrieved May 2, 2009 from www.nytimes.com/2009/03/22/business/22corner.html. "Best Global Brands," retrieved July 12, 2009 from www.interbrand.com/best_global_brands.aspx?year=2008&langid=1000.

15. Bryant, A., "The Keeper of That Tapping Pen," March 21, 2009, *New York Times*, retrieved May 2, 2009 from www.nytimes.com/2009/03/22/business/22corner.html, pp. 1–3.

16. Ibid.

17. Aaker, D., *Spanning Silos: The New CMO Imperative*, © 2008 Harvard Business Press, p. 38.

18. Ibid., p. 192. See also, Aaker, D. and Joachimsthaler, E., *Brand Leadership*, © 2000 David A. Aaker and Erich Joachimsthaler, The Free Press, pp. 313, 320–321.

19. The organization success factors stem from the same body of findings of the five ambassadors, both of which were part of the ongoing brand research from 2000 to 2009.

20. 1) Grupo Modelo SA de CV and subsidiaries, 2007, *Annual Report 2006*, retrieved February 12, 2008, from OneSource Database. 2) Research projects conducted by students at Singapore

Management University for their strategic brand management course between 2004 and 2008. 3) Irusta, M. A. L., April 23, 2007, *Grupo Modelo at the Beginning of the XXI Century*, case study, retrieved February 7, 2009, from www.ifama.org/conferences/2007Conference/ SymposiumPapers_files/1060_Case.pdf. 4) "History," retrieved February 2, 2008 from www. gmodelo.com.mx/index-1_en.asp?go=historia.

21. Ibid. See also "Roots of Grupo Modelo," retrieved November 15, 2007, from the World Wide Web: www.gmodelo.com.mx.

22. Ibid. See also Grupo Modelo SA de CV and subsidiaries, 2004, *Annual Report 2003*, originally retrieved September 30, 2007, from OneSource Database, updated February 3, 2009.

23. Ibid. See also, Armshaw, M. and Farris, C., 2001, *Grupo Modelo CEO visits Kellogg-Miami Program*, retrieved September 30, 2007, from http://kellogg.northwestern.edu/news/whatsnew/ grupo-modelo.htm, updated Feburary 3, 2009.

24. Ibid., pp. 15–16.

25. 1) Research projects conducted by students at Singapore Management University for their strategic brand management course between 2004 and 2008. 2) "IKEA in China— A Clash of Cultures?" completed November 2007, updated September 2008. 3) Ruppel Shell, E., "Just Don't Ask Why it's so Cheap," book excerpt from *Cheap: The High Cost of Discount Culture*, 2009, Penguin, retrieved on July 19, 2009 from www.theglobeandmail. com/life/just-dont-ask-why-its-so-cheap/article1223954/.

26. "Best Global Brands," retrieved December 1, 2008, from www.interbrand.com/best_global_ brands.aspx and supplemented by www.nokia.com.

27. 1) Retrieved December 1, 2008, from www.interbrand.com/best_global_brands.aspx. 2) Vogel, C., "Home Design; Modern Conveniences," December 6, 1987, *New York Times Magazine*, retrieved June 16, 2008 from www.nytimes.com/1987/12/06/magazine/home-design-modern-conveniences.html. 3) "China," September 21, 2007, retrieved March 19, 2008 from www.time. com/time/magazine/article/0,9171,1664358,00.html. 4) Leroux, M., "Madoff Casts Shadow over Rolex as Chief Executive Patrick Heiniger Quits," December 20, 2008, *The Times*, retrieved January 21, 2009 from http://business.timesonline.co.uk/tol/business/industry_sectors/ retailing/article5372593.ece. 5) Cartner-Morley, J., "What Is It with Men and their Watches?" December 1, 2005, *Guardian*, retrieved September 17, 2008 from http://business.timesonline. co.uk/tol/business/industry_sectors/retailing/article5372593.ece.

28 1) Research projects conducted by students at Singapore Management University for their strategic brand management course between 2004 and 2008. 2) "IKEA in China—A Clash of Cultures?" completed November 2007, updated September 2008. 3) Ruppel Shell, E., "Just Don't Ask Why it's So Cheap," book excerpt from *Cheap: The High Cost of Discount Culture* (Penguin, 2009), retrieved on July 19, 2009 from www.theglobeandmail.com/life/just-dont-ask-why-its-so-cheap/article1223954/. 4) Lewis, E., "Is Ikea for Everyone?" March 28, 2005, retrieved November 23, 2008 from www.brandchannel.com/features_effect.asp?pf_id=256. 5) Goodchild, S. and Cobley, B., "A Trip to Ikea could Save Your Marriage (No, Really)," May 15, 2005, retrieved November 23, 2008 from www.independent.co.uk/news/uk/this-britain/a-trip-to-ikea-could-save-your-marriage-no-really-490785.html.

29. Schmitt, B. H. and Rogers, D., "SAP: Building A Leading Technology Brand," retrieved February 11, 2007 from www4.gsb.columbia.edu/null/download?&exclusive=filemgr.download&file_id=10149

30. Kiley, D., "Poll: McDonald's and Google Top P&G for Brand Mgt.," July 16, 2009, BusinessWeek, retrieved July 18, 2009 from www.businessweek.com/the_thread/brandnew-day/archives/2009/07/poll_mcdonalds.html. "P&G's A. G. Lafley on Leadership, Brands, and

Innovation," Knowledge@Emory, September 14, 2006, retrieved on July 7, 2008 from http://knowledge.emory.edu/article.cfm?articleid=990. Aaker, D. and Joachimsthaler, E., *Brand Leadership*, © 2000 The Free Press, pp. 320–321. Rae, J., "P&G Changes Its Game," July 28, 2008, retrieved August 17, 2008 from www.businessweek.com/innovate/content/jul2008/id20080728_623527.htm.

31. "Best Global Brands," retrieved January 12, 2009, from www.interbrand.com/best_global_brands.aspx and supplemented by www.interbrand.com/best_global_brands.aspx and supplemented by www.nikebiz.com.

32. 1) *Fortune* magazine web site, retrieved February 23, 2009 from http://money.cnn.com/magazines/fortune/bestcompanies/2009/snapshots/12.html. 2) REI corporate, retrieved June 23, 2008 from www.rei.com.

33. 1) Research projects conducted by students at Singapore Management University for term projects in their strategic brand management course between 2004 and 2008. 2) MAS Holdings corporate web site, retrieved May 11, 2008 from www.masholdings.com/. 3) The author also visited the executive and toured factories for several days in 2005. 4) *Fortune* magazine online, retrieved February 2009 from http://money.cnn.com/magazines/fortune/bestcompanies/2009/snapshots/1.html. 5) "Great Places to Work Institute," www.greatplacetowork-europe.com/best/list-eu.htm. March 23, 2009 6) "100 Best Places to Work 2009," *Fortune* magazine, retrieved March 3, 2009 from http://money.cnn.com/magazines/fortune/bestcompanies/2009/snapshots/1.html. 7) Tansey, B., "Fortune Names NetApp Best Place to Work," January 23, 2009, *San Francisco Chronicle*, retrieved February 19, 2009 from www.sfgate.com/cgi-bin/article.cgi?f=/c/a/2009/01/23/BUQB15FEON.DTL. 8) "Best Workplaces in Germany," Great Places to Work Institute, retrieved May 17, 2009 from www.greatplacetowork.com/best/list-de.htm. 9) ConSol corporate web site, retrieved January 2009 from www.consol.com/company/awards/.

34. Ibid.

35. Davis, J., *Measuring Marketing: 103 Key Metrics Every Marketer Needs*, © 2007 John Wiley & Sons, Ltd., pp. 326–328.

36. Ibid., pp. 284–287.

37. Ibid., pp. 322–326.

Overview of Brand Experiences

8

Topics

- Preview
- What are Experiences?
- Four Subcomponents of Successful Brand Experiences
- An Experience Mandate
  - Senior Management
  - Marketing
  - Product
  - Support
  - Human Resources
  - Finance
  - Sales
  - Partners
  - Front Lines
- Experiential Marketing
  - Sense
  - Feel
  - Think
  - Act
  - Relate
- The Importance of Being Special
- The Importance of Creativity
- The Importance of Engaging and Relating
- Whole Brain not Half Brain
- Applicable to All?
- Measurement
  - Snapshot Surveys
  - Objective Scoring
  - Detailed Questionnaires
  - Direct Observation
- Summary
- Discussion Questions

> ## Preview
>
> Brands are clearly a more involving phenomenon than just a logo or a product. So what is needed to make them special for the customer? Knowing that an experience is more than just a product means that management must consider the ways customers interact with brands so that new associations can be created that add greater depth and distinctiveness. In this chapter we introduce the concept of experiences, a value-building approach that is subsequently explored in-depth in Chapters 9–10.

What are Experiences?

Experiences describes the complete range of associations, direct and indirect, a person has with a brand, before, during, and after the purchase of a product. The value of focusing on Experiences is the competitive advantage it confers on companies that develop it versus less ambitious rivals. To illustrate, consider two scenarios:

- *Scenario 1.* Imagine walking into any empty room without furniture or people, just bare walls and the door through which you entered. In the center of the room is a plate on the floor with your favorite sandwich on it. You are instructed to eat it.
- *Scenario 2.* Now change the situation to a party at someone's house, with music, games, a pool, dancing, and all your closest friends in attendance. On the dining room table is a selection of foods, including your favorite sandwich.

Of the two situations, which is likely to be a more enjoyable experience when eating the sandwich? Most people would choose the second scenario. The sandwich is the same in both situations but the atmosphere is livelier and more stimulating in the second scenario and more conducive to having a good time and creating positive memories.

Four Subcomponents of Successful Brand Experiences

For brands, creating experiences is analogous to the second scenario. Brand experiences connect the offering to other activities and touchpoints, creating numerous positive associations and memories that link back to the brand. Chapters 8–10 discuss brand experiences in depth, including the four subcomponents shown in Figure 8-1.

Figure 8-1   Components of Experiences

An Experience Mandate

Brand experiences are comprised of numerous factors and influences, both tangible and intangible, as illustrated in Figure 8-2:

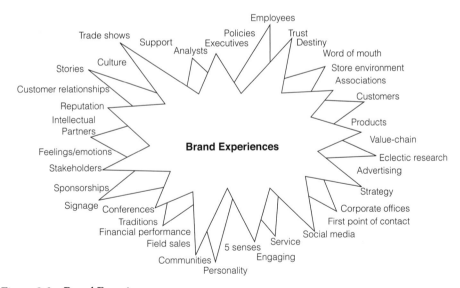

Figure 8-2   Brand Experiences

Figure 8-3   Brand Experience Mandate

For brands, coordinating the many complex factors is a sizable task beyond the scope of one department. Part of the effort to create successful brand experiences involves active, visible support from throughout the organization, as mentioned. Everyone in the company must recognize that creating brand experiences is an organizational imperative. We saw from Chapter 7 the importance of developing a deeply integrated company that works well across both formal and informal expectations and structures. When done well, employees take the initiative actively to participate in and shape their own brand experience. This instills a sense of vibrancy and dynamism that is reflected in the energy applied to planning the brand experience for the benefit of customers. This planning involves many areas, but developing successful brand experiences depends on a having a company-wide *mandate* that rallies everyone in support. Each of the areas shown in Figure 8-3 play a role in supporting the brand experience effort.

Senior Management

In any top brand, whether it is Virgin, Joie de Vivre, MAS Holdings, Nike, or Air Asia, senior management sets the tone and expectations, validating the need for creating a brand experience by making it a corporate mandate. They regularly demonstrate the importance of brand experiences through spoken communication and ongoing visible actions, such as in company meetings and daily "walking the talk," sending signals to employees their belief that building brand experiences is an invaluable and necessary imperative. Senior management states as well that brand experience building is more than a marketing-only responsibility and they explain why and how other parts of the company are expected to contribute. This effort includes removing obstacles to progress, pushing for and valuing creativity, and recognition and rewarding the accomplishments of those that exemplify the brand experience effort.

Marketing

Marketing in top brands applies the same vigor and tenacity to regular, internal marketing communications that they do to customer-facing activities. This was especially true in consumer goods *and* service firms, where brands are most visible. More than 70% of the marketing groups were involved in internal programs that had the professional flair of their consumer-facing counterparts. For B2B companies, the percentage was closer to 25%, partly because marketing is not always a clear department as it is in consumer products. The responsibility was often handled by business development, field sales, and/or account management and strategy. Top marketing departments work hard to make the brand experience special for employees by marketing inside their own companies, even going so far as to create internal campaigns and experience-based events that bring the brand to life for employees. New media, contests, and frequent meetings with other departments and other regions are used to keep the energy level high and ensure a consistent focus is on the brand experience effort. Interestingly, many brands, particularly software companies, involve customers in decision-making, although unsolicited involvement occurs naturally due to the advent of social networking tools. Just as with external customers, marketers survey fellow employees to gauge the pulse and commitment of the organization to the brand.

Product

People involved with product typically include designers, engineers, developers, although marketers may well be involved also. One of the challenges brands faced was how to get their product people out of the office and into the market. As simple as this sounds, a number of activities are dependent on their ongoing internal participation to ensure the product development process flows smoothly from conception to commercialization and distribution, leaving little time for travel. But when the product people traveled with the marketers to meet customers and generally observe behavior, they often interpreted the same event differently, adding richness and a degree of cross-checking to the insights marketers gleaned. Top product people worked hard to attend and/or speak at the latest conferences, even publishing their ideas, each of which boosted their own visibility and that of the brand. The travels sometimes inspired new prototypes as the product people witnessed first-hand how customers interacted with their products. This inspired more holistic ways of viewing a product, beyond just adding features.

Support

Customer support functions include customer service and technical support. Typically, companies see this as a component of customer relationship management (CRM), certainly an important need in any company, evidenced by the many sophisticated CRM software packages used to track a wide variety of customer data and designed to create a thorough customer profile. The resulting data can be used for developing trends and forecasts. But the key here is that with top brands the various customer support functions were usually united in a nontechnical way in their efforts to support customer experiences, not just relationships. They used recorded service calls, for example to discuss the tone of the conversation, not just the content, to raise sensitivity to emotion and the customer's overall state of mind. Customer support staff are regularly included in customer meetings as product planning sessions because they are listening every day to customer feedback. Bain & Company, the strategy consulting firm, states that customer satisfaction is influenced by three drivers:[1]

- A product meets the needs of the consumer.
- A product works as expected.
- Problems are resolved as expected.

When the customer experience goes awry, top brands discovered that a key indicator of winning them back was how the problem was handled by the company. Genesys is one of the leading contact center software companies in the world, a division of the French tele-communications company Alcatel-Lucent. Their software is designed to overcome frustra-tions that callers typically have with interactive voice response systems, which often subject users to extensive phone trees, endless selections, and dropped calls. Genesys focused not on designing software but on finding ways to improve the customer experience for companies. This led to innovative software design, including superb voice-activated commands, which streamlines the call-in process and allows callers to reach the appropriate area of interest faster. Such a solution facilitates smoother customer relations, reduces stress, and raises the chances strengthening the customer's long-term experience with the brand.[2]

Human Resources (HR)

Human resources serves as a valuable internal resource for reinforcing the brand experience. Of course its role in talent selection, as discussed in Chapter 7, is important (although in many companies HR plays more of a coordinating role and individual departments are responsible for hiring) but nearly all but 5% of the top brands had their HR groups helping developing and/or leading top-notch training programs that reinforce a number of corporate priorities, including brand experience shaping. For years, GE's Crotonville training center, Disney's learning programs, and McDonald's Hamburger U epitomized this effort. In the early 2000s, P&G introduced marketing "colleges" designed to help employees understand how to relate, perform important business tasks, and even mentor each other. One can see how the effort can help improve internal dedication to the company and thereby lead to improved products and customer experiences. Human resources also played a direct role in observing and acknowledging brand experience behaviors.[3]

Finance

Like the product people, travel and/or other direct contact with customers proved to be helpful to top brands, helping them think more holistically about the company's assets and how to support their deployment. In more than 64% of the brands studied, finance was active in reaching out and meeting with other departments, explaining their role and how department resource allocations work, which enabled employees to understand guidelines. Their presence was also helpful to marketers and other members of the customer team as it exposed them to new ways to understand and interpret budget and financing requirements.

Sales

Meeting with customers was a way for top-performing sales and account-management people to make the brand experience portable. They created an environment of psychological safety in which concerns could be discussed and appropriate adjustments could be made to fit the customer's needs, yet they allowed the products to be sold with confidence. They also identified and worked with channel partners whose own business practices complemented the company's brand experience approach. Sales departments were quite customer focused, as one would hope, demonstrating a remarkable ability to make customer situations as close to a top experience as possible. One key negative that was more distracting for sales people than for other disciplines was the pressure near the end of the quarter to bring in business. This is primarily a public-company phenomenon due to the quarterly analyst calls and reporting required. Sales practices during the last two or three weeks of the quarter became more aggressive and customers also knew that the sales people needed to make a sale, so there was more tension in that period of time each year than any other.

Partners

Important value-chain partners, such as suppliers, manufacturers, and logistics had an indirect but still valuable role in reflecting the brand experience. To make this effective required senior management and managers in charge of the partner relationship to work with the partner, discussing expectations, the brand's needs, and why they felt the partner was a good fit for supporting the brand experience effort. The sheer repetition of the message helped reinforce its importance to partners and that their ongoing relationship with the brand depended on their active support. Most of the top brands had significant experience working with partners, with long-lasting relationships and deeply embedded systems that simplified business exchanges due to the familiarity.

Front Lines

Front-line employees are often sidelined in company branding efforts but with support from the departments mentioned above and with HR training they were able to contribute to the brand experience. Even a simple greeting or the proper transfer of a phone call or the prompt follow-up to an unanswered question signaled that the brand experience was genuine.

Experiential Marketing

Columbia's Bernd Schmitt is one of the leading thinkers in experiential marketing. He posited that brands are far more than a mere product or corporate identity campaign. Schmitt cites philosopher Merleau-Ponty, who stated in his book *Phenomenology of Perception* that "The world is not an object such that I have in my possession the law of its making; it is the natural setting of, and field for, all my thoughts and all my explicit perceptions."[4]

Following on, Schmitt comments, "In other words, as a marketer you need to provide the right environment and setting for the desired customer experience to emerge."[5]

Reinforcing his point, he describes his experiential marketing framework, consisting of five strategic experiential modules (SEMs)[6] relating to different types of customer experiences:

- sense;
- feel;
- think;
- act;
- relate.

Sense

Sense marketing stimulates all five senses. Recall the example of Joie de Vivre Hotels and their philosophy of inspiring all five senses in the first five minutes. This typifies sense marketing. The impact on customers is direct and profound because the stimulation of the senses creates numerous inputs and responses that can make a brand experience positive and memorable. Of course, the converse is true as well. Exaggerated sense marketing, offensive smells, garish lights and sounds, unpleasant textures and tastes can quickly turn against brands that try to do too much.

Feel

Feel marketing taps into people's emotions, creating changes in moods and attitudes. The goal is to create positive emotional connections with customers that engender feelings ranging from warmth to joy to trust to security. Brands at holiday time in countries around the world run ad campaigns showing family reunions, beer companies advertise camaraderie with friends, and sports teams show highlights of team success to generate excitement with fans. Feel marketing is effective for public service announcements and/ or cause-related marketing, where it is important for the audience to *feel* the plight and desperation of the situation. Feel marketing can also be used to create feelings of discord or frustration, as politicians in the U.S. try to do during election campaigns by denigrating their opponents and running ads that create doubt in voters' minds.[7]

Think

Think marketing engages people by appealing to their intellect and creative side, compelling them to consider how the offering improves their life and/or engages them directly. Nike ID allows customers to customize shoes according to their own creative desires. This also involves customers more directly in the brand. Stikfas, a toy company based in Singapore, makes simple snap-together action figures with interchangeable parts. There are dozens of themes, from cowboys to rock stars to ninjas and more. Each figure comes unassembled, requiring customers to snap it together themselves. This has proven to be a superb marketing move because customers are directly involved in their own creations and, because the parts are interchangeable, there are innumerable potential combinations.[8]

Act

Act marketing is designed to modify or even transform people's lives by showing them how things can be better. Nintendo Wii showed that video games can be social, engaging, and even healthy, as opposed to the typical stereotypes of people locked away for hours playing video games by themselves. The Wii play station and wireless controllers allow users to do fitness routines and engage in friendly social competitions with friends. The controller's sensitivity to the user's movement often creates comical physical maneuvers that make the experience even more fun and memorable. Negative approaches can work in certain instances. In some countries graphic photos of cancer victims are placed directly on packs of cigarettes in an effort to change people's smoking habits (hopefully by reducing or quitting entirely).[9]

Relate

Relate marketing appeals to a person's self-expressive needs and their ideal sense of who they are or want to be. Cosmetics mogul Charles Revson once famously intoned: "In the factory we make cosmetics; in the store we sell hope."[10]

Other examples include Apple's iPod print and billboard ads featuring a silhouetted person with the iconic white ear buds dancing to the music and conveying a sense of personal freedom. While the silhouette does not move, it conveys movement, energy and vitality, suggesting that the iPod will bestow these same qualities on everyone else.

Think of this as the individual equivalent to the Ultimate Dream subcomponent in Destiny, where a brand's future is envisioned as far greater than its current situation, in which their contributions are extraordinary and meaningful.

The Importance of Being Special

Top brands are planned to be special and unique. It is part of what gives them a competitive advantage and, as we have learned from previous chapters, enhances brand value for all stakeholders.

The classic brand frameworks discussed in Chapter 3, are instructive guides for thinking about the fundamentals of brand structure. Experiences takes the two-dimensional brand architecture frameworks and adds the third dimension of depth—those inside spaces and experiences that take something from being ordinary and routine to being extraordinary and special. When we think about products we buy, we may find ourselves thinking of various associations attached to that brand—perhaps a provocative television ad, or a memory of a recent event in which the product was used. These associations add dimension, hopefully positive, to the brand, much of the time without additional prompting. The simple reason for focusing on the wide variety of inputs and influences that shape a brand experience is to raise the brand's attractiveness to customers. This, in turn, will improve the brand's performance *vis-à-vis* competitors.

To illustrate with an analogy, attractive people tend to be more favorably perceived than unattractive, however unfair that may be. Brand experiences are emphasized to create advantage for the brand by connecting to favorable touchpoints, an effort that may be distinctly unfair to rivals, but well-suited to standing out, improving business performance, and creating long-term brand value. Social science research has confirmed that attractiveness, personality, and grooming "has a positive and statistically significant impact on GPA (grade point average)."[11]

Brand building is similar. Chapter 5 discussed the importance of a brand's personality in influencing perceptions, whether inside or outside the company. The overall attractiveness of the brand is heavily influenced by a blend of its personality and its appearance ("grooming"). When building brands, actively conceptualizing, planning, and implementing brand experiences can transform the average performer to the top of the class.

The rationale for creating memorable experiences is evident from the various situations described in Example 8-1. To be among the best brands, every detail is important. When customers shop, they don't ignore the environment or other items in the store. While they may not interact with them at all times, customers are cognizant of their surroundings, and acutely aware when the environment is lacking or does not deliver fully on the experience. The emphasis on experience, therefore, helps make brands special.

The Importance of Creativity

Creativity is sometimes considered a dirty word in business. Creativity implies chaos, messiness, imprecision, unpredictability, and insubstantial outcomes. But at its root, creativity is found in some form or fashion in virtually every aspect of business. The factory worker who recommends a change to the production line that results in a 10% productivity improvement is exercising creativity. The entrepreneur who designs productivity software for consumers that was previously only available to expensive accounting firms is exhibiting creativity. The scientist who accidentally discovers a new adhesive, which is eventually used for office notepads is displaying creativity. The architect who designs a hotel that looks like a giant sail with a seemingly unsupported circular lounge at the top, and rests it on its own man-made island is also demonstrating creativity. Google's famous policy of allowing engineers to use 20% of their salary time to work on projects of their own choosing has inspired many new product ideas, including Google AdSense, Google Suggest, and Orkut (a social networking site).

In other words, creativity has many parents, not just the more common stereotypes of ad designers and artists.

Memorable brand experiences will not happen without creativity. Anybody inside the organization can conceivably be involved. To succeed, creativity does not need large budgets. As Walt Disney once famously said, "All your dreams can come true if you have the courage to pursue them."[12]

For brands, developing great experiences is an exercise of the imagination. As products are copied faster than ever, with quality now just the minimum cost of entry, distinctiveness takes on important new relevance for brands. Companies are moving beyond making things in favor of making things interesting. Doing so requires a different ability—a concerted effort to exercise creativity. While products are still made in manufacturing facilities, while service still means attending to customers, top brands are focusing on how to transform these by creating associations, setting expectations, fueling anticipation, and giving their offerings a personality. It may sound like so much trivial faddism but the evidence suggests otherwise. Consider the following examples.

EXAMPLE 8-1:

Singapore Airlines

Singapore Airlines is not selling airplane seats—it is selling travel hospitality with warmth. This subtle distinction is a leading indicator of the effort put forth throughout the organization to ensure the flying experience with them is unrivaled, beyond the luxury of the generous seats and meals in all classes of travel. The effort at creating an experience has paid off, with the airline winning annual awards as the world's best airline and consistently one the most profitable in the world as well. For customers, the benefit is a travel experience among the most consistent and very best in the world.[13]

Thunder Dolphin

Imagine yourself staring up at Thunder Dolphin, a roller coaster in Tokyo Dome City, near the heart of bustling Tokyo. Climbing up over 260 feet in the air, it is one of the world's tallest roller coasters. But unlike other roller coasters, Thunder Dolphin runs directly above the city traffic, with a track that loops through a building and other skyscrapers looming nearby. Then imagine riding in the front car as it is pulled up the first hill, feel the cool Tokyo air and slight breeze, notice the steep climb before finally cresting ever so slightly at the top as the steep plunge comes into view. You're hanging there momentarily, high above the noise of Tokyo, with thousands of people walking along the sidewalks 260 feet below, office workers in the neighboring skyscrapers, and you in a tiny roller-coaster car with a seemingly insufficient seat belt. All at once, you find yourself plummeting at high speed toward the bottom, wind and adrenaline combining to plaster a terrified smile on your face, then soaring back up as the track climbs over the roof of the Tokyo Dome mall, turning sharply right and causing you to lean sideways looking down at the city far below, then zooming directly through a hole in the wall of another building, followed by a few more twists and turns before the ride finally ends. Why do this at all? Because the experience is all-encompassing, testing your wits, stimulating your heart rate, feeling the sensation of seemingly death-defying high speed, hearing the nearby sounds of a chaotic city, seeing the mega-watt neon lighting that surrounds you, and listening to yourself and those around you scream in sheer, exhilarating pleasure. Too much to handle?

ExpressoConnection

Then imagine yourself eager for that first cup of coffee in the morning. Time and traffic won't allow you to drink your coffee in the coffee shop, so you use the drive through and you notice something unusual: the line for the drive-through is short, yet it is peak traffic time. As you pull up behind the car in front of you to place your order, you realize there is no remote microphone and speaker. So how will you place your order. Time is ticking away and you are feeling the stress about getting to work, so you contemplate backing out when a car pulls in behind you. Just then, a person comes bursting out of the door of the coffee place and skips merrily over toward your car with a big smile on her face. You nervously keep your window closed, not knowing who this person is or why they are coming toward you. Then, they knock on your window, still smiling. You roll it down slightly, just enough to hear her. "Good morning!" she exclaims enthusiastically, not a hint of insincerity in her voice. Just pure, genuine happiness. "Would you like to try a sample of our fresh baked pastries?" and she magically hands you a small slice, so you roll down your window more to take it. The sample tastes great, so you order a pastry, even though you originally only wanted coffee. She then tells you the coffee specials of the day, which all sound delicious and perfectly suited to the long commute ahead. You place your order, feeling good about the pastry and looking forward to the tantalizing coffee. As you roll up your window and prepare to drive forward to pick up your order, the attendant energetically knocks on your window one more time, so you roll it down. She continues smiling and asks, "would you like to hear the joke of the day?" a question that catches you so off guard that you stammer for a moment before saying yes. And she proceeds to tell you a very humorous joke that leaves you feeling great as you pull up to the pick up window to grab your order.

As you pull away you notice a second drive-through window on the other side of the coffee store, which explains the shorter lines during rush hour. A smart, yet simple solution that makes the customer's life easier. Suddenly, the traffic and stress of getting to work has diminished in importance greatly and you *feel* great, looking forward to the day ahead. Sounds preposterous? Well, EspressoConnection, a regional chain of specialty coffee stores in Seattle, Washington delivers this type of service every day to its customers. With the world's biggest coffee brand, Starbucks, nearby, EspressoConnection has found a way to compete that does not require thousands of stores, massive capital outlays, or ambitions to be the "third place" (a reference to Howard Schultz, Starbucks' founder, who envisions Starbucks as being the third place in customers' lives, after home and work). By focusing on their own brand of service, they carved a unique niche for themselves and created an utterly unique experience for their customers.[14]

Hermes International

Hermes International relies on its own ingenuity and creativity and not traditional market research such as focus groups to conceive and develop new products. As Patrick Thomas, who took over as CEO in 2004, commented, "We are an offering-driven, not a marketing-driven, company," Thomas said. "We're not trying to understand what the customer wants, but to bring our customers into our world, to convince them via the product."[15]

In fact, the company pursues a decidedly contrarian and original business planning process. They stopped using five-year financial projections because management believed it took the emphasis off of quality products and put it onto numbers. Unlike some of its luxury competitors, the company uses no celebrity endorsers in its marketing. Finally, to differentiate itself further still, Thomas does not see the company as a luxury goods firm, but as a maker of quality objects by craftsman and artisans. Despite, or perhaps because of, these counterintuitive business and branding approaches, Hermes International has seen steady revenue growth, from €1.43 billion in 2005 to €1.76 billion in 2009 and net income has increased from €247 million to €290 million during that time.[16]

Professional Sports

Professional sports teams around the world invest significant sums not just on playing talent but on making the experience for their fans exceptional with every game. In the NBA, teams use entertainment in short bursts during time-outs and breaks to keep fans engaged and make the atmosphere festive. In the English Premier League, many clubs have created interactive fan web sites with content about their favorite players, autograph sessions, and real-time game statistics beamed to mobile phones. Avid fans of the Boston Red Sox baseball team can become members of Red Sox Nation, a fan club with different levels of membership that includes two tickets to a home game, complimentary Major League Baseball audio subscription, merchandise discounts, eligibility for ticket giveaways, personalized photographs, early entrance to watch team warmups, and a tour of historic Fenway Ballpark (built in 1912). The Hong Kong Sevens Rugby tournament is a three-day sports extravaganza that takes place in March each year and features 18 of the world's top rugby teams. Each side is allowed seven players and seven minutes each way before the next game begins. The action is nonstop, with sideline entertainment part of the festivities. The fans are often passionate followers of their national teams, either flying in for the event, or local expats. Many strip down to shorts and socks, painting their torsos with national colors and chanting in rhythm for their team and passionately against their rivals. The event is more than just a sport: it is social, involves professional networking, is visually exciting, and the overall atmosphere is electric. A sizable percentage of fans returns every year, even though the distances are often great. The benefit for the Hong Kong Sevens organizers and teams is a steady following of fans whose passionate support and antics gives the three-day tournament a unique chemistry. The benefit for the fans is a first-rate competition during the contest, great entertainment throughout, and an ongoing connection with their favorite teams.[17]

Disney

Disney's success is not accidental. It seamlessly translates its brand into a consistent image and experience across continents, cultures and consumers. The company has a knack for transporting guests to a fairytale world in which imagination, color and good nature reign supreme. While Disney is a complex company with numerous divisions and businesses around the world, its historical emphasis on creating brand experiences has been the reason that its popular movies become new theme rides (and vice versa, in the case of Pirates of the Caribbean) and a successful line of merchandise and collectibles. Disney's innumerable touchpoints are magnets for consumer activity and the public's confidence in Disney is so high that it allows the company to be arbiters of taste—witness the success of the Jonas Brothers and Hannah Montana.[18]

Harry Potter

The Harry Potter books and movies are a cultural phenomenon that has connected millions of fans from around the world that share a common love for the stories. With the movies, merchandising, spin-off items (like author JK Rowling's book, *Tales of Beedle the Bard*), Harry Potter conventions, tours of Potter sites seen in the movies are among the offerings that make what was once a single book with a compelling story into one of the biggest brand success stories in years. Interestingly, as the books caught on, the author and publishers cleverly did not release advance copies, a normal practice for most new books. This heightened expectations. Rowling retained unusual control for an author over both the marketing for the books and approval for the movie scripts. Little or no advertising was done in advance. When the books were delivered to stores, explicit instructions were given to not sell the books before the official release date. Violators risked fines and jail. Security was increased at bookstores and the books were delivered in special vans, adding to the spectacle. Fans dressed in Harry Potter-themed costumes would line up days in advance and camp out in front of bookstores to be among the first to get copies. Fan blogs and web sites sprung up around the world. The books are the most successful commercial books of all time and the movies are among the highest grossing films ever. Even with the end of the book series, fans remain active around the world. The seventh and last book is being split into two movies to extend the magic a bit longer. The ensemble of actors in the films is an interesting combination of some of the world's most respected and successful actors as well as veritable unknowns. The three actors portraying Harry, Ron and Hermione have gone from invisibility to international stardom. Adding to the appeal of the entire Harry Potter franchise is the fact that the young actors remained remarkably normal and professional, despite the significant success they have enjoyed.[19]

Nokia

In 2004, Nokia created an experiential marketing campaign to raise awareness for its new Fashion Collection, which featured the Nokia 7280, 7270 and 7260 mobile phone models. In prior years the company had emphasized direct marketing, so the new campaign signified a departure from company practice. The campaign ran nationwide campaigns in the U.S. aimed at commuter nightspots such as bars, clubs, and hotels. The company had 40 000 matchboxes shaped like the Fashion Collection products and distributed throughout these locales, a clever device for making a statement directly to this particular target audience. At the same time, consumers were sent messages encouraging them to visit the company web site, driving additional traffic and interest in the brand. Nokia focused on emerging consumer trends as well, targeting those with an active lifestyle profile and an appreciation for offbeat urban music culture. Nontraditional marketing (see Chapter 10) was used, such as sponsoring live events and engaging customers through blogs and early social media, which helped attract even more of the leading edge of the youth market. In 2005 it was involved with the Prince's Trust Urban Music Festival at Earl's Court and the Isle of Wight Festival. These activities helped associate the brand more closely with the youth music market, adding credibility for the company to the younger audience. The company also began sponsoring free running sport and streetball, both popular sports. Free running, in particular, was rapidly growing an underground following of daredevil athletes and fans. The rich variety of marketing modes used were instrumental in shifting Nokia's marketing into a multidimensional experience.[20]

The Importance of Engaging and Relating

By now it is evident that focusing on brand experiences is a different approach to brand building, moving companies past one-way dialogs and toward ongoing interaction, facilitated by the advent of new media. It is helpful to set expectations by illustrating how marketing tools can help brands connect directly, quickly and massively with the market.

On Tuesday, November 4, 2008, Barack Obama was elected U.S. President, defeating Republican candidate John McCain. Obama received over 69 million votes (52.9%) to McCain's 59 million (45.7%). Each candidate had a compelling personal story, which helped drive interest. Aside from being the first African-American President, Obama was the first to use new media in a comprehensive way to reach voters and it helped build a strong voter base for his election. The statistics are interesting:[21]

- 13 million people on an email list that received 7000 variations of more than 1 billion emails;
- 5 million "friends" on more than 15 social networking sites;
- 8.5 million monthly visitors to main web site (at peak);
- 2 million profiles with 400 000 blog posts;
- 35 000 volunteer groups that held 200 000 offline events;
- 70 000 fundraising hubs that raised $30 million;
- nearly 2000 official YouTube videos;
- 440 000 user-generated videos on YouTube;
- 3 million people signed up for the text messaging program.

The purpose of showing the statistics is not to prove a political point. It is to demonstrate the power the new media tools have to engage people. The aggressive new media effort by Obama's team contrasted sharply with McCain's more traditional marketing approach—an approach that had worked well for decades—but was not sufficient to properly attract interest in 2008. The campaigns in many ways were reflective of their candidates: Obama was the younger, more technically savvy candidate whereas McCain was the seasoned veteran with more traditional views. Interestingly, their respective marketing approaches reinforced existing perceptions of the candidates, although in Obama's case his new media effort helped fill in detail for voters previously unfamiliar with him due to his emergence on the national stage only a few years before. The Obama campaign created buzz using new media, but not in the artificial "say anything to get noticed" sense of the term. In fact, Obama was often understated in his speeches, despite his reputation for rhetorical finesse. A campaign theme echoed this when it referred to him as "No Drama Obama." The buzz was propelled by voters and volunteers, who used the new media to reach out to voters everywhere. This corresponded with much higher online donations than ever before in a U.S. Presidential campaign. In fact, the total donations that he received were the highest in history. More than 3 million voters donated more than 6.5 million times, which means many voters donated more than once (a form of loyalty), and 6 million of those were less than US$100 each. The average donation online was US$80. In total, more than US$500 million was raised for Obama's election, allowing him to not only invest in new media but to also purchase extensive traditional media time as well.[22] Without the strength and flexibility of new media, the chances of Obama or any candidate to achieve equivalent figures is close to zero. Traditional tools are less flexible, less time sensitive and less personal (interactive) than new media. The 2008 Obama campaign highlighted the ability of new media to help build a brand. How the brand stays on top requires more than just a media campaign.

Whole Brain not Half Brain

Brands are multidimensional entities, so pursuing brand experiences is a concerted effort in activating the creative *and* logical halves of the brain. The entire organization is involved at varying levels. As such, marketing is no longer the only domain responsible for brand. Indeed, focusing on brand coupled with an experience requires involvement from most areas of the company. The top brands certainly have senior-level marketing and branding officers and they are still responsible for many of the traditional areas of marketing strategy and brand development. But their ability to develop a successful brand with high brand value is limited without the direct support of the rest of the company. As discussed before, marketers must market just as vigorously inside their own companies as they do outside to the market, which means other departments have to be persuaded, cajoled, and convinced to be an active part of brand building.

This whole-brain metaphor suggests that creating successful brand experiences does not result from incremental tweaks in service delivery or minor updates to products. Nor does it result from focusing only on narrow parts of the business or in isolated parts of the company. Creating brand experiences means effecting change across the organization, with members of senior management ensuring that their organizations are working in concert to make the experiences come to life for customers.

A brand experience describes the customer's interaction with multiple brand touchpoints. This means that creating a brand is more than just an exercise in advertising. A brand experience approach actually makes brand building more accessible to a wider range of companies, which previously considered such efforts the purview of only the wealthiest companies. Small companies can now look at their various touchpoints, from employees to products to partners, and use them to help build their brand in the absence of aggressive spending on advertising.

Applicable to All?

Can all companies benefit from a brand experience focus? The short answer is that every company is actually creating brand experiences, even if they are not aware of the term, simply because every touchpoint tells the market something about the company, however good or bad. Managing those touchpoints better can help even a poor performer or a quieter organization enhance its reputation with its core audience. Of course, some types of companies, such as consumer goods, automobiles and retail are obvious beneficiaries of strong experiences. Companies conducting sensitive research where publicity is discouraged, or working only with a small selection of other clients are still building a brand reputation by virtue of their actions and behaviors. An experience-based approach can help them improve the quality of reputation.

Measurement

No specific formulas are applicable here. However, a practical approach is surveys designed to gauge brand experiences. These can be applied to internal and external audiences.

Snapshot Surveys

Several brands used a real-time survey that we will term "snapshot," because it is intended to gain qualitative feedback from the customer at a single point in time. These surveys are given during product use, or immediately after, thereby getting quick feedback. They are most effective if they are short and ask customers to simply reply. Many companies asked permission to record the answers so that the interviewer could maintain eye contact with the interviewee. Management must recognize that the feedback is subjective and can be influenced by emotional extremes (a bad experience, for example), exaggerating the response. Nevertheless, when enough of these responses are collected and compared across similar times of day and similar customer situations, patterns can emerge that help pinpoint strengths and weaknesses in customer experience.

Objective Scoring

Hotels use guest comment cards, with a set of 5–10 questions and a multipoint ranking system (either a numeric or descriptive checkboxes) to assess simple customer satisfaction. These are not filled out by every guest. Indeed, many guests ignore them. Others only fill them out when they have a complaint, so the results are not statistically significant. But like the snapshot survey, such approaches can help businesses gain a better sense of how customers view the company's performance.

Detailed Questionnaires

More extensive surveys, with more questions and question variety (short answer, multiple choice, scoring) add greater detail, but the challenge is to find customers willing to spend the time answering them. Depending on the sample size and selection, these surveys can provide excellent and more in-depth feedback.

Direct Observation

Using video, social media, attending cultural events, participating in conferences and even leisure travel can all be productive ways to learn and observe how people respond to the brand.

Summary

This chapter introduced the concept of a brand experience to set the stage for Chapters 9 and 10, which explain brand experiences and how they affect brand value in greater depth. Brand building is an effort to show why companies and their offerings are special and attractive. Attractiveness is based partly on a brand's personality and its appearance. Judgment is often passed on an entity's attractiveness such that less attractive offerings are more harshly judged than attractive ones, even if the performance of the product is the same. Creativity certainly drives brand experiences but should not be pigeonholed as just an artistic expression. To build strong brand experiences requires creativity from multiple areas of the firm in order to imagine and then develop the right attributes and associations. We learned from Bernd Schmitt that experiential marketing involves the activation of strategic experiential modules (SEMs—Sense, Feel, Think, Act and Relate) to stimulate brands and create positive customer outcomes. To bring brand experiences to life is the equivalent of a whole brain activity requiring the creative and logical sides to work collaboratively to deliver on customer expectations. But to make this work consistently means that an organizational mandate must exist, genuinely promoted by senior management and then actively supported by key departments and decision makers throughout the company.

Discussion Questions

1. What is a brand experience?
2. How can companies manage the complexities inherent in creating successful experience?
3. Why is senior management support important? Why do you think the senior management of many companies does not do this? How would you persuade them to do so?

Notes

1. Speech by Michael McBrien, Senior Vice President-Asia Pacific Genesys at Singapore Management University in February 2009, retrieved February 23, 2009 from www.genesyslab.com/storage/msg/TRAC/2008Q1CSSG/CSSG_CustExper_v2_Screen.pdf.
2. Ibid.
3. 1) "Leadership and Learning," retrieved October 11, 2008 from www.ge.com/company/culture/leadership_learning.html. Material from Disney web site, retrieved October 11, 2008 from http://corporate.disney.go.com/careers/learning.html. McDonald's web site retrieved October 11, 2008 from www.aboutmcdonalds.com/mcd/careers/hamburger_university.html.

4. Merleau-Ponty, M., *Phenomenology of Perception*, Routledge & Kegan Paul, 1962.

5. Schmitt, B. H., *Experiential Marketing: How to Get Customers to Sense, Feel, Think, Act, and Relate to Your Company and Brands*, © 1999 by Bernd H. Schmitt, The Free Press, p. 60.

6. Ibid., pp. 64–69.

7. Pfanner, E., "Politicians Fail to Grasp Peer-to-Peer," June 14, 2009, *New York Times*, retrieved June 15, 2009 from www.nytimes.com/2009/06/15/technology/internet/15iht-cache15.html.

8. 1) Research projects conducted by students at Singapore Management University for their strategic brand management course between 2004 and 2008. 2) "Stikfas," research completed November 2006, updated February 2009. 3) "Marketing Lessons from the US Election," Seth Godin's blog, retrieved January 3, 2009 from http://sethgodin.typepad.com/seths_blog/2008/11/marketing-lesso.html.

9. 1) Casey, K. P., "Nintendo Hopes Wii Spells Winner," August 15, 2006, *USA Today*, retrieved July 11, 2008, from www.usatoday.com/tech/gaming/2006-08-14-nintendo-qa_x.htm. 2) Brenner, B., "Nintendo Storms the Gaming World," January 26, 2007, *BusinessWeek*, retrieved June 7, 2008 from www.businessweek.com/globalbiz/content/jan2007/gb20070126_278776.htm. 3) Nuttall, C., "Microsoft and Sony Take Aim at Nintendo Wii's Console Sales Lead," June 1, 2009, *Financial Times*, retrieved June 3, 2009 from www.ft.com/cms/s/0/5f90d77a-4e44-11de-a0a1-00144feabdc0.html.

10. Miles, S., Anderson, A., Meethan, K., *The Changing Consumer*, © 2002 Routledge, p. 155.

11. French, M. T., Robins, P. K., Homer, J. F. and Tapsell, L. M., 2009, "Effects of Physical Attractiveness, Personality, and Grooming on Academic Performance in High School," *Labour Economics*, 16(4), pp. 373–382.

12. Shipley, J., retrieved April 7, 2009 from http://vutimes.wordpress.com/2009/03/22/ "if-you-can-dream-it…you-can-do-it"-jake-klinvex-villanova-entrepreneur/.

13. 1) "World Airline Awards: Survey Methodology," retrieved January 28, 2009 from www.worldairlineawards.com/main/mthds.htm. 2) "Singapore Crowned Best Airline for Sixth Time, Singapore Changi Wins Best Airport, at the Twenty-sixth OAG Airline Industry Awards," June 4, 2008, retrieved January 28, 2009 from www.oag.com/oagcorporate/pressreleases/08+winners+of+the+oag+airline+industry+awards.html. 3) "World's Most Admired Companies," retrieved January 28, 2009 from http://money.cnn.com/magazines/fortune/mostadmired/2009/snapshots/8155.html. 4) "Our Achievements," Singapore Airlines information retrieved February 24, 2009 from www.singaporeair.com/saa/en_UK/content/company_info/news/achievements.jsp.

14. EspressoConnection was studied for research projects conducted by MBA students at University of Washington for their strategic marketing course between 2001 and 2003. The student teams studied a wide range of companies, each with excellent information about its branding and marketing efforts, including Intel, Amazon, Motorola, and Boeing. Interestingly, EspressoConnection stood out. The company has 15 stores in the Seattle region plus an affiliated business called SilverCup Coffee, which roasts and sells its own coffee beans. EspressoConnection was a remarkable story because of its service and strong overall performance in a market dominated by a much larger competitor—Starbucks.

15. "Hermes May Pose as New Luxury Model," by Vanessa Friedman, *Los Angeles Times*, January 10, 2005, retrieved November 12, 2008, http://articles.latimes.com/2005/jan/10/business/ft-hermes10?pg=1.

16. 1) Research projects conducted by students at Singapore Management University for their strategic brand management course between 2004 and 2008. 2) "Hermès Strategic Brand Management," research completed November 2008. 3) Hermès' Annual Report 2007,

Executive Management report, p. 26. 4) "Hermes International SA," retrieved January 30, 2009 from http://investing.businessweek.com/research/stocks/financials/financials. asp?ric=HRMS.PA.

17. 1) "Fenway Park," Major League Baseball web site, retrieved November 2, 2008 from http://mlb.com/bos/ballpark/index.jsp. 2) Material retrieved September 30, 2008, from www.ballparksofbaseball.com/al/FenwayPark.htm. Fenway Park, retrieved September 30, 2008 from www.ballparks.com/baseball/american/fenway.htm. 3) "History of Sevens," retrieved April 2, 2008 from www.hksevens.com/General-Info-History-History.htm. 4) "Fiji Wins Hong Kong Sevens," March 29, 2009, International Rugby Board, retrieved April 3, 2009 from www.irb.com/irbsevens/edition=5/news/newsid=2030394.html. 4) National Basketball Association (NBA), retrieved October 7, 2008 from www.nba.com/#. 5) Johnson, R. S. "The Jordan Effect," June 22, 1998, *Fortune* magazine, retrieved December 11, 2008 from http://money.cnn.com/magazines/fortune/fortune_archive/1998/06/22/244166/index.htm. 6) Koerner, B. I., "So Take Off All Your Clothes," March 24, 2006, *Slate* magazine, retrieved October 2, 2008 from www.slate.com/id/2138613/.

18. 1) Research projects conducted by students at Singapore Management University for their strategic brand management course between 2004 and 2008. 2) "Disney Final Research Report," November 2008. 3) Keane, T. W. and Trueman, W., 1999, "Autopoiesis in Disneyland," *International Journal of Advertising*, 1999, 18(4), pp. 519–536, retrieved October 11, 2008 from http://search.ebscohost.com.libproxy.smu.edu.sg/login.aspx?direct=true&db=buh&AN=12132910&site=ehost-live.

19. 1) Brown, S., "Marketing for Muggles: The Harry Potter Way to Higher Profits," *Business Horizons*, January–February 2002, pp. 6–11. 2) "Harry Potter Brand Wizard," July 18, 2005, *The Brand Channel and BusinessWeek*, retrieved May 4, 2008 from www.businessweek.com/innovate/content/jul2005/di20050721_060250.htm. 3) "Harry Potter, Marketing Magician," June 26, 2005, *Guardian*, retrieved June 17, 2008 from www.guardian.co.uk/business/2005/jun/26/media.books. 4) Bhatmagar, P., "Is Harry Potter dead?" July 11, 2005, CNNMoney.com, retrieved June 17, 2008 from http://money.cnn.com/2005/07/11/news/fortune500/brand_harrypotter/index.htm.

20. 1) Research projects conducted by students at Singapore Management University for their strategic brand management course between 2004 and 2008. 2) "Nokia," research completed November 2007, updated November 2008. 3) Masalin, L., March, 2003, "Nokia Leads Change Through Continuous Learning," *Academy of Management Learning and Education*, 2(1), pp. 68–72, March 17, 2008, from Business Source Premier database. 4) Carter, B., March 16, 2005, "Nokia in Experiential drive for Fashion Line," Marketing 00253650, retrieved March 17, 2008, available from Business Source Premier database. 5) Fletcher, M., May, 2005, "Only the 'Full Experience' will Link Brands with New Trends," retrieved March 17, 2008, available from Business Source Premier database. 6) Bond, C., November, 2005, "Centre stage for Nokia," trade event, retrieved October 23, 2007, from Business Source Premier database, updated March 17, 2008.

21. Statistics from speech by Gavin Coombs, Managing Director of FutureBrand Asia, at the BRITE Asia 09 Conference in March 2009, Singapore Management University. "Politics 2.0—The Obama Campaign," retrieved June 29, 2009 from www.i-policy.org/2009/06/politics-20-the-obama-campaign.html.

22. Ibid.

Brand Experiences: Customers and Solutions

9

Topics

Preview

In this chapter we will discuss the *customers* and *solutions* elements in creating a valuable brand experience. Creating a brand experience sounds both vague and complicated and both assessments hold some truth. Vague, because there is no precise definition of "experience," and complicated because many different business activities are used to create a brand experience, but the ingredients vary as do the ways they can be combined to make the experience special for customers. The example of Chip Conley's company, Joie de Vivre Hotels, provides a good example of a brand experience. Through a combination of uniquely designed hotels, branding that appeals to the five senses, and a quirky company atmosphere, Joie de Vivre has managed to create a memorable and highly valued brand experience for their guests. As successful as it is, their approach is unlikely to work at British Airways, Procter & Gamble, or Nokia. Each successful brand has a unique alchemy. Yet there are *actions* that any company can take to develop valuable and value-adding brand experiences.

Without clearly defined customers, any efforts to create a brand experience are likely to fail. Without relevant solutions for customers to purchase that also resonate with them, any profitable relationship development and brand loyalty is unlikely. Therefore, brand building requires researching and understanding the customer base and then developing solutions that address customer needs and marketplace opportunities. Analysis of customers doesn't just help obtain insights about product direction—it can also add salient detail about the different stimuli to which customers respond. This information can be used to identify more effective ways to create associations that help make a brand more memorable. Good customer data can also guide how a purchase can be leveraged so that the total market grows, share of customer wallet increases and the customer's loyalty to the brand deepens.

Of course, gaining a better and deeper understanding of customers has a purpose beyond determining how to position products and identifying which associations to create. Knowing what to position is vital. The effort expended to develop solutions, more specifically products (goods, services), is most effectively pursued when the entire product is considered. More than a physical offering or helpful service, a product is a set of expectations about its quality, support and usefulness. Customers expect a company's offerings to work as promised, and when they do not work, they trust that the company will fix it. Mismatches occur when products fail to connect with the market, because they are not relevant to needs and/or they don't resonate with the target audience. Mismatches can turn into negative associations quickly when a company mishandles a problem, such as failing to deliver on a warranty or making any effort to seek restitution onerous. Countering negative associations can be a significant obstacle and expensive to overcome. So the effort to create solutions involves planning thoughtfully about the expectations that will be created and how to address them. Pricing plays an important role in solution development, signaling quality and positioning. As brands develop through their lifecycle, the type of customer attracted to them may shift as well, placing an added burden of responsibility on tailoring the offering to suit the tastes of the new customer groups. Innovation plays an important role in his regard and whether it is incremental or breakthrough depends on customer knowledge and the brand's own reputation and is weighed against emerging opportunities. As these issues are explored in this chapter, keep in mind that the goal is to create memorable and positive customer experiences so that the brand has a competitive advantage over rivals.

Customers

Identifying, selecting, and attracting customers is important for any business. For brands, customer development goes beyond merely convincing people to buy your products. Brands are known identities, imbued with tradition and meaning and associated with tangible and

intangible qualities. Customers identify and relate to strong brands, often selecting a brand because it reflects their lifestyle and self-image. It is equally important to know which customers are not a good fit for the brand because such information will prevent resources from being used unwisely.

Of the more than 200 companies studied for this book, the most successful brands not only know who their best customers are but they know them *well*. This distinction is important. Too many businesses expend too little effort to identify and learn about their customers, falling prey to widely used category labels (i.e. "GenY," "Early Adopters") without diving below the surface to understand their customers more completely. In this chapter, we will revisit classic customer tools and add examples of how to dig deeper in developing insightful customer profiles that help brands grow stronger.

As discussed in Chapter 6, the 5 Cs are a marketing planning framework that examines strategic dimensions of the brand—and "customers" was one of the 5 Cs. Segmentation, Targeting, and Positioning break down the customer identification and selection analysis into sequential activities.

Segmentation, Targeting, Positioning (STP)

Segmentation, targeting and positioning (STP) emphasize identifying and selecting a target audience using a classic funnel approach, as shown in Figure 9-1, that starts with finding large segments that share common characteristics, narrows the market research toward the most attractive customers within those segments and then consistently communicates to the target audience using a variety of marketing communications modes, all in an effort to encourage the customer to purchase. Communicating well means that the message must be shaped to appeal to the target audience, communicated in a mode they use and help them relate to the brand as a result. Even when done well, not all targeted customers will buy, so an important element is developing the most effective marketing approach possible. The simplicity of the explanation belies inherent challenges. Marketers should be cautious in making early conclusions about the potential for different business scenarios without first conducting a more detailed investigation of the potential customer market so that they can then develop relevant positioning that ultimately appeals to and resonates with the selected target audience. Segmentation, targeting and positioning is the next step in the marketer's planning effort.

Done properly, detailed profiles of target customers will result, providing marketers with a better sense of customer needs, which will then help the creation of marketing programs designed to address those needs. Segmentation, targeting and positioning break the customer identification process into discrete phases, from a broad based analysis of common characteristics that defines each customer segment into the identification of the most attractive segments to target. Once the target segments are identified, marketers can then determine the most effective positioning strategy. The combination of segmentation, targeting, and positioning is instrumental in identifying the right groups of customers toward which the firm's brand building activities will be directed, ultimately resulting in a product sale. Let's begin with segmentation.

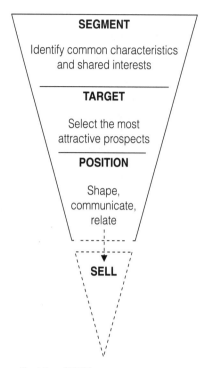

Figure 9-1   Segment, Target, Position (STP)

Segmentation

To identify market potential, marketers need a process for understanding and organizing customer audiences based on common attributes. Segmentation is a process for breaking the mass market into smaller, more manageable submarkets based on common characteristics, needs, and interests. Knowing these similarities helps marketers devise marketing communications that appeals to the most receptive group of customers. Kevin Keller describes segmentation bases for both consumer and business markets as shown in Figures 9-2 and 9-3.[1]

Consumers

Consumer is the term used to describe individual customers in the mass market who buy products for personal use. "B2C" (Business to Consumer) is a term frequently used to describe the transaction of businesses selling to consumers. To build a brand successfully requires marketers to develop a base of consumers that purchase the company's product. Purchases can be frequent, such as with less expensive commodities and/or necessities (such as food), or periodic, such as with premium branded goods and/or luxury items. Marketers use the segmentation bases to identify the characteristics most commonly shared by their target consumers, then using that information to tailor product offerings and marketing communications approaches that appeal most effectively to each segment.

```
┌─────────────────────────────────────┐
│      Consumer Segmentation Bases     │
│                                      │
│ Behavioral (aka Product Use)         │
│ User status                          │
│ Usage rate                           │
│ Usage occasion                       │
│ Brand loyalty                        │
│ Benefits sought                      │
│                                      │
│ Demographic                          │
│ Income                               │
│ Age                                  │
│ Sex                                  │
│ Race                                 │
│ Family                               │
│                                      │
│ Psychographic                        │
│ Values, opinions, and attitudes      │
│ Activities and lifestyle             │
│                                      │
│ Geographic                           │
│ Local                                │
│ Regional                             │
│ National                             │
│ International                        │
└─────────────────────────────────────┘
```

Figure 9-2   Consumer Segmentation Bases
Source: Keller, K. L., *Strategic Brand Management*, 3rd edn, © 2008 Pearson Education, p. 99.

```
┌─────────────────────────────────────┐
│      Business Segmentation Bases     │
│                                      │
│ Nature of Good                       │
│ Kind                                 │
│ Where used                           │
│ Type of buy                          │
│                                      │
│ Buying Conditions                    │
│ Purchase location                    │
│ Who buys                             │
│ Type of buy                          │
│                                      │
│ Demographic                          │
│ ISIC code                            │
│ Number of employees                  │
│ Number of production workers         │
│ Annual sales volume                  │
│ Number of establishments             │
└─────────────────────────────────────┘
```

Figure 9-3   Business Segmentation Bases
Source: Keller, K. L., *Strategic Brand Management*, 3rd edn, © 2008 Pearson Education, p. 102.

Business

Business (or *industrial*) describes customers that are other companies buying products for use in their businesses, and "B2B" (Business to Business) is the term that describes the transaction of businesses selling to other businesses. B2B marketers also want to understand common characteristics of their business buyers so that they can develop specific approaches to each business segment. For example, Figure 9-3 references ISIC code under the demographic base. The term "ISIC" refers to International Standard Industrial Classification, a United Nations designation that categorizes businesses according to type of economic activity (manufacturing, services, transportation, and so forth). Many, but not all, regions of the world have variations on the industrial classification designation. The U.S. segments according to the Standard Industrial Classification (SIC). The U.K. classifies using the United Kingdom Standard Industrial Classification of Economic Activities (UKSIC), Europe has the Statistical Classification of Economic Activities in the European Community (NACE), and Russia has the Russian Economic Activities Classification System (OKVED).

Communities

The advent of the Internet and digital technology has led to the birth and rapid growth of online communities whose participants do not easily fit into the more traditional segmentation bases. Communities are fast-responding people networks and subcultures, often with their own language and codes of conduct. Communities are simultaneously powerful, because of the millions of people using them, and fragmented, because the community members are spread around the world. They require the ability to filter chaff from useful insights. The ubiquity of social networking sites has fomented newer cultural practices where traditional social boundaries, such as income or age, dissolve and communities of shared interests emerge. Mobile technology has hastened the growth further, with people using messaging utilities like Twitter to send 140 character updates to others in their community, keeping the relationships alive wherever and whenever people want. As one can surmise, communities are hard for marketers to control, prone to exaggeration, yet potentially great for spreading the word and gleaning new trends. Without question, communities are an important, emerging opportunity and marketers need to understand them because they represent unique and increasingly large groups of potential customers.

Chapter 10 will discuss communities and social networking sites, such as Facebook, MySpace and LinkedIn in greater detail because they represent a growing area for marketing communications.

EXAMPLE 9-1:

Segmentation Classification Example: Vodafone[2]

Vodafone is a UK-based mobile communications brand. The needs of the company's consumers in general are changing as technology advances. This includes the desire for faster service, easy-to-use devices and mobile data services such as email and Internet access. Vodafone has built on their traditional voice and messaging services to include these features. Segmentation becomes important at this point because even these common requirements need to be fine tuned for specific customer groups. Vodafone uses psychographic-type designations in describing their customers:

- teens;
- young;
- active;
- fun;
- adult personal user;
- mature basic user;
- self-chooser users;
- company paid users;
- international business travelers.

One can see how these designations help brand building as they are descriptive terms and evoke images and associations beyond the label itself. For example, customers designated as *young, active, fun* want mobile phones with music and video capabilities, a *company paid user* may simply make work-related calls, and an *international business traveler* would be more interested in international 3G capabilities, platform agnosticism, and applications that that allow them to keep organized. The brand messages and mobile phone calling plans would, in turn, be tailored to appeal to each segment's particular characteristics.

Segment Analyses

Once segmentation bases are identified, marketers should then do deeper analysis by identifying needs, determining the relative share, and reviewing the financial contribution to their firm of each customer segment.

Segment Needs Analysis   One of the ways to better understand segments is to gather customer data and compare their needs. In Table 9-1, three segments (A, B, C) are shown, each with different needs.

Segment A is most interested in service, quality, and lifestyle, which suggests that this segment may be willing to pay a premium for higher value offerings. Segment B is attracted to low price and loyalty, suggesting that if they find the right product at an affordable price they will be regular customers. Segment C simply wants great service. Marketers should use this information when developing their marketing programs for each segment. If, for example, the company is shifting toward high-quality products at premium prices, targeting segment B would no longer fit because the company is de-emphasizing low cost/low price. Marketers must stay attuned to changes associated with each customer segment, as well as any strategic direction changes in their own firms, to ensure their marketing programs remain relevant to the customers and productive for their firm.

Table 9-1   Segment Needs Analysis

Needs	Segment A	Segment B	Segment C
Service and support	✓		✓
High quality	✓		
Low price		✓	
Loyalty programs		✓	
Lifestyle fit	✓		

Segment Share Analysis   Whereas market share tells marketers their percentage of the total market sales, segment share is the marketer's percentage of each segment's sales. Segment share is a useful metric because it uncovers useful information about the relative success of the company's product, marketing communications and service offerings mix in each segment, compared to the competition, as illustrated by Figure 9-4. Segment share information rarely exposes all the underlying details that led to each competitor's results but, as Figure 9-4 shows, marketers must look past the initial indicators and ask themselves several questions:

- Can we gain segment share versus our competitors if we succeed in winning over these customers?
- What are the segment share gains, if any, we can reasonably expect?
- Is it reasonable to expect any segment share gains in the short term?
- What is our competition doing that is affecting their success with each segment?
- Are there gaps or opportunities in our offering that should be addressed to improve segment share?
- Are the relative segment shares indicative of product quality, effective marketing communication, competitor tactics, service delivery or some combination of these?

Segment share analysis adds another helpful layer of understanding to the marketer's customer analysis. However, there is still more that marketers can and should do to evaluate their segments. Reviewing the financial contribution of each segment (or assessing its potential if it is a new segment) indicates where revenues and margins can be improved, or if servicing a segment is proving too expensive. Combining the market share analysis with a revenue and profit analysis gives the marketing team a more complete picture of each segment's potential.

Segment Financial Contribution Analysis   As marketers are accountable for their brand-building efforts, regularly assessing each segment's total revenues and profits offers insightful detail about the relative importance of each segment and, depending on the detail of the customer data gathered, its potential for profitable future financial contributions, particularly from new customers. Furthermore, marketers can then begin to gauge the effectiveness of their marketing programs in appealing to the various customer segments and whether financial performance and brand value can be improved by varying the marketing approaches. Several questions must be addressed:

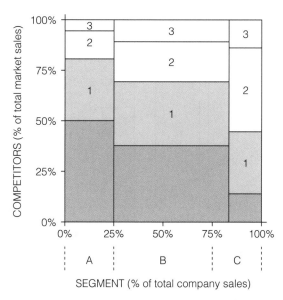

Figure 9-4 Segment Share Analysis
Source: Adapted from and executive education program co-taught by Sanjay Dhar, James H. Lorie Professor of Marketing, University of Chicago Graduate School of Business and the author. The executive education program was "Strategic Marketing: Creating Your Competitive Advantage," July 11–13, 2005 held in Singapore.

Revenues
- Is the segment (either business or consumer) large enough that our success with a few customers will enable us to continue developing growth opportunities?
- If not, then is the potential for revenue growth large with each individual customer?

Profits
- What is the profit we earn from the target segments?
- Are these customers high-end, high-margin customers with whom we can cultivate a premium image? Or are they volume customers requiring us to secure sizable contracts to ensure a reasonable profit?
- How does our emphasis on these customers affect our brand reputation?

Figure 9-5 illustrates how a company can graphically represent the overall contribution of its customer segments. The revenue and profit analysis for segments A, B, and C shows the relative financial contributions of each segment to the company's overall performance. This is a useful device because it provides a convenient and informative performance snapshot that can help marketers ascertain which customer segment(s) are performing well and, therefore, which should be emphasized in future marketing activities supporting the brand. The decision over which segment(s) to focus on may sometimes be counterintuitive.

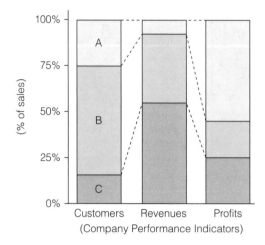

Figure 9-5 Revenue and Profit Contribution by Segment
Source: Adapted from: Sanjay Dhar, James H. Lorie Professor of Marketing, University of Chicago
Graduate School of Business, from an executive education program he co-taught with the author.
The executive education program was "Strategic Marketing: Creating Your Competitive Advantage," July 11–13, 2005, held in Singapore.

For example, a customer segment that contributes most of the profits might seem like a likely
candidate for an enhanced marketing effort because that high-margin segment is willing to
pay a premium. However, market trends may indicate that the weakest performing segment
should receive most of the marketing effort, perhaps because that segment offers the best
long-term growth potential despite the lower margins in the short term.

Segment A represents 25% of the company's customer base, approximately 10% of the
revenues, yet roughly 60% of the profits. Segment B is the largest customer segment overall, but its revenues are 30% of the total and its profits are approximately 15% of the total
profits. Segment C is about 20% of the total customer base yet it has more than 50% of
the revenues and 25% of the profits. Given the prior needs analysis that showed segment
A's preference for premium quality, service, and lifestyle fit, this analysis helps explain that
while they are not the dominant segment in terms of total customers, they dominate total
profits. Clearly, segment A is the high margin customer group that may be a best fit if the
marketer wants to develop a premium brand position and image.

The segment analysis may further prompt marketers to redirect additional marketing
resources toward this segment and perhaps toward segment C (whose key need was great
service), but leave segment B out of its customer marketing efforts in the future. However,
this graphic may also reveal opportunities the company has with segment B. How? Market
research may have indicated that segment B was trending toward more premium interests.
Perhaps their low price needs are less important than their interest in loyalty, for example.

In this instance, the marketing team may customize a marketing program to persuade segment B to deepen their relationship with the company. New loyalty programs could be marketed with the intent to convert a larger percentage of segment B to higher margin customers.

The benefits to deeper segment analysis can be vital for developing the marketing plan. An important lesson is that marketers must look beyond summary statistics and dig deeper into the factors that created the financial picture being reviewed. Part of what distinguishes superior marketers from the rest is their ability to see connections and relationships among various data and understand the potential implications, even though this information is not always clearly delineated. It is relatively easy to report numbers and describe trends, but it is far harder to explain what the potential causes and underlying influences are and where opportunities exist.

EXAMPLE 9-2:

ABSOLUT Vodka

ABSOLUT Vodka is positioned as a premium vodka, emphasizing sophistication and quality with memorable imagery of their iconic bottles in unusual settings and aligning with fashion, design, and fine art whose leaders influence ABSOLUT'S customers about their attitudes toward vodka.[3] This alignment suggests that drinking ABSOLUT helps customers be seen as cool, refined, and knowledge-able,[4] appealing to how customers associate opinion leaders with themselves. In 2002, *Forbes* named ABSOLUT the number one luxury brand in the world.[5]

The company uses psychographic and cultural segmentation,[6] rather than demographic, emphasizing the customer's lifestyle, beliefs, and attitudes.[7] The campaign targets attributes that would be most familiar and appealing to the target audience in that culture. For example, the *ABSOLUT Boston* ad shows cases of ABSOLUT Vodka in the shape of its iconic bottle floating in what appears to be Boston Harbor, linking to the famous Boston Tea Party of the 1773. The *ABSOLUT Rome* ad depicts a motor scooter, the front of which is shaped like an ABSOLUT bottle. There are subsegments within each segment, each receiving targeted approaches.[8] In 2006, rock star Lenny Kravitz recorded a new song, called *Breathe,* which was used in ABSOLUT advertising and was also made available as a free download from the ABSOLUT web site.

In 1988, ABSOLUT extended the product through flavored vodkas, including ABSOLUT Citron, tapping into consumer preference for choice and variety. In fact, ABSOLUT Citron remains the largest selling fruit-flavored vodka.[9] Today, ABSOLUT offers 10 different flavored vodkas (line extensions).[10] *ABSOLUT Mango* was launched in February 2008.[11] ABSOLUT has also been focusing on brand extensions to reach a broader client base. The ABSOLUT Spirits Co. launched *ABSOLUT Cut* in 2004, and entered the alcohol mixed beverages category.[12]

In summary, STP guides the thought process for identify common characteristics that can be exploited in the marketing plan in support of the firm's brand-building objectives. While perfect adherence to the sequence suggested by STP was not always evident (many brands know their customers quite well and bypass the segmentation stage, except when identifying possible new customer groups), the first step should yield customer characteristics that can be compared to the company's own capabilities (as outlined by the 5Cs), determining if a segment, while attractive at first review, is one that can be reasonably pursued using typical company resources.

Segmentation helps companies tailor their brands, products, and communications more effectively. But there is a tradeoff because narrower submarkets mean fewer potential customers, which may reduce the economic potential for the firm's offerings. If more resources are required to determine if this tradeoff is worthwhile, then senior management must be persuaded that further investment merits consideration. Furthermore, segmentation analysis identifies the relative financial potential and contribution of each segment. Top brands conduct ongoing research about each segment to determine whether the company should continue allocating resources to attract these customers.

Targeting

Most brands focus their planning on segments with the greatest potential, eliminating less attractive segments from further consideration. This is true for existing and potential customers. Existing customers may be invaluable as opinion leaders. Plus, their loyalty provides a source of ongoing revenue. On the other hand, they may have been lucrative in prior years, but changing industry conditions perhaps have made them harder to service and less rewarding. As older customers depart, new ones must be recruited. New customer acquisition is not always easy and often requires brands to be tailored to the needs of the potential new customers. This can be harder than it first appears because new customers may not view the brand favorably. Target market evaluation criteria can help marketers determine the most attractive segments to pursue.

Target Market Evaluation Criteria

The following evaluation criteria will help marketers identify which segments to target:

- strategic objectives
- market/segment characteristics
- capabilities match

Let's review each.

Strategic Objectives   The brand-building activities must be aligned with the company's strategic objectives and marketers are responsible for ensuring that this occurs. Strategic objectives will vary by firm but they might include financial, reputation, and awareness targets (for example). Financial targets include: revenues, profits, margins, units sold, and market share. Reputation objectives tend to state more intangible goals, such as "to be recognized as the most innovative company in our industry". Awareness targets refer to customer recall and recognition percentages. ("Have you heard of this company? Do you recall this brand? Do you recognize these products?")

1. Market/segment characteristics
   a. Are the segments large enough to warrant our attention?
   b. High revenue/profit potential?
   c. Market share growth potential?
   d. What are the needs of customers within?
   e. Early adopter/late adopter?
   f. Price sensitive/inelastic?
   g. Better ROI?
   h. High-cost/low-cost entry?
   i. Risk of competitor retaliation?
   j. Fast/slow growing?
   k. Risk-taking/risk-averse?
   l. Limited means/wealthy?
   m. Fair weather/casual/devoted customers?
   n. Functional/emotional orientation?
   o. Interests/behaviors/needs?
   p. One-time/loyal?
2. Capabilities match
   a. Can we deliver on promises we make?
      i. Infrastructure?
      ii. Support?
      iii. Meet demand?
      iv. Necessary financial resources?
      v. Previous experience with this market?
   b. Do we fit (loosely) the target customer's characteristics?
      i. If so, is the customer aware of this?
      ii. If not, do we believe our efforts will create the awareness needed?
      iii. Do they buy our products currently?
      iv. Will our effort be seen as credible?
      v. Is our reputation positive with this customer? Negative?

Several useful steps can be taken to help marketers assess the attractiveness of the new customers they wish to target. A simple ratings scale can be used for each segment and its characteristics. Figure 9-6 illustrates one such scale. In this case, the evaluation criteria

Figure 9-6　Target Customer Ratings Schedule
Source: Adapted from: Sanjay Dhar, James H. Lorie Professor of Marketing, University of Chicago Graduate School of Business, from an executive education program he co-taught with the author. The executive education program was "Strategic Marketing: Creating Your Competitive Advantage," July 11–13, 2005 held in Singapore.

the marketers use can be applied to each segment, comparing new segments to the firm's existing segments.

Once the target customer analysis has been completed, several sets of segment data will be available for a comparison. The marketing team can select the ideal target customer(s) based on the resulting scores. A higher, positive score is obviously desired.

Positioning

Having worked through the customer selection process using segmentation and targeting, the next task is to create and manage (position) how customers perceive the offering by attempting to associate one or two attributes about the offering in the customer's mind. Positioning success depends heavily on owning a unique space in the customer's mind and developing a memorable way to communicate it. Examples of clear positioning are given in Table 9-2.

Owning this unique space is directly related to our earlier discussion about differentiation: customers must recognize and understand what makes the offering unique, and if they do not, then the product is not adequately differentiated and any corresponding positioning efforts are likely to fail. As such, the key elements of the marketer's job should always be:

• understanding customer needs;
• determining if those needs could be turned into market opportunities;
• leveraging their own company's distinctive competencies;
• translating those competencies into distinctive offerings that customers value;
• positioning the offering by emphasizing one or two characteristics;
• communicating about the offering in a way that affirms its uniqueness.

If this is done thoughtfully, the marketer will have contributed to increasing the firm's brand value. Doing each of these things well is not easy. Indeed, significant thought and planning goes into this process, usually with a bias toward simplicity.

Table 9-2   Components of Distinction

Company	Country of Origin	Position
Apple	U.S.	Creative, lifestyle
Air Asia	Malaysia	Fun, low cost
Facebook	U.S.	The social network
IKEA	Sweden	Affordable design
Nintendo	Japan	Interactive play

Source: John A. Davis brand research, 2000–2009 and research projects conducted by students at Singapore Management University between 2005 and 2008.

While positioning planning varied by brand, with some approaches informal and others bordering on scientific, a useful positioning planning guide is as follows:[13]

1. To whom (target market)?
2. Relative to (frame of reference)?
3. Determine the customer value proposition.
   a. Affirm shared/known characteristics (points of parity).
   b. Identify a unique selling proposition (points of difference).

Let's look at each step.

To Whom (Target Market)?

Segmentation and targeting have identified the highest potential customers. As we have learned, this effort yields insight about the target segment, serving as a base description of that audience's profile. The more marketers know about their customer, the greater the likelihood that relevant offerings and associated marketing communications can be developed that attract and retain these customers profitably.

Relative To . . . (Frame of Reference)?

Consumers have two frames of reference with products:

1. Established
2. New

Established offerings are known by consumers based on past experiences and/or from what others have told them. Such offerings compete in known product categories (Nike competes in athletic footwear; Mercedes is a luxury car; Air Asia is a discount airline; NHN is a leading search portal in South Korea—70% of the search market, making NHN substantially more popular than Google in South Korea).[14]

New offerings are unknown, therefore the marketer's challenge is quickly establishing a category position so that consumers know how to understand and evaluate it. When Apple's iTunes first came out in 2001, the category of downloadable music was still relatively new and had been dominated by Napster, a free service that was the source of legal and ethical controversy. Apple's challenge was significant: how to convince users to pay for music they had been getting for free for several years. Apple's success in this category was partly due to creating a highly differentiated product that was easy to use *and* made consumers feel better about their music downloading (because the ethical issue of free downloading with Napster had been removed). iTunes has expanded into offering TV shows and movies and is tightly coupled with its iPod products, which are portable digital entertainment players, creating a great overall experience that fits in well with consumer lifestyles.

Determine the Customer Value Proposition

Affirm Shared/Known Characteristics (Points of Parity) Consumers will buy offerings they know more often than those they don't. This is fundamental to building a brand. The frame of reference connects the offering to a product category. Such a connection helps consumers understand how the product fits into the category, including associations shared by competitors in the category. Apple's iTunes points of parity with Napster included download-able music. Singapore Airlines (SIA) began service in 1972 at a time when the International Air Travel Association (IATA) regulated the airline industry. While membership was voluntary, most airlines were members, including SIA. IATA set standards for in-flight service specifications, including meal sizes and types of beverages allowed in each class of service. These standards were, in effect, the points of parity shared by most international airlines.

Identify a Unique Selling Proposition (Points of Difference)   To create a compelling value proposition, marketers must move past points of parity to those factors that create points of difference. Points of difference can give the marketer's offering a competitive advantage and, de facto, put competitors at a disadvantage. This is fundamental to building brand value.

Apple's iTunes brought legitimacy to downloading music, plus Apple's known reputation for design, added simplicity, and visual appeal that clearly distinguished it from other music downloading services.

Singapore Airlines' Destiny was based on superior customer service. A few years after its founding, SIA withdrew from IATA, choosing to set its own rules for service. The ensuing effort led SIA to create the most successful and profitable international airline in the world, establishing a reputation for unrivaled service and superior features in their planes at standards well above those prescribed by IATA. By leaving IATA, SIA was able to develop points of difference that distinguished it from rival carriers. Singapore Airlines rejoined IATA many years later but only after its market-leading position was well established.[15]

Determining the customer value proposition is a significant step in brand building. A successful value proposition helps clarify to customers why the offering matters to them, while simultaneously reaffirming to employees who the customers are, how the products satisfy needs, and why their company is doing it. Two questions help determine if a value proposition is successful with customers:

- Is it relevant to them (do they understand it and does it satisfy a need)?
- Does it resonate with them (does the offering connect with them emotionally and fit within their lifestyle)?

One challenge in positioning cannot be overlooked: beating incumbents. When a firm has a well-known market position, as Table 9-2 illustrates, challengers will have a difficult time dislodging a better known competitor, particularly if they compete on the same points of parity. Marketers earn their pay when they can identify points of difference that clearly separate their offerings from those of the competition and, correspondingly, cement a new position in the minds of consumers.

EXAMPLE 9-3:

American Express

American Express competes in the charge and credit-card markets with a distinctive set of offerings. Its two primary segments are the Global

Consumer Group and the Global Business-to-Business (B2B) Group. This example emphasizes the Global Consumer Group. When first launched in 1958, the American Express charge card was priced slightly higher than primary competitor, the Diners Club card. This helped position the card as a premium product. Exclusivity and prestige are key cornerstones of American Express's positioning. Visa is now the market leader with 54% market share, MasterCard with 29% and American Express with 13%. However, unlike Visa and MasterCard, which rely on generating income through charging interest on revolving credit balances, American Express focuses on increasing card member spending. In 2008 J. D. Power and Associates,[16] ranked American Express as the highest in customer satisfaction of the 10 largest credit card companies in the U.S. in vital customer satisfaction areas including problem resolution, rewards and benefits, and payment and billing processes, providing visible outside credibility about the quality of American Expresses offerings.

A primary source of revenue is called discount revenue, which are the fees earned from merchants that are processing customer transactions. The Gold Card was introduced in 1966 and the Platinum Card in 1984, signaling clearly defined market segments in American Express's business, in addition to the classic Green Card. Its Platinum and Centurion Cards followed in subsequent years and, depending on the market, are offered by invitation only. With its premium position, the company emphasizes value to the customer through a generous rewards program whose benefits vary by card type. Customers can earn points that are redeemable toward premier travel, retail, and entertainment products. Participating partners are equally prestigious, including BMW and Harrods' department store in the U.K. The programs encourage customers to spend more per card, driving discount revenue up and subsequent higher value to its customer over time. In 2004, the average American Express card member spent US$10 700 a year, as compared to $2900 and $2000 for Visa and MasterCard respectively.[17] In 2008 American Express increased card member spending 15% from the previous year.[18]

In the mid-2000s, American Express launched the "My Life. My Card" campaign, in which celebrities described how the American Express card fitted their lives. The campaign has garnered significant attention for the brand, reinforcing its premium image. In 2007, an ad featuring Ellen DeGeneres won an Emmy Award for Outstanding Commercial. An important point is that the campaign has been consistent with American Express's historical positioning as an exclusive card. Beyond the prestigious cards, American Express offers superior services and markets these as well. A television ad called "The Art of the Dispute" featured tennis star John McEnroe and was shown during the 2007 U.S. Open, highlighting American Express' dispute resolution services for card members, a humorous, ironic reference that enhanced the company's personality. Associating the product with famous celebrities, as the company's campaigns have done over the years, from professional athletes to movie stars, simply adds allure and appeal to the brand. The company's positioning still emphasizes prestige customers to this day, although the Blue card, launched in 1999, is targeted to younger working adults. The card has no annual fee and users have access to their own rewards program, which quickly boosted its popularity and market share. American Express does not enjoy the same market share as its competitors but it has successfully carved out a unique niche by focusing on a specific segment of the market, creating benefits tailored to their interests, consistently positioning itself as a premier brand.[19]

Nokia

Nokia is one of the most valuable and recognized global brands. Early on the company targeted consumers and not businesses, giving it a significant advantage over rivals such as Ericsson.[20] Nokia focused on the U.S. and European consumer markets during this time,[21] expanding in 1999 into China, India, Brazil, and Russia, to take advantage of their more rapid growth.[22] As mobile communications continued to grow, the business segment became an added area of focus, so in 2004 the company reorganized, adding three new segments: multimedia, enterprise solutions, and networks. This helped the company diversify its product range and enhance the features within.[23]

In the latter half of the 2000s, Nokia's strategy shifted increasingly toward rapidly growing emerging markets like India, China, and parts of Africa, with a goal of 2 billion new customers by the end of the decade.[24] Africa has one of the fastest growth rates, and the company expects to reach 200 million subscribers there by 2009/2010, doubling the amount since 2005.[25] Nokia's design studios take research insights from each region and incorporate those into new handset design. Cost and access is a limiting factor in many emerging markets, so the company is designing affordable handsets to appeal to these markets[26] by finessing its manufacturing and supplier logistics to keep profit margins healthy.[27] At the same time, the company is not ignoring mature markets, focusing on the replacements business for outdated equipment and slowing growth by focusing its manufacturing processes to be more nimble to take advantage of shifts in the market.[28] This segmentation approach has helped Nokia successfully differentiate itself from rivals.

Customer Cycle and Brand Growth

We are starting this discussion with the presumption that a company already has a new product and/or brand to launch into the market, so the sequence is specific to the attraction, retention and development of customers. As seen repeatedly with top brands, while they did not always perfectly fit into the flow shown in Figure 9-7, the pattern of customer-related activity and development was quite similar for the most part.

Managing the customer process involves a series of ongoing stages, represented by any of three outcomes at each stage:

- continue moving the relationship forward;
- lose the relationship;
- continue moving forward and refer a prospective customer.

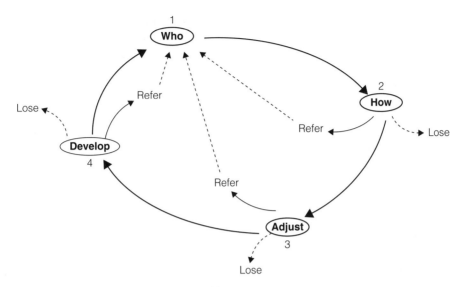

Figure 9-7 Customer Cycle in Brand Building

1. *Who.* The "who" has been addressed through the customer identification process, using STP.
2. *How.* "How" refers to brand positioning and the corresponding marketing activities used to communicate to customers. If the marketing efforts prove ineffective (wrong message, poor quality message), the customer will leave. This should trigger a review of the marketing efforts if either many customers react this way, or if those identified early on as having high potential leave. However, assuming this stage is successful, the customer moves along, their relationship with the brand growing as well. Ideally, the customer refers other prospective customers to the brand based on their early experience.
3. *Adjust.* This stage involves minor adjustments to the initial marketing campaign as more information comes in on customer feedback. Adjustments may include fine-tuning the message, subtly altering packaging and/or retail channel distribution, changing the frequency of the message and altering the marketing mode used. But this is not a stage for wholesale relaunching because customers have already voted in favor of the brand from the initial overtures. Customer loss at this stage should invite an analysis that examines which factors in the adjustments caused the customer to leave (or whether the loss was caused by competitor inroads). As before, referrals signal higher customer approval of the company, which is also leading to more positive word of mouth.
4. *Develop.* "Develop" is more than just a stage—it is an ongoing commitment between the brand and the customer. For the brand at this stage, nurturing customer loyalty becomes paramount. Focusing on building customer equity (the sum of the lifetime values of the brand's customers)[29] and increasing the brand's share of the customer's

wallet is the primary focus. This includes developing and adjusting the offerings to better fit customer needs and using a more familiar approach to marketing communication, because launch-style education is no longer appropriate or necessary. For customers, their interest in the brand is proven, expectations are growing and not diminishing, which begins to transition their interest from solutions to experiences ("I like the brand, so make it come alive for me"). If loss occurs at this stage this is a serious cause for concern because both brand and customer have invested significantly in the relationship at this stage. Assuming development progress, then more referrals and positive word of mouth are likely to continue.

EXAMPLE 9-4:

ComfortDelGro Taxi[30]

ComfortDelGro is the largest taxi company in Singapore. The company operates a 24-hour fully automated booking service whereby first time customers call the reservation number and tell the operator their location. The operator enters the data into an electronic dispatch program to which a nearby driver responds to by stating the amount of time until pickup (usually 5–7 minutes). Drivers are penalized for misstating or missing pickup times, so there is incentive for drivers to be accurate and customers know this, which makes the system more predictable and reliable. That first-time passenger is now entered into Comfort's dispatch database as is the location they used. The next time they call Comfort, the automated service automatically asks if they customer is in the previous location. If not, the customer can verbally describe a new location, which is also entered into the dispatch system. Customers calling from their homes have their addresses logged into the system and the automated voice response simply asks the caller if they want the taxi to come to their home, which alerts nearby taxis that confirm the approximate time of pick-up (again, usually 5–7 minutes). ComfortDelGro focused on improving dependability and trustworthiness.

EspressoConnection[31]

EspressoConnection (Chapter 8) cannot compete with Starbucks on size but its acclaimed reputation for high-quality service sets it apart. From the moment a car pulls up to the drive-through (recall that some stores have two drive-through windows, a thoughtful service design improvement that speeds up service during peak commute times), to the energetic employee who bounds from the store to personally take the order, to the joke of the day, EspressoConnection focused on how to improve the service while offering comparably priced coffee (to other specialty chains, including Starbucks). The result is higher customer loyalty.

Apple[32]

Apple's iTunes music service frequently upgrades and enhances its features. Evolving from music distribution initially, iTunes expanded to movies and TV shows. The service improved again by providing the artwork for each artist or video, creating a better visual appeal beyond the written description. More recently, iTunes added a "Genius Sidebar," which is intelligent software that analyzes the user's downloaded items and makes recommendations on other items that the customer might find of interest. These features enhance the customer's enjoyment of iTunes and further cement their loyalty. Apple focused on marketing seeking product improvement based on how customers think and use products, not on feature adjustments lacking a market.

Infosys[33]

Infosys, a large Indian IT firm with a reputation as a low-cost software development firm, sought a larger market for its services. It began investing in and offering high-end consulting services, in addition to vertical market software solutions based on consulting solutions that it had developed over many years. This enabled Infosys to compete more effectively against global giants IBM and Accenture. Had Infosys merely advertised that it was a viable alternative to IBM and Accenture, the chance of gaining new customers would have been low. Successfully entering new markets partly depends on actual changes to products and not just a marketing communications campaign with new positioning messages.

Ritz-Carlton[34]

Ritz-Carlton Hotels has a well-established reputation for managing high-quality luxury hotels. Their customers have strong, loyal connections to the brand, and the company has taken advantage of this by offering a range of Ritz-Carlton-branded merchandise ranging from bedding to apparel to bath products. By leveraging this customer loyalty, Ritz-Carlton merchandise has added a complementary revenue stream and has reinforced its brand connection to customers.

Throughout the customer cycle, acquisition and retention rates and costs should be measured. The further along the customer cycle in brand building, the more expensive a customer loss becomes. Conversely, each customer that continues with the company to each subsequent stage reduces the need to exphasize new customer acquisition programs, which tend to be more expensive relative to customer retention programs. Few companies eliminate new customer acquisition programs entirely, even with an enormous base of loyal customers, simply because internal growth needs, customer attrition, and competitor dynamics require ongoing development. For professional practice firms, such as physicians, accountants, and consultants, new customer growth is more closely tied to having a requisite number of experts available to service demand. A single doctor, for example, can only visit with a certain number of patients each day before time runs out. New customer growth, in this instance, is constrained by limited resources.

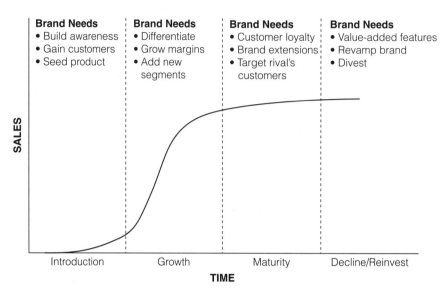

Figure 9-8   Brand Lifecycle Needs

Brand Lifecycle and Marketing Changes

Observing the customer cycle should raise the question of the brand's own changes over time. Needs evolve during the brand's lifecycle, as show in Figure 9-8. The best brands adjust their approach in each stage, although the stages are not nearly as neat and tidy as suggested by the figure. There are no direct signs or doors a brand passes through from one stage to another. Instead, business patterns shift (demand increases noticeably over prior weeks, inquiries into customer support areas increase, third-party channels step up their orders). As brands move from introduction to growth, the structure of the industry in which they compete changes, because new competitors enter in pursuit of their own share. This adds choice to the market, which also logically means that competitors will acquire new customers at this time. Firms must understand these dynamics for their brands so that appropriate marketing approaches can be developed to improve.

Introduction
The brand itself or the offering from the brand is new. The brand needs to build awareness and gain new customers. This can include seeding the product through samples and selected distribution channels to encourage customer trial. Awareness-related marketing is very different from more personalized approaches found in later lifecycle stages. Interestingly, awareness building does not necessarily mean only mass-market advertising. Field sales personnel can discuss the new offerings with customers individually or through

customer events. But the message they use would be introductory in nature since, logically, the market is not familiar with the offering yet.

Growth

The market is developing fondness for the brand, spreading the word and fomenting demand. Marketing campaigns grow broader and messages are typically more frequent. Message mode, timing, and delivery change as knowledge of the growing customer based improves. The effort here is to reinforce momentum and capture as much share as possible.

Maturity

With competitors in the market, customers have additional choice. Brands must refine and clarify how they are different and why it should matter to customers. Marketing communications shift toward more personalized appeals for the most loyal customers, recognizing their familiarity.

Decline/Reinvest

At this stage the primary choices are either revamping the product line through incremental and/or significant innovation, or divestment. Most of the global brands known today have been around for years, periodically refurbishing their image, offerings, and communication, as opposed to divestment or liquidation (unless there is a permanent, negative shift in the market, or a severe company crisis).

Arguably, had financial brands been more aware of customer segments' needs and lifecycles (such as ability to afford and pay for new mortgage products), and not focused on altering features to create new segments, this might have helped avoid the U.S. mortgage crisis in 2007 and 2008 that was a key cause of the global financial meltdown of September 2008. There may well have been a greater likelihood of identifying and avoiding unqualified buyers more effectively, in the earliest stages of segmentation. Unfortunately, in the late 1990s and early 2000s, as the U.S. liberalized banking and investment laws, a new class of home-loan products evolved that reduced the income and downpayment thresholds previously required by banks. This greatly increased the number of new customers with new home loans by making it far easier for previously unqualified customers to get a mortgage.

Questions for Customer Planning

1. What segments are being targeted?
   a. What do the customers have in common?
2. What is known about them?
   a. What are their needs?
   b. Your market share?
   c. Their contribution to the brand's revenues/profits?
   d. Does the segment match the firm's ability to deliver?
3. Has each customer target been evaluated and scored/rated?

Solutions

The term *solution* is selected purposefully because it conveys a complete answer to a need, which might include the core product plus partner products and service, whereas a product is confined to a narrower definition based primarily on its physical characteristics. Historically, a product has been viewed as an entity with certain features and benefits. "Product" was a useful concept in a less complicated world in which firms made goods, packaged and priced them, distributed them in stores, and then advertised to people in the market who listened to the messages and then purchased the products. The focus on features and benefits, however, restricts the concept of product to a simple offering that a company conceives on its own in the hope that customers will buy it and its use will give them satisfaction. "Product," as historically defined, does not describe what customers seek today, just as a logo is not an adequate description of a brand. A more engaged and connected society has developed more sophisticated expectations about what it wants. What is wanted is more than just being satisfied and/or having our needs met. Taken literally, those are relatively bland and nondescriptive terms anyway. People want more than just solutions for problems—they want solutions for opportunities that they didn't know existed. They want to be surprised (in a positive sense). They want to be connected with each other and they want to engaged and involved with life, not just observers of it. This has placed a unique challenge and tremendous opportunity on brands to become the catalyst for solutions, not just the purveyors of features and benefits. Rather than just solving problems, people are seeking brands to add more pieces to the puzzle, bringing it closer to completion but also allowing them to exercise their own ingenuity in putting the pieces in place.

The best performing brands studied for this textbook repeatedly referred to their offerings as solutions more often than product, although a product in its narrow sense was a part of it. In several instances, executives said they were purposely using the term to set an expectation inside their companies about how employees should perceive what they make, and a solution suggested a more dynamic, expansive interpretation of the company's offerings that actually helped inspire creative thinking on future solution development, organizational processes, and marketing communications. For example, Procter & Gamble's web site features a section called "Everyday Solutions" that has a wide range of articles and helpful hints on how P&G's products can contribute to a better lifestyle. The information ranges from recommended exercises to tips on how to throw a great party. Furthermore, solutions are important because they are one of the four subcomponents of an Experience. Finally, as reinforced throughout this book, Experience is one of four components of a strong brand.

However, the term *product* is still a key component of a solution and it is also a more common understanding for the majority of business people. We will discuss *product* because it is still the most commonly understood term and is useful for today's brands. But we also encourage brand building to encompass solution-oriented growth opportunities as future plans are developed.

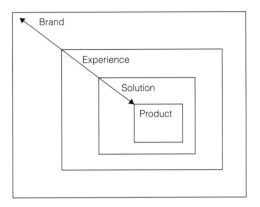

Figure 9-9 Product-brand Relationship

Brand-Product Relationship

Over the years, the business and academic literature has not always made a clear distinction between brands and products. However, this book argues that a brand is a much larger and more encompassing identity of which a product is a part, whereas a product is a generic entity to which a brand gives a personality and other value-enhancing qualities. This does not mean that products are less important. Instead, products are more tightly defined around solving a problem or satisfying a need. Figure 9-9 illustrates the product-brand relationship.

Let's look at each briefly before exploring the idea of product in greater depth. A simple illustration will help. A drill is a *product*; the hole it makes is a *solution*; the drill's ease of use and speed is an *experience*; and the resulting good feeling the customer has from using the drill enhances the company's reputation, which is *brand*. Table 9-3 defines the brand-experience-solution-product relationship in more universal business terms.

In the more conventional understanding, both brands and products have specific attributes that help define and distinguish their functions. A brand helps connect the product to a larger set of attributes, giving the product greater depth and meaning. For ex-

Table 9-3 Product-solution-experience-brand

BRAND	destiny, distinction, culture, experiences
EXPERIENCE	customers, solutions, marketing communications, environment
SOLUTION	product plus (+) added support, complementary offerings/bundle, resolution for need
PRODUCT	features, benefits, uses, tangible good, intangible service

Source: John A. Davis brand research, 2000–2009.

ample, a good cup of coffee can satisfy a consumer's need for a morning wake-up beverage. But when connected to the Starbucks brand, that cup of coffee takes on more characteristics and heightened expectations (customized drinks, comfortable chairs inside the store, games to play, friendly atmosphere). Psychologically, these additional attributes represented by Starbucks help customers justify the higher price they are paying. The core, a high-quality cup of coffee, is critical. But the larger brand identity adds significant intangible value.

Product Taxonomy

Products are typically classified by:

- *Product category/class*—a group of products sharing similar characteristics. Athletic footwear, juices, hair care, soaps, and sports cars are each product categories.
- *Product line*—a vertical line of products within a product category organized by price and functionality/ingredients/features. Nike Basketball is a product line within the athletic footwear product category.
- *Product*—a single offering within the product line. The Zoom Soldier III is a basketball shoe within Nike's product line.

Brand-Product Combinations

Combining the above with the brand relationship spectrum framework from Chapter 3, one can quickly see that a variety of different brand-product combinations are possible. An organization may have a brand over a single product (Bluetooth SIG—Special Interest Group), a branded product line (Apple iPods), several brands within a product class (P&G and soaps), or even a single branded house (Virgin). Figures 9-10 and 9-11 illustrate the brand-product combination for Procter & Gamble (P&G) and Apple. The P&G diagram in Figure 9-10

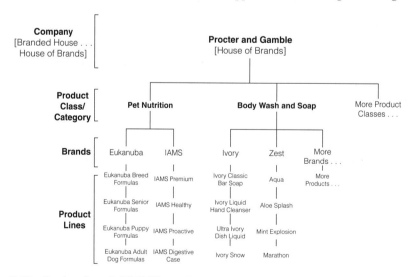

Figure 9-10   Product-brand: P&G Illustration
Source: P&G web site, www.pg.com, retrieved December 11, 2008.

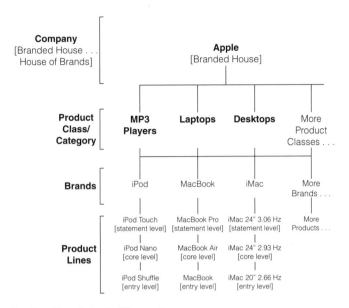

Figure 9-11   Product-Brand Apple Illustration
Source: retrieved March 30, 2009 from www.apple.com.

shows a selection of the firm's many different branded products within each branded product line. The Apple chart shows the price point levels within each branded product line.

The brand-product definitions and taxonomy are not absolute rules. In fact, many companies have multiple brand and product strategies. The point is not to tell companies to stay with one approach forever. Instead, the perpetual brand opportunity (and challenge) is deciding which strategy, or combination of strategies, is best for each company's needs and unique competitive situation. Furthermore, brand and product strategies can and should change over time as conditions warrant. The risk is that too much change too fast can prevent a brand from gaining sufficient market strength, undermining efforts to garner a loyal customer base and a stronger market position.

Product

The product (either a good or a service) is the core of the marketing mix. It is the main point of contact from the company to customers. The product must satisfy target customer needs and, ideally, do so uniquely well. The concept of product is often defined by more than the item itself and may include:

- *Variety:* does it come in different colors, sizes, or versions?
- *Quality:* is it best in class, or at least comparable to competitor offerings?
- *Design:* how does it look?
- *Packaging:* is the packaging plain, colorful, and/or consistent with the brand?
- *Features:* does it have the features customers expect? Any points of difference?
- *Services:* does it include or is it supported by helpful support?
- *Warranties:* does it perform as promised and are there remedies if it doesn't?

When consumers purchase a product, each of these factors is commonly associated with the product, and consumers assume it is supported by these and similar elements. Customers view products as *solutions* that satisfy a need or solve a problem. If the company is particularly skilled, then the solution the customer receives will be relevant to them while resonating with them as well. The result is not just a satisfied customer but a *delighted* one.

Marketing and Product Development

Successful brand reputations depend partly on regularly delivering reliable quality to the market and doing so supported by good execution in operations and marketing. During the brand-building process, some brands may be perceived as more innovative than others. Yet it is perfectly possible for multiple competitors to co-exist and succeed pursuing similar customers while having entirely different reputations for innovation. In the PC market, Dell competes against Apple, among others. Dell's reputation is based on its direct-to-customer, low-cost model, whereas Apple is perceived as more creative and innovative. Google competes against Yahoo! in the search business. While both started out seen as innovative leaders, Google has progressed into new businesses more quickly than Yahoo!, including Google Earth, GMail, Google Docs (office applications), and Google Mobile, while also keeping its core search business updated. Virgin Atlantic competes against British Airways on similar trans-Atlantic routes, with Virgin perceived as more fun and quirky, whereas British Airways holds a more traditional image.

Recall the bent arrow theory of marketing that described the inexorable shift from specialty to commodity status over time as more competitors enter the market and muddle differentiation points. The challenge for brand building is to turn the arrow back in the effort to recapture a distinctive specialty position. This is tougher to do than say. A great deal of success typically surrounds products that grow fast enough to shift from specialty to commodity, despite the pejorative connotation of the latter. As brands compete more as commodities, company operations must shift, focusing on lowering costs and meeting demand cost effectively. This takes the emphasis from state of the art innovation to managing a volume-based commodity business. There are other implications across the organization as well, as summarized in Figure 9-12, which illustrates both ends of the marketing and product development spectrum.

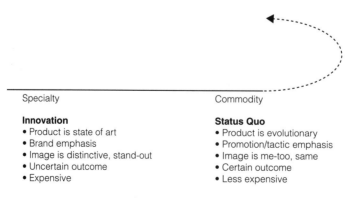

Figure 9-12   Bent-arrow Marketing and Product Development Issues

Building a strong brand does not have to only be for the purpose of returning to a pure specialty position. The point is that for a brand to remain memorable and strong, it has to find a way to either remain unique or return to being perceived as distinctive. Even commodity products can be successful brands. The strongest ones have a good reputation for quality and reliability, are familiar and are trusted. For them, the key is being *superior* at what they do, which may require an emphasis on innovation, but it may simply need minor modifications in product and/or marketing communications that help reveal the brand in a new light.

Specialty

Benefits

Looking at the far left end of the spectrum, there are many benefits for emphasizing a specialty brand position. Innovative products often reveal latent customer needs. Latent needs are not overtly known or understood by customers or the market at large. Instead, they are derived from inference and intuition, rather than straightforward surveys of customer needs. Examples of innovations that uncovered latent needs and created new markets include:

- Polaroid camera;
- Apple iPhone;
- Amazon Kindle reader;
- Virgin Atlantic service (massage, airport lounge, free limo service, bar on the plane);
- Tesla Motors all-electric car;
- Joie de Vivre Hotels;
- Fandango online movie ticket ordering;
- Starbucks;
- The Body Shop;
- Segway;
- Google;
- YouTube;
- Facebook;
- Twitter;
- Nintendo Wii;
- Minimally invasive surgical techniques (cardiac, knee, shoulder).

Risks

Innovation is higher risk and potential more expensive. Since the effort is placed on developing entirely new solutions, the market may not be ready or willing to embrace the new product at the beginning. Brands will need to educate the market about the innovation, why it is relevant, how it improves one's life (or work) and get it into as many people's hands as possible. Marketing costs will be higher with a new product because it is both unknown and untested (as far as consumers are concerned). Failure may tarnish a brand's image and reduce market confidence in future products. As discussed in Chapter 4, brand-building success is predicated on a company's ability to understand its capabilities. If a company is not known for breakthrough innovation, then claiming otherwise may prove problematic without investing in expensive marketing communications programs, R&D, and internal operations to support the innovation over the long term.

Status Quo

Status quo describes smaller and less dramatic changes to products.

Benefits

Incremental innovation is typically easier to undertake, requires less sophisticated technology and is less expensive. Most companies offer incremental innovation even if they also have examples of breakthrough products. Once again, Apple is a good example of this. Their breakthrough iPods, iMacs, and iPhone products have been supported by regular incremental innovation in memory increases, battery improvements, and exterior design. Customer needs should be regularly surveyed to gain the latest insights about a brand so that relevant incremental improvements can be made. Focus groups, which bring together customers to discuss ideas (ranging from current and new products to social issues to trends … and more), can also provide helpful information about market needs. The results are called *articulated* or *expressed* needs because the customer is able to describe what they prefer. When a buyer says she would prefer leather seats with lumbar support instead of standard cloth seats with no support, she is stating an articulated need. The basis for articulated needs stems from the customer's current understanding of the product, which they need in order to compare it to what they would like to have.

Risks

Incremental innovation carries lower risk than breakthrough innovation. However, any product change creates the potential for customer dissatisfaction if not executed and explained properly. Proper market research techniques are important here. It is beyond the scope of this book to describe detailed market research methodologies. However, understanding up front what the objectives of any market research are is vital to market research success. Target market selection, sample size, and survey design are each important to getting results that are statistically valid. Otherwise brands may make inappropriate or irrelevant product changes because of incomplete information. Survey questions must be structured in a way that is unbiased and does not overwhelm the respondent's time. Quantitative scoring systems with clear, unambiguous questions help make survey results easy to score and categorize. Opinion polls will reveal subjective insights, but are harder to assess statistically. Focus groups sometimes encounter the challenge of participants undermining the focus group by trying to guess the product or brand being discussed and thereby biasing the results. Focus groups need excellent facilitators to keep the participants on task. Whichever market research method is chosen, third-party market research firms are often the best resource to use for proper research techniques.

Keeping Growth Strong

The objective of product innovation, whether incremental or breakthrough, is to keep growth going as strong and long as possible. Over time, innovation will enhance brand

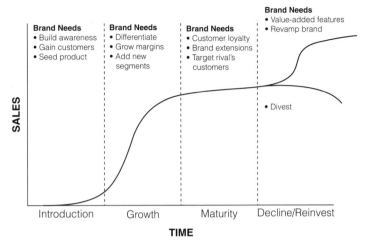

Figure 9-13   Brand Lifecycle Post-maturity Options

value, assuming of course that the product improvements are useful to the various customers in the market. Looking again at the brand lifecycle from Figure 9-8, it is clear the choices a brand faces when the post-maturity stage arrives. Figure 9-13 illustrates that if the brand is in true decline and little can be done to correct it, then divestment and/or liquidation are the probable outcomes. However, notice the other options of value-added features or revamping. These can breathe new life into the brand, a "reinvention" that can occur repeatedly far into the future. In other words, a brand does not have to die (unless there is a crisis or lack of desire).

Price

Price is the monetary value associated with the product and it is the driver of company revenues. The more units sold, the higher the revenues. If a brand has a superior image in the market, then its products can command a higher price versus competitor offerings with a lesser image. A higher price generally leads to higher profitability, which is why differentiation is critical in establishing a unique position in marketplace. There are several related components to price:

- list price: this is the recommended full price encouraged by the supplier;
- credit terms: good customers may be extended credit to buy now and pay later;
- allowances: these include buy-back guarantees if the product does not sell; or fees paid by a manufacturer to a retailer for guaranteed shelf space (also known as "slotting allowance");
- payment period: this is a pre-agreed arrangement to pay smaller amounts at regular intervals over a specified period of time;
- discounts: these come in many forms and include price reductions for customers that buy large quantities (volume discounts); temporary promotional prices to spark demand for a short period of time; and loyal customer reductions.

Each of these components affects the list price and, correspondingly, revenues and profits, which is why pricing strategy is a significant tool that directly influences the financial success of a company.

Cost

Customers view price as a *cost*, which, if the product does not perform as expected, looms psychologically large in the customer's mind due to the inconvenience and frustration from having to get the product fixed, returned, or replaced. Even if the product performs well, cost is a reduction in the customer's net worth at that moment. Convincing customers that the products are worth the cost is one of the marketer's biggest challenges because it is quite easy for a customer to switch but far harder for a company to recapture a lost customer.

Pricing Strategies

Pricing is not separate from other brand-building considerations. Instead, it is an important indicator of a brand's position and can have a significant impact on customer perceptions. We have defined a brand as the entire organization as seen through the eyes of stakeholders, so a number of factors affect customer judgment of a brand's value, beyond the product being sold. For now, let's isolate the brand-related price issues.

A brand's position can be described as falling into one of the following areas:

- premium;
- nonpremium;
- noncompetitive.

These simplifications are not intended to ignore the complexity inherent in product variation and corresponding pricing strategy. Nor is this describing innovations or commodities, or what's hot versus what's traditional. Furthermore, pricing theory is well covered in many other superb textbooks and marketing metrics guides. Instead, the important point is that premium and nonpremium brands are competitive in their respective domains, whereas noncompetitive are in deep trouble. As such, pricing is used to help competitive brands delineate and reinforce levels of product within, and can also influence whether noncompetitive brands recover.

Let's briefly examine these.

Premium

Premium brands cover high-end products, from super luxury to affordable luxury. The distinction between different levels of luxury is complex, owing to brand associations and brand reputation factors, which are discussed throughout this book. All brands try to be distinctive but an important characteristic of premium brands is the status and prestige attached to them. Customers are willing to pay the equivalent of a luxury tax for a luxury branded item, such as a designer leather bag, even if a perfectly acceptable nonleather bag could provide the same functionality. Customers are buying more than function—they are connecting to a set of very specific associations that give the luxury item added meaning.

Status and self-image are very important to these customers. LVMH, Hermes, BMW, and Mercedes are examples of luxury brands.

The pricing decision flexibility here is limited: premium brands are offered at entry-level prices. Furthermore, premium brands rarely discount as such a move would damage their reputation and it would anger customers who are devoted to the brand and who paid the higher price. Instead, value and image are closely linked and a premium brand's image is higher status, so customers expect to pay more. Such a premium pricing approach also serves to limit the brand's accessibility to the market since only a small percentage of customers can afford it. However, a premium brand can adjust its pricing slightly within a limited band. Such a strategy is called *price skimming*, which means that pricing is set at a high enough level that only a limited subset of customers can afford it, then the brand lowers the price slightly over time as costs are reduced through experience. It is important to ensure that prices are not lowered too much as the brand may jump down into a nonpremium category and risk losing the elite customers it first attracted. The important point is that premium pricing is commonly associated with premium brands and any other lower level pricing risks changing the brand's image. Consequently, premium brand pricing tends to stay at a premium level.

Nonpremium

Nonpremium brands encompass a wide range of products, from entry-level to just-below-premium, and most brands fall into this category. The common ingredient is that these products are simply not considered luxury or premium items. This is not an assessment of quality or value—nonpremium is not the same as noncompetitive. Indeed, quality and value are represented at both levels and top performing nonpremium brands offer superior quality (they have to, to remain competitive). Customers buying these brands tend to have more practical interests than social, although this depends on the type of product within the range. Companies with nonpremium brands in their portfolio include: Nestlé, Marriott, P&G, Dell, and Danone. Note that these companies may have premium brands as well, so one must be careful to clearly identify which brand within is being discussed. Marriott owns the Ritz-Carlton luxury hotel brand, Toyota owns Lexus, and Nestlé owns Haagen-Daz ice cream, a premium brand, for example.

The range of pricing choices here is wider and at the upper end of this category can be very close to premium for some brands. A skimming approach may work here as well, although it is more likely that companies will focus on comparable/parity pricing. Comparable/parity pricing means that brands set prices roughly in line with other competitors in the product category (not necessarily identical, nor is this condoning price collusion), consistent with market expectations. Pricing may increase slightly if a new innovation alters the product composition in a favorable way vis-à-vis competitors, or promotion/discount pricing may be used to attract new customers (and take away the competitions' customers). Top brands recognize the challenges such a pricing approach brings since it trains customers to wait for the next promotion before buying. Penetration pricing, which sets a low initial price to attract as many early buyers as possible, may be another approach. However, as with promotion pricing, it is harder to raise prices once they are set low, so if a brand is struggling with low margins, raising prices without a justifiable improvement in quality and features is likely to be much harder to accomplish.

Noncompetitive

Noncompetitive brands are in trouble. They may have once been luxury or nonpremium, but for some reason they have lost favor with the market and lost their reputation as well. Reasons typically include quality and/or reputation problems and these are hard to reverse in the short run. For noncompetitive brands, there are only a couple of pricing options. Customers here are mainly purchasing opportunity, meaning that the low price is too hard to ignore—they want to "get a deal." Conversely, the brand can be so tainted that no price will convince customers to return. Some would argue that the former "Big 3" U.S. automakers became noncompetitive over time, which led to declining product quality and brand reputation.

Pricing for noncompetitive brands typically comes down to a simple decision: assuming product design and composition cannot be altered significantly, can the company afford to drop prices low enough to spur significant increases in volume and hopefully begin to rebuild the customer base? If not, the brand is unlikely to survive much longer. Survival pricing is similar to a policy called "dumping," which involves pricing below the level of manufacturing cost. But dumping is a deliberate strategy to harm competitors and take enough of their customers so that the price dumper can control the market and raise prices later on, whereas survival pricing is a strategy based on desperation to keep the brand alive.

Brand Pricing Criteria

Whether a brand is premium, nonpremium, or noncompetitive, the pricing decision will be made based on three criteria:

- customer needs
- positioning needs
- company needs.

Customer needs

Customer needs encompass functional, emotional self-expressive, and social requirements and brands must *appeal* to these in a combination specific to the brand's position. Functional requirements address what the product is supposed to do (a hole needs to be drilled). Emotional requirements are concerned with evoking certain feelings in customers. Self-expressive requirements reinforce the customer's sense of identity and self-approval. Social requirements relate to the customer's broader social status and approval among peers, such as found in online social media sites (although social requirements can be satisfied in nononline environments, of course).

Positioning needs

Brand pricing will depend on its premium, nonpremium, or noncompetitive position. Pricing decisions for positioning are *driven* by:

- the brand's context (what are the overall market conditions like?);
- competitors (what are competitors currently doing, how are they likely to respond to us, and how can we improve our market share?);
- image/reputation (how is the brand perceived and/or how can the perception be changed?).

Company Needs

Pricing is also influenced by company *performance* in three areas: financial, overall reputation, and with stakeholders. Key financial considerations include revenues, profits, and units. Certainly, pricing will have a direct impact on all three of these. For strategic reasons, while a lower pricing might boost unit volume and revenues, it might also harm profits and the brand's image, particularly if it is at the high end of nonpremium, or premium, of course. Reputation is a key factor in brand value as discussed in Chapter 2. Much of the work of brand building also builds and reinforces the reputation. For a company to build a reputation, it must have credulity either in that product category or brand position (it is hard for a mass market brand to leap credibly to premium/luxury without a significant rebranding effort). Pricing signals a brand's value in the customer's mind, particularly if devoid of first-hand experience. Once the customer is loyal, pricing becomes more of a value reminder—if the product continues meeting or exceeding expectations and adding some level of value for the customer, then the price will be paid. But reputation is also more than just a quantitative figure—it is a qualitative statement. One does not hear of a "cheap" BMW for a very good reason: such a car would undermine the brand's reputation. Pricing also signals to stakeholders (employees, shareholders, value-chain participants) an important strategic and competitive decision made about the brand. Low price means high volume and a mass-market brand, whereas a premium price indicates a low volume exclusive brand.

The appropriate weight attached to each of these decision criteria will vary by brand, even within a brand position, but suffice to say that all three actually work together. Table 9-4 summarizes the brand position and brand price issues.

Pricing and the Lifecycle

Planning brand-pricing strategies is made easier by looking at the product lifecycle because each stage's competitive conditions are different.

Table 9-4 Brand Position and Brand Pricing Considerations

		Brand Position		
		Premium	**Non-Premium**	**Non-Competitive**
Brand Pricing Criteria	**Customer**	*Appeal to* • social status • self-image	*Appeal to* • social community • practical interests	*Appeal to* • 'getting a deal' • steep discount • desperation
	Positioning	*Drivers* • foster a premium reputation • exclusivity	*Drivers* • reaffirm quality • reinforce distinction • comparability	*Drivers* • survival • overcoming negative reputation
	Company	*Performance* • high margins • premium price levels • credibility	*Performance* • revenues • profits • market share • keep costs down	*Performance* • fix or die

Introduction

At this stage the brand must build awareness, so the choice of price decision will be based on whether the product is aiming for a premium or nonpremium position (it would be unlikely to aim for a noncompetitive position). For a premium brand, pricing will be set at a high enough price point to capture a very exclusive segment of the market, which will likely be wealthier customers and/or early enthusiasts who enjoy getting the latest, whatever the cost. If the price is set too low, the premium strategy will not work and may compromise the brand's long-term strategy. As stated, it is easier to reduce price than raise it, so a loose rule of thumb for premium brands is to start high and consider adjusting over time as the market grows and/or as costs decrease. This approach is also called price skimming. Alternatively, a premium brand may not choose to skim, focusing instead on establishing a firm long-term premium price. Such an approach suggests that the offering is utterly unique and the threat of competitors anytime in the near future low. Furthermore, the brand must decide that a small audience of exclusive customers is desirable over a growing customer base as the brand gains recognition.

If a brand is nonpremium, then the price at launch must be at a point that invites trial. This is tricky for several reasons. Unless there are competitors or comparable products, knowing the right price will be subject to some trial and error, even if using sophisticated pricing methodologies. If, however, the product is a new entrant in an existing market, then approximate pricing levels will be established, so the decision will be based on whether to be above, the same as, or below the competition. The most important point at introduction is that awareness is probably nonexistent, or most certainly low, for the product. So aside from a robust marketing communications campaign that explains the product and educates the market, price is an early signal about what to expect.

Growth

Once a brand demonstrates success during introduction, growth takes off and significant financial gain follows, assuming the company can meet demand. Even though the product is taking off, early concern over competitors will emerge, so price adjustments may be necessary to keep entrance unaffordable for rivals. For premium brands, pricing is likely to stay at or near the launch level, with minor adjusting due to either experience gained or a price-skimming approach that captures the next tier of customers, reducing opportunities for competitors. Premium brands do not want to adjust pricing down too much for fear of losing their brand appeal.

For nonpremium brands, pricing issues will be similar to premium, but less restrictive. The good news at this stage is that growth indicates acceptance of and possibly preference for the product, so pricing is likely to stay consistent rather than promotional.

Maturity

With competition much fiercer, differentiation becomes vital. To make this work, the brand must offer something compelling that continues to reinforce interest in the brand. A different challenge confronts premium brands at this stage, as there may be greater concern over whether the target audience still appreciates the status and exclusivity that the brand once enjoyed. Such concern involves more than just price (image, associations, self-expression, relevance). There are more options for nonpremium brands, ranging from product line extensions, stretching the brand vertically, and/or price promotions. Any of these can help brands by sparking renewed interest and perhaps convincing competitor customers to try the brand. By offering premium, core, and entry-level versions for example, a brand can command more retail shelf space (in the case of consumer goods) and crowd out competitors.

Decline

Brands either want to harvest any remaining business possible during decline, or reinvest if they are confident the brand can be revitalized (Figure 9-14). For premier and nonpremier brands, decline can be challenging to overcome. Either industry forces are influencing the decline, or customers have lost interest in the brands (perhaps for quality and reputation issues, or simply better offerings from competitors). Harvesting will include promotions to sell any remaining inventory and can provide a general lift (albeit temporary) to the parent company. Penetration pricing helps to clear inventory and undercut competitors. Premium brands may consider positioning the inevitable decline as an emerging collector's edition and thereby command a temporary premium.

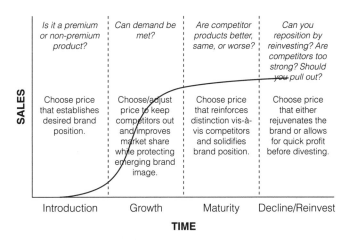

Figure 9-14   Brand Pricing and Position Decisions

Measurement

Without customers, there is no business or brand. Given this, brand builders have a complex and vitally important task in identifying, attracting, and retaining customers. Two important customer measures are per customer acquisition costs, and the retention rate. Knowing the investment required to attract a customer triggers many other strategic decisions, well before the first brand campaign begins. Most companies are not perfect, so customer attrition is a fact of business life. Some customer departures are welcome if they add no discernable value. Inevitably, good customers leave as well, although hopefully far fewer than remain. No specific measure can stop customer attrition, but knowing the customer retention rate helps explain whether the brand is heading in the right direction. With respect to customers in the aggregate, the segment profitability measure indicates the degree to which a segment is attractive and contributes to the margin and growth needs of the brand.

Solutions are more than features and benefits. As such, their pricing is subject to more quantitative rigor, which is beyond the scope of this book. However, both target-return and mark-up pricing offer instructive guidance for *thinking* about pricing decisions. Recognize, however, that pricing decisions involve a great deal more analysis than seeking a set profit level above cost. Pricing is a strategic tool that supports (or should . . .) brand positioning decisions. As such, a simple calculation will not fairly represent the total value represented by a solution or a brand. One must weigh competitor maneuvers, marketing conditions, the price of other solutions and/or brands in the company, and account for overall market perception of the company's reputation.

Two groups of measures will be discussed here: Customer and Price. The Customer Measures are:

- Per customer acquistion costs
- Retention rate
- Segment profitability.

The Pricing Measures are:

- Target return pricing
- Mark-up price.

Customer Measures

Per Customer Acquisition Costs

Metric
Per customer acquisition costs.[35]

Brand Experience Benefits
Helps determine the cost of reaching, attracting, and ultimately acquiring customers.

How
It is calculated by dividing total acquisition expenses by total customers acquired. More specific detail is usually needed, however, to capture the true cost of customer acquisition. The number of times a direct ad is run (or the number of direct mail pieces sent) is multiplied by the cost per insert (or per mailer).

Formula

$$C_p = \frac{A_g}{C_a}$$

Where
C_p = per customer-acquisition costs;
A_e = total acquisition expense;
C_a = total customers acquired.

Impact on Brand Experience

Customer acquisition costs vary across industries and media. As such, knowing the data allows for comparisons against industry benchmarks and/or specific competitors. Customer acquisition costs provide guidance on how to allocate brand resources in the future and how to design marketing programs accordingly. Other considerations are involved as well. The overall goal of the brand building efforts must be known (beyond the obvious desire to increase brand value). If the goal is to raise awareness in the market before specific marketing programs are deployed, targeted to a particular segment, then these awareness-building costs must be captured in the final customer acquisition cost calculation to give a more accurate picture. A market that has a high level of awareness will require less education-oriented communications in the direct-marketing programs. Conversely, if a customer-acquisition program is implemented in the absence of developing market awareness first, then the final customer conversion rate is likely to be much lower. Being aware of the relationship between these variables can maximize the return on the marketing investment down the road.

Not all customer acquisition efforts yield a satisfactory return, despite strong market development efforts with an attractive offer. Some companies from the dot.com era displayed, in retrospect, a disregard for the value of well-conceived marketing programs, making careless investments instead. CDnow (now owned by Amazon.com) spent nearly $40 to acquire each new customer. Purchase patterns revealed that these customers bought only $25 of products on average. Therefore, the costs outweighed the benefits.

A variation on this formula is cost per lead. A lead is a potential customer and there are companies whose business is selling their databases of customer lists. These are used for many forms of marketing, from mobile to email to direct mail. Buyers are charged a fee per name and the fees increase when more data is sought about each lead. The same methodology applies, but the numerator this time is *total advertising costs* and the denominator is *total leads generated*.

Retention Rate

Metric
Retention rate.[36]

Brand Experience Benefits
Retention rate is one of several indicators of customer satisfaction.

How
The number of active customers at the end of a given time period are divided by the number of customers at the start of the same time period.

Formula

$$Retention\ rate = \frac{C_e}{C_s}$$

Where
C_e = the number of active customers at end of time period t;
C_s = the number of active customers at start of time period t.

Impact on Brand Experience

A high retention rate indicates that customers find the brand remains attractive (for now). Customer retention (loyalty) is attractive because losing a customer costs money in terms of lost revenues and acquisition costs incurred to date. Retaining customers over time minimizes the expense of constantly prospecting for new customers and allows the company to focus more on improving the customer's experience. Furthermore, retained customers are generally less expensive to maintain because less education-oriented marketing is needed. However, the marketing expense does not go away. It often simply shifts to alternative communication, such as new media, one-to-one, or relationship-driven marketing. Additionally, loyalty is often perceived as verification that a company's products are accepted by customers over those of the competition. Loyalty is also an avenue to develop deeper and more profitable customer relationships.

Customer loyalty is an important and usually desirable objective but it must be in the context of *profitable* retention. This is a critical point for brands because loyalty, by itself, may not be financially attractive without a clear understanding of the cost of keeping and servicing those customers.

Segment Profitability

Metric
Segment Profitability[37]

Brand Experience Benefits
Segment profitability allows marketers to measure whether an attractive customer segment, from a revenue standpoint, will also be profitable.

How
Three formulas are used, each of which contributes to describing the overall understanding and attractiveness of the market segment in question.

Formulas
First, measure net marketing contribution because it indicates a given segment's profit potential and, therefore, its general attractiveness as a business opportunity.

$$C_{nm} = (D_s \times S_s \times (P_{pu} \times M)) - E_m$$

Where
C_{nm} = net marketing contribution;
D_s = segment demand;
S_s = segment share;
P_{pu} = price per unit;
M = percentage margin;
E_m = marketing expense.

Second, measure marketing return on sales because it is an important indicator of the efficiency of the business's operations. Marketing ROS describes the return on total sales, which is dependent on knowing the net marketing contribution. A lower marketing ROS signals either a decrease in pricing or an increase in expenses. This helps marketers understand whether or not the return is attractive from the perspective of total sales generated, and is an indicator of the effectiveness of the sales effort.

$$\text{Marketing ROS} = \frac{Cnm \times 100\%}{S}$$

Where
Marketing ROS = marketing return on sales;
S = sales.

Third, marketing ROI measures the total return on the marketing investment, indicating whether the expenditures on marketing are yielding maximum results.

$$\text{ROI} = \frac{C_{nm} \times 100\%}{E_m}$$

Where ROI = return on investment.

Impact on Brand Experiences
As the brand grows, the decision to target a segment is influenced by whether it has the potential to achieve a specific or desired level of profitability. Segment profitability is a useful method to assess the success of the marketing programs targeted to a segment, shedding light on whether the brand experience is having an impact. Segment profitability can help companies understand how their marketing investments affect profitability, which can guide marketing decisions for the future. Each segment, however, is likely to be unique and success or failure in one does not presuppose the same performance in another. As data comes back, components of the marketing mix should be adjusted to improve the brand experience and overall brand value proposition.

Pricing Measures

Metric
Target Return Pricing[38]

Brand Experience Benefits

Target return pricing is used to determine price for achieving a specified rate of return (usually specified by senior management and/or the product marketing plans).

How

The cost per unit produced is added to the expected return, multiplied by the capital invested. The result is then divided by unit sales.

Formula

$$\text{TRP} = \frac{C_{pu} + R \times I}{S_u}$$

Where
TRP = target-return price;
C_{pu} = cost per unit;
R = expected return;
I = capital invested;
S_u = unit sales.

Impact on Brand Experience

Target return pricing is not a direct indicator of brand experience satisfaction but the result can suggest whether the forecasted assumptions were even close to correct. If not, then significant adjustments in the brand experience elements will need to occur. Target return pricing is a guide for setting cost targets internally, but it is not a guarantee of achieving the target return. Unit sales will likely be different than forecasted for reasons not always in the company's control. Customer perceptions of value, competitor responses, and shifting economic conditions can all affect target return objectives. Furthermore, target-return pricing depends on the assumptions and expectations that went into it. The expected return may not be consistent with industry standards on similar projects, setting false expectations internally about what customers are accustomed to paying in the market and affect the outcome. Unit sales assumptions may be off target as well. In this event, determining break-even should be plotted at different sales volumes to see where a more accurate target-return price should be set. Preparing multiple scenarios is often the key to selecting an approach that works best.

Mark-up Price

Metric

Mark-up price.[39]

Brand Experience Benefits

It can help to ensure that a product can be sold at a profit. The approach adds a slight increase, or "mark-up," to the product's cost.

How

Unit costs are divided by 1 minus the expected return on sales

Formula

$$\text{Mark - up price} = \frac{\text{unit cost}}{(1 - \text{expected return on sales})}$$

Impact on Brand Experience

While mark-up pricing is a simple calculation based on covering costs plus adding a little margin, it is not ideal as a primary pricing guide. It ignores unique positioning opportunities that could help a higher end brand. Even if the goal were not to be a high-end brand, money may still be left on the table. The reason for noting the positioning goals is because pricing has a direct impact on consumer perceptions of the brand.

Summary

This chapter presented two of the four components of creating a brand experience: determining customers and developing solutions. In building brand value, significant investment and attention is paid to understanding customers. A company that strives to build a top brand and enhance brand value cannot ignore proper customer research and the segmentation, targeting, and positioning (STP) framework is a helpful guideline. Knowing which customer groups share characteristics provides an important clue about where the company may have an opportunity to sell its products and build brand awareness. Identifying common characteristics is a starting point to determining which customers within the larger segments are the most attractive targets. As this information is compiled, brand positioning objectives and development can begin. At the same time, the sequence of events used in the STP framework does not adequately capture substantial changes in today's markets. People have access to more information and new ways to communicate with each other. One by-product has been the formation of communities of shared interests that the formal STP planning process does not adequately capture. Part of the reason is because segments that may share common characteristics (age, income, ethnicity) do not necessarily share common interests (bicycling, music, astronomy). While this distinction has been known for years, and psychographic research helps address it, social media have led to the rapid formation of large, global communities of shared interests. For brands, this presents a significant opportunity not just for attracting new customers but for improving add-on sales. Marketing has a vital responsibility to evaluate the contribution that customers are making to the brand's growth and the financial health of the business. Examining existing customer groups can serve as a useful benchmark for evaluating potential new targets. At the same time, knowing the revenue and profit contributions of the brand's many customers can indicate where future growth and customer relationship development opportunities exist. Without this knowledge, those who develop brand experiences will have no specific understanding of what programs to undertake and what associations to cultivate. Deep customer knowledge also helps direct marketing communication.

We also learned about the role of solutions in the brand experience. The idea of a product as a collection of features that provide benefits is insufficient because customers today are seeking solutions that not only fit a core need (my teeth need cleaning, so I bought toothpaste) but address larger issues (I bought toothpaste from Tom's of Maine because they use earth friendly recycling). While there have always been pockets of customers with more expansive interests, today's online communities and global access to information connects people to news, issues, and trends, making customers far more engaged and informed than ever before. Consequently, they expect more from brands, including the creation of compelling experiences to make brands more attractive and relevant to their interests. Brands and products share characteristics, as we learned here and in Chapter 3. A product has a specific definition and set of attributes, including warranties and packaging (in the case of a good) that comprise the total offering. Brands can be both a product and a larger, more obtuse set of associations related to the brand's touchpoints (imagery, emotion, memories). As companies develop their brand growth plans, they face choices on how to innovate, position their brand, and price it. Innovation is either incremental and/or breakthrough. Incremental innovation is a more conservative approach that does not stress company resources as much, whereas breakthrough innovation is higher risk but may also lead to substantial gains in reputation and brand value. The brand position and pricing choices are based on a combination of customer, positioning, and company needs and are rarely as clear-cut as a standard pricing formula would suggest.

Discussion Questions

1. Describe the customers of a university library and compare them to the customers of an online search company like Google, Yahoo!, and Bing (from Microsoft). What are the similarities and differences? What overlap exists?
2. If you were marketing eyeglasses to the customer groups from question 1, what attributes would be most important to each group?
3. How would you position the product to each group? How would you price it?
4. What innovations might appeal to each group?
5. If your product dominated the eyeglass market, what pricing would you pursue as the market matures? What factors would affect your decision?

Notes

1. Keller, K. L., *Strategic Brand Management*, 3rd edition, © 2008 Pearson Education, pp. 99–102.
2. 1) Research projects conducted by students at Singapore Management University for their strategic brand management course between 2004 and 2008. 2) "Vodafone" April 2009 *Goldman Sachs Communacopia XIII*, Rep. 2004, Vodafone-Goldman Sachs, retrieved May 6, 2009 from www.vodafone.com/etc/medialib/attachments/external_conferences/2004.Par.55705.File.dat/goldman_sachs_2004.

3. 1) Research projects conducted by students at Singapore Management University for their strategic brand management course between 2004 and 2008. 2) "Absolut," research completed April 2009. 3) Remer, L., McLain, A., and McCaughey, J., "Absolut Parallel," April 29, 1997, retrieved November 9, 2007 from: www.lclark.edu/~soan370/Niche_Markets.html.

4. Ibid. See also, V&S group, "About V&S," retrieved February 11, 2009 from www.vsgroup.com/en/Om-VS/.

5. Ibid. See also Remer, L., McLain, A. and McCaughey, J., "Absolut Parallel," April 29, 1997, retrieved February 8, 2009 from www.vsgroup.com/en/Om-VS/.

6. Ibid. See also Perreault, W. D. and McCarthy, J., "Basic Marketing: A Global Managerial Approach," 14/e, McGraw Hill Online Learning Center Video Case Study, retrieved February 11, 2009 from http://highered.mcgraw-hill.com/sites/0072409479/student_view0/chapter6/e-learning_session.html#.

7. Ibid.

8. Ibid. See also, Geldner, O., "An Introduction to Overlook Hospitality Management Speed Shops—Comparing The Marketing Approach Used By ABSOLUT Vodka To Modern Lifestyle Hotels," January 31, 2002, retrieved February 11, 2009 from www.hospitalitynet.org/news/4010809.search?query=absolut+vodka+pricing+strategy.

9. Ibid. See also, Drinks International, "Consistency Gives Absolut Vodka the Edge," retrieved from: www.drinksint.com/articles/28070/Consistency-gives-Absolut-vodka-the-edge.aspx?categoryid=239.

10. Ibid. See also V&S group, "About V&S," retrieved February 11, 2009 from www.vsgroup.com/en/Om-VS/.

11. Ibid.

12. Ibid. See also, V&S Group, "A World Premier from Absolut: Absolut Mango," press release, October 23, 2007.

13. Adapted from Dhar, S. and Lorie, J. H., Professor of Marketing, University of Chicago Graduate School of Business from an executive education program he co-taught with the author. The executive education program was "Strategic Marketing: Creating Your Competitive Advantage" July 11–13, 2005 held in Singapore.

14. Tong-hyung, K., "NHN Braces for Japan's Search Market," January 19, 2009, retrieved January 28, 2009, www.koreatimes.co.kr/www/news/nation/2009/01/133_38129.html.

15. 1) Research projects conducted by students at Singapore Management University for their strategic brand management course between 2004 and 2008. 2) "Tiger Airways," in which the project studied the birth of Tiger Airways from the Singapore Airlines corporate umbrella. 3) "The Creation of Singapore Airlines," retrieved September 16, 2008 from www.singaporeair.com/saa/en_UK/content/company_info/siastory/history.jsp. 4) Allen, R., 1990, *SIA: Take-Off to Success*, Singapore: SIA. 5) Donoghue, J. A., "Superior, Innovative and Adept," *Air Transport World*, June 1994, pp. 30–39. 6) Leung, James, "Winging Their Way to Global Might," *Asian Business*, December 1996, pp. 24–34.

16. 1) Research projects conducted by students at Singapore Management University for their strategic brand management course between 2004 and 2008. 2) "Centurion American Express," research completed November 2008. 3) J. D. Power & Associates, September 3, 2008, *2008 Credit Card Satisfaction Study*, retrieved October 15, 2008, from www.jdpower.com/corporate/news/releases/pressrelease.aspx?ID=2008141.

17. Ibid. See also, Dykman, A., Locke, P., Richardson, F. and Vaccaro, F., 2005, *Next Chapter: A Guide to the New American Express*, L. P. Thebault.

18. Ibid. See also "American Express Company: Company Profile," *Datamonitor,* April, 2008.

19. Ibid.

20. 1) Research projects conducted by students at Singapore Management University for their strategic brand management course between 2004 and 2008. 2) Two Nokia projects were completed over two years: "Nokia," research completed November 2006, updated January 2008 and "Nokia Brand Development," research completed November 2008. 3) Wisk, M. and Wasserman, T. (October 16, 2000), "Fashion Statement," *Adweek,* New England edition, 37(42), p. 82, retrieved February 14, 2009, available from Business Source Premier database.

21. Echikson, W., 1994, "How To Win Markets Fast," *Fortune,* 129(11), p. 114, retrieved September 27, 2007, available from Business Source Premier database.

22. Ibid. See also, Reinhardt, A. and Ihlwan, M., 2005, "Will Rewiring Nokia Spark Growth," *Business Week,* February 14, retrieved September 6, 2008, available from Business Source Premier database.

23. Ibid. See also, Guyon, J., "Nokia Tries to Reinvent Itself—Again," *Fortune,* March 22, 2004, 149(5), pp. 65–66, retrieved September 6, 2008, from Business Source Premier database.

24. Ibid. See also, Lakshman, N., "Nokia: It Takes a Village to Design a Phone for Emerging Markets," *Business Week,* September 10, 2007, retrieved September 6, 2008, available from Academic Search Premier database.

25. Ibid. See also Beckman, K., "Nokia Outlines Low-cost Handset Strategy," *RCR Wireless News,* 24(23), p. 16, retrieved November 12, 2008, available from Business Source Premier database.

26. Ibid. See also, Segan, S., "Nokia Announces Prepaid Phones," *PC Magazine,* March 2006, retrieved October 1, 2008, available from http://findarticles.com/p/articles/mi_zdpcm/is_200603/ai_n19413457.

27. Ibid. See also, Carson, P., "Nokia Shows Smarts with Margins on Low ASPs," *RCR Wireless News,* 26(4), January 29, 2007, retrieved on July 11, 2008, available from Business Source Premier database.

28. Ibid. See also, Albanesius, C., April, 2007, "Nokia Still King in Shrinking Phone Market," *PC Magazine,* retrieved January 10, 2008, available http://findarticles.com/p/articles/mi_zdpcm/is_200704/ai_n19423935.

29. Rust, R. T., Zeithaml, V. A. and Lemon, K. N., "Customer-Centered Brand Management," *Harvard Business Review,* September 2004, © 2004 Harvard Business School Publishing Corporation, p. 4.

30. 1) Research projects conducted by students at Singapore Management University for their strategic brand management course between 2004 and 2008. 2) "SMRT" research completed November 2008; ancillary research on ComfortDelGro as a comparison to SMRT, the primary competitor in the Singapore transportation market; retrieved August 17, 2008 from www.comfortdelgro.com.sg/company/aboutus.htm.

31. Research projects conducted by MBA students at University of Washington for term projects in their strategic marketing course between 2001 and 2003. The student teams studied a wide range of companies, each with excellent information about its branding and marketing efforts, including Intel, Amazon, Motorola, and Boeing. EspressoConnection stood out. The company has 15 stores in the Seattle region, plus an affiliated business called SilverCup Coffee, which roasts and sells its own coffee beans. EspressoConnection was a remarkable story because of its service and strong overall performance in a market dominated by a much larger competitor—Starbucks.

32. 1) Research projects conducted by students at Singapore Management University for their strategic brand management course between 2004 and 2008. 2) "Sakae Sushi: Looking Beyond Singapore's Shores," research completed December 2006, updated December 2008, pp. 1–4. 3) "The Apple Core: What Makes it the Brand Today," research completed November 2007, updated December 2008. 4) "Creative Technology: Fighting Back," with Apple as the comparison company, April 2006, pp. 4–7. 5) Dyson, C. J., "Virgin Atlantic Experienced," April 1, 2002, retrieved November 17, 2007 from www.brandchannel.com/features_webwatch.asp?ww_id=66. 6). Martindale, N., "Virgin Atlantic's HR in Practice: High-flying Management," August 20, 2007, retrieved January 11, 2008 from www.personneltoday.com/articles/2007/08/20/41937/virgin-atlantics-hr-in-practice-high-flying-management.html.

33. 1) Research projects conducted by students at Singapore Management University for their strategic brand management course between 2004 and 2008. 2) "Infosys: The Challenge of Global Branding," pp. 1–2. Case: 950A01, Richard Ivey School of Business. © 2005 Ivey Management Services.

34. 1) Research projects conducted by students at Singapore Management University for their strategic brand management course between 2005 and 2008; two projects focused on Banyan Tree Hotels—one included Ritz-Carlton (and Four Seasons) as comparison companies to "Banyan Tree Hotels' Angsana Hotels"; "Colours of Angsana's Best Opportunity to Paint a Lasting Impression," research completed November 2006, updated December 2008. 2) Material retrieved December 21, 2008 from www.angsana.com/.

35. Davis, J., *Measuring Marketing: 103 Key Metrics Every Marketer Needs*, © 2006 John Wiley & Sons (Asia) Pte Ltd, pp. 95–100.

36. Ibid., pp. 126–130.

37. Ibid., pp. 84–89.

38. Ibid., pp. 171–174.

39. Ibid., pp. 167–171.

Brand Experiences: Marketing Communications and Environment

10

Topics

- Preview
- Marketing Communications
- Objectives
- Modes, Implementation, Measurement
- Traditional Marketing
  - Traditional Marketing Characteristics
  - Traditional Marketing Communications
  - Traditional Marketing Tools
  - Traditional Marketing Brand Planning
  - Traditional Marketing Costs
- Nontraditional Marketing (NT Marketing)
  - Nontraditional Marketing Characteristics
  - Nontraditional Marketing Communications
  - Nontraditional Marketing Tools
  - Nontraditional Marketing Brand Planning
  - Nontraditional Marketing Costs
  - Nontraditional Marketing Growth
- IMC Trends
- Impact on Consumer Decision-Making
- Communication Effectiveness
- Creative Execution
  - Creative Challenges: Getting the Point Across
  - Brand Lifecycle
- Environment
  - Implications for Brands
  - Environment Factors in Creating Successful Brand Experiences
- Measurement
  - Marketing Communications Measures
  - Environment Measures

- Summary
- Discussion Questions
- Case Brief

Preview

Continuing with brand experiences, this chapter discusses *marketing communications* and *environment* subcomponents of Experiences. Marketing communications are used by companies to inform stakeholders (customers, employees, shareholders, value-chain participants) about their brands. The marketing communications choices have increased since the advent of the Internet and digital media, which supplement the traditional media that have defined the field for more than 50 years. A rapidly developing practice is the integration of the various marketing communications pieces to improve coherence and consistency across dispersed markets, cultures, and geographic regions. Integration has also expanded into brand experiences, meaning that brands are finding ways to use marketing communications in conjunction with other brand touchpoints to more completely engage target audiences.

Environment includes both tangible and intangible components with which the public interacts whenever they are in contact with the brand. Tangible aspects are physical features, from store design to furnishings to corporate offices. Intangible components include atmosphere, service, and support-related issues. Controlling and orchestrating the brand's environmental factors is a complex responsibility but can yield powerful and positive improvements in brand value and reputation.

Marketing Communications

From Chapter 9 we gained insight into identifying the right market and gaining knowledge about specific customers. Brand building now depends on reaching those markets with the right communications. Marketing communications is a broad discipline encompassing a set of activities designed to persuade customers to purchase the firm's products. The right marketing communications are those that are relevant to each target audience, meaning that the communications may well vary depending on the customer segment, and each segment may perceive a brand differently. However, sample marketing communications campaigns can be tested for an approach that produces the greatest impact across

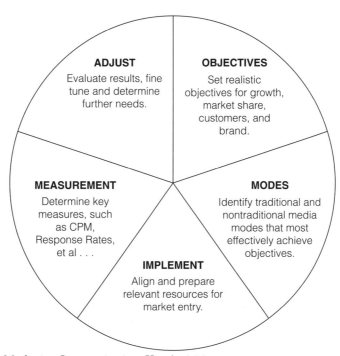

Figure 10-1   Marketing Communications Key Activities

diverse groups. Marketing managers rely on advertising agencies and market research firms to guide them through testing different communications approaches.

Let's look at marketing communications more closely. First, a summary of the main activities of marketing communications is depicted in Figure 10-1.

EXAMPLE 10-1:

Samsung

A quick illustration of integrated marketing will help. Samsung faced a significant shift in the market in the late 1990s. Coupled with its own struggles especially after the 1997 Asian Financial Crisis, Samsung refocused its business. Seeing digital technology as key to its future, the company focused on new stylish, easy to use new products and new marketing, around a campaign called "DigitAll Experiences":

> In 2000, Samsung started a management program with a new twist and aimed to stay ahead of the great waves of digital change now engulfing the world. We expect nothing less than to lead the digitization of society with our advanced technologies.[1]

The campaign was designed to link technology with lifestyle, connecting customers from different cultures together through the promise and excitement of digital. A global brand template was developed to facilitate consistent use of the corporate identity and message down to the detail of logo location in advertising:[2]

- Samsung logo on the top left;
- an ellipse under the Samsung name to help the mark stand out;
- use of DigitAll alongside complementary words to describe the benefit of the advertised product;
- a slogan "Samsung DigitAll: Everyone's invited" on the bottom right.

By 2002, advertisements with the new DigitAll campaign included: "DigitAllpassion," "DigitAllescape," and "DigitAllwow." Print and television, outdoor billboards, public transportation signage, and point-of-retail-purchase displays carried the new campaign and logo. Times Square in New York City displayed a new DigitAll television ad, with the usual array of neon and digital lights of the area adding to the spectacle. The campaign was designed to show how Samsung's products fit in with the emerging digital lifestyle. Online advertisements ran on more than 340 Internet sites, which included Fortune.com, Forbes.com, ABCNews.com, USAToday.com and similar business publications, creating more than 300 million impressions per month for Samsung. The company organized annual world tours called "DigitAll Inspiration" in Beijing, Singapore, Istanbul, New York, and Paris, which were intended to build direct awareness of the brand. Influential media and product enthusiasts (consumers and analysts) were invited to see the latest DigitAll products. The tours gave visitors a hands-on experience with the products, while also allowing people to mingle with Samsung leaders. Samsung also sponsored the Olympic Games, a relationship they began in 1997, leveraging both the Winter and Summer Games for raising brand awareness and launching new products. The sponsorship activities included setting up an *Olympic Rendezvous@Samsung* (OR@S) venue in which music and games were provided to athletes and their families. OR@S also showcased Samsung's latest wireless communications products, including an innovative information system called WOW (Wireless Olympic Works). Samsung also supplied nearly 22 000 wireless communication devices to athletes, media, and officials. Finally Samsung secured product placement in the two Matrix sequels "Matrix Reloaded" and "Matrix Revolutions," which collectively went on to gross more than US$1.1 billion at the box office, in addition to DVD sales, building additional exposure and awareness for Samsung.[3]

Results

The effort paid off. By 2004 Samsung showed a substantial improvement in its business:[4]

- Net margins increased to 10% yearly.
- Number one market share in memory chips (flash), memory chips (DRAM), and flat panel displays.

- Samsung's mobile phones moved ahead of Motorola in 2004, selling almost 23 million worldwide, for a 13.8% market share, second to Nokia.
- Samsung's brand value increased from US$6.3 billion in 2001 to US$17.6 billion in 2008.
- By 2008 Samsung had surpassed Sony in televisions and remained second in mobile phones behind Nokia.
- Samsung has won numerous awards since 2000, with more than 19 presented by Industrial Design Excellence Awards (IDEA), making it the first Asian company to win more awards than any European or American rival.

Samsung offers a useful example of an integrated marketing campaign. Let's now examine each of the integrated marketing communications key activities in greater detail.

Objectives

For any brand to succeed there must be a clear understanding of the central objective of the communication. Another way to consider this is to ask *what do we hope will be accomplished by our marketing communication?* This is an important question because the answer will affect the communication mode chosen. If the objective is to raise awareness, then that has different implications for communications design than if the objective is to increase sales by 5%. The amount of money to be spent on marketing communications is also critical. Few firms have the luxury to spend lavishly to promote their brand, so the money that is used has to be carefully allocated. The subtleties of nuance, understanding, and interpretation often take precedence over statistics. This is where the role of judgment assumes greater weight in decision-making simply because reams of market research data are unlikely to produce a marketing communications program that satisfies all customer groups. The complexities involved with creating successful marketing communications campaigns become readily apparent.

Modes, Implementation, Measurement

It is equally important to ensure consistency across the various marketing modes used. In years past the various marketing communications modes were often treated as separate and distinct disciplines. However, in recent years *integrated marketing communications* (IMC) has become predominant. Integrated marketing communications uses a combination of tools to create a consistent image for the brand as seen and experienced by consumers at every touchpoint. These tools take advantage of the company's investment in strategic positioning, customer targeting, product development, and messaging to create a memorable experience for customers. Research for this book revealed that successful brands are aggressive and rigorous in not just deploying unique combinations of marketing communications consistently and in a complementary fashion across markets and media but in regularly measuring and evaluating the results. Interestingly, underperformance or even negative outcomes did not necessarily cause the cancellation of the associated brand-building activities. Instead, companies used the measures and results to adjust their marketing and fine-tuning the strategies and tactics, rather than elimination. When elimination of a marketing activity occurred, it was only after carefully considering that activity's original intent, implementation, flaws, and potential for improvement. For brands, maximizing brand value is central to success and IMC is a means for accomplishing this. Each marketing activity should be assessed, as much as possible, on the value it adds in support of building a consistent and cohesive brand. Each marketing communications tool should have goals and measures attached to it.

Integrated marketing communication modes can be classified into *traditional* and *non-traditional* areas.

Traditional Marketing

Traditional marketing refers to a set of practices that have been part of academia and industry for much of the past 50 years. It emphasizes development of, and communication about, products, identification of customer types and their associated behaviors, and the competitive environment. The marketing messages are then either "pushed" onto consumers by company-led promotions and/or field sales forces selling directly, or "pull" campaigns, characterized by heavy advertising typically geared for building awareness.

Traditional marketing tends to be narrow in scope, focusing on features and benefits, and for most of the past half-century controlled by companies through advertising and promotions designed to tell consumers how great the products are. The marketing communications philosophy was predicated on building massive awareness and creating a lasting, indelible impression, often through the use of clever slogans, mascots, jingles, images, and similar devices that distilled a brand into a simple set of memorable ideas. During these years, consumers were more or less passive recipients of a company's marketing communications, because interactive two-way communication modes did not exist. They demonstrated their support by purchasing brands that they recalled from the advertising.

Bernd Schmitt of Columbia Business School, summarizes the characteristics of traditional marketing as:[5]

- functional features and benefits;
- narrow definition of product categories and competition;
- customers are rational decision makers;
- methods are analytical, quantitative, and verbal.

In this refreshingly simple summary, Schmitt's conclusions support the research findings in this book. Most companies pursue traditional marketing and are performing fine. But most companies are not top brands—they are very good but not the best. The traditional view of marketing is pervasive and reviewing it sheds needed light on why so few companies break out from the pack of competitors to truly stand out.

Traditional Marketing Characteristics

Traditional marketing emphasizes product features that are supposed to enhance the core product. For example, the core function of a cell phone is to enable mobile communication between people, and a feature might include the ability to surf the Web. Benefits might include uninterrupted access wherever the user travels. Narrow product and competitor definitions suggest that products compete against a limited set of alternatives in the market (for example, a cell phone competes against other cell phones only and not PDAs, cameras, portable music players). Customers are assumed to make logical decisions based on clear reasoning (personal needs assessment lead to research and comparison of alternatives, followed by purchase and use), devoid of emotional influences. Marketing and associated research methods rely on classic techniques, including surveys, focus groups, and associated models that usually reduce findings to quantitative figures that can be measured, from which logical business planning decisions are made.

Traditional marketing was often a more tactical, rather than strategic, approach to building brands (the company identifies an opportunity through basic research, develops a product to address it, and designs marketing communications to create market awareness and inspire buyer purchase). Strategic issues, such as overall fit of the new product with the company's reputation and long-term direction, were often considered indirectly because the primary concern was growing the individual product's business, and not the larger contribution that product might make over the long term to enhancing overall brand value and reputation.

Traditional Marketing Communications

Traditional marketing communications include television, radio, print, hospitality tents, team and/or event sponsorships, and outdoor advertising. These media are typically one way, from company to consumer, and are particularly useful for building brand awareness and brand image on a mass scale because the potential audience reach (defined as the number or percentage of people in the target audience reached by a single exposure ad/commercial in a specified period of time is large).[6] Customers cannot interact with these media beyond passive listening or viewing, which is why traditional marketing is most useful for conveying a simple message that requires little thinking or involvement on the customer's part. Nontraditional marketing, discussed following this section, is more effective for engaging and interacting with customers.

Traditional Marketing Tools

The following modes in Figure 10-2 are traditional marketing. They are familiar fixtures to businesses around the world and have been used for more than 50 years.

Television Advertising

Commercial TV advertising has been used for decades, particularly in mature markets like Japan, the U.S., and parts of Europe. Formats vary by market but TV advertisements

Figure 10-2   Traditional Marketing

are usually short, visually descriptive videos, ranging in length from 15 seconds to two minutes. In the U.S., 30-second ads are common on most television networks and cable programming.

Advantages

The medium is well suited for audio and visual communications that build awareness. Large audiences mean that there is significant reach. The cost per exposure is relatively low. A wide variety of programming options mean that advertisers have many choices for reaching target audience.

Disadvantages

Total cost is expensive (creative, cost of media/frequency) and length of audience exposure is brief. Viewers may even decide to use the advertising time to take a short break from watching the TV, negating any benefit to the advertiser. Ad message may lead to negative reaction from viewers. General viewing audience is large but ideal target audience is small, so effectiveness per exposure is low.

Measures

Reach (the number or percentage of people in the target audience reached by a single ad or commercial exposure in a specified period of time), frequency (the number of times an average member of the target audience is exposed to the same ad, commercial, or program over a given period of time),[7] and GRPs (an aggregate measure of the total amount or volume of advertising exposures a media campaign will generate via specified media vehicles during a specific time period—it is the product of reach % × frequency)[8] are the primary TV measures. Awareness measures, such as recall[9] (a test of overall brand awareness or of advertising impact where, given a product category, a consumer can name a brand or advertising campaign without further prompting) and recognition[10] (this asks if consumers have been exposed to a particular brand or product or ad campaign before) can also be used.

Radio

Radio advertising is somewhat similar in concept to TV advertising except, of course, that the medium is audio only.

Advantages

Radio advertising is less expensive than TV advertising. It is better for local coverage. The medium compels listeners to use their imagination to visualize the message, which can be a powerful way to connect to consumers.

Disadvantages

It may cause listeners to switch stations to hear other programming and avoid ads. As with TV, poorly executed creative work can adversely affect the brand.

Measures

Traditional reach, frequency, and awareness measures apply to radio as well as TV. With more radio stations online, Web-based metrics are also useful. Direct response that tracks purchase patterns from promotional offers is also useful.

Sales Promotion

Sales promotions are a concentrated, short-term communications focus, often in combination with a price discount, designed to boost demand.

Advantages

Done well, sales promotions can attract new customers and encourage existing customers to buy more products. Revenues increase, sometimes dramatically. Promotions can also create interest in the brand, generating word of mouth and increasing awareness of the brand. Market share increases can occur.

Disadvantages

The promotion may not generate enough volume to make up for the reduced profit. Consumers will quickly learn to watch and wait for the next promotion, creating erratic sales cycles, which can stress labor costs. Promotions can also cheapen a brand image. Consumers may perceive a promotion as a sign of a failing business and stay away as a result. GM's and Chrysler's bankruptcies in 2009 led to further erosion in consumer confidence. Dealers heavily discounted cars to rid themselves of excess inventory but buyers were wary, not knowing the long-term servicing needs of the cars.[11]

Measures

Since sales promotions are usually in the form of a discount program (such as a reduced price or bundled offerings), keeping track of changes in related customer and product variables is important. Useful measures include: markdown goods precentage (the percentage reduction from the original selling price); transactions per hour; hourly customer traffic; and the close-ratio (how many customers convert from shoppers to actual buyers).

Print

Print advertising is found in magazines, journals, and newspapers. The number of print vehicles is huge around the world and they range from general interest to narrow interest/ vertical market publications.

Advantages

High credibility. Good local and/or larger geographic coverage depending on publication. Newspapers are timely; magazines higher quality, longer shelf life. Newspapers relatively affordable, more opportunistic. Both mediums are good for either general or detailed ads, depending on publication and target audience.

Disadvantages

Newspapers have shorter shelf life; magazines are more expensive and require longer term advance commitment. Precise placement is harder to guarantee. Newspaper readership is declining. The market is cluttered with magazines.

Measures

Reach, awareness, recognition, recall, and impressions (which is the product of reach × frequency).

Direct Marketing

Direct marketing is advertising communications addressed directly to customers in a targeted market segment and designed to prompt a reply or action from them. This can be via direct mail, infomercial, or telemarketing.

Advantages

The message can be personalized. It is a good medium for short-term promotions or limited time discount offers—it can lead to a sharp increase in short-term sales. Target audience precision is high.

Disadvantages

The cost of quality mailing/emailing lists is high. Upkeep of audience addresses is time consuming and expensive. Telemarketing labor and equipment is expensive. Infomercial product and media-buy can be expensive, plus operational support costs of fulfillment. Direct mail is increasingly perceived as environmentally unfriendly. Cost per piece is expensive (design, postage, follow-up).

Measures

Direct marketing measures will vary slightly depending on medium (direct mail, infomercial, telemarketing). They include: revenue goals, profit goals, gross profit, net profit, response rate (number of people who respond to an offer relative to the number of people who received the offer), conversion rate (percentage of prospective customers or visitors to a web site) who both respond and buy a company's offerings, and ROI.

Team and/or Event Sponsorship

Marketing dollars invested in sponsoring sports team, conference, trade show, or other major event.

Advantages

Provides sponsor with visibility to targeted audience specific to event. Sponsor benefits from being associated with well-known event. Helps build credibility.

Disadvantages

Major sports team and events are expensive to sponsor. They may require multi-year agreements. A direct relationship with sales and market share increases is uncertain. Team or event scandals can tarnish sponsors.

Measures

Return on investment per marketing mode, awareness, sales increases, direct feedback surveys. In addition, Table 10-1 is a constructive set of deliverables that can help determine sponsorship attractiveness. There are many other possible benefits that a sponsor may seek, but this provides a useful starting point.

Event/Trade Show Booth

Industry-specific exhibitions/showcases featuring products and services of leading companies.

Table 10-1   Sponsorship Deliverables

Pre-event deliverables	Event day and related deliverables
• Access and usage of event images and trademarks • Publicity support by event management • Detailed event and venue guidelines for signage and other sponsorship exposure vehicles	• Tickets/tickets in preferred zones • Hospitality suites/facilities • Access to off-limit areas • Access to event management, support, and logistics
Association type deliverables	Facility/athlete/team deliverables
• Name association recognition—"official sponsor" • Industry association recognition • Sport association recognition • Athlete association recognition	• Use of facilities for corporate events • Athlete appearance deliverables • Athlete endorsement deliverables • Athlete image deliverables
Visual image deliverables	Ambush marketing protection
• At event site • At event surroundings • On direct transmission of event • On replays of events • Use in advertisements/promotions	• Aggressive stance against "ambushers" Post-event deliverables • Review and audit with event management • Preparation for next event/stage in relationship

Source: Davis, J. A. *The Olympic Games Effect: How Sports Marketing Builds Strong Brands,*
© 2008 John Wiley & Sons (Asia) Pte Ltd, p. 311.

Advantages

High visibility to selective audience. Potentially high volume of participants will visit booth. Can be used to meet with customers individually and/or give sneak previews to new products. Presence indicates that company is a competitor, and a larger booth suggests company is a major player. Gives customers confidence that company is substantial. Can convey credibility and reinforce brand image.

Disadvantages

The booth and labor to support it can be expensive. Marketing and PR materials also expensive to produce. Product demonstrations, travel and airfare add further to the cost. No guarantee customers will buy.

Measures

Trade show measures encompass customer counts, sales increases, and general awareness. Key measures are customer visits, new leads, new sales, referrals (potential customers referred by other parties), and awareness.

Sales/Business Development

Field-based selling activities led by specialized employees adept at increasing sales and developing relationships with new and existing customers. Business development is similar but may also include developing revenue-generating strategic partnerships with other companies in the value-chain, gathering competitive intelligence, sales business planning, and acting as a liaison between field-based personnel and corporate office.

Advantages

Creates direct, more personalized relationships with customers. Thorough understanding of customer issues. Top performers generate significant revenues and profits and act as brand ambassadors, representing the company and reinforcing a positive image. Work well with other people and know how to get things done. Have a thick skin that handles rejection better than other business people.

Disadvantages

This approach may push sales at expense of profits. The business may give away items like product support to win sales. Sales staff may become impatient with corporate marketing bureaucracy and may create their own marketing materials as a result, potentially harming brand image. Some sales people are loners and not strong team players, which might undermine solidarity.

Measures

Independent sales representative analysis (helps management compare costs between having independent and company sales forces), average sales per call, break-even sales volume, and sales productivity (total revenues per sales person).

Public Relations

Public relations (PR) is responsible for reinforcing a positive image, announcing relevant and important milestones, and managing crises and other challenges. Information of interest related to the brand is conveyed to the public. It is unpaid, meaning the company does not pay for the media's coverage of the information.

Advantages
Public relations is perceived as more credible than advertising because publicity appears in print and broadcast news media and is not seen as company-generated hype.

Disadvantages
Public relations coverage is erratic and subject to the whims of news editors who determine news worthiness. Poor management of a crisis can significantly harm the brand.

Measures
Hiring a tracking or news clip service (some PR agencies also do this) can provide updates on PR efforts. Measures to include: ratio of news stories printed versus sent, ratio of favorable to unfavorable stories, total number of news stories featuring brand, number of speaking engagements secured for key company leaders in the media and at conferences.

Hospitality/VIP Venues

Hire/rent venues to entertain customers and other VIPs.

Advantages
This approach has high visibility and can be associated with major team/event/conferences. It is ideal for exclusive, invitation-only events with company executives, which can enhance brand position and image. It can serve to thank and reward best customers, deepening the customer relationship. Memorable venues can become a popular tradition that customers look forward to.

Disadvantages
It is potentially expensive with room/tent rental, catering, A/V and other multi-media support, creation of marketing materials and the cost of flying and housing company executives. It may not lead to new sales.

Measures
Measures include: new business and customers gained, add-on business from existing customers, affinity/relationship survey (assesses how committed customers are to the brand) and awareness measures.

Outdoor Advertising

Outdoor advertising consists of billboards, wall boards, sandwich boards, street placards, banners, and external electronic displays.

Advantages

Exposure/visibility is high, particularly in congested areas with high traffic and/or urban density. It is less crowded than other mediums, providing advertisers with potentially unique locations. The cost is generally lower.

Disadvantages

The message may be peripheral to automobile drivers and tourists who are paying attention to other sights. Most displays are low-tech, reducing visual impact. The length of the message is constrained.

Measures

Outdoor advertising measures include: awareness, traffic volume (how many passersby noticed the ad), and reference ads (ads that ask consumers to refer to them when purchasing the advertised product).

EXAMPLE 10-2:

Use of Sponsorships and Events

Each of the traditional marketing vehicles offers unique benefits to brand building, depending on what the goals are. Let's examine how sponsorships and events can work.

PowerBar

In 2007, PowerBar signed a global sponsorship agreement with professional triathlete Luke Bell, three-time winner of the Ironman 70.3 series (70.3 represents the total number of miles raced in the event),[12] supporting him with performance nutrition products for his training and competitions throughout the 2007 and 2008 seasons. Bell was also integrated into the brand's ongoing sports nutrition product research and development projects. PowerBar featured Bell in integrated event and online marketing campaigns designed to educate recreational endurance athletes about the importance of proper training, sports nutrition, and hydration. PowerBar branding was featured on both his training and racing gear and Luke served as an international brand ambassador for the company's performance nutrition products.[13]

Since 2001, PowerBar has supported the Lance Armstrong Foundation (LAF) as primary energy product sponsor. Together, Armstong and PowerBar launched a sweepstakes and cultural tour of music, art, and wine festivals to promote healthy living. Kiosks with nutrition information were at the events as well. The PowerBar "Live Well Livestrong" sweepstakes helped to educate consumers about cancer risk, while increasing awareness for the LAF. The winner received a cycling jersey autographed by Lance Armstrong, health magazine subscriptions, and PowerBar products.[14]

> PowerBar donated $200000 to the LAF, adding images of the yellow Livestrong wristband to product packaging. P-O-P materials of the campaign were produced and displayed in select Whole Foods Markets and Wild Oats Markets, two stores closely associated with nutritional and healthy consumer products.[15]
>
> Both Powerbar and the Lance Armstrong Foundation used sponsorship and event marketing to create a more holistic approach to the market, benefiting both brands and acting in good faith to benefit society.

Traditional Marketing Brand Planning

Table 10-2[16] is a brand-planning template for traditional marketing communications. To illustrate how to use the templates, let's assume a brand has three primary target audiences for its traditional marketing communications (represented by A, B, C in Table 10-2). Research has shown that each of the brand's target audiences is most effectively reached using the media indicated.

The marketing communications choices for target audience A pays attention to TV, radio, print and event booths, whereas target audiences B and C respond to different traditional marketing tools. Communications programs for each brand must adapt to and fit the profile of each audience (assuming the company has the luxury of investing in multiple marketing vehicles to reach different customer groups). Once the media types are determined, a marketing activity planning worksheet such as that shown in Table 10-3[17] provides more detail about specific expectations for each mode.

Let's look at each element:

- *Message:* this company has chosen "Only the Best" as its brand message, using this theme consistently across the media types targeted to audience A.
- *Reach:* this measures the number or percentage of people that were exposed to a single ad during a specified period of time.
- *Frequency:* this measures the number of times members of the target audience is exposed to the same ad during the specified period of time.
- *Insertion date:* this refers to the start date of the particular media type used (i.e. magazine publication date, TV or radio broadcast date).

Table 10-2   Traditional Marketing Communications Brand Template

	TV	Radio	Print	Direct mail	Team/event sponsorship	Outdoor	Booth	Hospitality
Target audience A								
Target audience B								
Target audience C								

Table 10-3 Marketing Activity Planning Worksheet (Traditional Marketing)

Media type	Target audience	Message	Reach	Frequency	Insertion date	Ad. length or size	Gross rating points (GRP)	Total cost (creative, media buy)	Project outcome
TV	A	"Only the Best"	20%	6×	August 1	30 s	225	$3 000 000	15% awareness
Radio	A	–	40%	12×	July 1	15–30 s	300	$300 000	"
Print	A	–	25%	8×	June 15	1 page	75	$225 000	"
Outdoor	A	–		3 month contract	June 1	5 billboards	unknown	$125 000	"

- *Ad length/size*: this refers to the ad's key characteristics (time-length, physical dimensions).
- *GRP (gross rating points)*: these are the result of reach (percentage) × frequency and they describe the total number of ad exposures a marketing campaign will generate during a specified period of time.
- *Total cost*: this includes the cost of creative (producing the creative content either in-house or through an outside ad agency), the cost of media (fees charged by the media type to place an ad with them in a specified size, location, and time slot), and related support costs (other professional services).
- *Project outcome:* note that a key goal is to increase brand awareness 15% by the time the campaign has ended. This can be measured using different survey techniques before, during, and after this marketing campaign. The technique selected will depend on the research objectives but there are two primary types: probabilistic (random sampling of the population, from which the results can be reasonably projected to the rest of the population); nonprobabilistic (not a random sample and therefore not likely to represent overall population). Probability survey types include:

  - mail (questions mailed to respondents);
  - telephone (questions asked via telephone);
  - in-person (interviewer-led questioning);
  - mixed mode (combination of other modes).

  Nonprobability surveys are:

  - focus groups (facilitated discussion groups);
  - location interviews (respondents go to specific location);
  - convenience samples (respondents selected from busy areas such as shopping malls).

To calculate results requires data about the size of the customer audience from each of the media companies. Determining the project outcome is part science and art. Historical data for the brand may include past awareness levels (or whatever goal is used for the project outcome), which should guide the brand's longer term goal setting. If brand awareness has grown 1% on average in recent years, then setting a goal of a 95% increase in awareness would be unrealistic and overly ambitious. But settling for 1–2% suggests a lack of effort. This is where the art comes in since part of brand building is predicated on judgment born of other experiences, including historical knowledge of the brand's target audiences and responses to past marketing communication campaigns.

Traditional Marketing Costs

The cost of traditional broadcast coverage, such as television and radio, depends on the size and demographics of the target audience. For example, broadcast advertising rates in the U.S. are based on the size of the expected audience and the corresponding time of day. Peak TV watching occurs during prime time, which is between the hours of 7 to 11 pm, when most Americans tend to watch TV. The rapid growth of cable television during the past 25 years has changed U.S. viewing habits significantly, with the big broadcast networks (ABC, CBS, NBC) witnessing viewership declines. In more recent years, digital video recorders have further affected TV viewing because commercial advertising can be skipped and viewers can choose when they wish to view their favorite programs.[18]

With the increased sophistication of brand building the since the 1990s, IMC has taken on added importance in business planning and traditional marketing will continue to be an important, even dominant, aspect of brand building. IMC planning must look beyond tactical advertising campaigns by starting with the brand's strategic objectives—such as how to increase market awareness, then determining which communications modes and creative approaches would achieve this most effectively. Using broadcast television can help increase brand awareness to the mass market, while tactical marketing programs can then make unique offers to specific audiences with a message designed to inspire purchase (or other increases in usage).

Nontraditional Marketing (NT Marketing)

Nontraditional marketing describes newer marketing practices that facilitate interactive relationships between brands and customers. Nontraditional marketing is broader in scope, focusing not just on product features and benefits but also on customer emotions and interests. The marketing communications philosophy is based on two-way communication between brands and customers discussing a range of topics, including: brands, products, companies, and even consumer lifestyle interests. Awareness and customer loyalty are developed based on authenticity as perceived by the market. In essence, customers determine whether or not they believe in the brand, which serves as the source of the brand's success. Consequently, consumers are more actively involved in receiving and responding to the brand's marketing communications, making purchase decisions based on recommendations by other customers, as opposed to just company-initiated messages. This is a more customer-driven approach, facilitated by the Web 2.0/ digital media tools.

Nontraditional Marketing Characteristics

Nontraditional marketing emphasizes developing interactive relationships with customers to support the brand using techniques that evoke emotions, emphasize customer preferences, reinforce the brand's reputation and affirm trust between the brand and the market, in addition to focusing on product features and benefits. To illustrate, a cell phone maker would seek online feedback about how to improve its offerings, responding online in public to the suggestions so that anyone visiting the web site could see the discussion. Features, benefits, customer perceptions, and even previously unknown needs ("latent needs") can be revealed in these discussions. Plus, this two-way dialog helps the brand to be seen as more transparent and caring toward customers, building trust and deepening customer loyalty as well. Nontraditional marketing recognizes that brands compete against a broader set of offerings in the market (a cell phone competes against other cell phones as well as PDAs, digital cameras, portable music players). Customers are known to make logical *and* emotional decisions. They may choose a brand because they love what it means to them personally, even if the brand's offerings are no better than those of the competition. Methods used are not confined to traditional frameworks. Instead, NT marketing is more experimental, using a variety of approaches to determine what works best, modifying and adapting practices to fit each opportunity's unique circumstances. NT marketing offers brands more immediate data about customers and product popularity because every time a user types a message or clicks on an item, a digital "footprint" is recorded. When each visitor's digital footprints are added together over a period of time, trends and customer behavior patterns can emerge that help brands determine how the various marketing activities are performing and can make adjustments to the overall marketing strategy as a result.

Nontraditional Marketing Communications

Nontraditional marketing describes new media and/or unconventional marketing communications choices that have developed during the past 15 years as a result of technological advances in technology, such as the advent of the commercial Internet and the World Wide Web protocol, mobile technology, and social media. Nontraditional marketing consists of two-way, even simultaneous communication between the customer and the company. Software advancements and digital technology have given marketers and brands a wider variety of ways to reach the marketplace. Customers have more control now, which means brands must be attuned to trends and changes in the marketplace if they want to minimize negative word of mouth that can spread quickly via online modes such as blogs, podcasts, social media, and email. Traditional marketing, essentially company-controlled communications, is increasingly distrusted by consumers, especially if brand messages are contrary to actual customer experiences. A clever slogan or jingle can still help make a brand memorable but can quickly be undermined if negative perceptions grow. In essence, consumers today are far more actively involved in determining a brand's fate than ever before. They rapidly uncover falsehoods and misleading claims using the plethora of NT marketing communication tools available. For brands today, coordinating and using traditional and NT marketing together is likely to be the surest route for building long-term brand value. To make this alignment work best, brand builders have to ensure that they can deliver on the promises they make otherwise customers will quickly turn against the brand.

To illustrate, a Canadian musician named Dave Carroll used social media to complain about a frustrating customer service experience he had with United Airlines in March 2008. After a flight, he discovered that his $3500 guitar had been broken, the victim of mishandling during baggage loading. Despite a year of effort on his part, United turned down his claim for recompense. Frustrated, he wrote and recorded the first of three songs about his ordeal and uploaded a video to YouTube that received over 3.5 million views. He also blogged about his experience. His plight was subsequently picked up by other media, including the BBC, CBS, ABC, NBC, MSNBC, FoxNews, the *Los Angeles Times*, and the *Chicago Sun-Times*. Eventually, United said it was sorry and would fix the situation. United replied using Twitter, among other media.[19] Robin Urbanksi, a spokeswoman for United said "While we mutually agree this should have been fixed much sooner, Dave's excellent video provides us with something we can use for training purposes to ensure that all customers receive better service from us."[20]

As will be discussed shortly, NT marketing growth has been dramatic, illustrating the rapid and large-scale adoption of these tools by brands and customers alike. But while the term NT marketing is useful as a distinction from traditional marketing because it highlights the many new media choices available to marketers, in the coming years the distinction will be less relevant as NT marketing practices become more common. Marketing will have simply added more tools and media to its strategic arsenal.

Nontraditional Marketing Tools

Figure 10-3 shows the tools that fall under the NT marketing umbrella, each providing a different way to communicate a brand message and imagery.

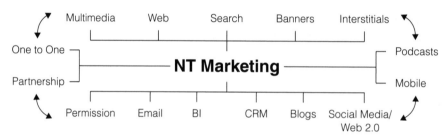

Figure 10-3   Nontraditional Marketing

Multimedia

Multimedia describes a combination of media and content presented in different forms, such as text, photographs, videos, online slide shows, animation, audio effects, and interactive features. For example, when visiting an online news source, such as BBCNews or the *International Herald Tribune*, visitors will see a range of these multimedia on the home page that are activated by a simple click of the mouse. These help bring an otherwise static page of written content to life and help create user "stickiness"—a term that describes how successful online content is in compelling visitors to stay and repeatedly visit with one site or feature before eventually moving onto another. Multimedia's ability to combine different media can be a significant tool for creating a brand experience because multiple tools are used to stimulate buyers. Multimedia can also include software that allows nonprofessionals to design web sites, DVDs, and digital songs, such as Apple's iWeb web site software and Garageband for recording and editing music.

Advantages
Multimedia can help present a brand in a richer, more visually interesting way that engages customers. Combining the various components has been made easier over the years with new software that does not require knowledge of programming to use it. These newer tools

are also far more affordable than in years past, enabling the average consumer to afford and use them.

Disadvantages
Despite their relative simplicity, multimedia tools can still be quite complex and time consuming to use relative to typical PowerPoint presentations. Sophisticated use of multimedia will probably still require brands to hire an outside firm and/or expert to develop these projects professionally, which can make them expensive.

Measures
The varied components that comprise multimedia have an equally varied range of measures. Engagement and abandonment, referenced following Table 10-4, can indicate whether the content is interesting and if it leads visitors to purchase products. Non Web-based multimedia, such as PowerPoint, demos, and DVDs, are harder to measure unless a specific request is made to the customer to reference it when making a purchase.

Table 10-4   Nontraditional Marketing Planning Template

	Multi-Media	Web	Banners	Blogs	Podcasts	Social Media	Mobile	CRM
Target audience X								
Target audience Y								
Target audience Z								

Source: John A. Davis brand research 2000–2009.

Web

The Internet is an enormous array of interconnected computers that communicate directly and easily with each other. The Internet is most easily accessed via the World Wide Web (designated by the www protocol in most web site addresses), which is a layer of software recognized by mostly commercial web sites offering a vast range of content, from business and nonbusiness sources alike. The Web has enabled companies to build sophisticated web sites that not only serve as digital brochures but interactive destinations between brands and the market place.

Advantages
The Web has evolved into a sophisticated source of information from commercial web sites to research on an enormous range of topics. It has become a key area where consumers around the world spend increasing amounts of time. Since the Web is comprised of code and accessed via computer commands and keystrokes, every action leaves a digital footprint, which means user activity and profiles can be tracked far more accurately than with

qualitative surveys or other research instruments. Well-planned and creatively designed web sites can be a powerful brand-building tool.

Disadvantages

The Web can appear cluttered and chaotic because there is no central index that outlines sections or topics. The content on the Web ranges from highly reliable with properly cited details to random opinions and unsubstantiated facts, so users may not always get reliable information. Good web sites can be expensive to produce and maintain, requiring a dedicated person or team of people responsible just for this one purpose.

Measures

Direct URL access, engagement, and abandonment are each useful measures (explained below). In addition, entry and exit pages, bounce rates, average sale price, profit margin, conversion rate, and total number of unique and repeat visitors (and buyers) are all useful for evaluating web site results.

Search

This refers to the practice of placing ads on search engine results pages.

Advantages

Search advertising places a brand's ad (paid or unpaid) on results pages with complementary or compatible products, increasing the chances that the brand's ad will be clicked on. For example, a wet suit manufacturer would seek placement on search results pages for products ranging from surfboards to scuba diving in the hope of attracting additional click through business.

Disadvantages

Active Web searchers may find search ads intrusive and distracting from their primary task.

Measures

Search measures include cost per thousand visitors (CPM), cost per action (CPA), and click through rates.

EXAMPLE 10-3:

Johnson & Johnson

Johnson & Johnson's advertising expenditures decreased 10% in 2006 to $1.9 billion. Traditional media expenditures dropped further—by 22%. Money was being shifted to search engine advertising and consumer-directed web sites. Many of the company's subsidiaries and healthcare brands shifted toward online marketing channels. For example, subsidiaries Depuy and Ethicon maintained web sites on movement-related products and surgical procedures. Despite decreased advertising expenditure, sales grew by 6% to US$53.2 billion in 2006, then climbing further to US$63.7 billion in 2008.[21]

Banners

Banners, or more specifically, banner ads, are a form of advertising found on web sites. While banner ads can be as large as a half page or more, most are simple strips ("banners") with a simple message designed to entice visitors to click on them. The visitor is then linked to the advertiser's main web site or item featured in the ad. Banner ads can be static or dynamic, depending on the software used to create them and the overall purpose of the ad. Over the years, banner ads have grown in sophistication, thanks to technology. Visitors can use their mouse to hover over a banner, which can trigger the banner to expand in size and provide additional content and/or dynamic media.

Advantages

Banner ads are a simple online version of billboard advertising. Their size limits the amount of information that can be stated about a brand, so brevity over detail works best. Banner ads are cheaper to create than longer, more detailed ads. Depending on the web site(s) where the banner is placed, their cost can be relatively less expensive as compared to more simplified traditional print, billboard, or broadcast advertising. When done well, banners serve as a point of entry for users who find the brand interesting enough to then click on it. Once clicked, the user is taken to the advertised brand's web site.

Disadvantages

Web site visitors may find banner ads intrusive and irritating, detracting from their enjoyment of the web site and conceivably creating a negative impression of both the web site and brand being advertised. The use of flash and other dynamic content can be distracting, further annoying users. Banner ad affordability can be deceptive because less expensive placement is usually the result of being placed on less popular web sites, or pages within web sites, reducing the number of people in the target audience. Since advertisers often pay based on click throughs, banner ad costs can increase quickly if a large number of visitors do so, yet buy little or nothing on the brand's web site. So the onus is on brand advertisers to invest more resources (money, time, people, effort) in developing a web site that entices people to buy.

Measures

Impressions (when a banner ad is displayed on a web page) and click throughs (the term that describes when a web site visitor clicks on the banner) are two of the measures used to evaluate banner effectiveness.

Interstitial

Interstitials ('in-between") are web pages that appear before the primary content page sought by the user is displayed, displaying advertising or other information (perhaps about the web site or the next section of the web site).

Advantages

Interstitial pages, like full page print ads, can be useful for providing more detailed content and/or more dynamic animation that can paint a more descriptive picture of the brand and create a more compelling user experience.

Disadvantages

Like banner ads, interstitials can be perceived by users as irritating, interrupting their navigation and enjoyment of visiting web sites. Interstitials can also be more expensive to produce and, if executed poorly, may harm the brand's image.

Measures

Similar to banners.

Blogs

Blogs, or web logs, are interactive online journals. Their use ranges from serving as opinion/ editorial to informational updates about specific topics (such as new products or events) to family diaries. They allow visitors publicly to log their comments and even critiques of the topics covered. Blogs are easy to set up and maintain because most of the software is free on the Web.

The most popular blogs have hundreds of thousands or even millions of followers who regularly spread the message through online sharing, also called viral marketing. Viral marketing is a form of marketing but it is not easy for companies to control. Nevertheless, it has become an important by-product of the Internet in recent years.

Advantages

Blogs can attract groups of people with shared interests in the topic, known as communities. The composition of communities often cuts across more traditional demographic boundaries, attracting people from a variety of socio-economic backgrounds whose common interest is the blog's content. Popular blogs can become sources of credible discourse and public opinion, helping brands develop a favorable image that spreads rapidly due to the two-way, immediate feedback design of the medium. Blogs can help brands by serving as a forum for engaging customers, interactively involving them and, as a result, facilitating their loyalty over the long term.

Disadvantages

There are millions of blogs and blogposts every day, so a company-initiated blog may not gain the following required to support the effort put in. Negative opinions can spread just as quickly as positive, harming a brand as a result. Controlling blogs is not possible due to the community-based, anytime/anywhere access. Because of their accessibility and potential for significant reach blogs can quickly undermine other company-controlled forms of brand building (traditional advertising, product development, field sales) by criticizing the company's efforts, presenting contrary points of view, and disseminating their feedback virtually instantly.

Measures

A blog's success can be analyzed using web site metrics plus a review of changes to the number of RSS feed subscribers, the number of RSS to email subscribers, top posts, top feed readers, trackbacks, and replies (RSS is short for Really Simple Syndication, and it is an easy way to automatically notify people of content changes to their favorite blogs and web sites).

Podcasts

Podcasts are digital audio and video programs similar to more traditional TV and radio programs, but developed specifically for online distribution. There are tens of millions of podcasts in the world, so the range of topics is extensive, and popular ones are slickly produced with dedicated fan followings.

Advantages

Podcasts reach specific audiences and, as such, can help brand positioning by reaffirming the brand's reputation or establishing a new image. As a form of programming, podcasts can develop loyal fan followings and provide useful content that creates a positive image for the brand.

Disadvantages

Like blogs, there are millions of podcasts and most do not have a significant following. A brand may expend unnecessary effort to develop a podcast series, yet have very few customers listening. Creating successful content on a consistent and regular basis requires significant effort, just as it does for successful television shows, and a brand can quickly turn people off if the programming quality is uneven.

Measures

Podcasts may use a mix of "classic measures" (total subscribers) with NT digital metrics (viral adoption rates).

Social Media and Web 2.0

Social media and Web 2.0 are terms that describe the second generation of Web-based tools that act as online social networking communities, although social networking is technically only one of the many uses. Collaboration, information sharing, software hosting, video sharing and more are each examples of Web 2.0 tools. Popular social networking web sites include Facebook and MySpace, although there are many more, designed to appeal to broad and narrow interests alike.

Advantages

The popularity of many of the better known social networking sites offers an attractive place for brands to reach large and influential audiences. The online discussions can provide rich, relatively unedited, and useful information where brands can learn more about public opinion and/or how their offerings and those of competitors are perceived. This information can help identify new opportunities and communities of users that may find the brand interesting.

Disadvantages

Opinions on these sites can be direct, emotional, and subject to extreme exaggeration, irrespective of accuracy. The viral nature of the medium, like other NT marketing modes, can undermine a brand's image as negative public opinion can spread rapidly and is notoriously hard to control.

Measures

Posting videos on the Web has become a popular tactic for getting messages out to market. Youtube.com provides statistics on views and even a basic five-star viewer ratings system. A small group of Lenovo employees produced several short, whimsical video spots about the superior qualities of their laptop computers that they uploaded to Youtube.com (such as the "Lenovo Skywalker" video). They set a goal of getting around 900 000 views (200 000 views is considered very good and 1 000 000 views is considered excellent) and did not inform their colleagues or senior management about their "project." Total views came to more than 3 000 000, indicating a major success. Senior management then noticed the potential power and reach of NT marketing.[22]

Mobile

Mobile refers to the software and hardware associated with portable communications and computing. Typically, however, mobile is associated most closely with cellular technology, including cell phones, pagers, and personal digital assistants (PDAs). An increasing number of cell phone handsets have software installed that enables Web surfing, small profile videos, games, digital photography, and GPS location systems. Mobile phones have also spawned a new communications tool called text messaging. Text messaging describes simple, short messages, often using colloquialisms to express words and ideas succinctly ("I love you" is "ily"). It is a quick and easy way to communicate with someone using another mobile device but without incurring the same fees as a more conventional phone call.

Advantages

There are nearly 4 billion mobile phone subscribers worldwide,[23] which means brands can directly reach an enormous global audience and/or pinpoint individual users for advertising and promotions. Brands can easily track the success of a particular promotion since mobile phones, like Web-based marketing communications, leave a digital footprint tracking usage patterns. For loyal customers of a brand, such as a favorite sports franchise, such technology can enable the team to send real-time score updates, promote specific products unique to individual players, and market upcoming games.

Disadvantages

Not everyone wants to receive advertising, promotions, or other information from brands, even if the mobile customer loves the brand. Marketing to consumers via mobile devices risks irritating and alienating them and tainting the brand as a result, and the viral effect can accelerate this process.

Measures

Several measures are useful for assessing mobile. Assuming a brand is providing content, either for sale or free, to customers, then download activity can be tracked. A brand may choose to offer free wallpaper featuring its logo (for example) and the resulting customer response will provide an indication of the brand's popularity. Cost-plus content is priced just above the cost to produce the content, such as ringtones. Fee-based content charges a higher amount for more sophisticated content, such as regularly updated product information, sports scores, games, and videos. Subscription services charge users over a longer time period for ongoing access to content. In each case, the download activity associated with each level can be measured directly. For mobile phones with access to the Internet, visitors, hits, page views, engagement, and abandonment are all relevant measures.

Customer Relationship Management (CRM)

Customer relationship management (CRM) is a term with two meanings. Generally speaking, CRM is anything having to do with proactively taking care of customers, from the behavior of field sales people to the responsiveness of customer service and support departments. However, CRM is more commonly associated with database software systems designed to track information about customers. This information includes the customer's profile, purchase history, order statistics, financing requirements, interactions with service, and support.

Advantages

Customer relationship management software has the potential to contain a customer's entire history with the brand, providing management with a comprehensive and centralized profile that is easy to access. Furthermore, depending on the CRM software used, management can run forecasts and projects based on customer data (individually and/or collectively). This is a powerful tool that facilitates decision-making, particularly as it pertains to customer account management, customer development, product development, and marketing communications.

Disadvantages

Customer relationship management software can be expensive and complex for many companies to implement. During the dot.com era, CRM-type projects were often the object of over-promising and under-delivery, creating early distrust of these systems. Since then, quality and reliability have improved, as has flexibility. Companies must be clear (and realistic) about what they want their CRM system to do before embarking on installing such a system.

Measures

Customer relationship management software is a powerful tool that benefits more than just marketing since the data touches on finance, operations, support, and logistics systems as well. As such, measurement of effectiveness is tricky. A better gauge is to regularly assess usage (frequency of use, type of use, ease of use, reliability of use) to determine how the system can be improved for more effective business decision-making.

Business Intelligence/Analytics

Business intelligence (BI) describes software that takes data from various company databases and organizes it into common themes, distilling the most relevant information that can help marketers determine possible business trends.

Advantages

Brands can benefit from BI because the information helps evaluate pricing, promotion, and direct response campaigns (among a wider range of findings), which can then be used to develop future forecasts and predict possible alternative scenarios.

Disadvantages

Like CRM systems, BI can be quite expensive. Companies must know what relevant information they need to extract from their databases in order to create a BI system that is useful.

Measures

Similar to CRM software. Another usage gauge would be usefulness, accuracy, and accessibility of forecasting data.

Personalization[24]

Personalization describes personalized communications and related actions directed to individual customers.

Advantages

Customers feel that brands know and understand them better when personalized marketing is used. It is made easier with CRM and BI software since those enable brands to gather detailed data about each customer, as well as trends in their respective markets. Visitors to Amazon.com experience personalized marketing whenever they return to the web site as it shows them what they bought before and previously viewed, making recommendations based on this profile.

Disadvantages

Software systems to support personalized marketing are complex and expensive and are only likely to be affordable for the largest companies. Personalization is more than a software implementation. It is an operating philosophy that is intensive, requiring a company-wide commitment from management to front-line employees if it is to be fully realized.

Measures

Since personalization is an online tool that essentially makes recommendations based on user behavior, measuring share of wallet (how much more of the customer's business was gained?), engagement (see Table 10-5), and conversion rates are all useful.

Table 10-5 Marketing Activity Planning Worksheet (Nontraditional Marketing)

	Target audience	Message	Direct URL access	Engagement	Abandonment	Cost	Purchase goals
Web	X	"Only the Best"	5000 ↑ per week	20%↑ in time spent on site	15%↓ in shopping cart abandonment	$250 000	15%↑ in purchases

Email Marketing

Email marketing is helpful in providing customers with updated information about the brand.

Advantages

Done properly, email marketing can be informative and personalized, helping customers learn about the latest offerings in a way that does not feel intrusive. Brands should ask customers whether they wish to receive email communications and, if so, what specific content is desired. This is known as permission marketing, which allows customers to decide whether they want to be reached via email.

Disadvantages

When done improperly, for example when permission marketing is not used, email marketing can quickly anger recipients and negatively affect the brand's image as a result. Email marketing has gained a negative reputation over the years due to spam, which is email generated by computer servers and companies designed to inundate the recipient's inbox with advertising and promotional messages. Email marketing has also been the mode used to transmit many software viruses, making customers suspicious of almost any message received, even if from a known and trusted source.

Measures

Email marketing measures include; response rates, conversion, click through, purchase volume and amount. Email marketing can also be used for delivery of surveys that determine awareness of the brand, customer satisfaction, and competitor comparisons.

Permission Marketing[25]

Permission marketing describes the practice of companies asking customers if they would like to be contacted or receive information about their brands. Customers then have the choice to say yes or no.

Advantages

When a customer gives permission to receive future information, they are indicating their interest in the brand. Having a motivated customer saves time and money prospecting because brand-building efforts can be directed toward maximizing the relationship with the interested customer. Deeper customer loyalty, higher sales, and profits will likely follow.

Disadvantages

Some permission marketers have abused the privilege, turning the customer against them by sending too much information and even spamming them. Maintaining brand consistency, relevance, and quality over the long term is hard and permission marketers put the brand at risk when these characteristics falter.

Measures[26]

Permission marketing measures include: delivery rate (which measures the number of emails sent minus those that bounced divided by total emails sent), unsubscribe rate (percentage of customers that unsubscribe from permission request), open rate (percentage of emails opened after delivery), and click throughs.

Partnerships

Partnerships marketing refers to two or more companies working together to reach a new market.

Advantages
Partnerships can give credibility to the participating firms suggesting that they believe in each other. Marketing costs will likely be shared, reducing the investment burden faced by a single company alone. Other costs may be shared too (operating, support, logistics, distribution, creative support). Partner firms can bring new customers, markets, and innovations to the business opportunity, thereby helping each learn from the other.

Disadvantages
Partnerships can be difficult to manage if clear expectations are not determined up front. Partnerships are usually more complex than envisioned and each unknown creates a potential point of failure. Each partner should openly discuss objectives, benefits, concerns, and even "walk-away" provisions but many firms are reluctant to share.

Measures
Partnerships are harder to measure directly. However, the following measures are good guidelines: cost takeouts (for redundant activities), new sales generated, units sold, revenues and profits, market share increases, brand image and awareness.

Nontraditional Marketing Brand Planning

Returning to our earlier illustration of marketing communications planning templates, three other target audiences X, Y, Z respond to NT marketing best, as shown by Table 10-4.

As with traditional marketing, a worksheet for each media type (web, banner) would be created with specific metrics as goals for each. A campaign planning worksheet for the Web is shown in Table 10-5.

This worksheet displays a possible way to evaluate the performance of the sponsorship's Web-specific campaign. Specific goals using select Web metrics are shown:

- *Direct URL access.* This describes the number of customers who access the company's web site by directly entering the URL, versus linking to it from another site. This can tell how well-known and sought after the brand is. The company wants to increase the number of people who visit the site using direct URL access by 5000 per week.
- *Engagement.* This refers to the length of active time a visitor spends on a web site (versus idle time, indicated by a page that sits for hours while a user has walked away). In this case, the marketers want the brand's web site to drive a 20% increase in engagement (as compared, for example, to other company web sites).

- *Abandonment* describes users who abandon a web site after a short time, or in the act of ordering a product. Here, the company is targeting a 15% reduction in shopping-cart abandonment (perhaps a feature of the shopping cart has been improved that streamlines the ordering process).

Cost: This is the total cost of web site development.
Purchase goals. These are the target sales increases forecasted based on the web site design and content.

With the power shift from companies to customers, brand building must include both one-way and two-way communications (traditional and NT marketing communications) choices if the brand wants to be perceived as relevant by today's customers.

Nontraditional Marketing Costs

Affordability is a key point of distinction from traditional marketing. Nontraditional marketing tools are typically less expensive up front. For example, many blog (short for web log) and podcast (shorter video and audio programming) applications are available for free or at very low prices, helping reduce the potential expenses associated with media placement. Nontraditional marketing should compel companies to communicate credible messages about their brands and their target customers should see them as relevant. The challenge here is that companies do not control the communications agenda with most of the digital tools available today—consumers do, through the use of blogs, podcasts, twittering, and similar digital tools. Nontraditional marketing fosters trust among consumers around the world, relying on each other's instant feedback to determine the attractiveness of a brand. Increasingly, advertising, historically one of traditional marketing's most successful tools for shaping public opinion about brands, is viewed skeptically because it is only the brand's message about itself, delivered directly to customers, with no mechanism for direct feedback. Consumers perceive advertising as unsubstantiated claims.

By comparison, most NT marketing is social and can be started anywhere by anybody— rather than initiated by the company. Consumers view NT marketing as more authentic and trustworthy because the communications are unedited opinions shared by people in the community (such as Facebook, MySpace, Twitter, LinkedIn). When news is reported about a company and its products, whether positive or negative, NT marketing fosters rapid viral growth and reputations grow and/or change rapidly as well. Harvard Business School's John Deighton has studied the impact of new media and related digital tools on marketing and suggests that the old style of bombarding consumers with messages simply will not work anymore in today's business world. His research, which included analyzing Dove's acclaimed "Real Beauty" campaign, which featured actual consumers and not models, says marketers must become comfortable with suggesting a topic, then letting customers respond. Deighton states: "When a brand adopts a point of view, rather than simply making a claim for softer skin, for instance, it can become a lightning rod for discourse. You have to be confident that your message can withstand reinterpretation."[27]

The important point is that combining traditional and NT marketing helps to convey more effectively a common brand image that is understood by various target audiences.

Nontraditional Marketing Growth

Various trends illustrate the growth of NT marketing, from mode adoption/usage to the way in which consumers spend their time online. Variations in NT marketing growth are due to a variety of factors, from innovation to the rate of technological adoption, to cultural beliefs, to business cycles to larger economic shifts. For brands, being aware of trends helps identify what, where, and how to communicate the brand message.

Figures 10-4 and 10-5 show broadband subscriber and penetration patterns, which can help brands determine the markets that have the largest numbers of consumers with broadband access, and which markets have the highest percentage penetration. Such knowledge may result in higher investment in online marketing vehicles for select markets.

The increase in broadband usage and penetration provides useful insight into the most desirable markets for NT marketing. But brand building success should compel marketers to learn why customers are online, what they are doing and which applications should be considered in a marketing campaign (this rationale is not limited to broadband as marketers would conduct a similar analysis for other NT as well as traditional marketing areas).

At the same time, knowing how consumers spend their leisure time signals different ways a brand can reach a target audience. Figure 10-6 shows how consumers are spending their leisure time. Online and digital activities have become a sizable percentage of the average person's leisure time. Data from 2006 shows both the attractiveness and uses of being online: 48% of the average consumer's leisure time was spent online overall. Online

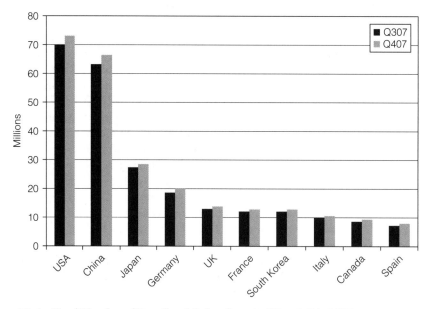

Figure 10-4 Total Number of Broadband Subscribers in Q3 and Q4, 2007
Source: Vanier, F., 2008, "World Broadband Statistics: Q4 2007," retrieved April 17, 2008 from http://point-topic.com/home/press/dslanalysis.asp.

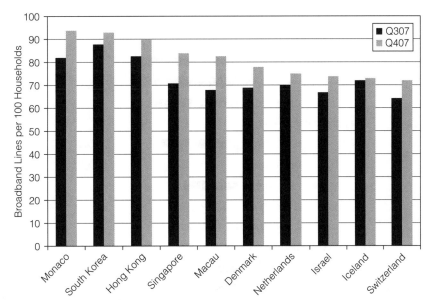

Figure 10-5   Broadband Penetration by Household Q3 and Q4, 2007
Source: Vanier, F. "World Broadband Statistics: Q4 2007," retrieved April 17, 2008 from http://point-topic.com/home/press/dslanalysis.asp.

usage is shown in Figure 10-7. Knowing how target customers spend their time when online helps brands determine the type of message that works, which web sites should be used, and the placement of messages within the web site. Varying the message and placement by web site can provide additional detailed data on which approach yielded the most effective response rates from customers.

Since brands appeal to a wide variety of markets around the world, careful attention must be paid to consumer statistics in each country or region so that IMC allocations reflect the level of acceptance and adoption of traditional and NT marketing. Note again the differences in Figures 10-4 and 10-5—the U.S. has the largest number of broadband users, followed closely by China (and gaining rapidly), whereas in the household penetration numbers the top 10 countries change significantly. Brands can use this data to adapt their IMC tactics accordingly.

Demographics show that the majority of consumers using new media are in their peak income years (35+) and are well educated, making broadband marketing an attractive mode of marketing the brand (see Table 10-6).

A quick review of mobile, blogs, podcasts, and social media provides further evidence of NT marketing's growth.

Mobile

According to Juniper Research, mobile entertainment is forecasted to grow to US$47.5 billion by 2010 from US$20 billion in 2007. China and the Far East are the largest markets,

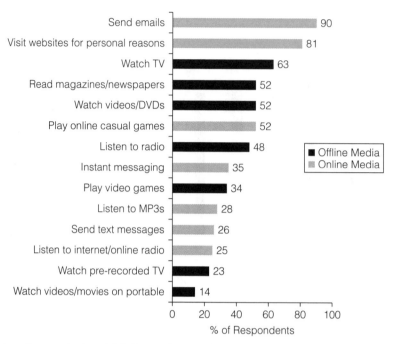

[n] Number of respondents = 4190. Base: all respondents.

Figure 10-6 Allocation of Consumer Leisure Time

Source: "Study: Brands Must Adapt to Shifting Media Habits of Users," Media-Screen, retrieved March 26, 2008 from www.marketingcharts.com/topics/blogs/study-brands-must-adapt-to-shifting-media-habits-of-users-369/.

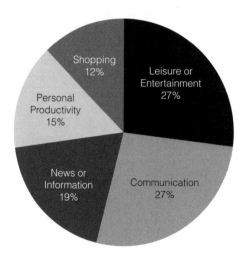

[n] Number of respondents = 4190. Base: all respondents.

Figure 10-7 Allocation of Total Time Spent Online

Source: "Study: Brands Must Adapt to Shifting Media Habits of Users," Media-Screen, retrieved March 26, 2008 from www.marketingcharts.com/topics/blogs/study-brands-must-adapt-to-shifting-media-habits-of-users-369/.

Table 10-6   New Media Consumer Demographics

Demographics Age %	
12–17	18%
18–24	11%
25–34	21%
35–44	22%
45–54	16%
54+	12%
84% college education	
24% advanced degrees	

Source: Data from speech made by Mitch Joel, CEO of Twist Image and Six Pixels of Separation, in a July 2007 presentation made to Singapore Management University's conference, PodCamp 2007. See: www.edisonresearch.com/home/archives/Internet&Multimedia%202006%20Summary%20Final.pdf and www.edisonresearch.com/The_Podcast_Consumer_Revealed_from_Edison_Media_Research.pdf.

contributing 41%, and they will remain in the lead through 2012 when the total mobile market will be US$64 billion, contributing 33% at that time. For brands, developing marketing programs that work effectively in mobile entertainment, such as games, small-profile videos, and real-time delivery of the latest content help further build the brand image.[28]

Blogs

In 2007 there were 71 million blogs in the world and 120 000 new blogs created every day; 1.4 million blog postings are added each day (58 334 per hour). More than 50% of Fortune 500 corporations blog. Blogs are growing because they enable anybody to have a voice online. Many of the blog tools are free, so cost is not an important consideration. For the lucky few, a blog that catches on does so quickly and can become an influential source of information.[29]

Podcasts

The number of podcasts grew significantly from 4000 in 2004 to 61 million in 2005 and 266 million in 2006. Podcast ad spending is growing globally, particularly in the U.S., due to the sheer number of Internet users and the maturity of the online customer market overall. Spending is forecast to increase from an estimated US$240 million in 2008 to US$435 million in 2012. Podcasting is growing rapidly because of its relative ease of use and ubiquity, the substantial concurrent growth in portable media players, information and entertainment-based content, and the affordable cost structure for content creation and deployment.[30]

Social Media

These companies have grown dramatically since 2006. Youtube.com grew approximately 1000% in 2006 and was acquired by Google in October of that year for US$1.65 billion.

Table 10-7   Social Media Usage

See what my friends are up to	86%
Sent a message to someone	79%
Posted/updated my profile	70%
Looked at profiles of people I didn't know	65%
Searched for someone that I used to know	59%
Send a friend/connection request	53%
Listened to music	47%
Read a blog or journal	51%
Wrote on someone's profile page	55%
Watched a video	40%

Source: "North American Technographics Media and Marketing Online Survey Q3 2007," retrieved April 22, 2008, from www.forrester.com/rb/consumertechno.jsp.

It had more than 100 million visitors per month in 2009, with 75 billion video streams served to 375 million unique visitors.[31] Twitter, one of the newer entrants, which enables short 140 character updates between people, saw total minutes spent "Twittering" increase 3712% from April 2008 to April 2009.[32] Facebook grew from 50 million users in 2007 to 200 million users in mid-2009, and was adding over 3 million new users per week.[33] Total minutes spent on Facebook grew 699%, from 1.7 billion to 13.9 billion minutes between April 2008 and April 2009.[34] Investors valued the company at US$15 billion. MySpace grew 72% to 125 million users in 2008.[35] Friendster grew 65% in 2007, and had 57 million users in 2008.[36] Juniper Research forecasts revenues rising in this market from $572 million (2007) to $5.7 billion in 2012, a CAGR of 59%.

Looking at Facebook's data more deeply, over 40% of their customers are over the age of 35 (their fastest growing demographic), college-educated, white-collar professionals, indicating that social media are not just for the youth. The average length of visit is 20 minutes, suggesting the social commitment level is high. Facebook's popularity has led to over 52 000 applications being deployed, many suggested by users and designed to make the site even more useful and customized. Its largest markets are in North America and Europe.[37]

According to Forrester, a technology and market-research firm, social media sites have become a central communications hub for users, as shown in Table 10-7.

As the center of social activity, these sites, along with blogs and podcasts, have become trusted sources of information. Trust and Trusted reputation, as discussed in Chapter 2, is essential to the long-term success of a brand.

IMC Trends

Nontraditional marketing will soon become a misnomer because these are not fringe media any more, having become part of the mainstream in the late 2000s. The growth is driven

Table 10-8   Ad Expenditures by Region – major Media (Newspapers, Magazines, TV, Radio, Cinema, Outdoor, Internet)

	2006	2007	2008	2009	2010
North America	181 816	186 667	193 606	197 921	202 605
Western Europe	103 576	108 287	112 559	117 253	122 249
Asia Pacific	91 811	98 842	106 980	113 937	122 520
Central and Eastern Europe	24 124	28 756	34 010	39 527	45 143
Latin America	22 725	25 627	29 025	31 941	34 540
Africa/M. East/ROW	13 480	16 657	18 715	21 976	26 063
World	437 531	464 837	494 895	522 555	553 119

Note: Figures shown are in US$ millions using 2006 currency average rates.

Source: "North American Technographics Media and Marketing Online Survey Q3 2007," retrieved April 22, 2008 from www.forrester.com/rb/consumertechno.jsp.

by enormous changes in the way in which individuals and companies use NT marketing tools. Global advertising patterns are changing at the same time, as the NT marketing tools become increasingly common. ZenithOptimedia, a media research firm, cites the following general advertising trends:[38]

- ad expenditure growth was 3.8% in 2008 in Europe and North America and 11.1% in the rest of the world;
- developing markets will keep global ad expenditure growth above the 10-year average;
- share of global ad market will increase from 27% to 33% for developing markets and these markets will be responsible for 63% of total global ad growth;
- the Asia Pacific region exceeds Western Europe in 2010;
- Internet advertising growth will continue, from 9.7% of total global ad expenditures in 2008 to 12.3% in 2010, and for several years thereafter.

Table 10-8 shows total ad expenditures by region.

The trends in advertising spending are clearly evident in Table 10-9, showing the differences in growth of each advertising medium. A quick calculation will show that advertising expenditure growth for the Internet from 2006–2010 is forecasted to be 132%, the largest percentage growth rate of all mediums.

Reviewing where the fastest ad expenditure growth is occurring reveals significant variation among countries, as Table 10.10 illustrates.

Shifting trends between traditional and NT marketing are evident, indicating that future brand-building investments will increasingly be in NT marketing. However, one should not declare the death of traditional marketing. Indeed, it will continue to play an important role in an integrated marketing communications mix.

Table 10-9   Global Advertising Spending by Medium

	2006	**2007**	**2008**	**2009**	**2010 est.**
Newspapers	122 795	125 030	126 327	127 583	130 070
Magazines	53 795	55 437	57 151	59 338	61 566
Television	161 633	171 823	184 212	193 673	204 559
Radio	35 834	37 251	38 587	39 927	41 246
Cinema	1882	2013	2197	2410	2700
Outdoor	26 802	28 952	31 676	34 475	37 330
Internet	28 818	37 795	47 544	57 106	66 903
World	431 561	458 301	487 695	514 512	544 375

Note: Figures shown are in millions US$ using 2006 currency average rates The totals here are lower than the totals in the previous table of advertising expenditures by region because that table includes total adspend figures for a few countries for which spend is not itemized by medium. That table also excludes some advertising that does not fit into the above media categories.

Source: "North American Technographics Media and Marketing Online Survey Q3 2007," retrieved April 22, 2008 from www.forrester.com/rb/consumertechno.jsp.

Table 10-10   Contributors to Global Adspend Growth 2007–2010

Country	**Growth %**
Russia	92.1
China	61.5
Pan Arab	54.2
India	52.2
Brazil	46.6
South Africa	45.8
South Korea	21.6
U.K.	19.5
U.S.	8.3
Japan	5.7

Source: "North American Technographics Media and Marketing Online Survey Q3 2007," retrieved April 22, 2008 from www.forrester.com/rb/consumertechno.jsp.

Impact on Consumer Decision-Making

The marketing communications decisions are central to clarifying the brand's image in the market. Developing a successful IMC program is challenging but achievable. Part of the solution includes knowing the customer's decision-making process. Chapter 9 introduced the segmentation, targeting and positioning framework (STP), a classic and important technique for understanding customers. This approach is company led and follows many traditional brand-building practices that start with company needs first, ultimately working their way toward the customers.

With the advent of NT marketing tools and the concurrent growth of consumer-led practices, brands need to adapt to continue to meet the needs of the rapidly changing consumer population. McKinsey, the global strategic consulting firm, offers insights into the consumer decision-making process.[39] Their research reviewed data on 20 000 consumers across five industries and three continents. In short, they learned that brands must find ways to more successfully manage word of mouth. To do this, marketers need to understand the current consumer decision-making process. Traditionally, this has been seen as a process of narrowing, from a broad range of choices to a final selection, following the classic segmentation-targeting-positioning approach discussed in Chapter 7. That approach can still work as it can reveal insights about how the brand is perceived at each stage of the customer's decision process but it must be considered in the context of twenty-first century factors such as technological change and sociocultural adaptation. Rather than a purely sequential decision process, the approach is more circular in nature. Interestingly, McKinsey's research found that, unlike conventional wisdom, which holds that consumers consider numerous brands at the start of their decision making, consumers actually begin with a narrower subset of competitors, partly because of the overcrowded market and onslaught of ongoing marketing communications. Those brands that stand out through the noise are the ones initially considered. Once a few choices are known, then consumers expand the number of brands being evaluated to ensure a proper set of criteria and examples are weighed. McKinsey states that brands that make the cut at the initial consideration phase have a significant advantage over other brands—they are three times more likely to be purchased ultimately.[40] The implication is that brands have an opportunity to add touchpoints at various decision-consideration stages to help keep them under active consideration. Another key finding, discussed elsewhere in this chapter, is that two-way, consumer-led dialogs are becoming more significant, with consumers doing research and gathering information that is helpful to their decision. As we have seen, companies no longer have as much control, whereas consumers have far more. Once consumers are satisfied with the information obtained, purchase follows. Historically, this is when most marketers have assumed that most of the marketing effort *ends*. But today, this is really where the marketing begins. How the brand handles the post-purchase experience will determine if the consumer returns for future purchases. Loyalty is never guaranteed, so brands have a responsibility to create an ongoing experience that is aligned with the pre-, during, and post-purchase phases of the consumers' decision-making process.

McKinsey's research is consistent with the research findings for this book. For brands to compete in the future, companies have to change and broaden their understanding of customers, whether in the B2C or B2B markets. Customers have many avenues to accept or reject brands and few are under direct company control any longer. Instead, organizations must become more flexible and quicker in their responses to market needs.

There is a natural tendency in organizations, indeed in people, to resist change. Change affects the existing order, potentially undermines existing investments, alters organizational needs, produces surprises, and places new demands on management and employees. But the magnitude of change represented by the shift toward NT marketing is the largest shake-up of marketing's traditional order in decades. Many companies are populated by generations of management schooled in traditional practices. While many understand the NT marketing opportunities, comfort with the traditional ways will still receive significant attention and support. Traditional marketing will continue to be important and will not disappear, nor should it, because many of its practices will always work. The important point is that NT marketing offers brands far more powerful tools and techniques for building reputations and gaining market share. When NT marketing is used in combination with traditional marketing, brands have a formidable and beneficial array of tools for connecting with the marketplace. Part of the brand-building process is knowing the right questions to ask about their marketing objectives and programs. We offer several guiding questions here:

Questions for Traditional and NT Marketing

1. What is the brand's mix of traditional and NT marketing?
   a. How will they be deployed?
   b. Who is in charge of media planning and purchase decisions?
   c. Is there a media insertion schedule?

      i. Who is responsible for it?
      ii. Who monitors the execution?

   d. Is there in-house digital media expertise, or will an outside agency be hired?

      i. Is there confidence that the outside agency can deliver?

   e. Are all logos and trademarks designed in appropriate formats for use in all media?
   f. Is brand and/or product image being properly conveyed?

2. Are the various marketing media integrated?

   a. Who oversees and coordinates this effort?

3. What are the contingency plans if a media provider does not deliver?
4. What is the understanding of the competition's equivalent marketing efforts?

   a. How might those affect brand planning, if at all?

5. What are the implications for the consumer's decision-making journey on brand marketing and brand touchpoint decisions?

Communication Effectiveness

For brands, clear communication is a necessary prerequisite to success. The effort required to prepare effective communication is substantial, yet the benefits can be great because a well-conceived position can be readily understood and spread virally from one person to the next. Communication effectiveness depends on aligning customer needs with brand offerings and supporting them with relevant creative support. The term "creative" can be misleading. Certainly, many brands are known for the humor and innovative visuals used in their advertising. Southwest Airlines, AFLAC, Orange, and IKEA have each garnered deserved reputations for creativity in their brand messages. But creative can also refer to the advertising agency's overall efforts to develop an advertising campaign, even if the tone is subdued and conservative.

Creative Execution

The creative effort is geared to producing memorable messages and/or images that the market perceives favorably, encouraging consumers to try the brand. Creative execution is among the most visible and common components of a brand. When asked what a brand is, many people reply that it is a clever advertisement, color, logo, and a memorable slogan. Brand building has historically been the responsibility of advertising agencies. When the business world was simpler (virtually any time before the present), brands were advertised in print publications, TV, and/or radio. Companies had a great deal of power while consumers did not. Today, consumers are armed with information from Internet searches, blogs, podcasts, and social media well before they decide to purchase a product. They might pay attention to an advertisement but only after their skepticism has been overcome through their own research. Power has shifted from companies to consumers (or any customer, for that matter), which makes creative execution much harder. Creative execution has grown increasingly complex, to include innovative distribution, merchandising, corporate identity/logo programs, mascots and, more broadly, integrated marketing platforms. A key driver of this shift has been the realization that creating compelling customer experiences, and not just clever advertising, helps make brands more memorable. As emphasized before, new media tools are an important part of this process.

Creative Challenges: Getting the Point Across

For example, in 2000 the annual SuperBowl game in the U.S. (an event in which the top two teams play for the professional title in American football) saw over a dozen dot. com companies spend $2.2 million each for a 30-second TV ad[41] that featured a cavalcade of odd sights including dancing chimpanzees and sock puppets. Many of these ads were bizarre, having little to do with the companies or their products, but the hope was that the cheeky cleverness would distinguish these hot upstart companies from all others and consumers would flock their way thereafter. While there is nothing wrong about using such unique imagery—it can work in some cases—it did not work for the 2000 SuperBowl dot.com advertisers, most of which subsequently went out of business (their demise was more the result of poor business plans and a lack of customers rather than the SuperBowl ads but the ads certainly did not advance their cause).[42]

Another example of provocative creative that was memorable, but yielded little or no long-term benefit, was a television ad for a dot.com called Outpost.com.[43] The ad featured a gentleman in a suit sitting in a leather chair. Next to him was a large ship's cannon with another person standing alongside firing gerbils (a small rodent) from it toward a sign on the wall that said "Outpost.com". The man in the chair said to the camera, "Hello, we want you to remember our name, Outpost.com, that's why we've decided to fire gerbils out of this canon through the 'o' in Outpost . . ."[44]

While he was speaking the camera panned over to the cannon with the other person firing away. The first gerbil missed, hit the wall and fell to the floor, scampering off stage. The man in the chair said in response, "cute little guy" then nodded his head toward the person next to the cannon and said "fire", whereupon several more gerbils were fired, each missing the hole in the 'o'. When the last gerbil went through the hole, a red light and siren went off and the man in the chair nodded his head in approval. The ad ended with the following onscreen words set against a black backdrop, "Send complaints to Outpost. com. The place to buy computer stuff online."[45]

This TV ad was certainly memorable, but it also left many viewers scratching their heads in wonder. While it was clever, did it boost awareness and, ultimately, sales? Awareness was boosted, but not of the company—only of the gerbil being shot out of a cannon. There was some recall of the company name, but not what the company did. The company was eventually acquired in 2001 for $8 million (roughly 25 cents per share) by a regional U.S. electronics retailer called Fry's. Outpost.com was started in 1995 and claimed to have 1.4 million customers but its sales had been declining in the years leading up to the acquisition. While relating the creative execution of Outpost.com's advertising to its decline and then eventual sale to Fry's is problematic at best, it is clear that Outpost.com's advertising might have benefitted from a more direct message.[46]

When the creative is disconnected from the company and/or the event as it appears to have been with the dot.com ads from the 2000 Superbowl and the Outpost.com example, then any potential benefits rapidly disappear, leaving a cautionary footnote about the dangers to a company's reputation from ill-conceived creative execution, but little or no evidence of success in growing the business or building a brand.

For creative execution to succeed today requires much more than a simple emphasis on bold visuals and clever copy for building awareness. In fact, bold visuals may have little or no impact, as the dot.com examples illustrate. As tempting as daring creative might be, it must be used in the context of longer term strategic objectives. Brands must evaluate their strategic objectives and the related reasons for marketing investments and the possible benefits to be derived. The benefits will include increased awareness, and superb creative can facilitate this.

Coca-Cola's Olympic sponsorship marketing campaigns since 1928 illustrate the many different ways they used creative execution to improve and reinforce awareness. Over the years, Coca-Cola has used the Olympics to launch new products and support other Olympic activities to help build its brand and be more closely associated with Olympic ideals. The brand's list of Olympic innovations is long, but a few highlights are shown in Table 10-11:

Table 10-11   Coca-Cola Olympic Marketing Highlights

Olympics	Coca-Cola sponsorship highlights
1932 Summer Olympics in Los Angeles	• Coke gave away a personal record keeper that allowed fans to compare athlete performances to Olympic records • 3 million miniature sports-action cutouts featuring Olympic records on back were given out across U.S. • Coke is endorsed by former gold medal winner swimmer Johnny Weissmuller in 1934

1952 Summer Olympics in Helsinki	• 30 000 cases of Coca-Cola shipped to Olympics in "Operation Muscle" • Coke donated most of its product to benefit Disabled Ex-Servicemen Association • Coke printed daily menus for athletes • Coke-logo'd sacks and cooler bags distributed
1964 Summer Olympics in Tokyo	• Coke produces street signs, tourist information, guide maps, Japanese-English phrase book. This idea continued at the 1968 Mexico City, 1972 Munich, 1972 Sapporo, 1998 Nagano Olympic Games
1984 Summer Olympics in Los Angeles	• Coke designed trading cards, similar to trading cards from other sports, featuring famous Olympians. Distributed with Coca-Cola beverages. • Coke launched the national Coca-Cola Olympic Youth Soccer Competition • Coca-Cola Olympic Games educational program for schools was introduced • Coca-Cola Olympic Youth Jamborees were developed, directed to underprivileged children • First corporate sponsor for 1984 games • Developed Olympic mascot called "Sam the Eagle"

2006 Winter Olympics in Torino	• Supported presentation of the Olympic Torch Relay
	• Created Coca-Cola Torch Exhibition Tour, an interaction road show
	• Coca-Cola-sponsored school and community programs were developed to select torchbearers
	• Developed "Get Caught Living Olympic" programs in Italy that featured:
	  ° Talking cans
	  ° Coca-Cola Polar Bear
	  ° Automobile prizes
	  ° Event tickets
	  ° Coke's Italian web site featured Olympic Games timeline and history, 2006 events calendar, daily torch relay information
	• Coke created full integrated marketing platform that included:
	  ° Outdoor messages
	  ° Special musical anthem
	  ° Olympic Pin Trading Center
	  ° Historical exhibits
	  ° Sports simulators
	  ° Video game kiosks
	  ° Postcard email booth
	  ° Mobile Coca-Cola Cruisers that gave away Coke products
	  ° 200 volunteers from 20 countries that rewarded random acts of kindness

(Continued)

Table 10-11   (Continued)

Olympics	Coca-Cola sponsorship highlights
	° Created "The Coca-Cola Award: Live Olympic" that celebrated people from around the world that lived the Olympic ideals everyday
	° Developed "Torino Conversations", a blog supported and written by university students who did interviews and posted regular updates about the Olympics
	° Developed program whereby fans in other cities could win trips to future Winter Olympics
	° Created Internet "Win Your Olympic Dream" contest in Austria; "Win Winter Fun" event in Switzerland; fundraising drive in Sweden; mobile phone contest in Belarus and Russia; GEORGIA® coffee promotion in Japan; "Drink. Watch. Cheer. Win" contest in the U.S.

Source: Adapted from: Davis, J. A. The Olympic Games Effect: How Sports Marketing Builds Strong Brands, © 2008 John Wiley & Sons (Asia) Pte Ltd, pp. 184–200.

Brands, whether product or company, rely on the creative execution of *message* and *imagery*, the two halves of creative success, to create lasting connections with customers.

Message

A well-conceived message, often more commonly known as ad copy (the actual verbal description in an ad), uses a mere few words to say a great deal and does so in a way that paints verbal pictures complementing the imagery used. Simplicity is key. Or, to summarize a quote attributed to the American writer Mark Twain, "I didn't have time to write a short letter, so I wrote a long one instead."[47]

Writing and/or speaking concisely (whether the communiqué is an email, a business plan, a proposal, or a verbal presentation) is far harder and requires greater effort than communicating excessively. Part of the magic of successful brand messages occurs when sweeping, positive themes that magnetically attract people while also presenting a persuasive point of view are created. Dense, detailed messages may well be informative, but the deep content can be counterproductive. However, a word of caution is important here. Content detail is a function of the media vehicle and target audience. General interest media, whether traditional or NT, is more effective for simpler vocabulary and messages with broad-based appeal because the audience is more diverse, whereas vertical publications and industry trade journals are conducive to penetrating ad copy and industry vernacular since the audience is more homogeneous and shares a common understanding of industry standards.

Written versus Verbal Messages

Marketing messages will differ in execution, depending if they are written (print, online) or verbal (broadcast, speaking engagements). Written communication, particularly print advertising, affords greater latitude in message since more detail can be provided. Verbal communication, particularly broadcast (radio, TV) is more appropriate for less verbose messages. However, while these are general guidelines, they are not hard and fast rules. With the advent of the Internet in the 1990s and the subsequent growth of online and digital tools, traditional guidelines have become increasingly situational.

Message Guidelines

There are four requirements for developing a successful brand message: *relevance, resonance, distinction,* and *simplicity.*

Relevance

The brand message must connect directly to the target audience. Whether the goal is a simple, three-word slogan or a multi-layered product description, the customer must be able to clearly understand it and recognize "that it is important to me." Without relevance, the brand message is unlikely to be successful, no matter how creative or lyrical it sounds.

Resonance

The brand message must evoke important and/or emotional imagery or sensation. Customers must *feel* that the message or information is right and is meaningful for them. Research shows that strong brands help customers reinforce their own identity and self-image, which helps explain why branding success today focuses on creating sensory experiences, and not just advertising, to develop relationships with customers.

Distinction

In Chapter 6 we learned from a strategic perspective why and how strong brands create distinction that leads to competitive advantage. Distinction is important at the brand message level as well. Furthermore, customers must recognize this distinction. This is not always a literal description as it could be a combination of evocative images as well.

Simplicity

The earlier reference to Mark Twain and simplicity can be expanded upon—a convoluted and/or verbose message risks boring or confusing the market, or both.

Focusing on one or two of these message requirements without the others restricts the message, making it incomplete and less effective. The challenge of developing a successful message should be readily apparent—it is not about being funny, loud, verbose, or different. It is about being relevant, resonant, distinctive, and simple.

Apple is recognized for having all three requirements and for paying attention to Twain's advice. The company's iPod products, for example, are relevant to customers who believe that having control over their listening choices is important to them. Their products resonate because they evoke a sense of personal freedom and imagery of an individualistic lifestyle and are distinctive from visual (well-known iconic designs), functional (they are famously easy to use), and socio-cultural (they are considered cool and hip) points of view. Apple's messages are simple and often have no words at all, just images that reinforce what the public already associates with the company. When a brand like Apple is so well known that it can develop message campaigns by not using words, then it has reached a rare position—that of being universally understood, requiring little or no explanation.

Imagery

Visual imagery is an important IMC tool because well-chosen images can be powerful, evocative and become easily associated with a brand. Relevance and resonance are important in image selection as well. Imagery is represented by advertising uses, identities-logos/landmarks, and even mascots.

Advertising

Consider Apple again—the iPod imagery has had a distinctive black silhouette of a person dancing to music wearing the iconic white ear buds, set against a single color background for years. We instantly associate these ads with Apple iPod. Nike's advertising imagery is replete with athletic scenes, as are UnderArmor's (a rapidly growing athletic apparel maker). McDonald's is known for showing people, particularly families and kids, enjoying themselves. Disney's castle and Mickey Mouse are classic images for which the company is widely known, as are many of their best known characters. Singapore Airlines has the renowned Singapore Girl. Manchester United's ubiquitous red color is used with creative identities targeted to different fan groups, with "Fred the Red" focused on kids and "The Red Devils" targeted to adults, not to mention the club's extensive merchandising, advertising and online communications efforts, all tied together thematically by the color red. Benetton is known for its "United Colors of Benetton" advertising that frequently uses arresting, controversial images.

Identities-Logos/Landmarks

The world's leading brands have instantly recognizable logos. This is not accidental but is typically a component of a carefully planned IMC program to support the brand. When customers see the logo of a well-known brand, images, emotions, and associations are triggered and either positive or negative perceptions are recalled.

For brands, logos are typically part of a detailed corporate identity program that describes appropriate legal uses of all logos and trademarks, from corporate stationery to podcast logos to sales literature to advertising. Corporate identities and logos are legally protected from unauthorized or improper use, as designated by each organization. One of the most recognized and protected logos in the world is the Olympic rings. The IOC has strict guidelines for proper and consistent usage of all logos and imagery associated with the Games. Even the order of colors in the Olympic rings is carefully prescribed to prevent a multitude of confusing variations in the marketplace (the blue, black and red rings are always across the top and the yellow and green rings are along the bottom). Doing so protects the Olympic trademarks and the sponsors that pay hundreds of millions of dollars to be associated with the Games, ensuring that they will have exclusive rights to use the Olympic images in their brand building.

Imagery is linked to landmarks and locations and can help strengthen the image of a brand. We do not have to see the name of a city or a country to know its name once we see a world-renowned landmark. The Transamerica building in San Francisco is an iconic, pyramid-shaped building that is recognized worldwide, and Transamerica was a leading financial services brand for years before its sale to the Dutch insurer, Aegon, in the late 1990s. The Eiffel Tower is a powerful visual structure that helps identify and brand the city of Paris, as does the Oriental Pearl Tower in Shanghai.

Logos and landmarks act as information filters, reminding us of how we feel about the associated brands.

Mascots

Mascots are intended to help put a colorful, memorable face on the organizations they represent. Many companies (and many more sports teams) use mascots to add personality to the brand. The mascots can also be used for public appearances through community outreach events to build deeper relationships with the public. Consumer marketing has long relied on mascots as a device for attracting young customers. Mascots, or a variation of them, can go viral, demonstrating another clever method marketers can use to reach the public. Jollibee, a popular Philippine-based fast-food chain, has a giant bee in a red blazer and chef's hat as its mascot and main corporate identity, reinforcing the chain's buzzing, happy family restaurants. NTTDoCoMo, the Japanese telecommunications company, has Docomodake—the smiling mushroom—as its mascot. When one thinks of Ronald McDonald, images of a yellow-suited clown in red floppy shoes with flaming red hair instantly appear. Jack-in-the Box's "Jack" is a quick-witted fast food CEO. Mars M&M's candy has turned the round green candy-coated chocolate treat into a much-sought after toy, complete with its own web site where visitors can make their own M&M's characters and then send them to friends (www.becomeanmm.com/). Sakae Sushi's frog reflects Asian-style tranquility. Arguably, Disney has perhaps been the company most responsible for turning mascots into more than just visual ambassadors for the brand. They have transformed mascots into a successful industry with stuffed toys, action figures, cartoons, and a dizzying array of related merchandise that generate significant revenues.

Sports mascots range from animals (such as the Chicago Bears) to gastropods (the University of California at Santa Cruz's Banana Slugs) to birds, such as Tottenham Hotspur's Chirpy Cockerell. Sports mascots have been a source of controversy, particularly when they appear as caricatures of ethnic groups, and a few more extreme observers have suggested the banning of mascots altogether because they serve as little more than a PR stunt that does not improve the quality of the team.

Mascots can help brands appear more playful and less serious, perhaps even more human, to endear themselves to the market. Whether they are absurd, surreal, or cute and cuddly, mascots are not a rocket science project designed to inspire deep thinking about the organization they represent. Mascots are simply a marketing device, nothing more nor less. They are intended to help reinforce the organization's identity by making it more memorable.

Merchandising

Many companies develop merchandise programs designed to extend their brands beyond their core products into a wider range of offerings, from apparel to office supplies to household items. BMW and Harley Davidson are two well-known examples.

> ## EXAMPLE 10-4:
>
> ### BMW
>
> **BMW has an online shop featuring a wide range of merchandise including: apparel, toys, luggage, yachting accessories, bikes, and golf equipment. Each is consistent with BMW's image as a premium brand and reflects the lifestyle tastes of their target audience.[48]**
>
> ### Harley-Davidson
>
> **Harley-Davidson features motorcycle-specific apparel for men, women, and children, in addition to motorcycle-specific accessories.[49]**

There is no magic set of guidelines that says which types of merchandise are best and which are to be avoided—each company needs to determine the items that lend themselves most effectively to extending their brand without diluting it. But too much merchandising can weaken the brand's focus, which might ultimately undermine the brand's integrity. Arguably, Starbucks' brand extensions into games, grocery items, kitchen equipment, music, publishing, and stuffed animals may have contributed to the brand's struggles in the mid-late 2000s. Rapid store expansion was a factor as well, of course. Any merchandising decisions must be evaluated based on strengthening the brand and improving brand value.

Questions for Creative Execution

1. Is the brand message clear?
   a. Is it designed to be funny/memorable/professional/instructional/other?
2. Is the brand message succinct?
   a. Can it be described it in a few words or seconds?
3. Is it relevant to the needs of the target customers?
   a. How do you know?
4. Does it resonate with them?
   a. How do you know?
5. Is the message distinctive?
   a. Is the distinction recognized by customers?
6. Is it simple?
   a. Do people "get it"?

7. What images/imagery should be associated with the brand and its message (follow the relevance/resonance/distinctiveness guidelines from above)?
8. What logos and trademarks will be used?
   a. How will they be used?
   b. Are they following corporate guidelines?
9. Mascots and merchandise
   a. Will either or both be used?
   b. What is the purpose of a mascot for the brand?
      i. Will it enhance or help the brand plan?
   c. How is the merchandise plan being handled?
      i. Design
      ii. Vendors
      iii. Quantities
      iv. Quality
      v. Price
      vi. Distribution
10. Is management comfortable with how these activities and plans are unfolding?

Brand Lifecycle

Mapping the lifecycle as shown in Figure 10.8 can help brand planning, particularly as it pertains to IMC, creative execution, and corresponding measures. Figure 10-8 is just a sample of how a brand changes over time. Each company is different, as are the actual marketing programs used. But the important point is that as brands grow, objectives and corresponding measures will change because both the market and the company's needs are changing. Static, one-size-fits-all marketing will not work. Brand building must be done in consideration of business context at the time.

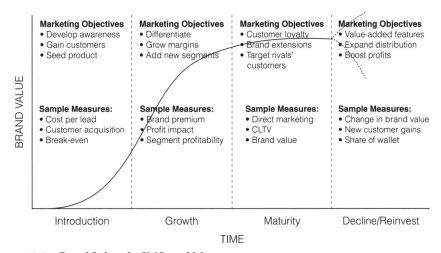

Figure 10-8   Brand Lifecycle, IMC, and Measures

Environment

One of the main reasons to build a brand is to differentiate from competitors in a way that is meaningful to customers by making the experience special. Environment addresses differentiation by orchestrating conditions surrounding the brand that reinforce its uniqueness, whenever it is in contact with the public. Such environmental coordination is pivotal to a successful experience.

Customers always have an experience when buying a product, whether it is great, average, or poor, and the environment in which the product is marketed can be a powerful influence. The challenge is how to manage the environment in a way that improves the customer's experience and enhances the brand's image. This is accomplished through the use of creative and innovative elements and can quickly become quite complex. The benefits apply to both B2C and B2B firms. These elements consist of tangible (furnishings, merchandise layout, facility/store design, products) and intangible elements (atmosphere, service, support).

C. K. Prahalad and Venkatram Ramaswamy describe experience as a higher level competitive space driven by innovation, above solutions and products.[50] This requires management to shift its thinking from a company to a customer perspective, ascribing product issues to the firm, solutions to the extended enterprise and its value-chain (because they depend on sources of professional expertise beyond the firm), and experiences to a larger networking including consumers (because they interact with all firm touchpoints). Having a quality product is essentially the minimum cost of entry. Improving the product with value-added features and services from collaborative value-chain relationships creates a more complete and distinctive solution. Innovation is important in all areas. But an emphasis on cocreating (firm, extended enterprise, consumers) experience environments ultimately determine a brand's success. As they state, "Companies can differentiate themselves not just through the quality and cost of their products and services, but also through their capacity to co-create unique experience environments with consumers."[51]

In their view, innovation does far more than develop products and enhance features. It facilitates the creation of great experiences, shifting the innovation emphasis from products to experiences where value is cocreated with customers.

Implications for Brands

This thinking has important implications for brands. Brand perceptions and even brand value are shaped by powerful experiences. Therefore, the purpose of brand-building activities is to support the overall environment in which the consumer interacts with the brand.

Environment Factors in Creating Successful Brand Experiences

The planning and design of environmental factors involves six areas as shown in Figure 10-9.

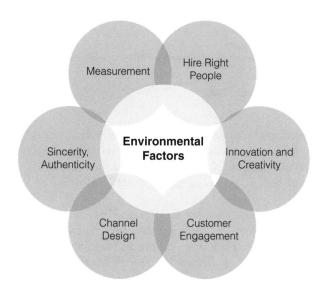

Figure 10-9   Environmental Factors in Brand Experiences

Hire Right People

As Chapter 7 discussed, having a strong brand culture is essential to creating long-term brand value and success. Customers interact with brands through the brand's customer service, sales, and corporate office employees, and quick impressions are formed, which affect brand perceptions and reputation. Management's task is to hire the right people, taking the initiative with each new employee to ensure the best possible employee-company fit. A necessary condition is a management commitment that any new hires will be made consistent with the brand building objectives. Four Seasons Hotels uses several guidelines when hiring employees:[52]

- The Golden Rule: treat others as they would want to be treated.
- Recruiting from other Four Seasons employees. This stems from the belief that a top-performing employee probably socializes with similar kinds of people. This streamlines recruiting and keeps initial costs lower.
- Attitude. Four Seasons wants people that are flexible and adaptable.

Once hired, employees are rigorously trained on the company's hundreds of service standards and procedures. Recognition includes employee of the month and year and team celebrations. Direct communication and front-line problem solving are part of the training and culture, creating a customer-centered service experience. Measurement is handled via annual evaluations.

Four Seasons evaluates management potential using the following criteria:[53]

- people leadership skills;
- sound analyzer and problem solver;
- implementation/action taker;

- good business acumen/operator;
- product and service obsession;
- versatility/flexibility/stress management;
- team player;
- interpersonal sensitivity and skills;
- public ambassador.

Each category is evaluated on one of four dimensions: *must improve, growing, solid,* and *exceptional.*[54] Four Seasons is consistently among the very top ranked hotel companies in the world for its consistently high level of service and their emphasis on hiring the right talent from the start has had an unquestioned effect on their superior performance and reputation.

It can be challenging to have a brand culture extend beyond the firm's immediate sphere of influence (its own employees) to indirect channel employees, such as those from a retailer. How can a brand protect its core culture and market its products and brand personality through the employees of another business? Nike offers one solution: *Ekins.* Ekins (derived from spelling Nike backwards) are Nike's technical representatives for retailers. Working out of each regional sales office, Ekins regularly run clinics for retailers and their employees, informing them of the latest products and technologies. Part of each Ekins' job is to be a corporate storyteller, sharing Nike's traditions with each retail account. This technical rep/storyteller combination serves two purposes: to help a retailer's employees be more effective at selling Nike products whenever a customer asks a question, and giving the retailer employees a sense of Nike's culture and traditions. While the retailer employees do not work for Nike, the Ekins' efforts help inject the company's culture more directly into them.

Whether it is in-house employees or inspiring the employees of an important value-chain partner, the service environment (the conditions and practices of the brand's employees when interacting with customers) has a direct effect on the customer's overall experience.[55]

Employee Behavior

Chapter 7 discussed the importance of the "five ambassadors" in shaping employee behavior. For customers, being treated well means a brand's employees exhibit elements of the five ambassadors, even though the customer and employee are not consciously thinking about those specific labels. Four Season's Golden Rule serves as a valuable guide to employee behavior. Although employee judgment at the moment of a customer interaction plays a vital role in shaping the customer's experience, management's support for building a strong brand culture, and all that implies, sets the foundation for encouraging the right employee behaviors in the first place.

Innovation and Creativity

Besides hiring the right talent, top brands tend to embed innovation and creativity in almost every internal area, particularly those responsible for improving the customer relationship.

Updating

Brand loyalty patterns have changed since the late 1980s, as have customer expectations. Staying relevant means that brands need to regularly update and refresh their products, solutions, and experiences. New products and/or updates can lead to changes in pricing, distribution choices, and marketing communications. As new products are conceived and developed, employees can and should be the first to receive information on all updates because they are responsible for reinforcing these changes whenever working with the public. Technology has enabled real-time updates for a wide range of online sites. For example, most professional sports franchises now have a section for live gamecasts and updates, allowing fans in remote locations to receive the latest information. Online shopping personalization engines help buyers keep instant track of their purchases, updating their account history and making recommendations for future purchases. Online merchandise assortments can also be shifted to reflect the buyer's latest purchases and preferences. Well-known U.S. direct marketers such as Land's End and LL Bean adjust their merchandise mixes every season, with lesser updates for special offers highlighted more frequently. If a customer has given permission, then online sites contact customers via email, twitter, or RSS feeds about offers in which the customer might be interested.

Channel Design

Channels describes where and/or how customers will find the product and in what variety. They include the chain of intermediaries that help get the product from the company to the customer. In the case of B2C markets, retail stores are a common place where products are sold. The Internet is another type of place, albeit in the virtual world. In B2B markets, place may be defined as supplier offices or warehouses, intermediary/vertical market businesses (such as VARs—value added resellers—in the software industry), or even any location where buying and selling teams meet to discuss a business transaction. Channel design includes:

- distribution: *direct selling, advertising, internet, retailer, distributor, agent, third party service provider;*
- coverage: *the extent to which each customer segment is reached by the channels design;*
- locations: *the geographic, or digital, location of each distribution point;*
- transport: *the movement of goods from manufacturer to distribution points;*
- assortment: *the combination of products offered in the distribution location;*
- inventory: *the depth of product in sufficient variety to satisfy demand.*

The number and quality of these channel components plays a significant role in brand development, from customer access to awareness to brand reputation. Among management's primary tasks is determining the proper channel design and alignment in support of brand goals. Several factors affect a product's success in the distribution strategy, including: location of the distribution points, reputation and brand image of the distributor, the use of the distribution point by the marketer's target customers, and even the popularity of the firm doing the distribution.

Physical design

Brands can be represented physically via stores, products, offices, and other customer touchpoints. The benefits accrue to all stakeholders—employees, customers, shareholders, and value-chain partners, each of which is likely to view thoughtful physical design favorably because it suggests quality and success. There is a reason premier law firms and consulting companies typically have highly professional, even luxurious office spaces, furnishings and multimedia features—because such amenities convey success and confidence. However, a different dynamic does occur with high-tech start-ups such as those in Silicon Valley, where venture capitalists would view opulent surroundings as a sign of misuse of capital. In these instances, physical design is simple, with only the bare essentials of desks, chairs, and telecommunications equipment, hopefully signalling that the firm is devoting its funding to product development and customer creation. Whether opulent or basic, physical design communicates a message about the firm that is ideally consistent with the customer's expectations. Joie de Vivre Hotel's clever use of fabrics, furnishings, decorations, and theme guest rooms creates a unique physical environment that sets the company apart. Merchandise layout within retail environments can affect brand perceptions as well. Nike's NikeTown stores are reminiscent of a modern town square, with unique pavilions for each sport, with the themes and interior merchandising changing as product lines are updated, players change, and sports evolve. Nike uses these stores as laboratories for merchandising innovations, where successful approaches can then be recommended to Nike's many retail customers. Urban Outfitters, a retailer positioned to the young adult market, features apparel, books, and eclectic merchandise in a stylized urban setting and pulsating with the latest music to create a multi-sensory experience. Virgin-Atlantic's airport clubhouses, which are lounges for the airline's frequent flyers, offer travelers theme areas for relaxing, massage services, a beauty salon, showers, game room, movie theatre, and several dining choices, making the pre and post travel experience complete. Singapore's Changi Airport is designed with travelers in mind, with each of the main terminals (1, 2, and 3) plus their budget terminal featuring state of the art check-in facilities, enormous public spaces, retail shopping that rivals any mall around the world, and immigration/emigration/customs services that lead the world in design and efficiency. Page One bookstores, part of the PageOne Group headquartered in Singapore, has uniquely designed stores in Singapore, Taiwan, and Hong Kong, featuring shelves at odd angles, different floor elevations, rich woods, and designer lighting to create a book retail atmosphere that is distinctive from Borders and Barnes & Noble.

Office building designs in most cities are witnessing a revolution, with environmentally savvy features, clever use of interior spaces, a host of composite materials, and architectural approaches that give owners and tenants utterly unique work environments.

Cities around the world are constructing office towers, residential communities, high-density transportation systems, and new cultural centers, in an effort to update their brand image. The layout of sidewalk cafes in Paris gives the city its unique social personality and reputation. Barcelona's Olympic Park, built for the 1992 Summer Olympic Games, created new public spaces along a previously inaccessible industrial area, connecting the waterfront to visitors and featuring new retail and cultural destinations. Boston's revitalized downtown, particularly its theater district, transformed areas that were previously unsafe into trendy shopping, entertainment, and restaurant locales. Singapore's two new integrated resorts feature iconic designs, family-friendly activities from theme park rides to museums, business-friendly convention facilities, along with entertainment venues and casinos.

Of course, products are launched, regularly updated, and redesigned, from consumer electronics to enterprise systems to cars to state-of-the-art airplanes like Airbus's A380 and Boeing's 787 Dreamliner. With consumer products, each new product affords channels an opportunity to revitalize displays, merchandise mixes, and related promotions. With industrial products, new offerings can increase loyalty from existing customers and garner interest from new customers. Suffice to say that environment design is a significant aspect of brand image and brand value.

Convenience

Buying a company's offerings must be convenient for customers, which is why distribution strategy is complex and, even when planned thoroughly, fraught with imperfection. It is simply impossible to be everywhere that is convenient for customers, yet convenience is partly what customers are buying.

Channel design is defined two ways:

- indirect;
- direct.

Figure 10-10 is a simplified illustration of the brand manufacturer's distribution options.

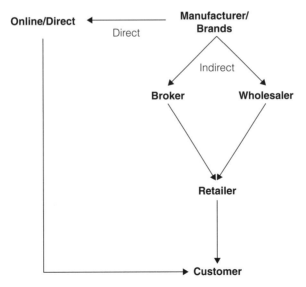

Figure 10-10   Distribution Flow

Indirect

This refers to the channel process in which products are sold indirectly from manufacturer to the customer through other businesses. This involves several related businesses: retailers, wholesalers, and brokers. Each of these provides a specialized service.

Retailers

Retailers are a well-known entity around the world, serving as the final distribution point to the customer. Retail strategy covers independent chains that sell multiple brands and product categories (Nordstrom, Carrefour, Footlocker) and specialty stores that focus on a niche market (such as hair care products, running products, or video games).

Wholesalers

Wholesalers are B2B businesses that buy large quantities of products from manufacturers, then resell them to retailers. Their expertise is strong in warehouse facilities, inventory management, storage, distribution, and logistics.

Brokers

Brokers are individuals or companies that act as a go-between between buyers and sellers. Their purpose is to facilitate the relationship between buyer and seller. A good broker would be sensitive to the needs of both parties, aware of the respective reputations and overall brand images, helping to ensure a compatible relationship since their ongoing role as a broker depends on their professionalism.

Direct

Direct channels are where products are sold directly from a manufacturer to the customer. This is both online and through-brick-and mortar locations. Direct bypasses third party intermediaries. For products distributed online through a non-brand-owned (third party) web site, an electronic order is sent from the Web to the manufacturer, without intervention from an intermediary. The non-brand-owned retailer receives a transaction fee from the sale without incurring inventory costs.

Online

The rapid growth of online marketing since the mid-1990s has made direct marketing an easier business to enter. Well-known brands in direct marketing cover a wide range, from pure online to hybrid (a mix of online, telephone, direct selling, and/or brick and mortar channels). Table 10.12 highlights a few examples:

Table 10-12   Online Stores—Pure and Hybrid

Pure Online	Hybrid
• Amazon.com	• Dell
• Peapod.com	• Apple
• eBay	• Toys R Us
• Craig's list	• Harrod's

- Cornerhardware.com
- Lastminute.com
- Gadgets.com
- Zuji.com
- Orbitz
- Play.com

- Barnes and Noble
- Sony
- GNC
- WalMart
- Nordstrom
- Bestbuy.com

Company-owned Stores

Many brands, such as Apple, Nike, Starbucks, and IKEA, have their own stores. Some have outlet stores as well, which sell excess inventory and off-season merchandise. Consumers can obtain reduced prices on selected items from prior seasons. These help the brand clear inventory in preparation for the next season's product offerings.

Theme Stores

Theme stores are housed within larger stores (such as department stores) and feature niche products or specific brands.

Create Areas where the Customer is in Control

Channel design includes creating places that require minimal or no employee supervision or interaction, where customers are free to take care of themselves and family members by using self-contained environments provided by the venue to encourage longer customer visits. Playgrounds in fast food outlets, coffee outlets in car dealerships, and entertainment zones in major international airports are each examples of how environments are created that support longer customer usage of the product or service.

Personality Themes and Atmosphere

A number of companies express their personalities through their stores and locations. Jordan's Furniture, located in the northeast of the U.S. has unique themes in each of its stores. One store features rock music and live performances, while another offers Jazz music and movies.[56] Joie de Vivre Hotels' properties are each individually themed to appeal to specific audiences. Themes include rock music, art, books, and even philanthropy and each hotel is decorated accordingly.

Themes are accentuated by music, visuals (such as background videos and interactive kiosks), and even smells. The secret to Joie de Vivre's ongoing success is the surprising attention it pays to every detail in each hotel. The company's founder and CEO, Chip Conley, believes in inspiring all five senses in the first five minutes, so every hotel visitor experiences an immediate (and subtle) multi-sensory welcoming. From fabrics to furnishings to food to music, Joie de Vivre makes each property come to life in a personalized and memorable way.[57]

Disney's theme parks continue to be leaders in creating personality-driven rides and attractions. From individual characters to themed "lands," Disney lives and breathes the idea of customer experiences.

Many movie theater chains are changing their designs as well by providing limited edition seating (sometimes called "Gold Class"), which are theaters with recliner chairs, blankets, and seat-side food service at a premium price.

Channel design affects customer perceptions of brands and companies have a responsibility to manage their channels in a way that improves the customer's experience, enhances brand value, and strengthens the brand's reputation. An important challenge is how to manage channels in a way that keeps all parties (brand, partners, customers, employees) happy. Direct channels are run directly by the company and many have the requisite expertise to do this well. Those that do not may want to stick with established indirect partners for getting their products to market. The challenge with indirect channels is getting the intermediaries to present the brand in a flattering way consistent with the brand's image.

Customer Engagement

Customer engagement encompasses physical retail environments and virtual environments. A theme often found in both is customer involvement in their own product creation, which strengthens the brand-customer bond.

Physical Retail Environments   Retail environments have been the subject of decades of research about the characteristics of superior design. Each store is different, with design influenced by the factors discussed throughout this book (Destiny, Distinction, Culture, Experiences). Customer expectations also dictate the success of retail design. Discount stores have different and often simpler designs than upscale, exclusive retailers. The colors, lighting, furnishing choices, sounds, smells, and general ambience each create an impression on each customer. Singapore Airlines' reputation as a top airline certainly reflects its consistent high level of service. But its interior designs and features add to the passenger's experience. Every passenger has a personal on-demand entertainment system with dozens of the latest movies and music, cabin colors are classic, seat fabrics and floor carpeting are clean and unstained, and even the bathrooms are kept meticulous. In fact, the clean bathrooms are the result of a unique combination of cabin crew cleaning schedules and passenger peer pressure. Such is the passenger care and loyalty that no one wants to leave the restroom unclean for the next passenger.[58] Apple-owned retail stores have become a cultural phenomenon, with their bright lighting, clean layout, easy access to products, and an almost museum-like zeal for captivating displays. Customers are encouraged to play with products, and an in-store "Genius Bar" offers customers a place to ask questions. The store environment is supported by well-trained and knowledgeable employees who carry portable payment units, eliminating long lines and further enhancing the customer's experience.[59] Cold Stone Creamery makes customers part of the product development process by letting them choose the ingredients to mix into their ice creams, which are then combined on the spot, helping customers feel engaged and more connected to the experience.[60] IKEA's unique store design guides customers through different theme areas, provides them with easy-to-use ordering forms and checkout areas, and has supervised children's play areas and restaurants to keep families happy during long visits. Customers pick up their purchases before they leave, and the products are ready to assemble at home, facilitated by simple designs and minimal parts, helping customers feel that making furniture is trouble free.[61] Stikfas, a Singapore-based toy brand, makes action figures with a ball-and-socket design. Customers buy their figure unassembled, putting it together themselves. With dozens of themes, the ball-and-socket design allows customers to put the toy together as they see fit, involving them directly in their own creation. Stikfas customers are so devoted to the brand that they post their hybrid creations on Stikfas own "Stik 'em up" blog, including homemade videos featuring their figures.[62]

Virtual Environments   Web sites offer customers a unique canvas for becoming involved with their favorite brands. Nike ID offers web site visitors the chance to customize their own product (footwear, apparel, and equipment), which is then delivered to their home. The company also has a New York-based design studio where customers can meet with consultants to customize their product.[63] BMW Mini allows customers to build their own mini by simply clicking on the "build" button on the web site. Visitors can then customize colors and options, and a real-time calculator updates prices based on the customer's choices.[64] Dell, of course, is well-known for its online ordering system that allows customers to start with a base design and then configure memory, software, processor, and other features, according to their needs. Apple does this as well. Skinnycorp.com describes itself as a technology company that thrives on coming up with new kinds of online communities. Among their many sites is one called "Threadless" (www.threadless.com), with the slogan "Nude No More." Threadless takes designs made by members of the community and turns them into T-shirts. Each day, more than 100 new designs are featured that can be purchase for around US$20. The community is inventing the product, not Threadless or Skinnycorp, creating a highly involving way for people to share ideas, see new products constantly, and make money. Another of their sites is called "I park like an idiot" (www.iparklikeanidiot.com) where community members submit pictures of bad and often comical parking jobs that can be turned into bumper stickers for people to purchase.[65] A different company called "Free Beer" (www.freebeer.com) from Denmark does not actually give away free beer. As their slogan says, "Free as in Free Speech". Free Beer gives away their beer recipe, treating it as open source code to be modified by other users. The recipe of Free Beer is a Creative Commons license, as are the brand elements. The only stipulation is that any derivative recipes and branding element changes users create must be published under the same license and their original work must be credited. After that, people are free to earn as much money as they can with their own recipes.[66] Many of the world's leading brands allow this type of customer engagement, creating physical and virtual environments in which customers can be the designers, further deepening their ties to the brand.

Authenticity and Integrity

Customers are more discriminating than ever before. In addition to memorable experiences in general, as Figure 10-11 shows, their brand loyalty decisions are influenced by several factors:

- proliferation of competitors;
- distrust of advertising;

- importance of word of mouth;
- products that overpromise and underdeliver;
- corporate behavior.

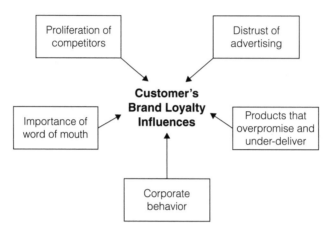

Figure 10-11   Customer Brand Loyalty Influences

Proliferation of Competitors

With so many choices and widespread access to information about brands, consumers are better informed than ever before and have the power to switch brands easily should they find a brand less than satisfying. For brands, the task is staying informed about the competitive landscape and knowing where opportunities and gaps lie that can be turned into long-term business gains. Brand is a powerful tool in creating competitive advantage, particular when so many products and solutions are of comparable quality. This is also why the idea of creating brand experiences has taken on new importance.

Distrust of Advertising

Over the years advertising has earned an uneven reputation, fairly or not. Whenever a brand makes a claim, it must follow through. Unfortunately, this does not always happen, which upsets consumers and harms brands as a result.

Products that Overpromise and Underdeliver

Similar to distrust of advertising, overpromising and underdelivering leads to customer dissatisfaction and can quickly snowball into customer abandonment and a poor impression of the brand.

Importance of Word of Mouth

Word of mouth has always been a source of credible information. As discussed earlier, the advent of social media makes word of mouth much easier to spread, which can be both good and bad for brands for obvious reasons.

Corporate Behavior

Since the early 2000s, corporate behavior has been under the microscope from consumers, governments, and media organizations. From accounting scandals to senior management ethical lapses, there have been numerous highly visible examples of egregious excess and poor governance. Such behavior tarnishes those directly involved, but also leads to back-lashes across other companies even if no transgression occurred. Poor corporate behavior undermines authenticity and integrity, which affects market trust overall.

Not every consumer is motivated to purchase products based on a personal perception of a brand's sincerity but people are increasingly looking into company claims and business practices before making a buying decision. To the extent that a brand builds a reputation for authenticity and integrity, consumers respond favorably.

There are a number of ways brands can gain a reputation for authenticity and integrity. Focusing on corporate social responsibility (CSR) is one important area. It requires companies to commit, beyond verbal support or financial donations, to improving the communities they serve and/or the quality of life overall. This can include giving employees time to work on projects either of personal interest, or of demonstrated importance to the company. The Body Shop is closely associated with natural ingredients and support of social causes. Ben and Jerry's Ice Cream donated 10% of pre-tax profits to social causes. Many companies sell only "Fair Trade" products, which supports sustainability by helping marginal producers from other countries become economically self-sufficient. Nike has a shoe recycling program called Nike Grind that takes the ground up old shoes and reuses the resulting material in sports surfaces from running tracks to court sports to playing fields. McDonald's has a large CSR program that includes the Ronald McDonald House Charities. Within, Ronald McDonald Houses provide healthcare and support of seriously ill or injured children. McDonald's was doing this several decades before CSR became fashionable as a business practice.

Measurement

As discussed throughout this book, measurement is vital to brand success, and this applies to the experience environment as well. Brick and mortar retailers can easily track which products sell best and in which parts of the store. Promotion tracking can help management understand when customers are most likely to shop. Customer service training can be gauged over time by changes in customer feedback. Atmosphere can be evaluated by asking customers their perception of the ambience. Returning to Joie de Vivre Hotels, the company conducts "split second surveys" of guests in their hotels to get a quick pulse check of their stay. This occurs during throughout the waking part of the day. While these are subjective reviews, they provide each hotel with feedback and even give insight into the guest's emotions and state of mind at the time. DaVita is a healthcare company providing kidney dialysis care through a large network of kidney centers around the U.S. The company is one of the most successful healthcare brands because of the total experience it provides patients, from top health care professionals to state-of-the-art facilities to a culture dedicated to make dialysis patients feel at ease. The company measures anything that can be measured, from dialysis equipment to productivity to patient satisfaction and more. Those items that cannot be measured are actively discussed at team meetings, serving as a reminder to employees that a measurement approach needs to be developed. The important point is that DaVita uses each measure to gauge how well their health care professionals deliver on the firm's stated promise to be the best kidney dialysis company in the world, as judged by patients. Measures include:

- ad-to-sales;
- ratio;
- response rate;
- conversion rate;
- share of voice;
- cost per thousand;
- cost per click;
- cost per order.

Marketing Communications Measures

Ad-to-Sales Ratio

Metric
Ad-to-sales ratio.[67]

Brand Experience Benefits
Measures how effective advertising campaigns are at creating sales.

How
Data on total advertising expenditures and total sales is required. The total ad expenditures are divided by total sales.

Formula

$$\text{ASR} = \frac{Ea}{St}$$

Where

ASR = ad-to-sales ratio;

E_a = total advertising expenditures;

S_t = total sales during time t.

Impact on Brand Experience
The ad-to-sales ratio varies by industry but generally a lower ratio is better than a higher one because it implies the advertising was likely to have been effective in getting people to buy. However, we cannot *conclusively* infer that a low advertising-to-sales ratio means ads are effective. There may be a "natural" level of interest and buyer attraction to the company's products anyway, and that the same, or nearly the same, sales level may have been achieved with little

or no advertising (although that is unlikely to last for very long). Nevertheless, the ad-to-sales ratio provides some guidance about the advertising portion of the brand experience.

Response Rate

Metric
Response rate.[68]

Brand Experience Benefits
The response rate is useful for measuring the percentage of people who respond to an offer relative to the number of people who received the offer. This helps gauge the offer's attractiveness and effectiveness.

How
The number of people that respond to an ad is divided by the number of people that received the ad.

Formula

$$R_r = \frac{Pr}{Pe}$$

Where

R_r = response rate;

P_r = number of people who respond to the brand's ad;

P_e = number of people exposed to the brand's ad.

Impact on Brand Experience
Customers are more likely to respond to a brand with an attractive offer, which can open the door to a more substantial and profitable customer relationship over time. Getting over the first hurdle of persuading customers to respond is key. Higher response rates are triggered when an ad offers a tangible benefit that can be easily obtained. Response rates also tend to be higher for shorter term promotions, such as limited time discounts or bundled offerings (such as two for one).

Conversion Rate

Metric
Conversion rate.[69]

Brand Experience Benefits
When customers purchase a product, they have converted from expressing interest and responding, to commitment.

How
The number of people that both responded and then purchased is divided by the number of people that responded.

Formula

$$C_r = \frac{P_o}{P_r}$$

Where
C_r = conversion rate;
P_b = number of people who both respond and buy;
P_r = number of people who respond to the ad.

Impact on Brand Experience

A high conversion rate is an indication that an ad was attractive enough to warrant both a response and a purchase. Achieving a high conversion rate depends on many variables, including the relevance and appeal of the offer to the target customer, how easily accessible the offer is, the visual design, appropriate price, and how it compares to competing offers. Each of these is an important factor in the customer's overall brand experience.

Share of Voice

Metric
Share of voice.[70]

Brand Experience Benefits
Share of voice measures the percentage of media spending by a company compared to total media expenditure for the product, service, or category in the market. This can be assessed, along with comparable percentages in market share, to gain a clearer sense of the brand performance against the competition and whether the brand is rising above the clutter.

How
The brand's advertising spend is divided by the total of all advertising spend for this category of product.

Formula

$$V_s = \frac{A}{\sum At}$$

Where
V_s = your share of voice expressed in percentage terms;
A = your advertising spend for a given product;
$\sum A_t$ = total of all market advertising spend for the same type of product.

Impact on Brand Experience
A high share of voice can lead to increased awareness, which can lead to increased sales and market share, indicators of a brand's strength. Share of voice provides insight on whether the type of audience being targeted, the time of day ads are run (for broadcast ads—in the

case of print, it would be theme of issue), and the type of publication in which the ads are run (mass market versus vertical publications). A high share of voice may indicate a larger amount of money devoted to advertising versus competitors; the relevance of the message to the target audience must be considered. It is not terribly useful to have the highest share of voice if the brand's message does not appeal to the target consumer.

Cost per Thousand

Metric
Cost per thousand (CPM).[71]

Brand Experience Benefits
This aggregates the cost per each single impression to help gauge the overall cost effectiveness per thousand impressions.

How
The cost of advertising is divided by the total number of impressions (in thousands).

Formula

$$CPM = \frac{CA}{I\,(thousands)}$$

Where

CPM = cost per thousand impressions;

CA = cost of advertising;

I = impressions generated (thousands).

Impact on Brand Experience
This is useful in comparing the efficiencies and costs of different marketing communications modes. When each marketing communications opportunity is evaluated, a key consideration will be the overall impact. More crudely, brand-building success is partly predicated on getting the biggest "bang for the buck."

Cost per Click

Metric
Cost per click.[72]

Brand Experience Benefits
Cost per click helps measure the cost of Web-based advertising.

How
The cost of advertising (in dollars) is divided by the number of clicks.

Formula

$$CPC = \frac{CA}{clicks}$$

Where

CPC = cost per click;

CA = cost of advertising (in dollars);

Clicks = number of click throughs made by web site visitors.

Impact on Brand Experience
Cost per click is a very accurate measure of the cost of Web-based advertising since more clicks mean a lower cost per click (and vice versa). This is a simple and effective measure of advertising success and can indicate the relative success of the ad's message, position, and design in generating interest.

Cost per Order

Metric
Cost per order.[73]

Brand Experience Benefits
This is another way to measure advertising costs but on a per order basis.

How
The cost of advertising (in dollars) is divided by the number of orders.

Formula

$$CPO = \frac{CA}{orders}$$

Where

CPO = cost per order;

CA = cost of advertising;

Orders = number of orders placed.

Impact on Brand Experience
Cost per order is useful for determining whether an ad led to an order being placed and a corresponding sales increase. A low order rate suggests that the ad was good but the product was disappointing by comparison, a red flag for any brand seeking to establish a quality reputation.

Environment Measures

Environment evaluation is ultimately concerned with two key questions:

- Was the customer satisfied?
- If so, were they happy enough to not only buy the brand again, but to recommend it to others?

A simple 1–5 scale (1 = not at all, 5 = yes, absolutely) for each of these questions will indicate how effective the brand experience efforts have been. Assuming the customer's experience has been strong enough to earn their continued business and willingness to recommend the brand to others, a key area of assessment is the various brand experience themes.

Experiential Marketing

Metric
Experiential marketing.[74]

Brand Experience Benefits
As discussed in Chapter 8, Bernd Schmitt's Experiential Marketing framework, *Sense/Feel/ Think/Act/Relate,* describes how brands can use *experience providers* ("ExPros"—tactical implementation components such as ads, store design, social media communication) to create the best brand experience. Measuring ExPros helps brands more effectively evaluate each of the five experience areas as defined by Schmitt.

How
The methodology uses questions in each experience area, measured by a simple seven-point rating scale (1 = not at all, 7 = very much). Schmitt mentions that since some of the questions are negatively worded, those must be coded reversely.

Formula
There is no formula. Instead, the framework in Table 10.13 shows a selection of questions designed to assess each brand experience area.

Table 10-13   Brand Experience Questions

Experiential Theme	Select Questions
Sense *Appeals to the 5 senses*	• The (ExPro) tries to engage my senses. (+) • The (ExPro) is perceptually interesting. (+) • The (ExPro) lacks sensory appeal for me. (−)
Feel *Appeals to customers' inner feelings and emotions*	• The (ExPro) tries to put me in a certain mood. (−) • The (ExPro) makes me respond in an emotional manner. (+) • The (ExPro) does not try to appeal to feelings. (−)
Think *Appeals to the intellect*	• The (ExPro) tries to intrigue me. (+) • The (ExPro) stimulates my curiosity. (+) • The (ExPro) does not try to appeal to my creative thinking. (−)
Act *Enhances physical experiences*	• The (ExPro) tries to make me think about my life-style. (+) • The (ExPro) reminds me of activities I can do. (+) • The (ExPro) does not try to make me think about actions and behaviors. (−)

(Continued)

Table 10-13   (Continued)

Experiential Theme	Select Questions
Relate *Appeals to the individual's desire for self-improvement*	• The (ExPro) tries to get me to think about relationships. (+) • I can relate to other people through this (ExPro). (+) • The (Expro) does not try to remind me of societal rules and arrangements. (−)

Source: Adapted from Schmitt, B. H., Experiential Marketing: How to Get Customers to Sense, Feel, Think, Act, and Relate to Your Company and Brands, © 1999 by Bernd H. Schmitt, The Free Press. pp. 231–232.

Impact on Brand Experience

The important takeaway from experiential marketing measurement is to force management to think differently about the ways they go to market. Statistics and figures are still important, such as measuring revenue and market share. But a more holistic and complete brand results when companies pay close attention to the means that lead to the financial ends. A critical means involves the many factors in brand experience development.

Summary

This chapter considered the remaining two components of brand experiences—marketing communications and environment. Several foundational topics were reviewed in both areas: marketing communications (traditional and nontraditional marketing) and environment (tangible and intangible components). These will continue to be important concepts as brands develop over the years for the simple reason that companies must regularly identify new ways to attract customers, position brands, and grow business.

The difference for modern brand building is that integration has grown beyond the coordination and alignment of externally focused communications to include internally focused communications (creating a holistic communications cycle) and environment-based factors. The purpose of this more complex, yet vital, attention to integration detail is to minimize disconnects between brand promises and the delivery of the customer experience. The management challenge is how to combine relevant areas of the company when much of business practice is still organized around departments and functional silos. For marketing communications, having clear objectives will determine the modes and measures used. For environment, identifying the right touchpoints (to be discussed further in Chapter 11) is followed by proper integration, activation, and regular monitoring.

The pitfalls can include poor or inconsistent integration that leads customers and even employees to wonder if the company knows what it is doing. But the benefits can turn a competitor with comparable products into a leader because every piece of the value-chain works in concert with every other. Employees sense it in the form of smooth practices and a sense of pride that ensures problems are fixed, and customers sense it in the quality and timing of follow-through on promises made.

Discussion Questions

Marketing Communications

1. Why is integration of marketing communications important? What are the challenges involved in making integration happen? How would you overcome those challenges? Identify and compare the IMC efforts of two or three companies. What are the characteristics of their respective campaigns? How would you evaluate their efforts: excellent, average, needs work? Why?
2. What are the ways in which IMC can impact a brand?
3. Can brands be built successfully without IMC? Can you identify any examples? If so, what are the examples? And are they truly unintegrated?
4. What actions would you recommend marketers make in developing their IMC efforts?
5. What are the components of a good brand message? Are there other factors you would consider? Is "message" the most important aspect of IMC? Why or why not?
6. What are the components of good visuals? Are there other factors that you would consider? Are visuals the most important aspect of IMC? Why or why not?
7. Is creativity more important than content? Or vice versa? How would you recommend balancing the two (cite an example)?
8. What are the challenges of IMC as companies grow?
9. Aside from the measures listed, are there other ways you recommend that marketing communications are measured? What are they? Why are they important to brand building?

Environment

1. Identify a large retailer and outline their environment touchpoints, both tangible and intangible. Evaluate the strengths and weaknesses of these touchpoints. How would you rate each touchpoint on a scale of 1–5 (1 = poor, 5 = excellent). Why did you evaluate them this way (what did you notice about their touchpoints that caused you to give them this score)?
2. What are the advantages of indirect channels in brand building? Disadvantages? How would you improve?
3. The Web and mobile communications have made direct channels more accessible for brands. What are the challenges brands face in utilizing these virtual channels?
4. Of the six areas in the planning and design of environmental factors, which are the most important? Why? Is it possible to manage all six simultaneously? If you were responsible for creating your brand's environment experience plan, how would you begin and what would you emphasize?

Case Brief

SAP: Building a Leading Technology Brand
Written in 2006 by Bernd H. Schmitt (Robert D. Calkins Professor of International Business, Columbia Business School; Faculty Director, Center on Global Brand Leadership, Columbia Business School) and David Rogers (Executive Director, Center on Global Brand Leadership, Columbia Business School; Columbia Business School Center on Global Brand Leadership). Used with permission.

Background
At the start of 2000, Hasso Plattner and Henning Kagermann, co-CEOs of software giant SAP AG, realized that their firm needed new direction for its brand. SAP's global messaging—from advertising, to logo, to web site—was sprawling, inconsistent, and confusing. In the hot new marketplace of the Internet, SAP was seen as being left behind. The buzz in the press was not on SAP.

The reality of SAP was much more impressive than its perceptions. The Germany-based company, founded in 1972 was already the leading enterprise software provider in every major market, with sales in more than 50 countries worldwide. SAP was the world's largest enterprise software company and the world's third-largest independent software supplier overall, with 12 500 customers and 25 000 software installations, predominantly within large companies.

SAP had a long history of market success, based on innovative product development. Founded by five engineers from IBM, SAP fostered an organizational culture that was highly product driven. Its first product in 1972 was a real-time data processing software, which was later named R/1. By the end of the decade, examination of SAP's IBM database and dialog control systems led to the birth of its big next-generation product, SAP R/2. In the 1990s, a new product using the client-server model and the uniform appearance of graphical interfaces was developed. It was named R/3. By its 25th anniversary, in 1997, the company employed nearly 13 000 people, with foreign sales accounting for the majority of customers. In 1998, SAP was listed on the New York Stock Exchange for the first time. As the company grew, SAP's reputation was built on its products and its heritage of market leadership and reliability.

By contrast, branding and marketing had never been a strong focus of the company's culture. Sales people and other employees spoke in complex jargon that often confused outsiders. Marketing had grown into a decentralized function, organized at the country level. Multiple advertising agencies produced independent local campaigns with inconsistent company and product messaging, and advertising was extremely product focused. Inside and outside of the company, there was no consistent way to answer the question, "What does SAP do?"

Weak Perceptions and Brand Image
In 2000, marketing fell under the board area of Hasso Plattner. It had become clear to him that strong marketing and brand management were key to maintaining the company's

position in the marketplace. SAP was perceived as a latecomer to the Internet. The marketplace had changed drastically; SAP found itself fighting for share with new "best-of-breed" Internet vendors such as I2 and Siebel. The Internet had led to a wave of hot new products, and companies of all sizes were entering the market looking for enterprise software. The *Wall Street Journal* wrote: "SAP was late to recognize the e-commerce boom, even as the Internet was transforming every aspect of its business." *BusinessWeek* asked, "What's sapping SAP? ... It has been left out of a flurry of deals."

It was in the face of this pressure that the company's new Internet-enabled suite of products, mySAP.com, was launched. The new product suite was strong. But there was concern that the company itself was viewed as *passé*. In light of hot new competitive products, this perception was so feared, that the decision was made to replace the corporate brand altogether with the new product brand. It was believed that this would be a strong signal to the market that the company was part of the Internet Generation. A sweeping overhaul in 1999 led to the replacement of the SAP logo with the new mySAP.com logo on the company's web site, brochures, product packaging, vehicles, and signage. By allowing a new product line to stand for the entire company, this change put SAP's own brand equity at risk. It also caused confusion. When the world looked for the SAP company web site, viewers were redirected to www.mySAP.com. Instead of finding SAP, the corporation, they found themselves at what appeared to be a product web site.

SAP also faced other branding problems. Its logo appeared in a profusion of variations across the world. Branding taglines were similarly numerous and constantly shifting, from "We Can Change Your Business Perspective" (1997) to "A Better Return on Information" (1997–8) to "The City of 'E'" (1999) to "The Time of New Management" (2000) to "You Can. It Does" (2000). Advertising campaigns in different markets resulted in inconsistent positioning for the company. The company was represented on the Internet by one global web site, more than 30 local country sites, and numerous subsidiary company sites—a total of 9000 Web pages with no consistent governance, design, or content creation across them.

The result was a weak and unclear brand promise. The challenge, as Plattner identified it, was how to transform SAP from a product-driven company into a market-driven company. To rebuild the SAP brand he would need to change the mindset of the entire organization.

The Global Marketing Office

Plattner began by radically changing the way marketing was led and organized within the company. In picking a leader for the new marketing mission, he broke several taboos: going outside the company, outside the software industry, and outside Germany. He hired an American, Martin Homlish, from Sony, to serve as SAP's new Global Chief Marketing Officer. Many were surprised by the appointment of Homlish, the man who launched the hit Sony Playstation, to lead marketing at a traditional B2B company. But Plattner was looking for a new vision.

At a board meeting in the Spring of 2000, Plattner and Homlish presented guiding principles for the repositioning of SAP. The brand would have a clear, relevant promise for customers; the promise would be communicated consistently; it would be delivered not just in advertising but at every customer touchpoint and the brand promise would have total alignment with the company's business strategy. Research indicated the brand possessed some very positive attributes that were consistent across all audiences—customers, prospects, analysts, and employees. More than anything, the new positioning would need to make SAP relevant to its customers and clearly convey the value of SAP's products and services. This new positioning would not manufacture hype, but would tell the truth about SAP.

In 2000, Homlish had a mandate for dramatic change as the new Global Chief Marketing Officer. He knew SAP had the potential for a great brand. "I saw SAP as a marketer's dream. We already had great products, a strong history of innovation, and a loyal customer base—all we needed to do was transform marketing." Based on the company's history, it is easy to see how SAP had gotten so far on the strength of its products. SAP transformed business, enabling companies across the world to leverage technology to improve efficiency, accountability, visibility, and ultimately, profitability of their businesses. Customers knew the value they received from SAP.

Homlish faced three large challenges in repositioning the brand for a global organization: communicating the brand consistently, aligning the organization, and creating a brand flexible enough to support changing business objectives within a dynamic industry. These three challenges could be further broken down into several issues:

1. Communicating the brand
   What should the SAP brand stand for? What is its brand promise?
   To what degree should SAP position itself as an "Internet" or "e-business" brand?
   What should be done with the SAP brand architecture, and what should be done with the logos?
   What should Homlish change first: the advertising, web site, logos, etc.?
2. Aligning the organization
   What elements of branding and marketing should be centralized at SAP? What should be localized?
   Where should the global branding function sit within the company's organization?
   How can Homlish communicate SAP's new brand positioning to personnel worldwide?
   How can SAP ensure consistent messaging, and consistent look and feel, in all SAP communications worldwide?
3. Leveraging the brand against changing business objectives
   How can SAP's brand be made flexible enough to respond if there is a shift to new customer targets?
   How can SAP leverage its brand to appeal to companies of all sizes?
   How will SAP know if it has succeeded in its rebranding?
   What measures should be used to gauge success?

Notes

1. "Timeline and History–2000 to Present," retrieved May 1, 2009, from www.samsung.com/us/aboutsamsung/corporateprofile/history.html.

2. 1) Research projects conducted by students at Singapore Management University for their strategic brand management course between 2004 and 2008. 2) "Samsung Brand Case," research completed April 2005, updated November 2008. 3) "Global Brands," BusinessWeek, retrieved May 11, 2008 from www.businessweek.com/magazine/content/05_31/b3945098.htm.

3. Ibid.

4. 1) Gardner, D. W., "Samsung Overtakes US Market Share Lead from Motorola," November 8, 2008, retrieved February 2, 2009 from www.informationweek.com/news/mobility/business/showArticle.jhtml?articleID=212001304 Samsung corporate web site. 3) "Investor Relations," retrieved May 1, 2009 from www.samsung.com/us/aboutsamsung/ir/financialinformation/financialhighlights/IR_Financial2006.html.

5. Schmitt, B. H., *Experiential Marketing: How to Get Customers to Sense, Feel, Think, Act, and Relate to Your Company and Brands*, © 1999 by Bernd H. Schmitt, The Free Press. p. 13.

6. Davis, J., *Measuring Marketing: 103 Key Metrics Every Marketer Needs*, © 2006 John Wiley & Sons (Asia) Pte Ltd, pp. 183–185.

7. Ibid., pp. 186–187.

8. Ibid., pp. 188–192.

9. Ibid., pp. 252–256.

10. Ibid., pp. 256–260.

11. 1) Hil, P., "GM Tailgating Chrysler Bankruptcy," May 30, 2009, retrieved June 2, 2008 from www.washingtontimes.com/news/2009/may/30/gm-tailgating-chrysler-bankruptcy/. 2) Levin, D., "Dealer Jobs Vanish as GM, Chrysler Bankruptcies Loom (Update 1)," April 21, 2009, retrieved May 2, 2009, from www.bloomberg.com/apps/news?pid=20601109&sid=aSefFiFMRV2I. 3) Simon, B. and Bullock, N., "GM Creditors Watch Chrysler Lawsuit," May 26, 2009 retrieved May 26, 2009 from www.ft.com/cms/s/0/6eddbdb2-498d-11de-9e19-00144feabdc0.html. 4) Woodyard, C., "What Happens to Warranties after GM's Bankruptcy Filing?" June 5, 2009, retrieved June 9, 2009 from www.ft.com/cms/s/0/6eddbdb2-498d-11de-9e19-00144feabdc0.html.

12. 1) Research projects conducted by students at Singapore Management University for their strategic brand management course between 2005 and 2008. Two projects focused on Banyan Tree Hotels—one included Ritz-Carlton (and Four Seasons) as comparison companies to "Banyan Tree Hotels' Angsana Hotels" and "Colours of Angsana's Best Opportunity to Paint a Lasting Impression," research completed November 2006, updated December 2008. 2) www.angsana.com/ retrieved December 21, 2008. 3) "Nestlé Powerbar Marketing Plan," research completed April 2008, "World Triathlon Corporation Launches Ironman 70.3 Series," March 2, 2006, retrieved November 29, 2008 from http://ironman.com/events/ironman70.3/world-championship-70.3/world-triathlon-corporation-launches-ironman-70.3-series.

13. Ibid. See also, "PowerBar Signs Luke Bell," July 19, 2007, *Triathlete* magazine, retrieved December 14, 2008 from www.triathletemag.com/Departments/News/2007/PowerBar_signs_Luke_Bell.htm.

14. Ibid.

15. Ibid. See also "PowerBar Launches Sweeps with Lance Armstrong," June 12, 2006, *Promo* magazine, retrieved December 6, 2008 from http://promomagazine.com/contests/news/powerbar_armstrong_sweeps_061206/.

16. Adapted from Davis, J. A., *The Olympic Games Effect: How Sports Marketing Builds Strong Brands,* © 2008 John Wiley & Sons (Asia) Pte Ltd, p. 293.

17. Ibid.

18. 1) "Audience," retrieved February 7, 2009 from www.stateofthemedia.org/2009/narrative_networktv_audience.php?cat=2&media=6. 2) "The Not-so-Big Four," April 8, 2009, *The Economist,* retrieved April 10, 2009 from www.economist.com/businessfinance/displaystory.cfm?story_id=13446620. 3) Schechner, S. and Dana, R., "Local TV Stations Face a Fuzzy Future," February 10, 2009, *Wall Street Journal,* retrieved March 9, 2009 from http://online.wsj.com/article/SB123422910357065971.html. 4) Gough, P. J., "The Case of the Disappearing TV Viewers," May 25, 2007, Reuters, retrieved November 15, 2008 from www.reuters.com/article/entertainmentNews/idUSN2523545420070525. 5) Gandosey, T., "TV Viewing at 'All-time High,' Nielsen Says," February 24, 2009, CNN.com/entertainment, retrieved February 26, 2009 from http://edition.cnn.com/2009/SHOWBIZ/TV/02/24/us.video.nielsen/.

19. 1) Jackson, C. V., "Passenger Uses YouTube to get United's Attention," July 9, 2009, Chicago Sun-Times, retrieved July 9, 2009 from www.suntimes.com/technology/1658990,CST-NWS-united09.article. 2) Newman, C., "Dave Carroll Tunes Up United Airlines over Broken Guitar Run-around," July 9, 2009, Shiny Objects Blog?—*Chicago Sun-Times,* retrieved July 9, 2009 from http://blogs.suntimes.com/shinyobjects/2009/07/dave_carroll_tunes_up_united_airlines_over_broken_guitar_run-around.html. 3) Christman, Z., "'United Breaks Guitars' a Smash Hit on YouTube," July 21, 2009, retrieved July 21, 2009 from www.nbcchicago.com/news/local/United-Breaks-Guitars-a-Smash-Hit-on-YouTube.html?yhp=1. 4) "Canadian's Song about United Airlines A Hit," July 10, 2009, MSNBC.com, retrieved July 10, 2009 from www.msnbc.msn.com/id/31836977/ns/travel-news/. 5) Fisher, L., "Musician Makes Music Out of Feud with United Airlines," July 9, 2009, ABCNews/Entertainment, retrieved July 9, 2009 from http://abcnews.go.com/Entertainment/Business/story?id=8043639&page=1.

20. Ibid.

21. 1) Research projects conducted by students at Singapore Management University for their strategic brand management course between 2004 and 2008. 2) "Johnson & Johnson: A Case Study," research completed November 2007, updated July 2008. 3) Depuy Orthopaedics, Inc., retrieved May 11, 2009 from www.allaboutarthritis.com/portal/DPUY/AAA. 4) Ethicon, Inc., retrieved May 11, 2009 from www.allaboutmyheart.com/. 5) "J&J Reallocates Budgeting in Favor of Online Marketing," July 2, 2008 , retrieved from www.bizreport.com/2007/03/more_indications_of_budget_shifts_for_large_firms.html.

22. Speech by David Shaw, Director of Brand/Asia Pacific for Lenovo at BrandFinance Forum in Asia, March 2008, Singapore Management University.

23. "Worldwide Mobile Cellular Subscribers to Reach 4 Billion Mark in Late 2008," September 25, 2008, ITU-International Telecommunications Union web site, retrieved November 6, 2009 from www.itu.int/newsroom/press_releases/2008/29.html.

24. Peppers, D. and Rogers, M., *Return on Customer: Creating Maximum Value—You're Your Scarcest Resource,* © 2005 Don Peppers and Martha Rogers, published by Doubleday, a division of Random House, Inc., Chapter 1, "An Open Letter to Wall Street," pp. 16–18. Return on Customer[sm] and ROC[sm] are registered service marks of Peppers & Rogers Group, a division of Carlson Marketing Group, Inc. Readers who are interested in a more comprehensive treatment of ROC[sm]

are encouraged to review Peppers and Rogers' book. Their web sites, www.peppersandrogers.com and www.1to1.com/ provide additional information about personalization.

25. Godin, S., 1999, *Permission Marketing: Turning Strangers into Friends, and Friends into Customers*, Simon & Schuster.

26. Ibid. See also, "E-mail Permission Marketing Fundamentals," March 2, 2009, retrieved March 5, 2009 from http://idaconcpts.com/2009/03/02/e-mail-permission-marketing-fundamentals/.

27. Hanna, J., "Authenticity over Exaggeration: The New Rule in Advertising," December 3, 2007, Harvard Business School Working Knowledge, retrieved January 12, 2009 from http://hbswk.hbs.edu/item/5812.html.

28. 1) "Mobile Music, Games and TV to Generate $34 Billion by 2010," March 2008, Juniper Research, retrieved April 11, 2008 from www.cellular-news.com/story/29857.php. 2) "Mobile Entertainment Markets: Opportunities and Forecasts" (second edition 2007–2012), pp. 5–6, retrieved April 11, 2008 from www.juniperresearch.com/.

29. Data from speech made by Mitch Joel, CEO of Twist Image and Six Pixels of Separation, in a July 2007 presentation made to Singapore Management University's conference, PodCamp 2007. See: www.edisonresearch.com/home/archives/Internet&Multimedia%202006%20Summary%20Final.pdf and www.edisonresearch.com/The_Podcast_Consumer_Revealed_from_Edison_Media_Research.pdf.

30. Verna, P., "Podcast Advertising: Seeking Riches in Niches," January 2008, retrieved March 23, 2008 from www.emarketer.com/Reports/All/Emarketer_2000474.aspx?src=report_head_info_sitesearch.

31. Schroeder, S., "The Web in Numbers: The Rise of Social Media," April 17, 2009, Mashable?—The Social Media Guide, retrieved April 23, 2009, from http://mashable.com/2009/04/17/web-in-numbers-social-media/.

32. Schroeder, S., "The Web in Numbers: Twitter's Phenomenal Growth Suddenly Stops," June 9, 2009, Mashable—The Social Media Guide, retrieved June 10, 2009 from http://mashable.com/2009/06/09/web-in-numbers-may/.

33. "Facebook Growth Continuing, Surpasses 150 Million Monthly Active Users," January 7, 2009, retrieved February 24, 2009 from www.insidefacebook.com/2009/01/07/facebook-growth-continuing-surpasses-150-million-monthly-active-users/.

34. Schroeder, S., "The Web in Numbers: Twitter's Phenomenal Growth Suddenly Stops," June 9, 2009, Mashable—The Social Media Guide, retrieved June 10, 2009 from http://mashable.com/2009/06/09/web-in-numbers-may/.

35. Arrington, M., "Facebook Now Nearly Twice the Size of MySpace Worldwide," January 22, 2009, retrieved January 28, 2009 from www.techcrunch.com/2009/01/22/facebook-now-nearly-twice-the-size-of-myspace-worldwide/.

36. "Top Facebook Application Developer Slide Building Virtual Goods Business, PaymentPlatform," June 26, 2009, retrieved June 26, 2009 from www.insidefacebook.com/category/friendster.

37. 1) Data from speech made by Mitch Joel, CEO of Twist Image and 6 Pixels of Separation, in a July 2007 presentation made to Singapore Management University's conference called PodCamp 2007, see: www.edisonresearch.com/home/archives/Internet&Multimedia%202006%20Summary%20Final.pdf and www.edisonresearch.com/The_Podcast_Consumer_Revealed_from_Edison_Media_Research.pdf. 2) Vogelstein, F., "How Mark Zuckerberg Turned Facebook Into the Web's Hottest Platform," September 6, 2007, retrieved March 18, 2008 from www.wired.com/techbiz/startups/news/2007/09/ff_facebook. 3) "Social Networking Goes Global," July 31, 2007, retrieved March 2, 2008 from http://www.comscore.com/press/release.asp?press=1555. 4)

Charny, B., "Even with Slowing Growth, YouTube Still No.1," March 21, 2007, retrieved March 2, 2008 from www.marketwatch.com/news/story/even-slowing-growth-youtube-remains/story. aspx?guid=%7B98FB4A03-0B53-4CFB-BA2D-716D2B59CAAB%7D.

38. "Advertising Boom in Developing Ad Markets Compensate for Credit-crunch Gloom in the West," March 31, 2008, p. 1. ZenithOptimedia, retrieved April 17, 2008 from www.zenithopti-media.com/gff/.

39. Court, D., Elzinga, D., Mulder, S., Vetvik, O. J. "The consumer decision journey", June 2009, retrieved July 2, 2009 from www.mckinseyquarterly.com/The_consumer_decision_journey_2373.

40. Ibid.

41. 1) "Super Bowl XXXIV," retrieved September 1, 2008 from www.super-bowl-history. us/superbowl-history34.html. 2) Taylor, H., "Widespread Belief that Super Bowl Players Use Steroids," Harris Poll #6, January 30, 2004, retrieved January 17, 2008 from www. quickinsights.com/harris_poll/index.asp?PID=435. 3) Horovitz, B., "Twenty highlights in 20 years of Ad Meter," February 10, 2008, retrieved November 11, 2008 from www.usatoday. com/money/advertising/2008-01-31-20th-super-bowl-ad-meter_N.htm.

42. Ibid.

43. See youtube.com for samples of Outpost.com's television commercials, including the gerbil commercial referenced in this section (www.youtube.com/watch?v=4hny1JSsZII).

44. Ibid.

45. Ibid.

46. Regan, K., "Goodbye COOL-Fry's Electronics Completes Outpost.com Acquisition," retrieved November 26, 2007 from www.ecommercetimes.com/story/14700.html?welcome=1209974781.

47. "Mark Twain (Samuel Clemmons)," *Senior Magazine*, retrieved December 3, 2007 from www. seniormag.com/whitt/mark_twain.htm.

48. "BMW Online Shop," retrieved May 2, 2009 from https://shop.bmwgroup.com/ is-bin/INTERSHOP.enfinity/WFS/Store-BMWShop-Site/en_GB/-/EUR/Shop-Start?MM=EXXRFBKLMA.

49. "Gear Up For The Ride," retrieved February 2, 2008 from www.harley-davidson.com/wcm/ Content/Pages/Accessories_and_Apparel/Accessories_and_Apparel.jsp?locale=en_US.

50. Prahalad, C. K. and Ramaswamy, V., "The New Frontier of Experience Innovation," Summer 2003, *MIT Sloan Management Review*, pp. 16–17.

51. Ibid.

52. 1) Research projects conducted by students at Singapore Management University for their strategic brand management course between 2005 and 2008. Two projects focused on Banyan Tree Hotels—one included Ritz-Carlton (and Four Seasons) as comparison companies to "Banyan Tree Hotels' Angsana Hotels"; "Colours of Angsana's Best Opportunity to Paint a Lasting Impression", research completed November 2006, updated December 2008. 2) Material retrieved December 21, 2008, from www.angsana.com/. 3) "100 Best Companies to Work For," retrieved May 7, 2009 from http://money.cnn.com/magazines/fortune/bestcompanies/2008/ snapshots/88.html. 4) Career page retrieved January 14, 2009 from http://jobs.fourseasons. com/Pages/Home.aspx. 5) Castaldo, J., "Now Hear This: Isadore Sharp, Founder, Four Seasons Hotels and Resorts," April 9, 2009, retrieved April 14, 2009 from http://jobs.fourseasons.com/ Pages/Home.aspx.

53. Ibid. See also, Medina, R., August 5, 2005, "Want to Work at the Four Seasons Hotel?" retrieved October 5, 2008 from www.epa.net/launch/comvcs/comrpts/item?item_id=594095.

54. Ibid. See also, 1) Sidman, S., "Lessons Learned from the Hotel Business . . . How Stellar Customer Service Can Assist with Tenant Retention," January 27, 2009, retrieved January 30, 2009 from www.buildingengines.com/index.php/Blog/lessons-learned-from-the-hotel-businesshow-stellar-customer-service-cabusinesshow-stellar-customer-service-can-assist-with-tenant-retention-assist-with-tenant-retention.html. 2) Phatak, A., Bhagat, R. S. and Kashlak, R. J., 2005, *International Management*, McGraw-Hill/Irwin. 3) "Best Practices in Service Quality," *Entrepreneur* magazine, retrieved October 4, 2008 from www.entrepreneur. com/tradejournals/article/69015997.html. 4) "Match Point," July 28, 2008, retrieved September 17, 2008 from www.humanresourcesonline.net/news/7352.

55. 1) Ransdell, E., "The Nike Story? Just Tell It!" December 19, 2007, *Fast Company* magazine, retrieved July 22, 2008, from www.fastcompany.com/magazine/31/nike.html. 2) Feit, J., "The Nike Psyche—It's Not Just a Job, It's an Attitude," retrieved January 12, 2009 from http://wweek.com/html/nike_psyche.html. 3) "Nike's Tattooed Ekins," May 22, 1994, *New York Times*, retrieved September 22, 2008 from www.nytimes.com/1994/05/22/magazine/sunday-may-22-1994-nike-s-tattooed-ekins.html.

56. "Jordan's Furniture Company," January 22, 2009, retrieved April 3, 2009 from http://investing. businessweek.com/research/stocks/private/snapshot.asp?privcapId=793786.

57. Information courtesy of interviews and emails with Chip Conley. Additional information was obtained from Chip's books: *Peak: How Great Companies Get Their Mojo From Maslow*, © 2007 Jossey-Bass, and *The Rebel Rules: Daring to be Yourself in Business*, © 2001 Fireside. Joie de Vivre's web site provides a thorough overview of the company's history, success, and business practices: www.jdvhotels.com. Jordan's furniture web site, retrieved April 3, 2009 from www.jordans.com/about/landing.asp. "Jordan's Furniture: Re-Imagine the Customer Experience" (Re-Imagine! series), retrieved October 17, 2008 from www.trainingabc.com/xcart/product.php?productid=17019. Peters, T., "A 'Finance Guy' Votes 'Top Line'!" December 8, 2004, retrieved October 5, 2008 from www.tompeters.com/entries.php?note=007094.php.

58. 1) Research projects conducted by students at Singapore Management University for their strategic brand management course between 2004 and 2008. 2) "Tiger Airways," in which the project studied the birth of Tiger Airways from the Singapore Airlines corporate umbrella. 3) "The Creation of Singapore Airlines," retrieved September 16, 2008 from www.singaporeair. com/saa/en_UK/content/company_info/siastory/history.jsp. 3) Singapore Airlines History retrieved September 16, 2008 from www.singaporeair.com/saa/en_UK/content/company_info/siastory/history.jsp. 4) Allen, R., *SIA: Take-Off to Success*, Singapore: SIA, 1990. 5) Donoghue, J.A., "Superior, Innovative and Adept," *Air Transport World*, June 1994, pp. 30–39. 6) Leung, J., "Winging Their Way to Global Might," *Asian Business*, December 1996, pp. 24–34 and www.singaporeair.com/saa/en_UK/content/exp/index.jsp, retrieved November 17, 2008.

59. 1) Research projects conducted by students at Singapore Management University for their strategic brand management course between 2004 and 2008. 2) "The Apple Core: What Makes it the Brand Today," research completed November 2007. 3) "Creative Technology: Fighting Back," with Apple as the comparison company, pp. 4–7. 4) Apple corporate web site retrieved December 1, 2008 from www.apple.com/retail/.

60. Based on ongoing research by John A. Davis. Reports on over 200 companies from around the world conducted from October 2000 to June 2008 and continuing. Companies come from multiple industries. The primary focus of the research was to understand the attributes and associations that underlie brands and to identify the programs and processes undertaken to

build brand value. See Coldstone corporate web site retrieved December 2, 2008 from www.coldstonecreamery.com/.

61. 1) Research projects conducted by students at Singapore Management University for their strategic brand management course between 2004 and 2008. 2) "IKEA in China-A Clash of Cultures?" completed November 2007, updated September 2008. 3) Ruppel Shell, E., "Just Don't Ask Why it's So Cheap," book excerpt from *Cheap: The High Cost of Discount Culture*, Penguin, 2009, retrieved on July 19, 2009 from www.theglobeandmail.com/life/just-dont-ask-why-its-so-cheap/article1223954/.

62. 1) Research projects conducted by students at Singapore Management University for their strategic brand management course between 2004 and 2008. 2) "Stikfas," research completed November 2006, updated February 2009. 3) Stikfas "Stik 'em up," blog retrieved June 3, 2008 from www.stikfas.com/cgi-bin/stikemUP.cgi.

63. 1) Research projects conducted by students at Singapore Management University for their strategic brand management course between 2004 and 2008. 2) "Adidas Sports Marketing," research completed March 2009. 3) Nike information retrieved January 19, 2009 from http://nikeid.nike.com/nikeid/index.jsp. 4) "Nike ID Design Studio," retrieved March 26, 2009 from http://architecturalrecord.construction.com/projects/bts/archives/interiors/05_nikeID/overview.asp.

64. BMW Mini web site retrieved October 23, 2008 from www.miniusa.com/?#/MINIUSA.COM-m.

65. Skinnycorp.com retrieved February 23, 2009 from www.skinnycorp.com/. Additional sites within their network include Threadless (www.threadless.com) and "I Park Like an Idiot" (www.iparklikeanidiot.com).

66. Freebeer web site retrieved April 21, 2009 from www.freebeer.com.

67. Multiple sources. Davis, J., *Measuring Marketing: 103 Key Metrics Every Marketer Needs*, © 2006 John Wiley & Sons (Asia) Pte Ltd, pp. 177–183. For advertising to sales ratio industry averages, refer to www.news-record.com/advertising/advertising/ratio.html.

68. Ibid., pp. 201–205. Also "Response Rate Report," by the U.S. Direct Marketing Association retrieved April 2, 2007 from www.the-dma.org/cgi/dispnewsstand?article=2891, and www.dbmarketing.com/articles/Art108.htm. See also MarketingProfs.com retrieved October 27, 2008 from www.marketingprofs.com/2/62percent.asp.

69. Ibid., pp. 205–208. Doyle, C., "Collins Internet-Linked Dictionary of Marketing," © Charles Doyle 2003, 2005 HarperCollins Publishers, p. 104. Also material retrieved October 27, 2008 from www.marketingprofs.com/2/ignoremarketing.asp.

70. Ibid., pp. 174–177.

71. Farris, P. W., Bendle, N. T., Pfeifer, P. E. and Reibstein, D. J., *Marketing Metrics: 50+ Metrics Every Executive Should Master*, © 2006 Pearson Education, pp. 265, 274–275.

72. Ibid., pp. 267, 294.

73. Ibid.

74. Schmitt, B. H., *Experiential Marketing: How to Get Customers to Sense, Feel, Think, Act, and Relate to Your Company and Brands*, © 1999 Bernd H. Schmitt, The Free Press, pp. 231–232. To gain a thorough understanding of Bernd Schmitt's assessment tools and detail on his experiential marketing framework, you are encouraged to read his book in its entirety. Not only is it one of the best books on the subject, it is also one of the first to address this important issue and make a significant impact.

Part III

Brand Leadership

Brand Leadership: Senior Management, Team, Planning, Mapping

11

Topics

- Preview
- Senior Management
- Team
  - Team Capabilities
  - Team Needs
- Planning
  - Principles
  - Brand Planning Framework
  - Brand Plan
  - Mapping
- Measurement
- Summary
- Discussion Questions

Preview

With brand value recognized as a desirable and advantageous asset to nurture, companies are spending more time, money, and resources to focus on brand building. The effort to do so has elevated brands and brand management and upward to a higher status in the organization. Brand leadership has supplanted brand management in guiding decision making. Understanding the skills and needs brand teams require helps in identifying the right talent to add to a team. Companies must also actively support brand building from the CEO on down if brand building is to be taken seriously.

The development of a brand is more than wishful thinking or skillful advertising. As we have discussed throughout this book, brands have evolved from a marketing responsibility and have become more of a strategic responsibility, with direct input and leadership from senior management and nonmarketing departments inside the company. Marketing still plays a vital role, indeed a driving role, in determining brand success. But marketing cannot and should not do it alone and the skills to build a successful brand require constant interaction and collaboration with other departments. The brand planning process can quickly become overwhelming if limits and expectations are not properly set about what is actually being planned. Yet brand plans risk failure if larger, company-wide issues are not addressed. Brand planning must reflect this new reality and include discussion of the role of Destiny, Distinction, Culture, and Experiences in the growth plans for the brand.

To facilitate a more complete understanding of the brand, brand teams must focus on the ingredients that comprise their brand, and how customers perceive them. Brand leadership must thoughtfully study their brands and markets to gain a holistic picture of the factors that shape perceptions and experiences. But this is more than an intellectual pursuit, it is a hands-on exercise in identifying specific factors and evaluating them individually to determine their contribution to overall brand value and reputation.

Senior Management

Top brands tend to make us think of their leaders as they are often covered extensively in the media and, if the brand is doing particularly well, these leaders are hailed as visionaries. The converse is also true—if misfortune befalls a top brand, the leader is the first to be blamed. Images of Steve Jobs, Richard Branson, Ho Kwon Ping, Martha Stewart, Sergei Brin, Chip Conley, Ingvar Kamprad, Oprah Winfrey remind us of their reputations and the reasons for their success and give us insight into their management styles. In the case of these names, they are also company founders. But equally notable leaders come from the nonfounder ranks as well. Anne Mulcahey, Sam Palminsano, Andrea Jung, A. G. Lafley, Indra Nooyi have successfully led their respective organizations for years and are recognized for having their own brand of distinctive leadership. The business world is populated by many more equally capable but lesser known leaders, successfully running their organizations. A key quality that they share is the ability to communicate the direction of the organization, clearly outlining their strategy and expectations. And they validate the importance of branding and marketing as a vital driving force of long-term value creation and success. They publicly give support to the development of brand as a strategic necessity for survival, let alone thriving. As the SAP case at the end of Chapter 10 shows, CEO support is instrumental to motivating alignment in support of brand building. For any organization intent on building a strong brand, the CEO and the senior management team must demonstrate their commitment to brand building. Such support was a constant theme at top brands. Interestingly, not all of the top brand CEOs were marketers by training but the common ingredient they each recognized as necessary is the ability to support and protect the brand's reputation. Anything short of CEO and senior management support and the chances of brand building succeeding diminish significantly, relegating branding to a lower level functional activity centered around marketing communications. Such poor insight into the importance of branding reveals why many companies fail to be recognized as brands by their stakeholders.

Team

The importance of a brand as a strategic asset has been the focus of this book. As such, brands need more than tactical oversight by managers, they need supportive leaders at the highest levels of the organization and extraordinarily skilled managers. They can, and most often are, marketing-trained people but they do not need to be. With the concept of brand expanded to encompass not just tactical management and strategic marketing issues but also whole-organization issues, nonmarketers can lead brands too. This reflects the fact that a brand is increasingly recognized as synonymous with the entire organization, which brings us back to the definition of a brand as discussed in Chapter 1: a brand is the entire organization as seen through the eyes of stakeholders.

We know that a typical brand leadership structure includes managers with responsibility for product lines, product categories, and/or brands. Indeed, brand teams can be organized in a variety of ways and populated by people with a wide range of expertise. The purpose of this section is not to cover detailed organizational structures, especially as such structures vary markedly across companies, even in the same industry. However, the capabilities of successful brand teams had ramifications for audiences inside and outside the company.

Team Capabilities

While team composition does vary, the knowledge areas shown in Figure 11-1 are likely to be found on brand teams.

Business/Brand Strategy (and Likely Team Leader)

This person is the likely team leader, setting the strategic direction and leading the planning effort for the brand, including authoring the business/brand plan. In larger companies, such individuals may be in charge of multiple brands and/or product categories. They are the primary conduit between the team and senior management, although they may also be members of senior management. They interface with the field sales force and make presentations about the business at company-wide meetings, to analysts and to the channel community. Profit and loss (P&L) responsibility is usually part of this role. At a minimum, they are responsible for financial projections and budget planning. Historically, they have a marketing background. They may also be category managers.

Category Management

Category managers are responsible for all brands within their product category. They help ensure that there is minimal overlap between brands, develop merchandising plans, and

Figure 11-1   **Brand Team Knowledge Areas**

monitor consistency. They may also have P&L responsibility for all brands under their supervision.

Product Management

Product management covers several disciplines. In the context of branding, a product manager is responsible for developing individual products and building product lines, some or all of which may be brands as well. But their expertise is the product. This includes working with people in development, engineering, and design. Product management may also be directly responsible for those disciplines, depending on the size of the company. Product management makes sure that the products meet specifications and pricing constraints, so materials sourcing plays a significant part in their success.

Creative Management

Creative management turns the business goals and ideas into designs, helping bring new products to life. They have to translate ideas into commercial products. Beyond creative design, they have to work closely with product management, in particular, to ensure the designs can be produced cost effectively.

Marketing Communications

This role is responsible for the various marketing communications disciplines, from traditional to NT marketing. They may be the primary team members in charge of the relationship with the advertising agency, if the firm has one, although the team leader may also perform this role. This role plans the media campaign, recommends spending allocations, and leads the process of writing the marketing communications brief, a document that describes for internal audiences and external service firms the expectations for the communications campaign. They may also be in charge of public relations if an outside agency is not used for this purpose.

Marketing Research

This role is designed for people trained in research techniques, statistics, social, and/or consumer behavior. Their primary task is to understand the customer markets, both existing and emerging, by conducting research and/or partnering with a third-party market research firm. They are also involved in data mining, tracking, and interpreting historical data on behalf of the company/brand.

Business Development

Business development people are responsible for strategic partnerships and negotiations with value-chain suppliers, working with outsourcing partners (such as overseas manufacturing) and developing alliances with complementary businesses to create new business opportunities. On occasion, they may also lead or be part of teams in mergers and acquisitions.

Team Needs

In Chapter 7 the characteristics of successful organizations and teams were analyzed in the context of developing a brand culture. Here, we will briefly discuss the kinds of things that need to be done when focusing on brand management, particularly as it pertains to performing effectively inside the company. Each requires fulfilling several business needs, shown in Figure 11-2, that are pertinent to leading the brand to success.

Strategic Insight

Teams must understand the role of the brand in the organization consistent with its Destiny. They are collectively responsible for setting of goals and objectives for the team.

Brand "Ownership" (Who is Responsible/Accountable?)

The best performing teams in top brands had a strong sense of ownership of the brand and individual responsibility in ensuring each member performs their part well. This ownership

Figure 11-2   Brand Team Needs

reinforced a team culture of accountability as well as for each member individually. In successful teams studied, no one wanted to disappoint the others.

Customer Proximity

No top brands ignored customers or their needs. At the same time, brand teams were focused on finding gaps and developing better offerings that more effectively met existing needs and/or seemed to address unmet/latent needs. Most team members spent several days each month visiting with customers and even visiting locations to just observe people. Many teams invited customers to join them, either on a regular basis or to get feedback for new initiatives.

Tactical Management/Execution

The motivation to get things done occurred in concert with brand ownership. Teams regularly met deadlines and expectations because to not do so was simply unacceptable. This was often displayed in a sense of self-induced stress, but not in a debilitating way.

Instead, teams were eager to implement plans and tactics to see what did and did not work so that they could quickly adjust and fine tune.

Expertise/Specialists

Top brand teams are given broad latitude to organize themselves according to their needs. As such, common organizational approaches were found within companies, a sensible outcome given the need for efficiency but divergent approaches were seen between companies in the similar industries.

Alignment and Collaboration

Teams were the catalysts for rallying other parts of the organization in support of their efforts. This included identifying ways to more effectively align resources and collaborate with experts in other departments.

Measurement/Review/Adjustment

The discipline of ownership and tactical management was matched by a strong desire to evaluate performance. The strongest brand teams were hungry for success and a commitment to measurement and review helped them improve.

Planning

Principles

Researching leading brands from around the world revealed several important principles that steered brand decision making across cultures:

- *The brand's traditions are honored and respected.* Regardless of country of origin, top brands celebrate their traditions, sharing successes with stakeholders and deftly using selected highlights to communicate the brand's story to the market. Time and again, brand leaders used the traditions to honor the brand's past and inspire generations of employees and customers. Understanding traditions and passing them on to new generations of employees helps management evolve brands in a way that does not violate society's understanding of the brand and its deeper meaning, while also staying relevant to the times.
- *Strong values guide behavior and actions.* Considerable discussion was devoted earlier in this book about the importance of having strong corporate values that are not just displayed on the corporate web site but permeate the organization and are demonstrated by employee actions. Every organization stands for something beyond making money, and values dictate what that "something" is. Knowing and reinforcing core values helps brands avoid artificial or forced growth opportunities.

- *They are brutally honest about their capabilities.* Knowing what the organization is good at doing assists the process of identifying brand-building opportunities that offer the best potential. Furthermore, this self-knowledge positively affects relationships with other businesses in the brand's value-chain because management is not deluded into believing it has all the answers and/or is smarter than their competitors. Instead, they are motivated to find complementary skills that enhance the overall product offered.

- *They focus on fulfilling needs distinctively to create strategic benefits.* Top brands are fully aware that their long-term health is predicated on delighting customers. While many companies talk about taking care of customers, far fewer take the leap and put in the work to actually do it well. Short-term sales and profits can be increased but are often temporary in the absence of a guiding set of objectives that provide a sense of direction. At the core of those objectives is addressing customer needs, whether articulated or latent, by developing truly distinctive products.

- *Their plans encompass pre-during-post plan activities and follow-up.* This is where daily accountability is rooted. Long-term strategy is realized when short-term tactics are executed not just effectively, but in interesting and memorable ways. This is where many managers and marketers get into trouble. Successful planning requires not just descriptions of what is to be done but assignment of responsibility, setting of deadlines and accompanying deliverables, establishing measures of success, and preparing options if and when programs need adjusting. Managers must "own" their piece of the plan and teammates must be accountable to each other and to the company's overall objectives. Reviews of the plans at predetermined stages must occur if accountability is to have any teeth.

- *They are flexible but core principles are never compromised.* Every brand faces risks and disappointments. Planning a risk-free or failure-free brand is impractical if not impossible. Hundreds and thousands of judgment calls made every day will determine success. A rule of thumb repeatedly observed in the research of top brands was a simple one: if it is illegal, unethical, immoral, or simply against the organization's core values, then don't do it, no matter how attractive and tempting the short-term benefits might be. When ethical compromises are made then the ultimate dream suffers. Management knows when they have a strong brand when their own customers help keep them focused on the ideals for which the brand stands. New media are certainly a useful way to stay in touch with customers to ensure the brand's compass heading remains set on true north.

- *They have a palpable commitment to authenticity and excellence.* Interviews with dozens of senior managers around the world produced variations on a common theme: brand success occurs when the people inside the organization dedicate themselves to being world class.

Brand Planning Framework

With the research completed, brand management's task is translating the information into a useful plan that can be understood and acted upon throughout the organization. Temptation may lead plans toward deep detail and extensive analysis. But before plotting such an ambitious path, recall a few lessons from this book.

First, do preliminary research on your own organization. Understand its background, learn about current leadership, pay attention to resource allocations. Knowing this is vital to conveying knowledge about the limitations and competencies the company has. Second, relevance remains a decisive factor. Just as customers want to understand the relevance of a brand to their lives and needs, so too do decision makers inside the company. Choose the information most relevant to growing brand value and brand reputation. Third, resonance remains important as well. The plan's content will need to resonate with decision makers, which means the company's pain points must be addressed. Pain points are the areas of the business most at risk from competitor inroads, internal underperformance, or rapidly changing customer needs. At the same time, resonance also needs to excite decision makers, helping them commit to the course of action recommended. It remains surprising how many marketers ignore the tools of their trade when trying to sell their plans inside their own firm. Internal branding starts here. But as Chapter 7 pointed out, internal branding must continue deep into the organization. In essence, marketers must market inside if they are to succeed outside. Fourth, use the tools and frameworks, but don't become slaves to them. New insights were gained about how top brands perform, which showed the much deeper commitment they have toward becoming holistic enterprises. But no single company practiced all approaches discussed in this book. They modified traditional frameworks, adapted measures, shifted strategies, all in an effort to get closer to their Destiny. A great deal of experimentation occurs within the top brands and not all of it is related to product innovation. Much of it deals with process innovation, decision-making authority and the willpower to reshape, not just throw away, brand-building approaches that do not meet expectations.

To help management, the following brand plan is a useful guide for incorporating many of the lessons discussed in this book. A selection of more in-depth tools, measures, and questions covered in each chapter should be chosen to tailor a planning approach specific to each user. For top brands, brand plans were not large dissertations. They were succinct directional guides that senior managers and those who were not brand experts could easily understand and incorporate into their own business responsibilities.

Brand Plan

Overview

Provide one to two paragraphs of plan highlights. Briefly describe where the brand will be in a few years and what it will be like if the plan works. Set the stage by discussing brand awareness data.

Measures to consider include:

- awareness;
  - brand recall;
  - brand recognition;
- brand development index;
- category development index;
- brand scorecard.

Brand Analysis

Destiny

Review the four components of the company's Destiny and discuss briefly how each affects/colors the brand plan. This is done to keep the brand aligned, even loosely, with the company's overall direction. Consider the following:

- What is its ultimate dream?
- How does it create value?
- What are the values and how are they demonstrated in the brand?
- How does the personality relate to the brand?
- How will the influence of Destiny be measured/evaluated?

Measures to Consider

- Destiny diagnostic.

Distinction

Focus on why the company and/or brand are distinctive. If they are not then describe how they will become so if the plan is followed. Keep each of the subcomponents of distinction in mind:

- How does the company's heritage influence the strategic objectives set forth in this plan? Has it been a niche, national, or global leader? Is it an innovator or follower? Are you proposing a change? Why?
- What are the goals and objectives?
- What is the context of the brand's situation? Summarize the most important issues in the brand's market. Identify at most three to five main points. The purpose is to inform, but not inundate, decision makers with accurate appraisal of outside factors affecting the brand and how your plan makes the brand distinctive.
- How has the brand positioned and is repositioning proposed? Discuss why repositioning is or is not needed.
- How will Distinction be evaluated? How will goals and objectives be measured?

Measures to Consider

- Market share.
- Market growth.
- Share of requirements.
- Market penetration.

Culture

Describe the key attributes of the company's culture and their influence on the brand's ability to deliver on promises made to the market. Consider the following:

- Identify the company's and/or brand's known competencies and how those relate to current needs. Are they sufficient? Do new competencies need to be developed? If so, how? What new knowledge is needed to succeed?

- How do the team and people within behave? Are there behavior-types missing that are needed to balance out the team?
- Is the organization's structure conducive to meeting the brand's needs? If not, what do you propose? How will this affect the culture? What will the company learn? Is the team's structure complete, or does it need to be reorganized? Who leads the team? Are roles and responsibilities clear?
- Describe how the social fabric of the organization is a help or hindrance to helping the brand.
- Does senior management support the brand? Evidence?
- What assessment criteria will be used to determine the culture's influence?

Measures to Consider

- Recruiting.
- Sales/profits per employee.
- Turnover rate.

Experiences

Identify the experiences that the brand wants to create/has created. Think expansively, not just in terms of traditional marketing tactics. Consider the tangible and intangible elements.

- What are the customer needs? What is important and relevant to them? Have these been fulfilled by the brand or competitors before? Where are the opportunities?
- Are the brand's solutions relevant? How do we know? What is the reputation of the solutions in the market?
- Are the marketing communications clear? Persuasive? Authentic? Original? Memorable?
- What are the environments like in which the solutions are presented? Engaging? Do they inspire the senses?
- Which measures will be applied and when will results be evaluated?

Measures to Consider

- Mark-up pricing.
- Target-return pricing.
- Customer acquisition costs.
- Cost per lead.
- Retention rate.
- Segment profitability.
- Ad-to-sales ratio.
- Response rate.
- Conversion rate.
- Share of voice.
- Cost per thousand.
- Cost per click.
- Cost per order.

Financial Analysis

Summarize the brand's financial history the past five to 10 years, including high points and low points.

- What are the projections for future performance?
  - Revenues, profits, cashflow.
  - Include income statement, balance sheet, cashflow statements.
- What has brand value been in recent years? Projections based on this plan?
  - How are any changes related to this plan?
- What criteria will be used as warning signs of trouble, or indicators of success?

Mapping

Mapping refers to techniques for visually depicting brand-related attributes and their relationships to each other and to the market. The exercises provide clear benefits by helping participants see the world through various stakeholders' eyes. They break complex businesses into manageable parts and create visual associations that show relationships among departments and services inside the company.

While many techniques exist, the brand touchpoints map and the customer experience journey map capture strategically vital elements of the brand, seen through internal and external points of view. These techniques can be used separately but a helpful approach is to map the touchpoints first, followed by the customer experience journey map, because touchpoints often show up in both maps. Having identified the touchpoints first can ensure that the customer experience journey map has more helpful detail. Each has been used in dozens of executive education programs over the years for leading companies, helping shed new light on existing businesses and opportunities for improvement.

Each mapping exercise involves several steps. To make these exercises effective, they should be done away from the office at an off-site location (even better if it is held at a resort or similar retreat-like place). The group should take breaks at the end of each step, perhaps doing a team exercise or some other group activity, to keep the group as fresh as possible. However, making phone calls and answering emails should be avoided, otherwise distractions will begin to consume the group, reducing their focus on the exercise.

Brand Touchpoints Map

The topic of touchpoints has been discussed throughout this book. Recall that touchpoints are the points of contact between a brand and stakeholders (customers, employees, value-chain participants, shareholders). While the term touchpoint implies something that one can touch, they actually take numerous forms, both tangible and intangible. Recall that touchpoints trigger a range of associations, from emotional to social to intellectual, which help anchor the brand in the customer's mind.

For brands to be more fully developed and their potential value enhanced, identifying the brand touchpoints is a powerful exercise. All brands should be evaluated using this tool, whether the brands are corporate, family, or individual (or master, sub-brand, endorsed brand and so forth). Some will have more touchpoints than others and companies with multiple brands will quickly find numerous connection points and interrelationships among the various brands. This latter point must be emphasized: interrelationships are important for management to see, understand, and evaluate because resources are often shared across the organization and without a visual understanding of the relationships, resource constraints will not be nearly as obvious.

The brand touchpoints map is important for another reason as well: it can help identify the importance of a touchpoint to the company and to the customer and/or stakeholder. An interesting finding is that companies will often perceive a touchpoint as vital, yet customers will see it as incidental, or not recognize its importance at all. Management would then need to decide whether these perception gaps should be addressed and, if so, how.

These connections can be revealing to management because relationships between various parts of their company are not always obvious in the course of daily activities. Yet when mapped and even scored, management often discovers why the impact of a touchpoint differs from expectations and, furthermore, what other areas of the company might influence that difference.

How to Create a Touchpoints Map

There are six steps in creating a touchpoints map:

1. *Brainstorm.* The management team should begin by brainstorming every conceivable touchpoint possible related to the brand being reviewed. This will quickly become complicated as flip charts and white boards become crowded with everyone's input. But the key is to list *everything* that comes to mind. A natural point will come at which the group will conclude that the task is complete, but this will not happen for a while, possibly several hours. One thing is certain: if a team finishes this initial step in less than an hour, then it will not have spent enough time thinking and discussing touchpoints deeply. This is not an exercise for the impatient who want to "cut to the chase." This is an exercise to fully enumerate every conceivable touchpoint. Organizing and pruning comes afterwards. The reason for this "no-holds barred" judgment-free approach is because each addition to the touchpoints list may trigger another person's input. But if artificial constraints are set, then the team would gravitate toward discussing only those areas within the constraints.

2. *Organize.* Once brainstorming has been completed, the group must collectively organize all of the touchpoints into categories, based on common characteristics. A vigorous discussion may ensue debating where touchpoints belong and possible areas of overlap. If a touchpoint fits in more than one category, then place it there as well. Rigid perfection is not the goal here. Developing a clearer sense of common themes is.

3. *Prune.* Once the common themes are more-or-less identified, the group should prune. It is tricky to do this well because there is no magic number of touchpoints that should be targeted. Outlandish touchpoints are likely candidates, although defining "outlandish" will differ slightly by person. Some will be tempted to remove overly creative touchpoints or the most extreme intangibles. But keep in mind that the goal

is not perfection. The touchpoints list must be an honest appraisal of the brand, which means that good and bad items should be included. If the group is open and communicative, then the resulting list of touchpoints will reflect as comprehensive and honest an assessment as possible. Experience dictates that less pruning is better than more, because as the map is created in Step 4, group members often add back removed touchpoints or even new ones not previously considered.

4. *Create map.* The map begins with the brand being discussed at the center, and it should be circled. Each of the main themes are then added outside the brand. Draw smaller circles around each theme. Solid lines are then drawn from the brand to the main themes. From each theme, individual touchpoints as listed from Step 3 should be written, with even smaller circles drawn around them, and lines then added connecting each touchpoint to each theme. As groups discover, the interrelationships between themes and touchpoints become readily apparent. Levels of touchpoints, or subtouchpoints, are usually added as the map takes shape and the visual cues spark additional insights. Relationships among various touchpoints usually emerge as the group is freed from more traditional, silo/org. chart brand structures that make product lines and categories appear as discreet, self-contained entities. The reality is that a great deal of overlap exists, with different brands and products dependent on many shared resources, internal services, and external value-chain participants. Dotted lines should be drawn when interrelationships and dependencies are revealed.

5. *Score each touchpoint.* Once the touchpoints and connections are mapped, the group has an opportunity to look at the brand with fresh eyes. It can now see the many different dimensions of the brand and the relationships. The next task is to score each touchpoint from two perspectives: company and customer, as follows:

   Company perspective: importance of the touchpoint to the brand (1 to 5 scale; 1 = low, 5 = high).
   Customer perspective: ability of the brand to provide/deliver the touchpoint successfully (1 to 5 scale; 1 = low 5 = high).

   Ideally, companies should have customer surveys and research that tells them how the brand is perceived and the importance of key touchpoints. However, as these data may be hard to obtain, especially the first time the exercise is run, an alternative is to invite a representative selection of customers into the mapping session to spend a day with the group discussing and assessing the touchpoints. The least attractive alternative is to have the management group assume the customer's point of view and score accordingly. However, one can readily see the potential problems arising from this latter approach because bias is more likely despite claims of impartiality and customer knowledge. Nevertheless, two scores are important to have for each touchpoint.

6. *Discuss and address gaps.* The map will now be quite busy. The task at this point is to discuss the findings and identify opportunities as well as problem areas. An easy way to start is to review each pair of extreme scores, for example: (1, 5), (5, 1), (2, 5), (4, 1), ask why the discrepancies exist and if fixing them is important to increasing brand value and progressing toward the brand's Destiny. Each discrepancy should be recorded and responsibility for fixing it assigned, along with a timeline for updates, completion, and review. The same is true for any other opportunities identified by the group.

When this exercise is pursued in-depth, it can take several hours or even days, creating a rather complex spider-web of touchpoints, connections, and scores. The end result is a detailed picture of the brand's touchpoints, each of which give shape to the brand's reputation and ultimately affect brand value. The overriding benefit is that groups begin to identify bottlenecks, shared needs, and opportunities/gaps that can be addressed.

This exercise should be repeated each year to review progress since the previous session and determine current needs. The touchpoints map is unlikely to change dramatically from one year to the next but there will inevitably be changes within specific touchpoints, as there should be. Significant changes will be more obvious over many years.

Figure 11-3 shows a simplified example of a touchpoints map. The two aforementioned scores are noted by the numerical scores in parentheses adjacent to each touchpoint (*company perspective: importance of the touchpoint to the brand*; and the *customer perspective: Ability of the brand to provide/deliver the touchpoint successfully*). This is not comprehensive, as there would be many more touchpoints in reality. The theme areas would also be labeled based on the topics from the actual brainstorming session. Bear in mind that the themes must be determined *after* the initial brainstorming session otherwise participants will simply fill in touchpoints based only on the themes already identified, nullifying the benefit of considering the wider range of touchpoints that affect the brand. Experience with companies around the world shows that themes run the gamut from familiar business labels (services, products, organization, brands, experiences, marketing communications, people) to softer labels (empathy, sensitivity, personality, and even humor). But again, themes should never precede the touchpoints discussion.

Impact of Nontraditional Marketing

The many NT marketing tools discussed in Chapter 10 are each potential brand touchpoints, adding new points of contact between the brand and the customer. As the Joie de Vivre's "Inspire All Five Senses in the First Five Minutes" example illustrates, NT marketing goes beyond new media, embracing dynamic new service practices that are revolutionizing customer experiences. Joie de Vivre's Hotel interiors avoid the trappings of cookie-cutter hotel designs by viewing every attribute of each hotel as a brand touchpoint. Unique fabrics, textured walls, subtle scents, perfectly themed music, devoted staff, innovative themes, and Yvette the Hotel Matchmaker all reinforce the brand's eponymous philosophy that their name declares.

Customer Experience Journey Map

The customer experience journey is specific to the brand being analyzed and, as the name implies, it evaluates the sequence of events in the customer's interaction with the company before, during, and after purchase. The customer experience journey map helps management understand what the customer's experience is like when interacting with the brand. (An interaction is loosely interpreted here. It can refer to a basic spontaneous purchase of a packaged good at a supermarket, a more involving research effort to narrow down which automobile to buy, a complete sensory experience such as staying at a resort hotel, or shopping at sophisticated theme stores.)

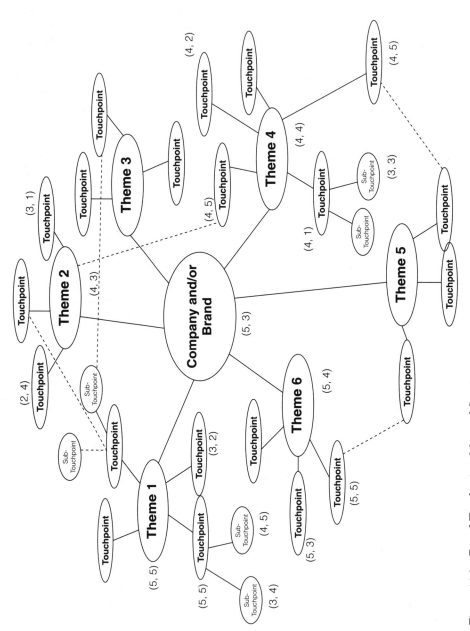

Figure 11-3   Brand Touchpoints Map and Scoring

How to Create a Customer Journey Map

There are six steps in the process. The resulting map provides a remarkably detailed breakdown of a customer's experience, as we will see:

1. *Identify the customer's needs.* Determine what the customer needs and why they need it. Market research will help develop insights. Write each need on the customer journey map. For B2B companies there may be multiple buyers (customers) during the purchase process. Each of their needs must be identified.

2. *Determine the company's response to each need.* Each need, however simple, will have a corresponding response from the company. Identify who is involved with the response, what resources are needed and any related touchpoints. Add these responses to the map.

3. *Score each response.* Score each response using two scales: a competitor comparison and a customer assessment. The competitor comparison should be based on known, verifiable data or, at a minimum, market knowledge from past experience and customer feedback. The customer assessments should come from satisfaction surveys. However, using recollection of prior customer can serve as a temporary assessment until more statistically valid data are available. The idea is for management to be actively considering and weighing their customer responses and having transparent discussions about their own strengths and weaknesses. For multi-resource responses (in which the company response involves several inputs), score each resource individually as this will help clarify relative contribution toward satisfying the customer's need. For the closest competitor use the scale in Figure 11-4. For the customer assessment, evaluate the brand's response on a 1 to 5 scale (1 = poor 5 = excellent) as in Figure 11-5. Participants will notice that many touchpoints from the previous exercise will be among the responses. This is important, particularly because touchpoint scores from the first exercise will likely be correlated with how the customer perceives that stage of the journey (a positively viewed touchpoint should also be reflected in a positive step in the customer journey sequence and vice versa).

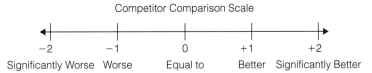

Competitor Comparison Scale

−2	−1	0	+1	+2
Significantly Worse	Worse	Equal to	Better	Significantly Better

Figure 11-4 Customer Experience Journey Scoring—Competitor Comparison Scale 2000–2009

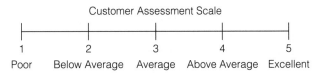

Customer Assessment Scale

1	2	3	4	5
Poor	Below Average	Average	Above Average	Excellent

Figure 11-5 Customer Experience Journey Scoring—Customer Assessment Scale

4. *Identify gaps, problems, and opportunities.* Each need/response pairing along the customer journey map will have a score compared to the closest competitor.

5. *Determine plan of action.* There are always ways to vary and improve the customer's journey. Once the journey has been outlined, responsibility for any changes must be assigned, scheduled, and measured, as was done for the brand touchpoints map.

6. *Review.* Periodic reviews will help management remain attuned to how customers are being treated.

As with the brand touchpoints exercise, the customer experience journey is not a one time only activity. It should be repeated on a regular basis, so that benchmarks can be established and improvement more easily tracked.

Figure 11-6 shows a hypothetical customer experience journey. It is divided into three phases: "pre-," "during," and "post-" (shown on the right side). The "pre-" phase designates the effort exerted by the customer to learn more about the brand and whether it is the right fit for them. The company's response(s) determines whether customers continue to purchase and usage, or leave prior to purchase. Assuming they do not leave, the journey shifts into the purchase phase, which, depending on the product, may involve several steps (the transaction, delivery, and installation, for example ...). The final phase is the post-purchase phase, which includes post-purchase courtesy follow-ups, surveys, and ongoing support. The company's responses are scored throughout, using the two measures in parentheses (comparison to closest competitor; and customer perception of response).

Impact of NT Marketing

The success of the customer experience journey determines whether the customer views the brand favorably or not. Brand marketing over the years has taught us that favorable outcomes usually lead to repeat purchases and ongoing satisfaction builds loyalty. Each exposure to the brand during the customer's subsequent journeys exposes them to more touchpoints and consequently builds and reinforces new associations. This is still generally accepted wisdom but NT marketing has increasingly influenced this process. For example, at each step of the journey the customer has the ability to connect with other people via mobile communications to ask specific questions about what they should expect and to even comment briefly (such as via Twitter) about the impressions of their experience as they progress. Such real-time information exchange can influence the course of the purchase decision, despite the company's best efforts to control the customer situation at that moment. Companies, too, can use NT marketing to influence the customer's decision. Customers may be considering purchasing the brand precisely because they received a video clip about the brand on their mobile phone attached to a movie preview they were watching. Companies can also send immediate thank you notes post-purchase to the customer's mobile phone and/or email. After purchasing from an Apple store, customers receive a thank you note at their preferred contact address, followed a few days later by a survey seeking customer service and product satisfaction feedback.

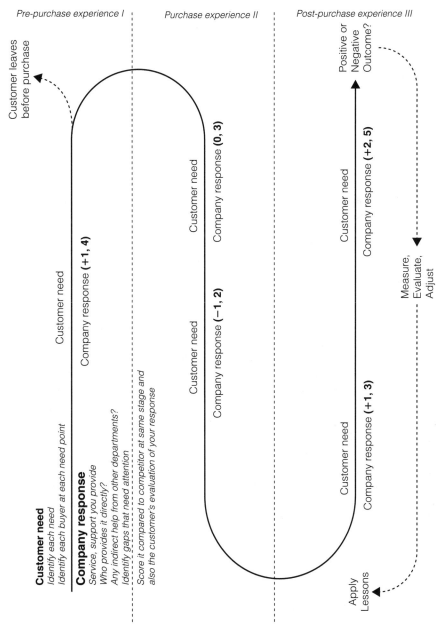

Figure 11-6 Customer Experience Journey Map

Measurement

Measures and assessment tools have been described throughout this book, specific to the particular area of brand building being addressed. The mapping techniques discussed in this chapter add an important component to the assessment list because they are designed to capture the customer's (and other stakeholders) perspectives about the brand's points of contact and its success at creating a memorable experience for customers.

Summary

Brands have become strategic assets and must be managed accordingly. This chapter discussed the need to lead brands, not just manage them, which suggests the importance of long-term strategy and not just using tactics to achieve growth. The days of brand managers being lower status, entry-level managers are long gone as companies have come to realize the significant importance and benefits building a strong brand brings. As such, brands require senior leadership support and a deeply talented team to run the brand and continue building the business. Today's brand teams need several important skills from functional to visionary to keep their brands strong and relevant. At this stage, the obligation is on management to assemble brand-building ingredients based on the needs of their organization. Brand planning is still a requirement, just as any business needs a plan for growth. But the content and structure of brand plans has changed to accommodate the more progressive and holistic aspects brands have. In developing brand plans, management should use mapping tools to help them understand the brands for which they are responsible. Brand touchpoints identify the many different points of contact between brands and the marketplace and provide a useful visual guide to the attributes that ultimately shape the brand's reputation. The customer experience journey enables management to see more easily the way customers are treated and evaluate the company's performance based on responses to customer needs by working through each step of the customer's journey. Scoring techniques assess where the brand is strong and surface areas of weakness as well as opportunities. The combination of the two maps provides visual insight and added depth to management, giving them a deeper understanding and appreciation for the brand and serving as invaluable ongoing tools for updating and adjusting their brand-building programs.

Discussion Questions

1. LVMH is a leading luxury branded house, with dozens of top individual luxury brands within as well. What kinds of skills would you look for in their brand teams? How will those help?

2. Why isn't there a commonly agreed organizational structure for brand teams? How would having one affect brand building in companies around the world?

3. Select a popular mass consumer brand, either national or global, and create a brand touchpoints map. Based on your own assessment, score each touchpoint using the scoring criteria from this chapter. Which touchpoints are most influential for the brand? Where does the brand need to improve?

4. Answer the same question above, but use a B2B brand. What are the differences in touchpoints? Are there areas where the two brands can learn and benefit from each other?

5. Choose a well-known hotel where you have stayed and recreate (to the best of your recollection) your own customer experience journey. How well did the hotel perform in responding to your needs? If you were put in charge of the hotel, what would you change and improve? How would this affect their reputation?

Index